GODS OF MONEY

WALL STREET AND THE DEATH OF THE AMERICAN CENTURY

F. William Engdahl

edition.engdahl
Wiesbaden

Edited by Margot L. White

Published by edition.engdahl
Wiesbaden, Germany
0049-611-505-6169

ISBN 978-3-9813263-1-4

Printed in USA

To Stephen J. Lewis who taught me that in the world of international finance things are rarely what they seem and whose years of tutoring in the workings of political economy informed this book

And to John Williams, whose relentless dedication to economic honesty sustained my own work for the past two decades

Table of Contents

Author's Introduction

This is not a book that explains how to survive the financial crisis or perhaps why gold is a sound investment in times of turmoil. Others have done that better. This book is not a conventional account of money and banking or even economics. Rather, it is a history of power, more precisely, of the colossal abuse of power in the hands of a tiny elite who have constituted themselves as the "Gods of Money." This book is a history of the tiny clique of international bankers who created Wall Street and who control it today, as they did the City of London until the First World War.

This volume is a chronicle of the rise to positions of unheard-of power on the part of individuals who considered themselves a power onto themselves, separate and above the mere laws of man.

The Book of Matthew in the *New Testament* states, "No one can serve two masters. He will either hate one and love the other, or be devoted to one and despise the other. You cannot serve God and mammon." (Matthew 6:24). From the very beginnings of the founding of the United States as a Constitutional Republic in 1789 following the War of Independence against Great Britain, powerful money interests resolved that Biblical conflict by anointing themselves as simply the "Gods of Money," a higher law unto themselves, above all other mere mortals. Step-by-step, through the power of their money, they sought to corrupt the foundations of the Constitution, attempting to recoup by credit and financial fraud what they had lost on the field of battle.

In a November 2009 interview with the London *Sunday Times*, Lloyd Blankfein, the Chairman and CEO of the world's most profitable bank, Goldman Sachs, defended his bank's record profits at a time when most financial institutions were struggling to survive. He commented that he was merely a "banker doing God's work." More than a century earlier, John D. Rockefeller, the founder of the Standard Oil monopoly, when asked by a naïve reporter how he had become the world's wealthiest man, snapped back without hesitation, "God gave me my money!"

Books have been written attempting to define the most fundamental question, "what is money?" The fact that so many different answers and so many different books exist demonstrates that the true nature of something most of us take for granted, is not at all clear at least to academic economists.

The reason is the fact that contemporary study of economics as taught in all major universities in the Western world today has little or nothing to do with economic reality, nor with the political role of international finance, and its geopolitical agenda, in shaping that economic reality. That should not be surprising, as the financial powers, the great and powerful international bankers of the City of London and of Wall Street and their kin, have endowed the appropriate professorships to ensure that what is taught will protect their order, even going so far as to endow a Nobel Prize in Economics to serve their interests.

Money is nothing more and nothing less than a political creation, a promise to pay between two or more parties, enforced, to a greater or lesser degree by the power of a state. Ultimately money, especially in a world where money is a pure paper commodity—fiat money so-called—is a question of "confidence," confidence ultimately in the "full faith and credit of the Government of the United States of America." And that confidence has been backed always, ultimately, by military power, political power, power to buy or control the lawmakers and administrators—Presidents, Congressmen, judges.

The edifice that has developed within the United States over the course of the past one hundred and fifty years is one where an inordinately powerful small circle of international bankers, the powers of Wall Street and the money center banks allied to it, has shaped the lives of the American public, prepared them for wars far from American shores, literally controlling what people buy and produce and most dangerously, even what they are allowed to think. The late American historian, Carroll Quigley noted, *"The aim of the international bankers was nothing less than to create a world system of financial control in private hands able to dominate the political system of each country and the economy of the world as a whole. This system was to be controlled in a feudalist fashion by the central banks of the world acting in concert, by secret agreements arrived at in frequent private meetings and conferences."* (Tragedy & Hope, p. 324).

In 1862 in the early months of the American Civil War, a memo was discreetly circulated among England's wealthy aristocrats and bankers. It stated the cold assessment of the banking powers of the City of London regarding events in the United States:

"Slavery is likely to be abolished by the war power and all chattel slavery abolished. This I and my European friends are in favor of,

for slavery is but the owning of labor and carries with it the care of the laborers, while the European plan, led on by England, is that capital shall control labor by controlling wages. The great debt that the capitalists will see to it is made out of the war, must be used as a means to control the volume of money. To accomplish this, the bonds must he used as a banking basis. We are now waiting for the Secretary of the Treasury to make this recommendation to Congress. It will not do to allow the greenback, as it is called, to circulate as money any length of time, as we can not control that. But we can control the bonds and through them the bank issues." (cited in Lindbergh, Banking, Currency and the Money Trust)

In 1913, Minnesota Congressman Charles August Lindbergh Sr., father of the famed aviator, wrote *Banking, Currency, and the Money Trust*, in which he accurately described the political agenda of the Wall Street international bankers who were shaping the creation of a new central bank and with it, control over the nation's economy.

As a Republican member of the US Congress Lindbergh wrote exposing the secret machinations of powerful Wall Street financial interests, their efforts to sneak through a piece of legislation that, more than any other single bill, has shaped the future history of the nation and much of the World—the Federal Reserve Act. It was passed by an almost empty Congress and signed into law by President Woodrow Wilson—a crony of Wall Street—on Christmas Eve, 1913. Lindbergh described the influence of what he accurately named the Wall Street Money Trust in that de facto bankers' coup d'état:

"Ever since the Civil War Congress has allowed the bankers to con-trol financial legislation. The membership of the Finance Committee in the Senate (now the Banking and Currency Committee) and the Committee on Banking and Currency in the House have been made up chiefly of bankers, their agents, and their attorneys. These com-mittees have controlled the nature of bills to be reported, the extent of them, and the debates that were to be held on them when they were being considered in the Senate and the House." (Lindbergh, op. cit, Appendix).

In 1917 Lindbergh wrote a widely read pamphlet, *Why is Your Country at War?*, in which he laid the blame at the door of "high finance" for America's involvement in what came to be known as World War I. For his courage and accurate expose of the role of the Money Trust in leading America into the war, the press, controlled by Wall Street, labeled Lindbergh a traitor. His political career was destroyed by the Money Trust he had fought.

One international Wall Street bank, J. P. Morgan & Co., in violation of US neutrality, became the banker to Britain and France at the outset of the war in Europe and, through its influence on Woodrow Wilson's administration, was able to manipulate the media accounts of events to create a war fever in an unknowing American populace that had been deeply skeptical of the need to go to war.

The US Secretary of State, William Jennings Bryan, an unappreciated figure in American politics, gained a large national political following by opposing Wall Street "plutocracy" and defending the Western states' silver interests of that day against the Wall Street and London gold standard. Bryan resigned as Secretary of State in 1915 in protest at what he rightly saw as a cynical manipulation by the President and his advisers—especially the press controlled by Wall Street bankers close to Morgan, to bring the United States into the war at a time the House of Morgan faced possible financial ruin owing to its huge loans to Great Britain and France. The Money Trust of Wall Street saw war as the entrée to financial influence in Europe, filling the vacuum left by a bankrupt Britain. It was the first step in creating what became the "American Century."

Between the creation of the First Bank of the United States by Treasury Secretary Hamilton in 1791 as a private bank, and the creation of the Federal Reserve in December 1913—also a privately-owned central bank—a small group of extremely wealthy families had emerged, earlier referred to as America's Sixty Families. The wealth and power of these families were tied to their ability to control the money of the new nation, to create shortages of money at will, leading to panics and even depressions, in order to expand and consolidate their power over the nation. It was they who financed wars and the expansion of the United States beyond its borders when, after the Spanish-American War of 1898, America became a de facto imperial power by annexing the Philippines as a gateway to the lucrative trade of China and Asia.

In the period from the outbreak of the "war to make the world safe for democracy" in August 1914, until the end of the Second World War in May 1945—contrary to the claims of standard and 'approved' history texts—the world underwent a titanic struggle between two world powers, the United States and Germany, over which would succeed the failing British Empire as global hegemon. The interests that shaped the American challenge were above all concentrated in Wall Street, among the Gods of Money. The individual faces changed. The House of Morgan dominated until its crisis in 1931. Thereafter, the

Rockefeller group and their banks emerged as the unchallenged leaders of the emerging American domination of the globe, proclaimed as "The American Century" in 1941 by one of their own, Henry Luce of *Time-Life*.

Since 1945 American hegemony, or more accurately an American imperium, has rested on two firm pillars of support. The first pillar has been the role of the dollar as unchallenged world reserve currency in which New York's Wall Street is the center of global finance, the "banker to the world." The second and complementary pillar has been the role of the Pentagon and the unchallenged dominance of American military power.

What is poorly understood is how the two pillars fit together seamlessly within one and the same power structure, a power structure that is driven by the money interests. It is driven above all by Wall Street and the special breed of international bankers who institutionalized their rule in organizations such as the Pilgrims Society, the Council on Foreign Relations, the Bilderberg Meetings, the Trilateral Commission and other private and select organs of their control.

The crisis which broke in summer of 2007, initially around the securitization of high-risk "sub-prime" home mortgages has rocked the foundations of the financial system as no other crisis in history to date. For those wishing to understand how the same Wall Street banks that caused the crisis through their unfettered greed and drive for ever greater control over the world, emerged—at taxpayer expense—even more profitable, this book provides an introduction into the inner-workings of the money power.

The book is the result of some thirty years of research and writing on the theme of money and power. It follows the sequence of books I have written relating to the statement in the 1970's attributed to then-Secretary of State Henry Kissinger, a protégé of the powerful Rockefeller circles. He declared, "If you control the oil, you control entire nations; if you control the food, you control the people; if you control the money, you control the entire world." In my two previous books—*A Century of War: Anglo-American Oil Politics and the New World Order*, and *Seeds of Destruction: The Hidden Agenda of Genetic Manipulation*—I undertook to analyze the first two of Kissinger's now famous dictum. This book analyzes the third, the attempt to control the money of the world.

The book chronicles the rise of the American Century from the period following the Civil War, as J. P. Morgan emerged as a force in New York finance, to the debacle today that signals, as harsh as it may sound, the death of that American Century. Much as with the Roman Empire in the third and fourth centuries, the causes of that decline were the same—a system based increasingly on power and plunder, extension of empire, whether formal as with Rome or informal as with the American Century.

A former Goldman Sachs Wall Street banker described the culture that dominates Wall Street as *"completely money-obsessed. I was like a donkey driven forward by the biggest, juiciest carrot I could imagine. Money is the way you define your success... It's an addiction."*

The ultimate question is what will follow the crisis of the dollar and of Wall Street. As we begin the second decade of this century, it is increasingly clear to much of the thinking people across the world that the American "sole Superpower," so triumphantly proclaimed at the end of the Cold War twenty years before, was in deep crisis. Its financial power had become a pale shadow of what it had been only three years before. Its military, awesome in technology, was cracking at the edges, stretched to the breaking point in wars its own citizens little understood. In 2010 the American Century was in a crisis more profound and fundamental that its elites would recognize, at least publicly.

As President, Barack Obama made clear he was every bit as much beholden to the powers of Wall Street and the big banks as was Woodrow Wilson and most every President, with the possible exception of John Kennedy, since the Civil War. Only when a disease is fully diagnosed and understood can it be treated. This book is an attempt to help ordinary citizens in that diagnosis.

–   *F. William Engdahl, February 2010*

CHAPTER ONE:

An American Money Oligarchy Emerges

Money will cease to be the master and become the servant of humanity. Democracy will rise superior to the money power.
  – Abraham Lincoln shortly before his assassination in 1865[1]

A global crisis with a long history

On July 29, 2007 the head of the German banking regulator, Bafin, and the German Minister of Finance held a press conference to announce that the State, together with leading private and public banks, was organizing an emergency rescue of Germany's IKB *Deutsche Industriebank*. IKB was a bank originally set up in 1924 to facilitate payment of German industrial war reparations under the Dawes Plan. The latest crisis marked the second time in its history that the IKB played an historic role in the context of unsound American banking practices.

This time, however, much as the collapse of the Vienna Credit Anstalt in 1931 had been the proximate trigger for a global chain-reaction banking collapse that led to the Great Depression and ultimately to world war, the 2007 collapse of the relatively obscure Duesseldorf business lender triggered a similar global chain reaction. The chain reaction from the collapse of the mid-size IKB created a global systemic financial crisis which, by 2009, looked likely to exceed the tragic dimensions of the Great Depression before its ravages would be complete.

IKB's troubles had originated with its investment in the new, exotic high-yielding securities issued by New York banks called subprime mortgage-backed securities. What were these? Where did they come from? Subprime mortgage-backed securities were created from a convoluted process, as follows:
  – taking hundreds, or thousands, of ordinary real estate home mortgages, bought at a discount from issuing American banks;
  – using the monthly mortgage payment flows to create an entirely new synthetic bond or debenture;

- insuring its component payment flows from possible default through specialized insurers, including AIG;
- and having them rated by the only three rating agencies which enjoyed a de facto monopoly on such ratings (all three based in New York);
- Finally, selling the new Mortgage-Backed Securities, now rated AAA to governments, pension funds and unwary investors around the world in search of high gains. Thereby banks believed they had found a magic route to risk-free super-profits.

Subprime mortgage-backed securities were the culmination of the growing usurpation by private American banks of power – not merely over the economy of the United States, but over the economy of the entire world. The process, dubbed "securitization" by its creating Wall Street banks, was intended to give a new lease on life to the overwhelming American domination of global capital markets, the major pillar of American power since the country emerged victorious in 1945.

"Securitization" -- the idea that normal bank debt risk could be removed from the bank's own balance sheet and organized to spread risks of loan defaults so widely that it could never again threaten the kind of crises that had spread after Credit Anstalt collapsed in 1931 -- was a mad illusion. Asset-backed Securitization was based on fundamental assumptions about future American power, assumptions that dated all the way back to the emergence of the United States as the major industrial rival of the German Reich following the American Civil War in the 1860's.

The global crisis that was triggered by the payment problems of a small German bank in 2007 had roots in a deeply flawed financial and banking power called the Dollar System, earlier referred to as the Bretton Woods System. To understand the true origins of America's colossal global financial power requires going back to the 1860s when the United States emerged from the Civil War. That period is key to grasping the significance of the July 2007 collapse of IKB *Deutsche Industriebank*.

Before exploring the Civil War in relation to the emerging powers of banking, we have to go back briefly to an even earlier period that is central to an understanding of the unique political character of American banking.

America's private 'National' banks

The very term "national" bank or "central" bank in America was the kiss of political death to anyone advocating one at the beginning of the 20th Century. Since the adoption of the US Constitution in 1787, the United States of America had had two abortive experiences with central banks in its first hundred and twenty years of existence as a republic.

The first national bank was designed by the nation's first Treasury Secretary, Alexander Hamilton. In 1791, Hamilton proposed the establishment of a Bank of the United States, modeled, however, on the privately-owned Bank of England. Benjamin Franklin, being familiar with the Bank of England, understood all too well the dangers of a privately owned central bank controlling the issue of the nation's currency. Franklin effectively blocked the chartering of a privately-owned central bank until his death in 1791.

Before Franklin's body had long been laid to rest, Hamilton pushed through legislation that same year that would charter the First Bank of the United States, to be situated in Philadelphia.[2]

Hamilton's national bank was no United States Federal Government bank. By its charter, it was 80% owned by private investors, including -- remarkably enough for a young nation not yet healed from the wounds of an independence war from that same City of London -- investors from the largest British banks.

Nathan Rothschild, at the time London's and the world's most powerful banker, invested heavily in the first Bank of the United States, becoming by some accounts its largest shareholder. By guiding the activities of the Bank of the United States from behind the scenes, the London bankers set about to control financial activity and credit in America, something many Americans viewed as tantamount to re-colonization by Britain by financial and economic means.

Hamilton wrote to the Congress that the bank should be "a National Bank which, by uniting the influence and interest of the moneyed men with the resources of government, can alone give it that durable and extensive credit of which it stands in need." [3]

Unite those interests it certainly did, but not in the general interest of the people of the United States.

The Bank of the United States was used to deposit US Government revenues from its tax collections and to issue bank notes to increase the money supply as the Bank saw fit. The Bank had a capital stock of $10 million, with 80% of the bank being owned by private investors, as noted. A mere 20% of the bank's stock was owned by the United States Government. The Bank was administered by a President and a twenty-five person Board of Directors. Twenty of the twenty-five directors were elected by the stockholders, 80% of whom were private groups. Only five were appointed by the Government. The US Government in effect handed over to private bankers control over its money and agreed to pay those bankers interest to boot on money it borrowed.

Thomas Jefferson vehemently opposed the bill to create a privately controlled central bank. Nevertheless, George Washington signed it into law on February 25, 1791. President Washington did so on Hamilton's advice, despite the fact that the US Constitution clearly placed control of the nation's currency in the hands of Congress, and made no provisions for Congress to delegate that authority. [4]

That explicit Constitutional provision had been designed specifically to keep the American money supply out of the hands of the private banking industry, and keep it directly in the hands of what Jefferson, the drafter of the Declaration of Independence, called the most republican of the three branches of government, that of the elected Congress.

In 1811 the US Congress defeated the renewal of the charter for the First Bank of the United States by one vote in each house. The Bank was regarded as responsible for a significant rise in wholesale prices in the country.

In 1812, in a bizarre turn of events, the United States Congress, at the urging of President James Madison, declared war against Britain. To finance the War of 1812 as it became known, the US Government went deeply into debt. The national debt rose from $45 million to $127 million in just four years, an increase of near 300%. During the rush of patriotism generated around the war, state-chartered banks expanded their loan base in a lending boom, with little regard to gold or silver reserves.

To address the problem of the rampant inflation that resulted, Congress was urged by a convergence of interest groups -- above all the private banks -- to create a new national bank. In 1816, Congress acquiesced and created the Second Bank of the United States, based on the same principles as the First bank and also seated in Philadelphia. It had a charter for twenty years until expiration in 1836.

The Second Bank of the United States also permitted only 20% of its stock to be held by the Government, with 80% of shares -- the control -- in private ownership. And highly important, it was mandated to create a single national currency; it could buy most of the US Government debt and receive US Treasury funds as deposit, a huge advantage over private or state rivals. These privileges were unique to the privately owned Second Bank as they had been with Hamilton's previous First Bank.

Thus, on May 10, 1816, after five years with no national bank and after the 1812 war with England, President James Madison signed the bill creating the Second Bank of the United States. Its new charter raised its capital stock to $35 million. It authorized the creation of Bank branches and the issuing of money, notes in denominations larger than $5.

The new Bank thus had the power to control the entire fiscal structure of the country.

In 1819 the US Supreme Court, in an opinion written by Chief Justice John Marshall, declared the Second Bank of the United States to be Constitutional, finding with dubious logic in *McCulloch v. Maryland* that Congress had the "implied power" to create a national bank – a power that the state of Maryland had challenged. The Second Bank was controlled by Nicholas Biddle, a wealthy Philadelphian and the bank's President after 1822. He and his shareholders renamed it the Bank of the United States.

President Andrew Jackson vetoed the bill to re-charter the Second Bank in 1832. A popular military hero of the War of 1812, Jackson distrusted the privately held Bank of the United States and feared it gave too much power to foreign investors and that it favored New York and Boston investment banks over the western and southern agrarian parts of the country.

To assure the Bank's demise, Jackson ordered the Secretary of the Treasury to remove all Government deposits from the private national Bank and to deposit them in the state banks. In retaliation against Jackson, Biddle contracted the money supply and triggered a nationwide recession in 1834 to force Jackson to re-charter the private national Bank. Biddle did so by demanding the immediate repayment of old loans and by making no new loans, a total choke on national credit.

Biddle's blackmail attempt failed. On January 8, 1835, Jackson paid off the final installment on the US National Debt for the first time in America's history. The Treasury accumulated a surplus of $35 million, which was distributed among the States.

In another attempt to force a re-chartering of the Bank of the United States, Nicholas Biddle, aided and abetted by leading London and European bankers, engineered the Panic of 1837. In his autobiography, Wall Street banker Henry Clews revealed in 1888 that,

> *The Panic of 1837 was aggravated by the Bank of England when it in one day threw out all the paper connected with the United States.*[5]

The dominant figure in the policy council of the Bank of England at that time was Nathan M. Rothschild, a close ally of US Bank President Nicholas Biddle, and a major shareholder in the Bank of the United States. [6]

London bankers control the US bank

The Rothschild banking dynasty in Europe, headed by Baron Nathan in London, with brothers in Vienna, Naples and Paris, was the most powerful financial group in the world at the time. Its power was based on absolute control of family dynastic ties so extreme that it was common practice for the brothers and their descendants to marry first cousins to guard the family wealth and secrets.

Nathan in London and James de Rothschild in Paris held major stock shares of Biddle's Bank of the United States. Nathan Rothschild was even for a time the official European banker for the US Government. As historian Gustavus Myers stated, "The law records show that they were the power in the old Bank of the United States." [7]

The manipulated panic in 1837 however also failed to get the charter through, and the Bank died. When the Bank was finally forced to close its doors in 1841, it left two London merchant banks, Baring Brothers and N.M. Rothschild's, with $25 million in claims, a staggering sum for two private banks, even for a Rothschild bank. [8]

In 1841, President John Tyler vetoed two bills which would have re-chartered the Bank of the United States. Repeated attempts by the money interests to re-establish control over the nation's money through a central bank under their private control continued without success right up to 1913.

Enter London's powerful Rothschilds. Amid the financial panic of 1837, Nathan Rothschild had sent August Belmont, Sr. to America, as his private agent. Belmont founded the investment bank, August Belmont & Co. with Nathan Rothschild of London as his silent backer.

Rothschild was forced to operate through agents rather than in his own name after the defeat of the Second Bank and the negative publicity surrounding it. However, August Belmont was so effective in protecting Rothschild's financial interests that he later became a financial advisor to US Presidents and head of the Democratic Party, all the while taking extraordinary measures behind the scenes to foment the American Civil War. (Belmont's son, August Belmont, Jr., would later work with J.P. Morgan to create the Panic of 1893, paving the way for the third Bank of the United States— which would be called the Federal Reserve System.)

In the 1860s during the course of the Civil War, President Abraham Lincoln said:

> *Money is the creature of law and the creation of the original issue of money should be maintained as an exclusive monopoly of National Government. Government possessing the power to create and issue currency and credit as money and enjoying the right to withdraw both currency and credit from circulation by taxation and otherwise, need not and should not borrow capital at interest as the means of financing governmental work and public enterprise.*

> *The Government should create, issue, and circulate all the currency and credit needed to satisfy the spending power of the Government and the buying power of consumers. The privilege of creating and issuing money is not only the supreme prerogative of Government, but it is the Government's greatest creative opportunity. By adoption of these principles, the long-felt want for a uniform medium will be satisfied.*

> *The taxpayers will be saved immense sums in interest, discounts, and exchanges. The financing of all public enterprise, the maintenance of stable government and ordered process, and the conduct of the Treasury will become matters of practical administration. The people can and will be furnished with a currency as safe as their own Government. Money will cease to be master and become the servant of humanity.* [9]

Lincoln's words were not at all well received in the City of London, where the powerful House of Rothschild and other City banks planned to entice a desperate Lincoln Government to accept war loans at usurious interest rates. Lincoln, who had won the Presidency on his strong support for industrial protectionism, was faced with the secession of Virginia and six other Southern cotton-growing slave states immediately after his election.

At the time, the London banks, led by the House of Rothschild, were the major creditors to the Southern cotton trade, the vital source of raw cotton for the Manchester, England textile mills. The Southern secession had been discreetly encouraged by August Belmont, still serving as Rothschild's personal agent in the United States, and now a major figure in American politics. Belmont regarded Lincoln's protectionist policies as anathema. US protectionism and high tariffs would have destroyed England's lucrative cotton business with the slave states.[10]

Abraham Lincoln had understood very well why the framers of the US Constitution had vested the money power with the duly-elected Congress and not exclusively with private bankers. He had been a long-time supporter of the pro-industry protectionist tariff policies of Whig (National Republican) party leader, Senator Henry Clay. Lincoln was also a close friend of Pennsylvania protectionist economist Henry C. Carey, a follower of the famous German economist, Friedrich List.[11]

Rather than establish a new Third Bank of the United States -- again to be controlled by private bankers, as leading London and allied New York bankers wished -- Lincoln used the powers of the Constitution to convince Congress to authorize the issue of interest-free Legal Tender Notes in the amount of $150 million (an enormous sum at that time), backed by the Full Faith and Credit of the United States Government.

Under Lincoln, the Legal Tender Notes were issued by the US Treasury. The Notes paid no interest but were to be used for "all debts public and private except duties on imports and interest on the public debt." They came to be nicknamed "Greenbacks" for their distinctive design and color.

During the course of the Civil War, the volume of these government-authorized Greenbacks in circulation was increased to $450 million. The Greenbacks could not at the time of issue be redeemed in gold. They were US Government fiat paper notes—i.e., promises to pay the bearer in gold or silver at some unspecified date in the future. The holder of the note was, in effect, betting on the future existence and prosperity of the United States.

Issued by President Abraham Lincoln on State Paper Currency, Greenbacks enabled the Union to finance the Civil War independent of the London banks and their New York partners. It likely provoked his assassination hours after the end of the war.

The Greenbacks allowed Lincoln to finance war costs independent of London or New York bankers who were demanding an exorbitantly high interest rate – as high as between 24% and even 36%.[12] Lincoln's Greenbacks financed the war and avoided entangling the Union in large war debts to the private bankers, something that made him bitter enemies in London and New York banking circles.

The influential *Times* of London reacted vehemently to Lincoln's Greenback issuance. In an editorial clearly written on behalf of the City of London bankers, it declared,

> *If that mischievous financial policy, which had its origin in the North American Republic, should become indurated down to a fixture, then that government will furnish its own money without cost. It will pay off debts and be without a debt. It will have all the money necessary to carry on its commerce. It will become prosperous beyond precedent in the history of civilized governments of the world. The brains and the wealth of all countries will go to North America. That government must be destroyed or it will destroy every monarchy on the globe.* [13]

On April 14, 1865, Abraham Lincoln was assassinated, shot down in cold blood in a Washington theatre just five days after Confederate General Robert E. Lee surrendered to Grant at Appomattox Court House, Virginia. As with the assassination of John Kennedy almost a century later, a 'lone gunman,' John Wilkes Booth, was blamed. There was no serious Congressional investigation into the issue of conspiracy and who might have been behind the assassination.

Though the truth may never be provable, persuasive evidence suggested that Lincoln's assassin, John Wilkes Booth, had been hired for the job by Judah Benjamin, Treasurer of the Confederacy. Judah Benjamin was a close associate of Benjamin Disraeli (1804-1881), British Prime Minister and an intimate of the London Rothschilds. After the murder of Lincoln, Judah Benjamin fled to London, becoming the only member of the Confederate cabinet who never returned to the United States.[14]

That all suggested that Lincoln was killed as a result of his monetary policies. Lincoln needed money to finance the Civil War. European bankers led by the Rothschilds had offered Lincoln loans, but at usuriously high interest rates. Rather than accept the loans, Lincoln found other means to fund the war effort using the powers of the State. More importantly, the British bankers opposed

Lincoln's protectionist policies. Some Englishmen in the 1860's believed that 'British free trade, industrial monopoly and human slavery travel together.'[15]

Lincoln's policies, if continued after the Civil War, would have destroyed the Rothschilds' commodity speculations. Lincoln's plans for recovery after the war included a mild Reconstruction policy that would have enabled a resumption of agricultural production in the southern states. That in turn would have drastically weakened the ability of London bankers to raise world grain and especially prices and profit. Moreover, Lincoln's wartime experience with issuing Government Greenback currency independent of the stringent terms of the New York bankers suggested he would have bitterly opposed returning the United States economy to a London-controlled Gold Standard.

The Rothschilds, however, wanted the opposite: a Reconstruction policy towards the South that would be tough and harsh, resulting in high prices, especially for commodities like raw cotton. Lincoln was viewed as a threat to the Rothschilds' established order of things, and his assassination would be viewed as likely to weaken the United States, assisting the Rothschilds and their New York banking allies to take over its postwar economy. [16]

In 1934 a Canadian attorney named Gerald G. McGeer obtained highly sensitive information about the identity of John Wilkes Booth – evidence that had been deleted from the public record at Booth's trial. The evidence was provided to McGeer by Secret Service Agents after Booth's death; it showed that John Wilkes Booth was a mercenary working for the international bankers. In a speech to the Canadian Parliament, reported in the *Vancouver Sun*, May 2, 1934, attorney McGeer stated,

> *Abraham Lincoln, the murdered emancipator of the slaves, was assassinated through the machinations of a group representative of the International Bankers, who feared the United States President's National Credit ambitions. There was only one group in the world at that time who had any reason to desire the death of Lincoln. They were the men opposed to his national currency program and who had fought him throughout the whole Civil War on his policy of Greenback currency.* [17]

Following the assassination of Lincoln, a battle ensued in the US Congress to eliminate the US Government's issuance of Greenbacks and replace them with a gold specie-backed currency. The goal was to allow those holding monetary gold -- namely, London and an elite circle of allied New York international bankers -- to control the US currency by locking US currency issue to gold.

At that time, most of the world's central bank gold was in the hands of the Bank of England and the London banks.

In 1875, under pressure by East Coast bankers advocating the gold redemption of Greenbacks and the future issue exclusively of gold-backed US Government notes, the US Congress passed the Specie Resumption Act. The key Senator pushing the bill through Congress was Senator John Sherman of Ohio. Henry Stoddard, publisher of the *New York Republican* Newspaper, noted that Senator Sherman's "relations with the First National Bank of New York were so close during the resumption crisis that the institution was popularly called 'Fort Sherman.'" [18]

The founder of First National Bank of New York was George F. Baker, who went on to become a member of the elite Pilgrims Society, founded in 1902 as the guiding forum of the emerging axis of Anglo-American financial power located on Wall Street. Baker later became a close ally of J.P. Morgan, himself also a founding member of the Pilgrims Society.

The lobbyists behind Baker and Sherman's campaign to resume specie or gold payment for US bank notes represented New York, Boston and Philadelphia banks that specialized in financing international trade. The pro-gold lobbyists also included international shippers and importers who were forced to pay for goods in specie to British and other European suppliers.

What would later come to be known as the American East Coast Establishment had its origins in this internationalist banking-centered group of powerful New York and East Coast families. They organized pressure on Congress through their lobby organizations including the New York Chamber of Commerce, the Boston and Philadelphia Boards of Trade and the National Board of Trade.

The East Coast internationalists were bitterly opposed by the powerful Western and Southern agriculture interests, by a major share of the nation's iron industry, as well as small businessmen. Economist Henry C. Carey, who had earlier been one of Lincoln's economic advisers, represented the nation's iron manufacturers who feared specie resumption would raise interest rates and make US iron and steel less competitive against cheaper British imports.

Carey wrote that the East Coast "commercial states" had "established a monopoly of money power without a parallel in the world." He pointed out that while interest rates in the banking states of New England and New York were low, the rest of the country's manufacturers and farmers had to pay from 10% to 30% for money.[19]

The Specie Resumption Act was highly controversial and bitterly opposed by farmers and small manufacturers who feared a major deflation of the economy and contraction of the money supply. They rightly complained that as the New York and New England bankers held the bulk of the nation's monetary gold, and the distribution of the nation's currency was skewed towards those same East Coast banking powers, that Specie Resumption would most benefit those banks at the expense of the rest.

Specie Resumption

A syndicate of New York and London international banks finally pushed through the Specie Resumption Act in 1875. The international bankers in the syndicate included August Belmont & Co. representing London bankers N.M. Rothschild & Sons; J. and W. Seligman & Co. representing Seligman Brothers; Drexel, Morgan & Co., whose partner was J.P. Morgan and who represented Junius S. Morgan & Co. of London, the bank of J.P. Morgan's father. The syndicate also included Morton, Bliss & Co. representing Morton, Rose & Co. And it included the only New York commercial bank in the syndicate, George F. Baker's First National Bank of New York, the predecessor to Citigroup. [20]

The Specie Resumption Act specified that by January 1, 1879, all Greenbacks in circulation could be redeemed for gold specie. The Resumption Act was a major step towards bringing the US economy under the control of London and New York international bankers because they controlled the lions' share of the world's monetary gold in private hands.

But even this was not sufficient for their long term plans and intentions: total control over the issue of money in the United States of America.[21]

That goal would be accomplished later, as we shall see, through the 1908 Aldrich Commission on Monetary Reform, set up after the Money Trust organized the Panic of 1907.

Endnotes:

[1] Abraham Lincoln, officially cited in, 76th Congress, 1st Session, Jan 3 - Aug 5, 1939, Senate Documents #10304, Vol 3, Senate Document 23, *"National Economy and the Banking System of the United States,"* by Robert L. Owen. Accessed in http://www.basicincome.com/basic_practice.htm.
[2] For a detailed description by Treasury Secretary Hamilton to Congress of the bank proposal, see Alexander Hamilton, *The Second Report on the Further Provision Necessary for Establishing Public Credit (Report on a National Bank),* December 13, 1790, reprinted

in Jacob E. Cooke, ed., The Reports of Alexander Hamilton (New York: Harper Torchbooks, 1964), pp. 74-82.

[3] Alexander Hamilton, *The Continentalist,* No. IV, August 30, 1781.

[4] The Constitution of the United States Article I: The Legislative Branch, Section 8. The relevant section states, *"The Congress shall have Power To lay and collect Taxes, Duties, Imposts and Excises, to pay the Debts and provide for the common Defence and general Welfare of the United States...To borrow Money on the credit of the United States...To coin Money, regulate the Value thereof, and of foreign Coin, and fix the Standard of Weights and Measures..."*

[5] Henry Clews, *Twenty-eight Years in Wall Street* (New York: Irving Co., 1888), p. 157.

[6] Ibid.

[7] Gustavus Myers, *History of the Great American Fortunes* (New York: Random House, 1936,) p. 556.

[8] United States Treasury, *Frequently Asked Questions: Buying, Selling and Redeeming Currency*, in www.treasury.gov/education/faq/currency/sales.shtml, accessed July 7, 2006.

[9] Abraham Lincoln, op. Cit.

[10] Reinhard H. Luthin, Abraham Lincoln and the Tariff, The American Historical Review, Vol. XLIX, No.4, July 1944, pp. 610-627.

[11] Ibid., pp. 626-629. The former Tuebingen professor of economics, List, known in Germany as the father of the Zollverein (Customs Union), had been brought to Pennsylvania in the 1820's by Matthew Carey's Pennsylvania Society for the Promotion of Manufacturing and the Mechanical Arts. While in Pennsylvania, List wrote an attack on the British free trade doctrines of Adam Smith and Ricardo titled "Outlines of American Political Economy," which Carey, father of Lincoln adviser, Henry C. Carey, published. Interestingly the name List today has been all but expunged from the study of economics since the dogmas of Milton Friedman's neo-liberalist free trade became dominant during the 1970's.

[12] R. Mac, *A Brief History of Banking System*, February 9, 2009, accessed in http://www.fairloanrate.com/2009/02/09/a-brief-history-of-banking-system/#more-266.

[13] Ibid.

[14] John E. Kovacs, *Two Presidents who died defying the Rothschilds*, The National Educator, September 1990, p. 9.

[15] Burke McCarty, introduction to, *The Supressed Truth About the Assassination of Abraham Lincoln,* (Health Research Publishing, 1993), accessed in http://healourworldnow.org/how/forum/index.php?topic=365.0;prev_next=next.

[16] Lincoln Assassination Conspiracy, accessed in http://home.att.net/~rjnorton/Lincoln74.html.

[17] Gerald G. McGeer, The Vancouver Sun, cited in R. Mac., op. cit.

[18] Henry L. Stoddard, *As He Saw It*, cited in Ferdinand Lundberg, *America's Sixty Families* (New York: The Vanguard Press, 1937), p. 59.

[19] Henry C. Carey, *The Finance Minister, the Currency and the Public* (Washington, D.C.: Collins,1868), pp.13-14.

[20] Irwin Unger, *Business Men and Specie Resumption*, Political Science Quarterly, Vol. 74, March 1959, No.1, p. 68, footnote 95.

[21] Ibid., pp. 46-70.

CHAPTER TWO

J. Pierpont Morgan, America's First 'God of Money'

The rights and interests of the laboring man will be protected and cared for, not by the labor agitators, but by the Christian men to whom God in His infinite wisdom has given control of the property interests of the country.
  – George 'Divine Right' Baer, JP Morgan railroad executive in 1902 [1]

As the vast British Empire went into a prolonged and seemingly irreversible decline following a major economic Depression beginning in 1873, a challenge began to emerge from across the Atlantic. Powerful American industrial and banking families grouped around J.P. Morgan and John D. Rockefeller concentrated the wealth and control of American industry into their own hands.

In their rise to unprecedented heights of power, the Morgan and Rockefeller interests deployed fraud, deceit, violence, and bribery -- and they deliberately manipulated financial panics. Each financial panic, brought about through their calculated control of financial markets and banking credit, allowed them and their closest allies to consolidate ever more power into fewer and fewer hands. It was this concentration of financial power within an elite few wealthy families that created an American plutocracy or, more accurately, an American oligarchy.

Aristotle used the term "oligarchy" to describe rule by the wealthiest families, where voting power in the state was related to the size of a family's fortune. Whether it was called an oligarchy or a plutocracy—government by a wealthy "class"—the real power in the spectacular rise of the American Century at the end of the 1890s did not rest democratically in the hands of the majority of citizens. It did not even lie in the hands of a broad, educated and growing middle class. Power, together with control over the nation's economy, was being ruthlessly centralized in the hands of the wealthy few, every bit as much as it had been in the days of Imperial Rome.

The more centralized that power became in the hands of an aristocracy of wealth, the more it wrapped itself in the rhetorical garb of American "democracy." In one respect, and one respect only, the new American oligarchy was democratic: it did not restrict entry to those of noble birth and bloodline, as had been the case with the decadent nobility of ancient Rome or pre-revolutionary France.

The American Constitution prohibited inherited titles of nobility and aristocracy. It did not, however, prohibit an aristocracy of wealth—either inherited or created. Like Britain around the time of the founding of the private Bank of England in 1694, this "open admissions" aristocracy would turn out to be a key factor in the dynamism of the emerging American empire—the "American Century" as Henry Luce was later to name it.

In the closing decades of the 19th Century, anyone clever, determined and ruthless enough to win the Darwinian survival of the fittest award by amassing a huge fortune -- and holding onto it -- was eligible for membership, almost regardless of class, religion or national origin. Race, however, remained a barrier to entry to the higher circles of power in America for at least another century.

This oligarchy used its immense economic power, often secretly and in coordinated fashion, to orchestrate events that generated waves of bankruptcies and severe economic depressions, even panics. The emerging American oligarchy cynically corrupted and co-opted state legislatures, governors, US Congressmen, judges, newspaper editors and even Presidents to serve their private interests. Those interests were served by wars their captive press helped trigger, wars from which that oligarchy profited while thousands of young Americans perished for causes they knew nothing about.

The prevalent myth claimed that a rugged American frontier inspired the democratic and entrepreneurial spirit of the United States in the remarkable industrial expansion after the Civil War. In reality, by the late 1870s, after the enactment of the Specie Resumption Act of 1875 which fully took effect in the year 1879 -- and which, in effect, put the United States on the London Gold Standard -- few countries had financial and economic power so concentrated in so few hands as did the United States.

By the 1880s two colossal groups had emerged within the United States' wealthiest families. Initially they were bitter, hated rivals. In the end they became allies, not out of love but out of practicality, in one of the greatest concentrations of financial and industrial power ever seen. The two families, Rockefeller and Morgan, created a combination of wealth and control so powerful in its influence over the economic and financial life of the United States at the beginning of the 20th Century that Congressional critics named it the Money Trust.

The engineered Panic Of 1893

The emergence of the Morgan group as the decisive money power in the United States required years of covert and usually corrupt machinations. The Panic of 1893 led to a severe US economic depression that lasted four years. It exemplified the lengths to which the emerging Money Trust around J.P. Morgan was willing to go to amass concentrated power.

Following the American Civil War, right up to the end of the 19th Century, the United States Treasury recognized silver as well as gold as monetary metal. The monetary system was, in effect, a bi-metallic system. Silver existed in abundance in the Western United States. Farmers and small shop owners advocated using silver to expand cheap credit to allow the economy to grow. It made sense if expansion of the monetary base through the Federal Government were carefully guided.

However, the influential New York bank syndicate, headed in the 1890s by the House of Morgan, took the opposite position. They saw gold, especially in light of their close ties to leading London banks, as their best road to dominant power over the money supply of the United States. Supplies of monetary gold were controlled by a handful of New York banks and by the financial powers of the City of London -- above all, by the banking group of Lord Rothschild.

The New York bankers wanted no competition from silver. Their banking allies in the City of London, the heart of the world gold standard at the time, wanted America exclusively on a gold standard where their influence would be vastly greater. London's New York banking allies -- J.P. Morgan, along with Rothschild's US banking agent, August Belmont, and others in New York finance -- shrewdly used their London banking associates to control American credit markets to their own exclusive advantage and to the distinct disadvantage of the general American public. It was no easy challenge, but they were single-minded in their determination regarding the gold standard.

The infamous Panic of 1893 was in fact manipulated by Morgan interests, in collusion with August Belmont, in order to end the role of silver and to consolidate the gold of the nation into the hands of the private New York banks. In the course of manipulating several financial panics, the same bankers also gained unprecedented control over the nation's steel and railroads—the heart of the economy.

The point man for Morgan and company was John G. Carlisle, Secretary of the Treasury under Democratic President Grover Cleveland. Cleveland, a mediocre New York City politician before getting the financial backing of

Morgan and friends to become President, was on intimate terms as President with two frequent private White House guests.

The two were J.P. Morgan and August P. Belmont, Jr., son of (London) Rothschild's official banking agent in the United States. August P. Belmont, Sr. had been rumored in London society circles to be the illegitimate son of Baron Karl Meyer Rothschild, who, in any case had adopted the young Belmont as if he were his son, dispatching him to manage the Rothschilds' American business interests under the less-controversial Belmont name.[2]

The one hand washes the other....

Morgan's takeover of America's gold reserves began in 1893. Following Cleveland's second inauguration as President in early 1893, Morgan and Belmont secretly instigated a run on the US Treasury's gold reserves. Colluding London banks, acting via instructions from Morgan and Belmont, right on cue, sold the millions of US Treasury securities they held, and demanded payment in gold.

At the time, the Treasury by law was allowed to pay for redeemed bonds in either gold or silver. The powerful silver lobby naturally urged that the Treasury pay in silver not gold.

Under the law, the decision was left to the Treasury Secretary's discretion. But Secretary Carlisle was getting his advice secretly from Morgan and Belmont. As a result Carlisle refused to redeem the bonds for silver, which would have ended the gold hoarding panic. Instead, he redeemed the securities exclusively in gold, feeding further panic as US Government gold stocks disappeared rapidly.

The consequence was that the US Treasury's gold reserves vanished. By April 1893 the reserves of gold fell below $100 million for the first time since resumption of specie payments in 1879. The trap had been masterfully set.

J.P. Morgan and August Belmont, Jr. had convinced Cleveland to have his Treasury Secretary, John Carlisle, issue US Treasury bonds exclusively to Morgan and Belmont. In exchange, the private bankers paid the Treasury with gold that was urgently needed for the Government's foreign reserves. The prevailing practice was to maintain US Treasury minimum gold reserves of $100 million; anything below that being grounds for alarm over the stability of the dollar.

Cleveland's Treasury Department sold the bonds to the private Morgan banking syndicate at a steep discount. The bankers in turn immediately resold the bonds at much higher prices to the investing public—small regional banks, insurance companies and others—pocketing the huge profit from what amounted to an insider trade. To complete the circle of corruption, President Cleveland's former law partner F. L. Stetson represented J.P. Morgan & Co. for whom he negotiated the terms of the bond issues with the US Treasury. To call this arrangement a conflict of interest and violation of the public trust would be mild.

Cleveland managed to sell a staggering $162,000,000 of such bonds to the Morgan private syndicate at sweetheart prices before the anti-corruption *World*, the newspaper of journalist Joseph Pulitzer, exposed the deals forcing an end to the highly profitable operation.[3]

By May 1893, full-scale panic had broken out across the United States. Some weeks later the government of India, then a British colony, announced that it would no longer accept silver to mint for coin. India, largely as a result of the earlier machinations of the British Opium Wars against China, had become the world's largest holder of silver bullion.

The Indian colony's rejection of silver gave an added boost to the London-New York bankers' plot to destroy once and for all the monetary role of silver in America. It led to a catastrophic 50% fall in the international price of silver, including in the United States. There was more than a little suspicion within US circles hit by the money panic that certain banking houses of the City of London and New York which stood to gain handsomely from the gold panic had encouraged the Indian government, the crown jewel of Her Majesty's British Empire, to reject silver purchases.[4]

In early 1895, the US Treasury had again been emptied of its gold, which it had just purchased at usurious rates from J.P. Morgan & Co.'s banking syndicate.

Where had the gold gone? Records of private gold holdings of the New York banks show that in January 1895 twenty six New York banks held in their vaults a hoard of $65 million of gold. US Treasury reserve minimum for gold at the time was $100 million. To fall below that level, as noted, was considered dangerous for US financial stability. President Cleveland reportedly cried, "the banks have got the country by the throat." He was careful not to reveal to the ignorant citizenry his help in giving the banks the rope.

At the critical moment, a syndicate appeared with a "generous" proposal. Led by J.P. Morgan & Company, August Belmont & Company representing the London Rothschilds, and James Speyer of Rockefeller's National City Bank, the syndicate offered to sell their private gold to the US Treasury—for a handsome profit of course.

The 'worst depression in US History'

The gold hoarding Panic of 1893 resulted in a contraction of bank credit across America that triggered the worst economic depression in US history up to that time. By law, holders of US paper currency could redeem in gold from the US Treasury. As a result of the panic, most banks feared to lend.

Between May and October 1893, national bank loans contracted by an alarming $318 million. Rates on bank money hit 70% as banks and private individuals frantically sought gold. Exports of gold from the United States to the City of London were the heaviest in US history as London banks demanded gold as security for their US loans. The gold panic severely cut into US Government tax revenues, increasing the deficit, and forcing the Treasury to use its increasingly scarce gold reserves to pay current expenses, further impacting gold reserves.

The Depression of 1893 which followed from the orchestrated bank panic of 1893 was deliberately manipulated by J. P. Morgan and New York bankers in collusion with their London bank allies to tighten their control over money and the economy.

The credit crisis led to a wave of business failures and bankruptcies across America from East to West as banks called in their loans. Western farmers and silver miners blamed Eastern gold banks whom they believed secretly sought to discredit silver. They were right.

On cue, in August 1893 President Cleveland, advised by Morgan and Belmont, called a Special Session of Congress to repeal the Sherman Silver Act, under which the US Treasury had bought silver in exchange for US Treasury notes that in turn could be exchanged for gold by their bearers.

The Sherman Silver Act had originally been passed under pressure from farmers and small businesses that faced depression and ruin as a result of the forced shift to an exclusively gold-backed dollar.[5] Cleveland successfully argued that by ending the Government's silver purchase, the nation would avert financial disaster. Predictably, the opposite proved to be the case as silver, which was in abundance, was no longer a practical alternative to gold.

The Sherman Silver Act was immediately repealed, despite hefty protests from western and southern farmers and small businesses. New York banks, above all the Morgan-Belmont syndicate, had triumphed. Presidential candidate William Jennings Bryan later dramatically characterized this as being "crucified on a Cross of Gold." [6]

The victory of J.P. Morgan, Belmont and their Wall Street cronies was formalized into law. A Monetary Commission was set up in January 1897. The Gold Standard Act, introduced into the House of Representatives in December 1899, was passed by Congress and became law in March 1900. The Act confirmed the gold dollar as the standard of value, with silver as only a subsidiary coinage. [7]

President Cleveland arranged for Morgan to create a private syndicate on Wall Street to supply the US Treasury with $65 million in gold, half of it from Europe, to float a bond issue that restored the treasury surplus of $100 million. The Treasury bonds were sold at rock-bottom sweetheart prices exclusively to the Morgan-Belmont syndicate, not to the general public. Morgan then resold the bonds at hefty premium to smaller regional banks and insurance companies, making a handsome profit at both ends of the deal at the expense of the economic health of the nation.

During the ensuing Great Depression of 1893, lasting for four full years, spending for capital goods collapsed, profits plunged, and depression hit the cities en masse. Over the course of this depression 15,000 businesses, 600 banks, and 74 railroads failed. There was severe unemployment and wide-scale protesting, which in some cases turned violent. At the peak of the ensuing unemployment, an unprecedented 14.5% of the active labor force was out of work. Some estimates put the jobless figure as high as 25%.

The deliberately engineered economic collapse of the Philadelphia and Reading Railroads had been the first step in the oligarchy's consolidation of railroad ownership. J.P. Morgan had organized a credit boycott of the railroad, triggering a sharp fall in the rail's stock, at which point Morgan quietly bought controlling shares at dirt-cheap prices. The rail was linked to vast anthracite coal deposits in Pennsylvania.[8]

Meanwhile, in the midst of the gold panic, by May 15, 1893 stock prices in the New York Stock Exchange reached an all-time low. This included major railroads, many of which -- such as the Union-Pacific, Northern-Pacific and Santa Fe railroads -- were forced to declare bankruptcy. The chain of major railroad bankruptcies across America provided the "golden opportunity" for the highly solvent banks of the Morgan-Belmont syndicate to consolidate their iron grip over the expanding US railway network, at that time the heart of the American economic expansion.

America's Oligarchy—The Sixty Families

America's business tycoons emerged in the economic boom years following the Civil War of 1861-65 and the Specie Resumption Act of 1875, accumulating and consolidating vast fortunes largely through fraud, bribery of public officials and Congress, corruption, forced bankruptcies and other noble practices.

Railroads were the heart of American economic growth, and they fed the expansion of a large and growing steel industry. The telegraph also required huge tonnages of copper for the wires across the nation as rail ties expanded from East to West.

Most of the great railroad lines were built not with Morgan money but with public taxes and gifts of public lands. J.P. Morgan then captured these railways and thereby achieved vital control over the entire United States economy. By 1901 the Morgan Group controlled the Southern Railway, Mobile & Ohio Railroad, Queen & Crescent, Georgia Central, Georgia Southern & Florida, Macon & Birmingham, Philadelphia & Reading, the Erie, the Central of New Jersey, and the Atlantic Coast Line -- a total of more than 55,000 miles of steel rail track that controlled railroad rights of way, access to coal lands, terminals, competing lines and steamship connections.

The emerging caste of American oligarchs draped themselves in the rhetoric of American 'democracy.' They carefully fostered the myth of 'rugged individualism' and 'free enterprise' to justify their huge gains and cover their fraudulent origins.

By the end of the 1890's Morgan and Rockefeller had become the giants of an increasingly powerful Money Trust controlling American industry and government policy. There was little room for the actual practice of democracy in their world. Power was the commodity of their trade. It was the creation of an American aristocracy of blood and money, every bit as elite and exclusive as the titled nobility of Britain, Germany or France – despite the Constitutional ban on titled nobility in America. It was an oligarchy, a plutocracy in every sense of the word—rule by the wealthiest in their self-interest.

Some 60 families—names like Rockefeller, Morgan, Dodge, Mellon, Pratt, Harkness, Whitney, Duke, Harriman, Carnegie, Vanderbilt, DuPont, Guggenheim, Astor, Lehman, Warburg, Taft, Huntington, Baruch and Rosenwald—formed a close network of plutocratic wealth that manipulated, bribed, and bullied its way to control the destiny of the United States. At the dawn of the 20th Century, some sixty ultra-rich families, through dynastic intermarriage and corporate, interconnected shareholdings, had gained control of American industry and banking institutions.[9]

One of the wealthiest of the new American oligarchs was Cornelius Vanderbilt who created his fortune through bribing state legislators to ignore laws prohibiting preferential freight rates to preferred customers. Vanderbilt at the time controlled all rail lines that connected to New York City. To promote and benefit from the greater profit margins of large enterprises, and squeeze out the smaller ones, Vanderbilt used a variety of tactics. Among his methods was to impose a 50% tax on small farmers to ship milk on Vanderbilt's railroads. Farmers were not preferred customers; emerging large agribusiness groups who got Valderbilt's preferred rates were. Vanderbilt later became an appendage of the J.P. Morgan circle.

Another fortune of the day built on fraud and bribery was that of the Phelps and Dodge families and their Phelps Dodge Company, importers of metals such as tin, copper and lead needed to feed the American construction boom of the 1880s and beyond.

Founded in 1834 by Anson Greene Phelps and William E. Dodge, the company went to great lengths to cultivate the image of being run by God-fearing Christian businessmen who donated their efforts to the Young Men's Christian Association and other philanthropy. In reality, as an 1873 US Government trial determined, the Phelps Dodge fortune was built on a mountain of fraud, illegalities and bribery. A US District Court in New York fined the company $1 million --- a huge sum in those days -- for defrauding US customs by undervaluing the copper that Phelps Dodge imported from Peru and Chile. The company had bribed US Customs officials to facilitate the deal, depriving the US Government of significant import tax revenue.[10]

The list of American fortunes built on such fraud, corruption and bribery of government officials was long. It included the most famous names in America, men who donated money to the nation's museums, endowed its finest universities like Princeton, Yale, Harvard with professorships, or had buildings and sometimes entire universities named after them. In this way, they created the image of philanthropy and "good works" while the reality was quite different.

This small, elite group included railroad magnate, Edward H. Harriman, father of Averell Harriman, US diplomat, spy and confidential adviser to Franklin D. Roosevelt. E.H. Harriman used illegal means to gain control of the Union Pacific trans-continental railway, along with his Southern Pacific Company. By watering down stock shares and using bookkeeping tricks that would make Enron's auditors envious, Harriman built an empire that controlled no fewer than seventeen major US railways. A 1907 US Government report stated that Harriman's aim in acquiring so many rail lines was "to eliminate competition between them in transcontinental business." The monopolistic restraint of competition violated both Federal and state laws. [11]

'Anti-Trust' Act turned against Labor

Such abuses became the focus of newspaper investigations and public outrage towards the end of the 19th century, culminating in the Sherman Anti-Trust Act passed by Congress in 1890. The law appeared to be aimed at reining in the practices associated with the Standard Oil Trust, the US Steel Trust of Morgan, the Sugar Trust, and the like.

The trusts had been formed as a way for large corporations to protect their profits by combining with their competitors to set prices and control production. The first trust had been Rockefeller's Standard Oil, formed in 1882. Soon, similar combinations or trusts were formed in tobacco, beef, whiskey, steel, mining, sugar and other industries. On the surface, the Sherman Anti-Trust Act seemed to be aimed at corrupt monopolists like Morgan or Rockefeller or Harriman. The reality was just the opposite.

As early as 1895, the Supreme Court diluted the effect of the Sherman Act by ruling in *United States v. E.C. Knight* that manufacturing was not considered "interstate commerce" even though the manufactured goods were shipped all over the United States. This decision effectively put key industries beyond the reach of government regulation. A wave of mergers at the end of the 19th century engulfed most of US manufacturing, resulting in a few hundred huge corporations dominating the landscape. The biggest trust was Northern Securities Corporation of New Jersey; it was the umbrella enclosing 112 corporations worth $22 billion in assets and it was controlled by J.P. Morgan and John D. Rockefeller.

In an apparent assault on this particular trust, the US Supreme Court declared in its 1904 decision, *Northern Securities Co. v. United States,* that "all combinations in restraint of trade" were illegal. While it broke up one railroad trust, the ruling clearly benefited others, particularly E. H. Harriman.

The Sherman Anti-Trust Act never in the least hindered Harriman or the other corporate giants. The law was a political charade to defuse public anger. The influential Harriman and his friends remained exempt from anti-trust prosecution while numerous small business owners were sent to prison under the act.

Egregiously, the Sherman Anti-Trust Act was also turned into a weapon to block the expansion of trade unions in the US, as the Supreme Court ruled that striking unionists were a 'combination in restraint of trade.'

The climate fostered by Morgan and his oligarchic cronies against any attempt by their workers to organize for better working conditions or wages or even unions was repressive in the extreme. The US Supreme Court was a bastion of oligarchic conservatism. In 1905, in *Lochner v. New York,* the Court ruled that states were not allowed to restrict working hours in private businesses, and three years later in the 1908 Danbury Hatters' case, it ruled unions were forbidden to boycott to obtain better wages and working conditions.

In 1902, indicative of the prevailing climate, George Baer, the man J.P. Morgan installed as head of his Philadelphia and Reading Railway, was named by the Pennsylvania coal operators to lead negotiations with striking coal miners. Anthracite coal was transported to numerous cities via the Philadelphia & Reading. In the decades before the dominance of petroleum, coal was the essential energy source used for home heating, cooking, powering factories and generating electric power.

The mine workers were demanding an eight hour day, a ten percent pay increase and recognition of the United Mine Workers union as their future bargaining agent with management. They resorted to the only weapon they had—withholding their labor to press for relief.

Baer won the nickname, George 'Divine Right' Baer when he sent an open letter to the press at the start of talks with the striking miners, declaring, "The rights and interests of the laboring man will be protected and cared for, not by the labor agitators, but by the Christian men to whom God in His infinite wisdom has given control of the property interests of the country." [12]

Baer, like Morgan, Rockefeller, Carnegie and most of their peers at the time, was a convinced social Darwinist who believed God had 'chosen' them, as they had manifestly proved 'superior' to their workers by virtue of their control of their businesses and their accumulated wealth. Baer told President Teddy Roosevelt, who had been called in to negotiate a solution, that there was "nothing to negotiate." Only when Baer's stubbornness threatened a national backlash in favor of the striking miners did Morgan intervene together with the politically shrewd Roosevelt to force a settlement with labor, one that gave concessions on hours and pay, but refused union recognition.

The anthracite strike and the Supreme Court rulings indicated the extremely one-sided nature of labor-management relations in turn of the century America. It was an oligarchy that ruled by bribery, threats and brute force. They had yet to learn the subtle skills of co-optation and liberal reform to maintain their grip on power. With public sentiment overwhelmingly behind the cause of the miners, Theodore Roosevelt proclaimed his "Square Deal" between management and labor:

> *Let the watchwords of all our people be the old familiar watchwords of honesty, decency, fair-dealing, and common sense...We must treat each man on his worth and merits as a man. We must see that each is given a square deal, because he is entitled to no more and should receive no less* [13]

The "Square Deal" established the principle of Presidential intervention in certain strikes and it made for good press, while Roosevelt, the "Rough Rider," continued his backroom deals with J.P. Morgan and company. TR, as he was popularly known, was the self-proclaimed "hero" of the Battle of San Juan Hill in the Spanish American War of 1898, a nakedly imperialist venture that had made Roosevelt a popular political candidate.

That tactical shift towards at least some of the demands of the miners won for the Republican Roosevelt major blue-collar support from ordinary working Americans whose vote was becoming increasingly significant. But Teddy Roosevelt had in no way changed his allegiance to the powers of great wealth. He was merely a shrewd politician who sensed which way the winds of change in the country were blowing and masterfully exploited it to retain Republican control of the Executive.

This period would be misleadingly labeled the beginning of the "progressive era" in American politics. In reality the oligarchic families controlling the nation's wealth were beginning to become more sophisticated about how they projected their image. None was more shrewd in that endeavor than J.P. Morgan. No American business giant of that day could hold a candle to the greatest fraudster and swindler in American financial history at that time— Junius Pierpont Morgan.

Endnotes:

[1] George Baer, , cited in *The Gospel of Wealth*, accessed in http://www.digitalhistory2.uh.edu/disp_textbook.cfm?smtID=11&psid=3818.

[2] Robert McElroy, *Grover Cleveland* (New York: Harper & Bros., 1923), vol. II, pp. 21, 999.

[3] Gustavus Myers, *History of the Great American Fortunes* (New York: The Modern Library, New York, 1936), pp. 578-581.

[4] Paul Studenski and Herman E. Kross, *Financial History of the United States* (New York: McGraw-Hill Book Co.,1963), pp. 217-221.

[5] Gustavus Myers, op. cit., p. 558-9.

[6] Paul Studenski et al, op. cit., pp. 219-220.

[7] John Chown, *A History of Money* (London: Routledge, 1996), p. 264.

[8] *Testimony before the House Committee in Interstate Commerce*, US House of Representatives Reports, Fifty-second Congress, 2nd Session, 1892-93, vol.i.

[9] Ferdinand Lundberg, *America's 60 Families*, New York, The Vanguard Press, 1937, pp. 26-27.

[10] Gustavus Myers, op. cit. pp. 428-434.

[11] Ibid. p. 531

[12] George Baer, op. Cit.

[13] Theodore Roosevelt, Speech, New York State Fair, Syracuse, September 7, 1903, quoted in http://www.theodoreroosevelt.org/life/quotes.htm.

CHAPTER THREE

The Bankers' Coup D'état creates a Federal Reserve

"The market prices of commodities vary from day to day and often several times a day. This occurs when there is no radical difference in the proportion of the supply and the natural demand. This fact is conclusive proof that our system is controlled by manipulators and fundamentally wrong. I have... suggested a plan which, if adopted, would make the people the master of the world, instead of the present master—THE MONEY TRUST."
  – Congressman Charles A. Lindbergh, 1913[1]

Morgan Emerges as King

J. Pierpont Morgan, as a result of his machinations with Belmont in the crisis of 1893, had emerged by the end of the 1890's as one of the most powerful bankers in the world. He had begun his business career at the age of 24, fraudulently selling back to the US Government its own Army surplus rifles for the Civil War – obsolete rifles which he had initially purchased from the US Army Arsenal in New York City through dummy representatives.

Morgan's agents had secretly bought the 5,000 defective and obsolete rifles for $3.50 apiece and had then sold them for a price of $22 a gun to Army Headquarters in St. Louis, misrepresenting the rifles as 'new and in perfect condition.' His spectacular career of fraud, deceit and corruption had gotten off to a rousing start. 2

At the time Pierpont Morgan was busy swindling the US Government on rifles for the Civil War, his father Junius S. Morgan, a partner in the bank Morgan, Peabody & Co. had moved to London to join American banker George Peabody as Financial Representative of the United States Government in England.

At the time Morgan joined him Peabody was US Representative in London during Lincoln's struggle to win the Union cause against the southern Confederate states. Despite ostensibly representing the Lincoln Administration, however, the two men were widely regarded in England and even in the US as pro-Confederate.

A respected Massachusetts newspaper, the Springfield Republican, reported in October 1866 that Peabody and Morgan "...gave us no faith and no help in our struggle for national existence. They participated to the full in the common English distrust of our cause and our success, and talked and acted for the South rather than for the nation." Moreover, The New York Times had this to say about the London deeds of Morgan and Peabody:

> No individuals contributed so much to flooding our money markets with the evidences of our debt in Europe, and breaking down their prices and weakening financial confidence in our nationality than George Peabody & Co., and none made more money by the operation.

Under the Constitution of the United States, the London financial manipulations of Peabody and Morgan in time of war constituted palpable treason. [3]

Just like his father, son J. Pierpont Morgan would go on to build a colossal banking and industrial empire in America on fraud, treason and deception, all the while taking care that his press coverage portrayed him as a man of philanthropy and Christian rectitude.

As we shall later see, J.P. Morgan, whose bank emerged at the beginning of the 20th Century as the most powerful financial institution in America, was behind the creation of the Federal Reserve in 1913, as well as the creation of the New York Council on Foreign Relations, the private think-tank that shaped American foreign policy throughout the 20th Century. Morgan's Bank also engineered the Dawes Plan for repayment of German war reparations after World War I, the terms of which arguably created conditions for the rise of Hitler and World War II.

But this is running ahead of our account.

The role of J. P. Morgan in the Panic of 1907 was absolutely decisive for all that followed – from the emergence of an American oligarchy, through two world wars to defeat a German challenge and to build, on the ashes of war, the new American Imperium, the successor to the bankrupt British Empire.

Morgan and Rockefeller Engineer the 'Panic Of 1907'

The panic of 1893, it will be recalled, was caused by a run on gold engineered by the bankers themselves. The powerful winners that emerged from that panic were Morgan, along with James Stillman, then head of National City Bank in

New York—the bank of Rockefeller's Standard Oil Trust—and a handful of brokerage houses led by Belmont and Kuhn Loeb & Co.

J. Pierpont Morgan had used the crisis to gain control of the most strategic steel and railroad industries of the United States. In 1901 he gained control of US Steel, which he created out of mergers of Carnegie Steel and others to form the world's largest steelmaker. In creating US Steel, Morgan floated "watered" stock in nominal value of a staggering $1,402,000,000 for his new steel trust, the world's first corporation to be valued at more than a billion dollars.

An investigation by the US Bureau of Corporations determined that of the stock capitalization sold to the public, more than half or $727 million had been issued in excess of any visible property value. The stock price was based, in effect, on capitalized future profit, much as notorious companies like Enron or Worldcom were to do during the stock market mania of the late 1990's. In addition Morgan created the vast General Electric Company, International Harvester and countless other major industrial groups on top of which sat the all-powerful bank, J.P. Morgan & Co.

Meanwhile, Stillman's National City Bank (Citigroup), the bank of John D. Rockefeller's Standard Oil Trust, had emerged as the largest commercial bank in the United States. The Morgan and Stillman gold 'rescue' after 1893 had saved the US Treasury, but badly hurt President Cleveland with the agrarian wing of his Democratic party. Cleveland's relationship with the banks became an issue in the election of 1896, when the banks came under attack from silver advocate and fellow Democrat, William Jennings Bryan.

Standard Oil magnate John D. Rockefeller, along with J.P. Morgan and his fellow Wall Street bankers, all donated heavily to Republican William McKinley, who was elected in 1896 in a sound defeat of silver advocate Bryan.

McKinley came from Ohio, the home of Standard Oil, and his career was made by Rockefeller associate, Mark Hanna, a school friend of John D. Rockefeller and later Rockefeller's business associate. McKinley's election as US President in 1896 was the result of a secret meeting between the Rockefeller and Morgan Wall Street factions represented by Hanna for the Rockefellers, and railroad-man James J. Hill for the Morgan interests. With McKinley, the presidency was in a safe pair of hands as far as the interests of Morgan and Rockefeller were concerned.

McKinley was re-elected in 1900 on a gold standard platform. Thanks to the Panic of 1893, the bi-metallic silver faction had been destroyed and the way was clear for Morgan and a tight circle of New York and allied London banks to take over the finances of the United States.

By 1907, the Morgan and Rockefeller financial groups were ready to launch their next financial attack on the country's economy -- what came to be called the Panic of 1907. This was to be the needed final push to their greatest coup of all—passage in 1913 of the Federal Reserve Act in which a largely unwitting US Congress turned control of its power to print money over to a consortium of private bankers.

The background to 1907 events originated with a New York bank called the Knickerbocker Trust Co., a medium-sized bank for those days, headed by an aggressive wheeler-dealer named Charles T. Barney. Barney and his business partner, Frederick A. Heinze, set out to corner the market in copper by buying up the stock of United Copper Company, a major supplier of copper, a metal in extraordinarily strong demand. In doing so they ran up against the powerful Rockefeller group that controlled the huge Amalgamated Copper Company and had little interest in an upstart outsider rival like the Montana-born Heinze.

Heinze had created his own bank in New York, the Mercantile National Bank. He had used its assets to challenge the Rockefeller-dominated copper market. On October 14, 1907, the stock of United Copper Company soared past $62 a share. Two days later it closed at $15, and F. Augustus Heinze was on his way to financial ruin. Rockefeller had unloaded millions of pounds of copper onto the market, precipitating a collapse of copper prices and with it, the price of Heinze's United Copper stock.

Heinze had one glaring defect as a businessman—he was a head-strong outsider and not part of the plutocrats' cartel. He was an aggressive maverick who paid no heed to the power of Morgan or Rockefeller until it was too late.

It turned out Heinze, in addition to his own Mercantile National Bank, was also linked to six other medium-sized New York banks. The news of Heinze's ruin and his bank links was leaked to the New York press, causing panic with-drawals from all six banks, as well as from the Mercantile National.

The full-blown panic, however, was triggered by news that the President of the third largest savings bank in New York, the Knickerbocker Trust Company, had business links to Heinze's Mercantile National Bank. That news triggered an immediate panic run on the large Knickerbocker Trust as well.[4]

The impact on Knickerbocker Trust was immediate. The bank was forced to beg for a bailout from the private banks' Clearing House Association. The head of the Clearing House Association was none other than J. Pierpont Morgan.

J.P. Morgan demanded an audit of Knickerbocker's books before agreeing to any bailout or rescue. The audit was headed by Morgan crony and employee, Benjamin Strong, the man who later became the powerful first Governor of the Federal Reserve. The result of the audit was that Morgan refused to extend emergency credit to Knickerbocker to stop the depositors' panic, and rumors of its insolvency spread. A wave of panic withdrawals spread to other trust banks.

The ensuing panic, according to a 1911 Congressional investigation, had been carefully fed by false rumors deliberately planted by Morgan cronies in newspapers they controlled, including the New York *Evening Sun* and *The New York Times*. The press reported alleged runs on select trust banks such as the Trust Company of America, which Morgan and Rockefeller wanted out of the way.

There had been no run on the Trust Company of America until the press reports appeared. The bank in fact was solvent, but it coincidentally also held a large bloc of stock in the Tennessee Coal and Iron Company with rich ore deposits (one of the largest known iron reserves in the US) coveted by Morgan's newly formed US Steel Corporation. Morgan made sure that the Trust Company of America got the liquidity it needed from the Morgan bankers' syndicate only in return for agreeing to release as collateral all its shares in Tennessee Coal and Iron.

To seal the deal, Morgan sent two of his lieutenants, Henry Clay Frick and Elbert Gary of US Steel, to meet President Theodore Roosevelt in order to secure Roosevelt's agreement to suspend US anti-trust law. The public story was that this was done to "save the country." In point of fact it was really to allow US Steel to swallow Tennessee Coal and Iron in contravention of the Sherman Anti-Trust Act.

Roosevelt, who had campaigned on the nickname "trust-buster," in actual fact was deeply entrenched with the Money Trust, especially to the Morgan interests.[5]

As President, the Republican Roosevelt made it a practice to run his major public policy pronouncements past key representatives of either the Rockefeller or Morgan group, or both. He submitted the draft of his Third State of the Union address to Rockefeller's personal banker, James Stillman of National City Bank, promising to alter the section on the currency question to suit Stillman, if needed. In October 1903 Roosevelt had invited J.P. Morgan to the White House for a private discussion, and secretly corresponded with railroad mogul E. H. Harriman over political appointments and campaign contributions. [6]

Psychologically devastated by the collapse of his Knickerbocker Trust Co., Charles Barney committed suicide a month later. The New York stock market crashed as cash-desperate trust banks sold stocks to raise capital. The country was plunged into yet another severe economic depression, this one lasting thirteen months.

Across the country regional banks refused to redeem deposits for gold as required by law, fearing loss of 'hard money.' In some respects it was similar to the interbank collapse of trust that erupted a century later, in 2007 -- only in 1907 the public "lender of last resort" had not stepped in.

The 1907 panic subsided almost miraculously when Roosevelt announced his suspension of US anti-trust laws. John D. Rockefeller and his banker James Stillman, eliminated the copper competition from Heinze. As soon as Morgan got his hands on the much-desired Tennessee Coal and Iron ore resources from Trust Company of America, the press rumors stopped and the bank returned to normal business.

The gullible public was told of a "heroic and courageous rescue" of the nations' banking system by the selfless J. Pierpont Morgan. One of the few men who was not convinced of the altruistic motives of Morgan, Rockefeller and their Wall Street cronies was the pro-silver Democrat William Jennings Bryan. Bryan declared, "Blame the unscrupulous financiers who have piled up predatory wealth and who exploit a whole nation as high finance." [7]

An unwelcome Treasury proposal

Rarely mentioned in the debate about the recurring bank panics was the fact that the Government of the United States of America, through its Secretary of the Treasury, already had the power to step in and lend to the credit-starved banks. The Treasury could easily have played the role of lender of last resort and kept the nation's credit process under federal guidance and public control, as was explicitly mandated in Article 1 of the United States Constitution. It would only have required that the Congress fund an emergency reserve that would be at the Treasury Secretary's discretionary disposal.

In a US Treasury Report in 1906, a year before the 1907 Panic, US Treasury Secretary Leslie M. Shaw, a strong advocate of greater use of the US Government's powers to control crises in the money market, wrote:

> *If the Secretary of the Treasury were given $100,000,000 to be deposited with the banks or withdrawn as he might deem expedient, and if in addition he were clothed with authority over the reserve of the several banks, with power to contract the national bank circulation at pleasure, in my judgment no panic as distinguished from industrial stagnation could threaten the United States or Europe that he could not avert. No central or government bank in the world can so*

*readily influence financial conditions throughout the world as can
the Secretary under the authority with which he is now clothed.* [8]

The US Treasury Secretary's proposal for making the Government's Treasury Department the banking 'lender of last resort' in times of liquidity crises was no far-fetched fantasy. By 1899 just before the turn of the century, the US Treasury held gold reserves larger than any central bank in the world including the Bank of England and the Bank of France. The US dollar was one of the world's strongest currencies and the management of its gold standard was under the direct control of the US Treasury, not private banks as was the case in Europe and England.

Morgan, Rockefeller and the elite interests behind the Money Trust of that day, however, had no interest in a public or government solution which they might not be able to direct to their advantage. They were determined to use the panic and the crisis atmosphere to move forward their most audacious plan yet—capturing from the Federal Government of the United States its power to coin, print and control the supply of money. Their plan was to create a national bank that would be entirely in the private hands of bankers J.P. Morgan, Rockefeller and friends.

Treasury Secretary Shaw conveniently retired in March 1907, several months before Morgan and Rockefeller precipitated the Panic. Shaw's post was filled by George B. Cortelyou, a close Morgan crony. With Cortelyou in place, Morgan and his friends on Wall Street had little to fear.

J.P. Morgan emerged from the crisis a hero. He was proclaimed by the friendly financial press as the 'saviour of the day' when, at the opportune moment that prices had become extremely attractive, he publicly announced his 'confidence' in the markets by buying shares of major corporations to add to his vast industrial empire.

Morgan had already emerged as the dominant power controlling America's private railways, as noted earlier. He had done this in 1889 by secretly calling together the heads of all major rail lines to forge an illegal price-fixing cartel to drastically increase freight rates. According to leaked minutes of the meeting, Morgan secured the price-fixing cartel by threatening to freeze new loans to uncooperative railroads. He was foreshadowing the methods employed decades later during the debt crises of the 1980s and 1990's by New York bankers acting through the Washington-based International Monetary Fund and World Bank: "Play by our rules or perish..."[9]

The bank panic of 1907 had led many banks to call in their loans to real estate ventures and to business companies. The large Westinghouse Electric Co.

sought bankruptcy protection. In 1908 Wisconsin Senator Robert La Follette charged that "a group of financiers who withhold and dispense prosperity, deliberately brought on the late panic" for their profit. Morgan was silent.

Morgan had help in managing the 1907 crisis. US Treasury Secretary George Cortelyou, after a late-night meeting with Morgan's partner, George Perkins, announced formal support for the house of Morgan during the crisis, offering the extraordinary sum of $25 million dollars in additional liquidity. "Not only has the stability of the business institutions impressed me deeply," Cortelyou said, "but also the highest courage and the splendid devotion to the public interest of many men prominent in the business life of this city." On leaving the Treasury, Cortelyou was rewarded for his loyal service by being named president of the Morgan-Rockefeller Consolidated Gas Company of New York. [10]

Boxes of gold and satchels of greenbacks from the federal vaults at the New York Sub-treasury office were delivered to select banks approved by Cortelyou. John D. Rockefeller Sr., founder of the Standard Oil Trust, assured Morgan of his willingness to help. Rockefeller deposited $10 million with Morgan's Union Trust Company, and promised additional deposits of $40 million, if needed.

Morgan successfully led the Wall Street banks' attempt to avert a general financial collapse following the stock market panic of 1907, a collapse he had deliberately engineered. He headed the group of bankers who took in large government deposits and he decided how the money was to be used for financial relief. Morgan then proceeded to reward friends and punish enemies. [11]

In 1911 a US Congressional Committee undertook an investigation into the control of the nation's commerce by what they called the Money Trust. Their investigations found that members of the firm J.P. Morgan & Co. controlled no fewer than 72 directorships in 47 major US corporations worth a combined $2,104,000,000, a staggering sum in its day. [12]

Morgan-Rockefeller 'National Monetary Commission'

The outcome of the 1907-08 crisis, in addition to monumentally expanding the financial and political influence of J.P. Morgan, was the formation of a National Monetary Commission to study the banking crisis and make recommendations to Congress to prevent such panics in the future. President Theodore Roosevelt signed into law the Aldrich Vreeland Act, creating the commission in 1908. Its mandate was to come up with a plan to end money panics in the financial markets.

The Commission was rigged from the outset. It was headed by US Senator Nelson Aldrich, chairman of the influential Senate Finance Committee, father-in-law of John D. Rockefeller, Jr. and namesake of Governor Nelson Aldrich Rockefeller. Senator Nelson Aldrich was known to insiders as "Morgan's floor broker in the Senate." [13]

Senator Aldrich was also no stranger to corruption. In a 1905 article, *McClure's* magazine revealed that Aldrich dominated the corrupt Rhode Island political machine, and that the majority of the state's senators had been bought by Aldrich's machine. In 1881 Aldrich gave up a family grocery business to run for US Senate with a declared net worth of $50,000. When Senator Aldrich died after thirty years in politics, mostly in the US Senate, he was worth an impressive $12,000,000, a fortune that was not the result of frugal savings of his paltry Senate salary.[14]

Morgan and Rockefeller could perhaps not have found a finer candidate to steer their desired "monetary reform" through a sceptical Congress. Aldrich would be responsible for steering the passage of the most fateful political *coup d'état* in American history: the Federal Reserve Act of 1913. Who backed him and how they orchestrated the coup, few were to know.

The Bankers' Coup D'état

In 1908, a year after the creation of Aldrich's National Monetary Commission, the most powerful bankers in America met in highest secrecy to draw up plans for the greatest financial and political coup d'état in the history of the United States. The plan was to rob from the US Congress its constitutionally mandated powers to create and control money. The coup was to usurp those Constitutional powers in order to serve private special interests, even at the expense of the general welfare of the population of the United States.

The men who drew up the plans to take control of the nation's money were no ordinary bankers. They were a breed apart within the American banking world.

They were primarily international bankers who patterned themselves on their London cohorts. The bankers who orchestrated "the money coup" included J. Pierpont Morgan; German émigré Paul Warburg of the New York private bank Kuhn Loeb & Co.; August Belmont & Co.; J.& W. Seligman & Co.; Lee, Higginson & Co., and others. In London these international bankers called themselves "merchant bankers." In New York they preferred the title "investment bankers." Both were working the same track.

By the nature of the business, international bankers were not loyal to any fixed national space. Their world was not a particular nation state, but wherever their influence could alter events to their financial advantage. As a consequence, secrecy was essential to their success and paramount in gaining the advantage over rivals. They had discovered over centuries, going back to the Venetian Empire, that lending to governments or monarchs was far more profitable than lending to private borrowers, not least because the subject loan was backed by the power of the state to tax its citizens to guarantee debt repayment.

To gain entry to the halls of power, money was an extremely effective door-opener. Credit—or cutting off of credit—could be used to control entire nations or regions. Money, or more precisely, control of money, was the bankers' strategic goal. Control of countries through control of their central or national banks was essential to their power. Ultimately, the elite cabal of international bankers sought nothing less than control of the entire world as their goal and purpose. As Henry Kissinger was said to have put it in the 1970s, "Control the money and you control the entire world."

International bankers with names such as Barings, Rothschild, Schroeder, Morgan, Warburg, Schiff, Mallet or Seligman were focused on establishing close, confidential ties to governments, foreign or domestic, that issued debt. They traded government-guaranteed bonds for a high premium.

They operated in absolute secrecy, lest the general public understand how the banks' money manipulated political decisions behind the scenes, including decisions to go to war or to keep the peace. The traditional preference of international bankers for utmost secrecy became a hallmark of their practice and allowed intrigue, political manipulations, buying of politicians and judges, financing of coups to eliminate an uncooperative sovereign here, a head of state there, all to make way for governments more amenable to the bankers' dictates.

During the Civil War in 1863 Congress had passed a National Banking Act followed by the National Currency Act. The bill was largely drafted by Treasury Secretary Salmon P. Chase. A consequence of the new law was that certain banking centers across the country were designated as "Reserve Cities" – such as Chicago, St. Louis or Boston. Regional banks could hold a part of their required minimum reserves of 25% in the form of deposits and bank notes in "National Banks" in their regional Reserve City.

The so-designated National Banks in New York City, however, held a special status and were required to hold 25% of their reserves of legal tender in the form of gold or silver coins or bars. Under the law, New York City was designated uniquely as the "Central Reserve City" under the new banking act, amounting to recognition that it had already become the nation's money center, and a harbinger of its future role under the Federal Reserve Act of 1913.[15]

Because local and regional banks could earn interest by placing their funds in New York banks, capital flowed from the regional banks into New York banks, up to the beginning of the 20th Century. New York National Banks grew disproportionately as a result.

In addition, the new banking laws granted Federal banking charters to two New York banks -- the First National Bank and later the Chase National Bank. The latter, named for Treasure Secretary Chase, became the bank of the Rockefeller Standard Oil empire.

In addition to the large national banks there was a small but highly influential group of private banking houses, international banks that did not sell their stock to the public and therefore were not limited to doing business locally. They did not need any state charter to do business. They exploited a gaping loophole in the Federal banking and state laws.

Unlike the state-chartered stock banks, these "unincorporated banks" were not permitted to issue banknotes. But because of this, they were largely unregulated, free to do business wherever they found opportunity.

For decades before the end of the 19th Century, these un-regulated investment banks, which became the international banking firms such as J.P. Morgan, Kuhn Loeb, Lazard Frères, Drexel and a small number of others, were free to organize the largest financial dealings for building of the national railroads and for financing the expansion of large industry across state boundaries.

Because they were not regulated or restricted to state boundaries, these banks made their fortunes by organizing capital, largely from London and Paris banks, to finance the huge costs of building America's railroads. These were America's international bankers.[16]

In this elite world of international finance at the end of the first decade of the 20th Century two giants, one British and one American, stood well above the rest of the international banking elite—Nathaniel Lord Rothschild's N.M. Rothschild & Co. and J. Pierpont Morgan's J.P. Morgan & Co.

The two were by no means always on amicable terms with one another. Initially the two houses worked in close cooperation, with Morgan discreetly representing Rothschild's interests in the United States. Then, as the first decade of the 20th Century drew to a close and war in Europe neared, an inevitable rivalry began as it became clear that British industry and the British Empire were in definite decline and that Morgan, who initially had cooperated closely with Rothschild, sought to build his own independent financial imperium.

The creation of the Federal Reserve System was designed to establish control over the United States money system by Morgan and a small circle of private, allied, international bankers in New York. It was done with extreme care and preparation. As far back as the ratification of the United States Constitution -- which placed the power to coin money explicitly in the hands of the US Congress -- private banking interests had been battling unsuccessfully to gain popular acceptance for a national bank. Early in the 20th Century, things changed.

A Georgia island 'duck hunt'

The group of international bankers who drafted the Federal Reserve Act of 1913 acted with utmost secrecy and deception, lest their role in crafting the new central bank be discovered as a "bankers' plot."

Recall that President Theodore Roosevelt had named Republic Senator Nelson Aldrich to head a National Monetary Commission in 1908 following Morgan's and Rockefeller's manipulated Panic of 1907. Two years later, in November 1910, the same Aldrich traveled by private train with a group of the nation's leading financiers to a private resort owned by Morgan at Jekyll Island off the Georgia coast.[17]

This group of the country's most powerful bankers and their trusted official cronies had agreed that, if discovered, they would use as the excuse for their gathering that they were going duck hunting. They neglected to say what kind of ducks.

The secret cabal of Wall Street "duck hunters" who joined Aldrich included Frank Vanderlip, President of Rockefeller's National City Bank of New York; Henry P. Davidson, senior partner of J.P. Morgan & Co.; Charles D. Norton, President of Morgan-controlled First National Bank of New York; Benjamin Strong, Vice President of Morgan-controlled Bankers Trust; Paul Warburg, a German immigrant and senior partner of Kuhn Loeb & Co.; and A. Piatt Andrew, Assistant Secretary of the Treasury of the United States.

The powerful Rockefeller faction had two influential representatives at Jekyll Island at that November meeting. One was Paul Warburg of Kuhn Loeb & Co., the second most powerful private investment bank after J.P. Morgan & Co. and, at the time, the leading investment house for John D. Rockefeller, as well as being the house bank of Rockefeller ally, E.H. Harriman of the Union Pacific Railroad.[18] The second representative of the Rockefeller faction at Jekyll Island was National City Bank President, Frank Vanderlip.

Jekyll Island Club Hotel, owned by J. P. Morgan, was the site of secret meetings by a bankers' cabal to draft the Federal Reserve Act of 1913 that enabled America to finance World War I.

Years after creation of the Federal Reserve, Vanderlip described his view of the secret meeting. "I was secretive indeed, as furtive as any conspirator...Discover, we knew, simply must not happen, or else all our time and effort would be wasted. If it were to be exposed that our particular group had got together and written a banking bill, that bill would have no chance whatsoever of passage by Congress."

The Secret of Jekyll Island

In 1916, after the Federal Reserve had become a reality, B.C. Forbes, founder of
the financial magazine by the same name, wrote about the secret Jekyll Island
gathering, using only the first names of the men who participated:

> *I am giving to the world for the first time the real story of how the
> famous Aldrich currency report, the foundation of our new currency
> system, was written...The utmost secrecy was enjoined upon all. The
> public must not glean a hint of what was to be done.*
>
> *Nelson [Aldrich-w.e.] had confided to Henry, Frank, Paul and Piatt
> that he was to keep them locked up at Jekyll Island, out of the rest of
> the world, until they had evolved and compiled a scientific currency
> system for the United States, the real birth of the present Federal Re-
> serve System, the plan done on Jekyll Island...Warburg is the link
> that binds the Aldrich system and the present [Federal Reserve-w.e.]
> system together. He, more than any other one man, has made the
> system possible as a working reality.*[19]

The irony was that Paul Warburg, the man who played such a decisive role
in formulating the model of the Federal Reserve, was a German. Warburg would
later be appointed to the first Board of Directors of the new Federal Reserve in
1914, and then be made its Vice Chairman, sitting until 1918. The irony lay not in
the fact that Paul Warburg was a German, but rather in the fact that his Federal
Reserve became the financing instrument that enabled the ultimate defeat of
Kaiser Germany in 1918.

At the secret Jekyll Island gathering in 1910, Kuhn Loeb's Paul Warburg had
proposed a deception to get the new national bank act passed by Congress. It
was deliberately not to be called a "national" or "central" bank, he insisted, but a
more harmless sounding "federal reserve bank association." The argument
would be advanced that, unlike the Bank of England or other European central
banks, the United States model would be decentralized and insure maximum
regional banking and monetary control. The ruse also would disguise the private
ownership of the member banks of the Federal Reserve System.

The dominant influence of New York, the nation's largest banking and
money center, would be concealed by creating twelve "independent," regional
banks – in San Francisco, Kansas City, Minneapolis, Atlanta, Boston, etc. Each of
the regional banks would be privately owned by the most powerful banks or

corporations in their region. As Philadelphia banker Leslie Shaw told a Congressional hearing on the Aldrich Plan in 1913:

When you have a local organization, the centered control is assured....When you have hooked the banks together, they can have the biggest influence of anything in this country, with the exception of the newspapers. [20]

In its January 11, 1911 issue, *The Nation* magazine noted of the Aldrich-Warburg central bank plan developed at Jekyll Island:

> *The name of Central Bank is carefully avoided, but the 'Federal Reserve Association', the name given to the proposed central organization, is endowed with the usual powers and responsibilities of a European Central Bank.* [21]

Warburg's plan proposed that the stock of the twelve member banks of the Federal Reserve Association, as he called it, would be owned by private stockholders. The private stockholders in turn could use the credit of the US Government for their own private profit. The Federal Reserve Association would control the nation's money and credit; it would be a bank of issue, meaning it could create currency or money at will, and it would finance the Government by mobilizing credit in times of war. Senator Aldrich later admitted in a magazine article,

> *Before passage of this Act, the New York Bankers could only dominate the reserves of New York. Now we are able to dominate bank reserves of the entire country.* [22]

Warburg, the only one present at Jekyll Island who had had direct experience with the functions of various European central banks, modeled his reserve bank on the private Bank of England. In its 1943 entry for the Bank of England, the *Encyclopedia Americana* described it this way:

> *Its weakness is the weakness inherent in a system which has developed with the smallest amount of legislative control...its capital is held privately, and its management is not in any way directly or indirectly controlled by the state.*

The description then noted a decisive feature of both the Bank of England and its progeny, the Federal Reserve:

On the other hand, during its whole history, it has been more or less under the protection of the state; its development has been marked by successive loans of its capital to the state in return for the confirmation or extension of its privileges...The Bank of England is controlled by a Governor, deputy-governor, and a court of twenty four directors who are elected by the proprietors [i.e. the private stockholders-w.e.] on the nomination of the directors.... [23]

The Bank of England had been granted a royal charter in 1694, by William III to regularize the monarchy's finances. The scheme was invented by a Scot promoter and privateer named William Paterson, to create a bank with a 'fund for perpetual interest.'

A perpetual money machine for the British Government was created. The idea of a permanent National Debt was born. The Bank of England would finance the emerging empire from the City of London. Never again would lack of money, or liquidity, hamper the British Empire under normal economic conditions.

"Fractional reserve banking" – another mechanism embedded in the Federal Reserve system—was created on the model of the Bank of Amsterdam almost a century before founding of the Bank of England, along with the radical monetary concept of a "monopoly" bank which would create money for loans that would in effect never be repaid.[24]

The dirty secret of 'Fractional Reserve Banking'

Fractional reserve banking was first introduced at the Bank of Amsterdam in the middle of the Seventeenth Century. It was done in strict secrecy, lest a depositors' panic ensue, which it ultimately did. But the deception succeeded for more than a century and a half.

The Bank of Amsterdam was founded in 1609 under protection of the City of Amsterdam for a very specific purpose. As gold and silver coins were bulky to carry and risked robbery, merchants created the bank to accept both foreign and local coinage at their real, intrinsic value. The bank deducted a small coinage and management fee, and credited clients in its book for the remainder. This credit was known as "bank money."

Always in compliance with mint standards, and always of the same value, bank money was worth more than real coinage, which deteriorated with age, losing some of its gold or silver specie content. At the same time a regulation was introduced, according to which all bills drawn at Amsterdam worth more than a set amount must be paid in bank money. This regulation removed all uncertainty from the bank bills and compelled all merchants to keep an account with the bank. That in turn occasioned a demand for bank money of the Bank of Amsterdam.

Soon the bankers of Amsterdam realized that at any one time only a small portion of their deposits were withdrawn. So they secretly set out to determine the minimum deposits needed to meet that demand on average, and to lend out the rest in order to make money on their borrowed deposits. Initially, being naturally cautious lest they be discovered, they lent a small fraction of all deposits. Then, as that seemed to work, increased it to more than fifty percent. Were the general public to learn that only 50% of their gold was in safe deposit with the Bank, a panic would ensue -- which it did in 1791, ending the Bank.

The abuse of its depositors' trust had been possible because the Bank of Amsterdam had not been required to make any public disclosure. It was the beginning of the principle of modern banking that, under a system of fractional reserve lending, the value of a bank or an entire banking system rests on one ethereal value—depositors' confidence. The essence of fractional reserve banking drives banks to lend to the maximum to maximize earnings until credit excess leads to a market collapse. Because the bank lends funds it does not own, the credit mechanism leads to creation of money *ex nihilo*—out of nothing—through simple bookkeeping entries.

Such was the history of the repeatedly engineered bank panics during the century prior to the creation of the US Federal Reserve. Morgan and the elite bankers in his circle wanted a central bank that their own chosen people would permanently control, an institution to act as the overseeing governor of the credit system, the central cop to keep individual banks in line with the interests of the banking system as a whole.

To control this system, to raise or lower credit, required changing levels of bank reserves for their fractional lending. The power that the Federal Reserve gave to the New York Money Trust banks was a quasi monopoly over the nation's credit. This power was to prove awesome.

The group at Jekyll Island reached a consensus behind what was called the Warburg Plan, which we will explain presently, which for political reasons was dubbed the Aldrich Plan to give the appearance it was the brainchild of the Republican Senator.

Before they could advance their plan to take control of the nation's money, however, they faced a new challenge in the form of a growing popular revolt against the concentration of money power.

Democrats investigate the 'Money Trust'

In 1912, some months after the secret meeting at Jekyll Island, Minnesota Congressman Charles Lindbergh, Sr. introduced a resolution into the US House of Representatives calling for an investigation of Wall Street Power. Lindbergh, a fiery and very accurate critic of the workings of that Money Trust, as he called it, was blocked by the bankers and their Congressional friends in his call for an independent inquiry.

Instead, as Lindbergh documented in a personal account written in 1913, the influential bankers of the Money Trust, using their friends in Congress, diverted the call and sent it to a banker-friendly Louisiana Congressman, Arsene Pujo, who named a Wall Street lawyer, Samuel Untermyer, to do a harmless pseudo-investigation. The cynical result of the hearings was so orchestrated as to lead to the creation of the very goal the Money Trust had in mind with the Aldrich Plan, namely a private central bank whose power would lie firmly in the hands of that New York Money Trust.[25]

The House Committee on Banking and Currency convened hearings beginning May 1912, known as the Pujo Committee for its chairman, Louisiana Democrat, Arsene Pujo. The Pujo Committee's mandate was ostensibly to investigate banking and currency conditions in the nation.

The Committee issued subpoenas to J.P. Morgan, James J. Hill, and the two co-founders of First National City Bank -- George F. Baker and William Rockefeller, brother of Standard Oil's John D. To avoid testifying, William Rockefeller actually went into hiding on his New York estate and then claimed he could not testify as he had "throat problems." Morgan and the others in the Money Trust appeared, but refused to disclose anything of substance.

The Pujo Committee report concluded with a harmless statement to the effect that a cabal of financial leaders was abusing the public trust in order to consolidate control over many industries. They confirmed that there indeed had been an increased concentration of control of money and credit in the country, both through the consolidation of bank ownership in a few hands and by the banks putting hand-picked allies on the boards of directors of industrial trusts or groups it had financed and in which it held large stock shares.

The Pujo Committee documented that the Money Trust as had come to be called, had six major financial houses at the top. Those six controlled the largest steel, railroads, public utilities, oil and refining companies, as well as other major industrial groups. The concentration of wealth and ownership was completed by the Money Trust's control of America's major media, enabling them to disseminate propaganda favorable to their special interests. It was a system of interlocking directorates, the Committee said, and it was controlled by six private banking houses:

- J.P. Morgan & Co.
- First National Bank of New York
- National City Bank of New York
- Kuhn Loeb & Co.
- Kidder Peabody & Co. of New York
- Lee Higginson & Co. of Boston

The Committee's report revealed that at the very top of this vast pyramid of economic, political and financial power over the United States in 1913 stood the private investment bank, J.P. Morgan & Co. Pujo's report documented that Morgan, through shareholdings and seats on the boards of directors, held controlling positions in virtually all of the country's largest corporations, including: US Steel Corporation, American Telephone & Telegraph, Western Union, General Electric Company, International Harvester, Bankers Trust Co., Guaranty Trust Co., National City Bank of New York, the New York Central Railroad, Northern Pacific Railroad, Great Northern and Baltimore & Ohio Railroads. In all, the Pujo Committee documented 112 such companies under the effective control of the J.P. Morgan group in 1913.

The report pointed out that Morgan also had extensive international ties as a partner in the London banking house of his father, J.S. Morgan & Co., later Morgan Grenfell, as well as in the Paris banking house Morgan, Harjes & Co. Morgan was called to testify, but he refused to say anything of substance. He regarded himself as a power above and apart, not subject to the quaint laws or demands of republican government.

Morgan's power within the six financial institutions named above included not only his own bank, but major interests in National City Bank and shared control with Rockefeller of National City Bank. Morgan also controlled the next largest bank, Bankers' Guaranty Trust. These four banks in which Morgan had full or shared control via corporate directorships and stock ownership corporations were worth a staggering sum of $22 billion.

The Pujo revelations, however, as noted, were no sincere or serious attempt to challenge the power of the Money Trust, something well within Congress' Constitutional powers. Instead, it was a calculated ploy backed by the Money Trust itself, to lend populist credibility to the newly elected Democratic Congress, to push the Democrats' version of a national bank act, the Owen-Glass Federal Reserve Act of 1913.

Contrary to Lindbergh's intention, the Pujo investigation was a ruse by the Money Trust to push their desired banking control bill through a Democratic-controlled Congress, Democrats whose campaigns in many cases had been quietly financed by the same Money Trust.[26]

The Pujo hearings were used to manipulate public opinion to back passage of the fateful Sixteenth Amendment to the Constitution permitting the Federal Government, in divergence with the Constitution, to levy a direct personal income tax, something that was to prove decisive later in financing US entry into World War I and beyond.

Decisively, the hearings and the orchestrated press treatment of them were also used to set up a phony debate that led Congress to pass almost verbatim the private plan hatched by the bankers on Jekyll Island.

To deepen the deception, Pujo Committee lawyer, Untermyer, whom friendly press had built up as an anti-trust "friend of the little guy," was given the task of drafting the text of the 1913 Federal Reserve Act. The bill was snuck through Congress in the sheep's clothing of a Democratic reply to the Republican bankers plan, the Aldrich bill. The wolves of Wall Street had got their prize.

The Owen-Glass bill was largely drafted by Democrat lawyer Samuel Untermyer, the chief staff investigator for the Pujo Committee. The Republican Aldrich Plan was lambasted in the Morgan-controlled press and the Owen-Glass Federal Reserve Act was praised as a fair democratic alternative, allegedly a way to limit control by the New York Money Trust. [27]

The reality was exactly the opposite.

Republican Bankers buy a Democrat to do their Coup

By 1910, J.P. Morgan and the Money Trust had decided it was necessary to have their own version of the confidence game that the privately-owned Bank of Amsterdam had run -- underwritten not by the City of Amsterdam, however, but by the full faith and credit of the Federal Government of the United States of America.

Given the widespread, dislike of the Money Trust among the public and in the Congress, particularly among Democrats such as Charles Lindbergh and progressive Republicans such as Robert La Follette, it required a charade of deception to advance the Warburg central bank scheme by appearing to attack Senator Aldrich's National Monetary Commission and the Aldrich plan as "putting voting control into the large banks."[28]

While denouncing the Aldrich plan as a "central bank plan" Congressman Glass's own Federal Reserve Act fulfilled precisely the functions of such a central bank under private control by the Money Trust. It was exactly what Warburg had outlined at Jekyll Island in 1910. The Warburg Plan and the Aldrich Plan were essentially one and the same. Not surprisingly, Paul Warburg was given the task of drafting the text of the "alternative" bill for Glass and the Woodrow Wilson White House, with the aid of Wall Street lawyer Samuel Untermyer. [29]

The new Federal Reserve Bank's stock would be owned by private stockholders who then could use the full faith and credit of the Government of the United States for their private profit. The Federal Reserve proposed by Glass would control the nation's money and credit, in direct contravention of Article One of the United States Constitution which vested such control explicitly in the US Congress, originally conceived as the most representative of the three branches of government.

Moreover the Federal Reserve, as proposed by Glass, would be a "bank of issue" which meant that it could issue money "out of thin air" and could finance the Government by mobilizing credit "in times of war." Effectively, the Federal Reserve System ceded the Congress' right to print money to a legalized cartel of private banks, affiliated with the banks of the City of London, above all N.M. Rothschild & Co., through the agency of the Rockefellers, Kuhn-Loeb, and J.P Morgan. [30]

In sum, Carter Glass' bill gave the Morgan-led cabal of private bankers total monopoly control over note issue, over money.

Not surprisingly, the Owen-Glass Federal Reserve Act of 1913 won the warm endorsement of the American Bankers' Association, a fact downplayed in the popular press.

In 1910, Republicans lost control of the US House of Representatives, and in the national elections of 1912 they also lost control of the Senate as well as the White House to the Democrats. The election of Woodrow Wilson in 1912 was the work of a small group of men who engineered a split in the Republican Party by financing a third party, the Progressive Party, nicknamed the "Bull Moose" party for its Presidential candidate former Republican President Teddy Roosevelt. [31]

It was Morgan and Rockefeller money that put 'reform' Democrat Woodrow Wilson in the White House in 1912. Since 1898 when Wilson was president of Princeton University, he had been promoted into national politics by a powerful group of bankers led by Princeton man Cleveland Dodge of Phelps Dodge copper, and a director of the Morgan-Rockefeller National City Bank. Wilson was on such personal terms with Dodge that he wrote letters addressed simply, "Dear Cleve."[32]

When the Morgan group decided that Wilson would be more likely to pass an essentially Republican national bank act into law than would a Republican President, they orchestrated a national media campaign around Wilson. Through newspapers that the Morgan group controlled, Morgan's group hailed Wilson, then the Governor of New Jersey, as the "liberal reformer" candidate. Wilson's nomination was bought and paid for by National City Bank's Dodge, by Cyrus McCormack of International Harvester Co., and by Jacob Schiff, senior partner of Paul Warburg's investment bank, Kuhn Loeb. [33] In other words, Wilson's election was bought and paid for by the Jekyll Island cabal.

He wouldn't disappoint his patrons.

On December 23, 1913, the day before Christmas Eve, the Federal Reserve Act, also known as the Glass-Owen Bill, was passed by Congress with scarcely a debate. The Republican controlled Senate pushed the bill through when many members of the US Congress were home for the Christmas holiday. Democratic President Woodrow Wilson signed it into law one hour after it was passed by the Congress.

The Federal Reserve System was set up as an independent central bank. Although the President of the United States appointed the chairman and governors of the Federal Reserve System, and the appointment had to be approved by the United States Senate, the presidents of the 12 private reserve banks controlled the system and none was more powerful than the President of the New York Federal Reserve Bank, *the primus inter pares* or first among equals of the twelve.

The key provision of the Federal Reserve Act stipulated that decisions of the Federal Reserve were not to be ratified by the President, or anyone else in the Executive branch of the United States Government or the Congress. Instead, buried in the legislation was the granting of total power over the monetary policies of all US banks in effect to the privately-owned New York Federal Reserve Bank and its directors—the most powerful names on Wall Street of the Money Trust.

Stock not held by member banks was not to be entitled to any voting power. This clause guaranteed that no outsider would seek to buy shares in the Federal Reserve. It was strictly an insiders' or Old Boys' Club, controlled by the Money Trust. [34]

A few months after the initial passage of the Federal Reserve Act of 1913, the newly named New York Federal Reserve Bank President, Morgan's man Benjamin Strong, along with Federal Reserve director and author of the bill, Paul Warburg, went to the White House and to Congress to successfully argue for passage of an amendment to the original act. The amendment would allow the newly-established central bank to destroy money as well as to create it. With that, the way was now clear for the Federal Reserve and the private bankers controlling its policies to create economic boom periods, mobilize the economy for wars, and to create deflationary recessions and depressions, all of which it proceeded to do with a violence that exceeded anything the individual bankers of the Money Trust had ever succeeded in doing in the century prior to creation of their private Federal Reserve System. The resulting lurches from economic boom to bust were given a pseudo scientific explanation called the theory of "business cycles" as if these phenomena were somehow inevitable.

They weren't, by any means.

The most essential use value inherent in the new Federal Reserve, however, was that it allowed private banks, most especially the House of Morgan and its allies, to take risks never before imagined. Their ventures – no matter how risky – were now backed by the "full faith and credit" of the Government of the United States of America and its unwitting taxpayers. The first test of the vast new powers of America's third National Bank since 1787 was not long in coming. England and France were soon to appeal for massive credits from the United States to finance their war in 1914 to destroy the German Reich and Austro-Hungary, a process that became known as The Great War.

Endnotes:

[1] Charles A. Lindbergh, Sr, Congressman, *Banking and Currency and the Money Trust*, C.A. Lindbergh, Little Falls, Minnesota, 1913.

[2] Ibid, p. 552.

[3] *New York Times*, October 31, 1966.

[4] Kevin J. Cahill, *The U.S. Bank Panic of 1907 and the Mexican Depression of 1908-1909*, The Historian, vol.60, 1998.

[5] Ferdinand Lundberg, op. cit., pp. 90-95.

[6] United States Senate Committee on Privileges and Elections, *Hearings of the Sub-committee on Campaign Contributions*, 62nd Congress, 3rd Session, 1913, pp. 453 ff. The background on the Roosevelt contacts with Stillman and Morgan are in, Henry Pringle, *Theodore Roosevelt* (New York: Harcourt, Brace & Co., 1931), p. 350.

[7] Cited in The Federal Reserve Bank of Boston, *The Panic of 1907*, p.8.

[8] US Department of the Treasury, *Annual Report on the Finances*, 1906, Washington D.C., p. 49. The US Treasury's debt management powers then, as Milton Friedman pointed out were "comparable to the Federal Reserve System's ability to conduct open market operations. See Milton Friedman & Anna J. Schwartz, *A Monetary History of the United States 1867-1960* (Princeton: Princeton University Press, 1963), p. 150, footnote 24.

[9] Gustavus Myers, op.cit. p. 586-572.

[10] Ferdinand Lundberg, op. cit., p.92.

[11] Details of the actual workings of the 1907 Panic have been obscured by later Morgan-friendly accounts. Useful in piecing together actual events in that decisive event in the emergence of the Federal Reserve System in 1913 as the pillar of an American Century, in addition to the work by Gustavus Myers cited above, is the book by James Grant, *Money of the Mind: borrowing and lending in America from the Civil War to Michael Milkin,* Farrar Straus Giroux, New York, 1992. As well, Milton Friedman & Anna J. Schwartz, op. cit.

[12] Report of the House Banking and Currency's *Committee to Investigate Concentration of Control of Money and Credit,* Washington D.C., 1913, pp.56-91, cited in Gustavus Myers, op. cit., p.634. This is the so-called Pujo Committee headed by Louisiana Democrat, Arsene Pujo, whose chief counsel, Samuel Untermyer in 1911 coined the term, "Money Trust" to describe the power of the group around Morgan and Rockefeller.

[13] Henry Pringle, op. cit., p.244.

[14] Walter Davenport, *Power & Glory,* Colliers' magazine, February 7, 1931.

[15] Karl Erich Born, *Geld und Banken im 19.und 20.Jahrhundert* (Stuttgart: Alfred Kroener Verlag, 1977), p. 173-5.

[16] Ibid., pp. 172-173.

[17] Eustace Mullins, *The Secrets of the Federal Reserve* (Staunton, Virginia: Bankers Research Institute, 1983), p.1.

[18] Ron Chernow, *Titan: The Life of John D. Rockefeller, Sr.* (London: Warner Books, 1998), p. 373, 377.

[19] Bertie Charles Forbes, *Current Opinion,* December 1916, p. 382, cited in Eustace Mullins, op.cit. p. 2.

[20] Cited in Eustace Mullins, op. cit., p. 14.

[21] Ibid., p. 12.

[22] Nelson Aldrich, Senator, after the creation of a private central bank the Federal Reserve 1913

[23] Encyclopedia Americana, *The Bank of England,* Vol. 13, 1943 edition, cited in E.C. Knuth, *The Empire of 'The City'* (Milwaukee: The Noontide Press, 1946), footnote p. 27.

[24] E.C. Knuth, op. cit.

[25] Charles A. Lindbergh, Sr. op cit. Lindbergh describes the successful attempt of the Money Trust and their allies in Congress to defuse the Lindbergh call after it had gained too much popular support to be killed outright: *"Secret meetings were held by the representatives in Congress of the trusts and bosses. The doors of the innermost and least suspected offices were barred to the public, and so guarded that none should enter who were interested on behalf of the public. In these offices plans were laid for the drafting of a new resolution, the purpose of which was to defeat the appointment of a special committee, and to substitute for it the Banking and Currency Committee; which was chiefly composed of bankers, their agents and attorneys, and the interests expected that that committee would faithfully protect the wrongs committed against the public, in so far as it could be done without arousing public suspicion. It could not whitewash the whole of the Money Trust operations, but much could and would be concealed by that means, and was in fact, as was shown by subsequent developments.*

"The next step was to secure the passage of this substituted resolution, which really amounted to the investigation being made by the secret friends of the Money Trust. This committee, as well might be expected, . . . because of the special personal interest of its members, . . . did not select an attorney to aid them from among the many able attorneys who are Members of the House and who would serve without further pay than that to which they are entitled as Members, . . . but they selected a Wall Street attorney, paid him a very high salary, allowed him to manage the whole investigation and practically draft the committee's report." The Wall Street attorney for the Money Trust hearings of House Committee on Banking and Currency chairman, Louisiana Congressman Pujo, was

Samuel Untermyer who would later draft the text for the Money Trust of the Federal Reserve Act of 1913.

[26] Ibid.

[27] United States House of Representatives Committee on Banking and Currency, *Report of the House Committee (The Pujo Committee) Appointed to Investigate the Concentration and Control of Money and Credit*, Washington D.C., 1913, p. 64.

[28] Eustace Mullins, op. cit., pp. 14-15.

[29] Ferdinand Lundberg, *America's Sixty Families* (New York: The Vanguard Press, 1937), p. 122.

[30] Eustace Mullins, op. cit., p.15.

[31] The details of the creation of the Bull Moose third party in order to rob Republican Howard Taft of the Presidency in favor of the more amenable Woodrow Wilson is related in detail by Ferdinand Lundberg, America's Sixty Families, "The Politics of Aggrandizement: 1912-1920," pp. 106-120. Following the successful 1912 victory of the bankers' man, Woodrow Wilson, the completely synthetic Progressive Party dissolved and Teddy Roosevelt quietly rejoined the Republican Party.

[32] Ferdinand Lundberg, op. cit., pp. 109-121.

[33] Ibid., p.109.

[34] Wayne N. Krautkramer, *The Federal Reserve - Its Origins, History & Current Strategy*, 15 September 2004, in news.goldseek.com/GoldSeek/1095269452.php.

CHAPTER FOUR

Morgan's Fed Finances a European War

'This is a war to make the world safe for Democracy'
- President Wilson's Committee on Public Information, 1918

Imperial Overstretch

On the eve of the Great War in 1914, it was in no way apparent, at least on the surface, that the mighty and colossal Pax Britannia, the 'Empire on which the sun never set,' was rotten to its core and in terminal economic decline.

In 1899 the British had fought a war with the aid of Cecil Rhodes, a highly eccentric British mining magnate, in order to wrest control of the vast gold riches of the Transvaal in South Africa away from the Boer settlers. South African gold had given the City of London a new lease on life. In 1897 Queen Victoria celebrated her Diamond Jubilee, 60 years as Queen of the world's most powerful empire. The British Empire appeared to be at its zenith in power and prestige.

The High Commissioner of Cape Colony in South Africa, Alfred Milner, was a close associate of Lord Rothschild and Cecil Rhodes, all of whom belonged to a secret group calling itself 'The Society of the Elect.'

The Milner group wanted the economic power inherent in control of the gold mines in the Dutch Boer republics of the Transvaal and the Orange Free State. They also wanted to create a Cape-to-Cairo confederation of British colonies to dominate the mineral-rich African continent.[1] They saw Africa as the key to future British global hegemony.

N.M. Rothschild & Co. in London secretly financed Rhodes, Milner and the South African war cause. Cecil Rhodes had a plan to obtain Royal backing for a British South Africa Company modeled on the British East India Company. Rhodes was convinced that the gold and minerals of South Africa would be sufficient to guarantee that the City of London would be the world's unchallenged financial center for decades to come.

Rhodes and Milner and an elite circle of Empire strategists founded a secret society in 1910 whose purpose was to revitalize a flagging British imperial spirit. The society, many of whose members were graduates of All Souls College at Oxford University, would secretly steer the strategic policies of the British Empire up until the end of the Second World War. They called their group the Round Table, a reference to King Arthur's medieval table surrounded by his select knights, and gave their magazine the same name.[2]

The British won the Boer War. But in the course of events, they lost their Empire.

The British army fought ill-armed Boer farmers and almost lost a bloody Boer War for control of South Africa's gold in 1899-1902. The gold was key to the future of the City of London as world finance center.

The war was not a quick, easy affair as had been first anticipated in London. England's last war with a European foe had been the 1853 Crimean War against Russia. Since that time the British Army had spent four decades fighting ill-armed and ill-trained native forces around the world, hardly a serious challenge. A bit like the initial swagger of US generals following the fast victory of Operation Shock and Awe to occupy Iraq more than a century later, the Boer War in 1899 was treated in London as just another 'splendid little war,' that would be over in a matter of weeks.

In the end, the Boer war was as devastating to Britain as the Iraq war would be for the United States a century later. The Dutch Boer settlers fought fiercely, using tactics of irregular or asymmetric warfare against a far better equipped and better-financed opponent. England, as was her tradition, brought troops from her colonies to do her fighting for her. The Boers were quick and highly mobile as a guerilla force, using the new smokeless cartridges in their German Mauser rifles which concealed their positions.

Boers employed hit-and-run tactics that not only caused losses the British couldn't afford, but they also thoroughly frustrated the Empire's view of a 'fair fight,' a war as 'gentlemen' would fight it. The Boers were no gentlemen; they were fighting for their land and their homes.

That war dragged on for three bitter years and England's nominal victory in the end was pyrrhic. It demonstrated to the entire world that the mightiest Empire on the earth was unable to defeat a small, inferior fighting force determined to defend their homeland, a lesson the American elite was to learn bitterly in Vietnam in the 1970s.

As the costs and casualties in the Boer campaign mounted, Her Majesty's generals stubbornly insisted that the end was near. British public opinion soured. Due to British incompetence and neglect, some 25,000 Boers and 14,000 natives—mainly women and children— died in 'concentration camps,' a new term which first appeared in the context of civilian internment during war. The Boer war was a watershed that began the long decline of support for the Imperial idea in England.[3]

Two rivals for England's global role

At the time England was showing signs of terminal decay, two potential contenders emerged, at first imperceptibly, as challengers who might fill the role of the British Empire. One was the German Reich. While few among the German elites thought of surpassing Britain in 1900, Germany's industrial growth, its educational system and its science were already leaving England far behind. Little remained of England's power except the role of the City of London as dominant over the terms of world trade.

The second emerging challenger to the role of Great Britain as the dominant global empire was the United States of America. In 1898-99, America had just fought her first imperial war of acquisition against Spain to secure the Philippines and Cuba. The undeclared geopolitical contest among Britain, Germany and America would require three decades and two world wars to be finally decisively resolved.[4]

In America, the elites who controlled the Money Trust and the great industrial trusts around Morgan, Rockefeller, Harriman, Schiff and others, began to see the possibilities for achieving real and dominant global power.

In 1902, Brooks Adams, grandson of President John Quincy Adams and one of the most ardent and influential advocates of American Empire, wrote,

> *During the last decade the world has traversed one of those periodic crises which attend an alteration in the social equilibrium. The seat of energy has migrated from Europe to America...American supremacy has been made possible only through applied science...Nothing has ever equaled in economy and energy the administration of the great American corporations.*

By "corporations" Adams clearly meant the US Steel of Morgan, the Standard Oil of Rockefeller, and the railroads and other industries they controlled. Adams continued,

> *The Union [the United States-w.e.] forms a gigantic and growing empire which stretches half round the globe, an empire possessing the greatest mass of accumulated wealth, the most perfect means of transportation, and the most delicate yet powerful industrial system which has ever been developed.* [5]

In his geographic analysis, which foreshadowed Halford Mackinder's landmark 1904 speech, the *Geographical Pivot of History*, Adams added a Darwinian touch,

> *The United States now occupies a position of extraordinary strength. Favored alike by geographical position, by deposits of minerals, by climate and the character of her people, she has little to fear*

either in peace or war, from rivals, provided the friction created by
the movement of the masses with which she has to deal does not
neutralize her energy.... Masses take the form of corporations and
the men who rise to the control of these corporations rise because
they are fittest. The process is natural selection.[6]

A 'Manifest Destiny'

Adams echoed the ideas of Frederick Jackson Turner, the theorist of what was
known as America's 'Manifest Destiny.' Turner argued that America's uniqueness was the product of an ever-expanding frontier. He defined American
historical existence as perpetual geopolitical expansion toward new frontiers in
the West: "The existence of an area of free land, its continuous recession, and
the advance of American settlement westward explains the American development," Turner insisted. "The universal disposition of the Americans, an expanding people, is to enlarge their dominion." It was a precursor of a later German
notion of *Lebensraum*, but one imbued with a messianic religious veneer of
America's 'God-given' mission.

Turner argued that the ongoing geopolitical enlargement was "the actual
result of an expansive power which is inherent in them." As he put it, "the
American energy will continually demand a wider field for its exercise." [7]

The writings of Turner and Adams provided the ideological justification to
America's elite families for their global agenda of expansion from the 1890s and
beyond. America's Manifest Destiny—as seen by the financial powers around
Morgan and John D. Rockefeller at the onset of the European Great War in
1914—was to fill the vacuum in global affairs left by a declining British Empire.
In his book, *The New Empire*, written at the turn of the century, Adams envisioned nothing less than an emerging American World Empire, including the
conquest of all Eurasian geopolitical space.[8]

Adams and Turner were social Darwinists, as were Rockefeller, Carnegie,
Morgan and most of the American plutocrats. They extended the 19th Century
notion of America's 'Manifest Destiny' of God-willed expansion across the
Continent to the 20th Century task of an American domination of the rest of the
world, just as the sun was setting on the decadent and moribund British Empire.

In his enlargement of Turner's frontier to include the entire world, Brooks
Adams was openly anti-German and pro-British. He argued that the German
Reich was the only rival to America's emergence as the successor to the British
Empire. His solution was an American alliance with the weaker rival, Britain,

against the stronger, Germany. This would be the strategy for the rise of American power on the ashes of a great European war. However, it didn't happen all at once.

The Casus Belli

The ill-fated miscalculation of the British military and diplomatic leadership that led it to go to war in August 1914 have been covered in some detail in my earlier work, *A Century of War: Anglo-American Oil Politics and the New World Order*.[9] The world war was not a response to violation of solemn international treaty agreements following the assassination in Sarajevo of the Archduke Francis Ferdinand. It was the result of a strategic decision taken well beforehand in Whitehall and Ten Downing Street, first with France in 1904, followed by an entente with Czarist Russia in 1907. The aim of this emerging Triple Entente was the military encirclement and isolation of their mutual foe, Germany.

Leading British policy circles at the time were influenced by two major factions. One was around Lord Robert Cecil who drafted the outline for the postwar League of Nations.

The second and even more influential war faction was grouped around the exponents of Alfred Milner's Round Table group. Using editorial control of the London *Times*, the Round Table had come to the conclusion that the German Reich, by its dynamic growth and its very existence, posed a mortal threat to continued British domination of the seas and control of world trade and finance. The Round Table group argued that a pre-emptive war was called for to stop the otherwise inevitable German march to world domination on the ashes of the British Empire.

There were two immediate *casus belli* for the war. First, and perhaps most decisive, was the decision of the German banking and political leadership to complete a rail link from Berlin to Baghdad in Mesopotamia, a part of the Ottoman Empire. This posed a threat to British oil supplies in Persia as well as to British control of the passageway to its crown jewel colony, India. The threat was aggravated in the eyes of prominent British military thinkers -- including a young Lord of the Admiralty, Winston Churchill -- by the second cause, the decision of the German Reich to build a deepwater navy to defend German trade routes against the British control of the seas.

The heart of the British Imperial strategy since the Napoleonic Wars had been to dominate and control the strategic sea-lanes and trade routes of global commerce.[10] The decision to go to war against Germany and Austro-Hungary, and later Ottoman Turkey, was not made out of the strength of the British Empire, but out of a realization of its fundamental weakness. It was based on a calculation that it would be better to get it over with sooner rather than later, when it would be far more difficult for England to challenge the rising hegemony of Germany. The decision proved to be the undoing of Rule Britannia, although it would take years, and a second world war, before Britain's elites reluctantly acknowledged the reality.

'He kept us out of war...'

On the outbreak of war in Europe, more than one-third of all Americans were immigrants, mostly from Germany, Ireland and Italy. Eight million German-Americans lived in the United States. Aside from the small banking and corporate elite with business dealings in London or France, the overwhelming majority of Americans had no interest in getting involved in what was clearly a European war, and which in no way threatened the security of the United States.

In 1916, Woodrow Wilson, the President who had colluded with the Money Trust to create the Federal Reserve in 1913, was re-elected by the smallest of margins, and again with help from the Money Trust and the Progressive Party. Meeting in 1915 at the home of US Steel's Elbert Gary, the cream of the Money Trust (August Belmont, Jacob Schiff, George F. Baker, Cornelius Vanderbilt) decided to back the re-election of Wilson. Also at the secret meeting were former President and 'Bull Moose' Progressive operator, Theodore Roosevelt, and George W. Perkins, a 'bag man' for political bribes and a former partner of J.P. Morgan.[11] US Steel, whose business boomed in the course of the war, was a Morgan company.

Wilson was discreetly backed by unreported campaign funds from Morgan circles.[12] Still, he barely won re-election, and only with the suspicious shift of the California Progressive Party vote to Wilson the day after the actual vote.

In January 1916, the re-elected President Wilson gave a press conference. His sole campaign slogan, "he kept us out of war," had been calculated propaganda, designed by his shadowy adviser Colonel Edward M. House. Wilson boldly declared, "so far as I can remember, this is a government of the people, and this people is not going to choose war." Little more than a year later the American people still had not chosen war, but Wilson, at the urging of the Money Trust, had.

Morgan does a lucrative business

At the onset of war in August 1914 the finances of Great Britain were in ruin. The economy was in a depression and gold reserves of the Bank of England had dwindled to alarmingly low levels. England was in no position industrially to produce sufficient war equipment and munitions for a full-scale war.[13]

In October 1914 the British Government sent a mission from its War Department to Washington to procure military supplies from private American companies. The United States was officially neutral. The British procurers quickly selected a private investment bank in New York to be its Sole Purchasing Agent—J.P. Morgan & Co. On the surface it was extraordinarily risky to make a private bank in a neutral country its official purchasing agent.

Conveniently, however, the newly created Federal Reserve opened its doors in 1914, making the risks more manageable through their control over future US Government debt as well as control over the nation's money supply. E.W. Kemmerer , a noted Princeton economist and Wall Street adviser during and after the war noted, "As fiscal agents of the Government, the federal reserve banks rendered the nations services of incalculable value after our entrance into the war. They aided greatly in the conservation of our gold resources, in the regulation of our foreign exchanges, and in the centralization of our financial energies. One shudders when he thinks what might have happened if the war had found us with our former decentralized and antiquated banking system."[14]

Conveniently enough for Morgan, Rockefeller, Carnegie and the very wealthy who stood to earn billions on entering the European war, an amendment to the US Constitution, the Sixteenth Amendment had been ratified in 1913, the same year as Wilson signed the Federal Reserve Act into law. The very rich avoided most taxation by protecting their wealth in new tax-exempt 'charitable' foundations such as the Rockefeller Foundation, created the same year as the income tax. The passage of a broad-based tax on income would allow Wall Street to finance the war through issuance of US Treasury bonds, so-called 'Liberty Bonds' whose debt service would be assured by the taxpayer, the ordinary citizens who were also called to fight and die in the trenches of France in a war 'to make the world safe for democracy,' or better said, safe for the House of Morgan..

Morgan served as intermediary for His Majesty's Government in arranging purchases of munitions, arms, uniforms, chemicals, in short all that would be needed to wage a modern war in 1914. As Financial Agent for the British Government, J.P. Morgan & Co. not only organized the financing of war purchases and decided which companies would be the suppliers, but it also set the

prices at which the equipment would be supplied. Not surprisingly, corporations directly in the Morgan and Rockefeller groups of companies were the
prime beneficiaries of Morgan's astute purchasing.[15]

The British war Office asked Morgan's new chairman, J.P. Morgan Jr., who
had succeeded his deceased father in 1913, how President Wilson would react to
such an obviously partisan action by America's most prestigious bank -- openly
aiding the British war cause. Morgan reportedly replied that it definitely would
not embarrass the Administration's professed neutrality because the Morgan
business with the British War Office, and later with the French Government, was
a commercial arrangement to increase trade and not a political or diplomatic
arrangement. In January 1915 J.P. Morgan met with President Wilson at the
White House to discuss the matter of the Morgan-British role and Wilson
confirmed that he had no objections to any actions by the Morgan group or
others "in furtherance of trade." [16]

Trade it furthered, like nothing before.

In 1915, at the beginning of the European war, E.I. DuPont de Nemours &
Co. of Delaware received $100,000,000 of British money through J.P. Morgan &
Co. to expand DuPont's explosives division. Within months DuPont rose from
being a small, unknown company to a primary international industry. Hercules
Powder and Monsanto Chemical Company grew accordingly. The iron and steel
industry blossomed. Crude iron prices rose 300% in three years, from $13 a ton
in 1914 to $42 a ton by 1917. Bethlehem Steel, US Steel, Westinghouse Electric
Co., Remington Arms, Colt Firearms—all had bulging order books. Profits at US
Steel alone rose from $23 million in 1914 to $224 million by 1917. Between 1914
and 1917, William Rockefeller's Anaconda Copper Co. saw its net income rise
from $9 million to $25 million. The assets of Phelps Dodge & Co. - the Dodge
who had put Wilson in the White House—increased some 400% from $59
millions in 1914 to $241 millions in 1918.[17]

In 1916 alone American industry, despite the nation's official neutrality,
exported a staggering $1,290,000,000 worth of war munitions to England and
France. By the eve of America's entry into the war, J.P. Morgan & Co. had
organized the export of some $5 billion worth of war matériel to the English and
French, and later Italian, governments, all bought on credit organized by J.P.
Morgan & Co. Such an amount—equivalent to about $90 billion in contempo-
rary dollar value—had never before been transacted by a private bank group.

It was enough to cause a major banking crisis should the loans default.

In April 1915, two years prior to America's entry into the war, Thomas W.
Lamont, a partner in J.P. Morgan, delivered a remarkable and little-noted
speech before the American Academy of Political and Social Science in Phila-

delphia. Lamont told the academic audience about the enormous profits American industry was drawing from financing and supplying munitions and war matériel to Britain and the allied powers in Europe. Lamont noted approvingly that J.P. Morgan and its Wall Street cronies would benefit handsomely should the war continue much longer. He enthusiastically cited the benefits of war:

> ...[W]e are turning from a debtor into a creditor...We are piling up a prodigious export trade balance....Many of our manufacturers and merchants have been doing a wonderful business in articles relating to the war. So heavy have been the war orders running into the hundreds of millions of dollars, that now their effect is beginning to spread to general business...As a climax to all this improvement, America is becoming a large factor in the international loan market.

That was J.P. Morgan's prized area, international government loans, and they were to turn it into a geopolitical weapon of staggering dimensions in the postwar period. Lamont rhapsodized further,

> Now what of the future? Many people seem to believe that New York is to supersede London as the money center of the world. In order to become the money center of the world, we must of course become the trade center of the world. That is certainly a possibility....

In explaining how such a course of events might happen and which rival nation Morgan and Co. saw as the major threat to such a US global dominance, Lamont bluntly warned:

> This question of trade and financial supremacy must be determined by several factors, a chief one of which is the duration of the war. If...the war should come to an end in the near future...we should probably find Germany, whose export trade is now almost wholly cut off, swinging back into keen competition very promptly.

Lamont then elaborated specifically on the war's financial implications;

> A third factor, and that too is dependent on the duration of the war, is as to whether we shall become lenders to foreign nations upon a really large scale...Shall we become lenders upon a really stupen-

dous scale to these foreign governments?... If the war continues long enough to encourage us to take such a position, then inevitably we would become a creditor instead of a debtor nation, and such a development, sooner or later, would tend to bring about the dollar, instead of the pound sterling, as the international basis of exchange. [18]

In this extraordinary speech, dutifully ignored by the nation's media, Morgan's partner Lamont outlined the strategy of Morgan & Co. not only for the war but also for the postwar era, right up until the outbreak of the Second World War.

War was spectacularly good for business, particularly for J.P. Morgan & Co. and their favored war industry companies. It was so good, in fact, that in 1934, two decades later, Senator Gerald Nye, a North Dakota Progressive Republican, held hearings to investigate the role of the munitions industry and finance in dragging the United States into the First World War.

Nye called the war industries "merchants of death." He was especially critical of DuPont and other large chemical and munitions dealers, claming that they were willing to sacrifice American soldiers in order to make larger profits from sales. Senator Nye's final report in 1936 concluded,

[T]he American munitions companies investigated have at times resorted to such unusual approaches, questionable favors and commissions, and methods of 'doing the needful' as to constitute, in effect, a form of bribery of foreign governmental officials or of their close friends in order to secure business.[19]

War to 'make the world safe' for J.P. Morgan

From the point of view of Lamont and friends, their "unusual approaches" during the war were working handsomely for them. Then, in late 1916 and into the first months of 1917, their prospects suddenly turned catastrophic. In February 1917 the Russian Czar abdicated as the exhausted military staged a mutiny at St. Petersburg (Petrograd). The Russian Army leadership was powerless to suppress the mutiny. Were Russia's forces to leave the war, Germany would no longer be faced with a devastating two-front war and could focus her forces on the Western Front.

Junius Pierpont Morgan, the most powerful banker before World War I, was responsible for creation of the privately-owned Federal Reserve in 1913 that made possible US entry into World War I to rescue Morgan's loans to Britain and France.

With more than $1,500,000,000 in direct war credits organized to Britain, France, Russia and Italy, and the underwriting of some $5 billion in supplies to Europe's belligerent nations, Morgan & Company began to fear that the unthinkable might happen, namely that Germany might after all win the war.

The Russian front against the German Reich had collapsed and a Bolshevik regime headed by V.I. Lenin, threatened to take power and withdraw Russia from the war. In a daring gamble financed by the German General Staff, the Germans decided to transport Lenin and the Bolshevik leadership—then in exile in Switzerland—in a special sealed railcar from their Swiss exile by train back to Russia, together with enough gold bars to fund a revolution against the Czar. [20] The Germans hoped this would get them a regime hostile to the Anglo-French cause, one that would agree to sue for separate peace with Germany. It did, but at a heavy price.

France was then exhausted, but Britain rejected French pleas for reinforcements, even though the British military had one million soldiers under the British flag in the Middle East, preparing to carve up the untapped oil treasures of Mesopotamia, that could have been re-deployed to France. With a ceasefire

on the Russian front, the German troops would be able to regroup for a final
push through the Maginot Line across France.[21]

Wilson's Ambassador to London at the time was Walter Hines Page who had
been a trustee of Rockefeller's General Education Board before being named
Ambassador to the Court of St. James. On March 5, 1917, Ambassador Page sent
a confidential dispatch to President Wilson in which he stated,

> *I think that the pressure of this approaching crisis has gone beyond*
> *the ability of the Morgan Financial Agency for the British and*
> *French governments. The need is becoming too great and urgent for*
> *a private agency to meet....*

Page added that the outlook in Europe was "alarming" to America's industrial and financial interests.

> *If we should go to war with Germany, the greatest help we could give*
> *the Allies would be such a credit. In that case our Government*
> *could, if it would, make a large investment in a Franco-British loan*
> *or might guarantee such a loan....*

Then, to be perfectly sure Woodrow Wilson did not mistake where Page was
going, the Ambassador concluded, "Unless we go to war with Germany our
Government, of course, cannot make such a direct grant of credit...." He added
that the alternative to war was domestic collapse of the US economic and
financial structure.[22]

Four weeks after Page's alarming letter, Woodrow Wilson, who had been re-
elected as a peace candidate in 1916, led America into the First World War in
April 1917. He appeared before Congress to ask for a formal declaration of war
against Germany, citing as grounds Germany's renewal of unrestricted subma-
rine attacks on US and other neutral shipping to England and French ports.
Congress overwhelmingly gave him the powers with the only dissenting votes
coming from a handful of principled neutrals including Senator Robert LaFol-
lette from Wisconsin.[23]

The US Treasury, assisted by the newly created Federal Reserve, whose New
York Federal Reserve Bank president was Morgan's Benjamin Strong, began to
raise unprecedented sums by selling so-called Liberty Loans to the public. From
the first sales of such Liberty Loans, J.P. Morgan & Co. was paid $400 million to
satisfy the Britain's debts owed to Morgan. In other words, Wilson used the US
taxpayers to pull Morgan's large chestnuts out of the proverbial fire.

From the time of its official entry into the European war in April 1917 until the signing of armistice with Germany on November 11, 1918, the United States Government lent the European Allied Powers what Lamont had called a "really stupendous" sum: $9,386,311,178. Britain received the lion's share of $4,136,000,000. France got $2,293,000,000.

The Full Faith and Credit of the United States of America, backed by the new Federal Reserve, was being mobilized to defeat Germany. The $9 billion, however, did not go to London or Paris. Rather, it went directly to American industries, most of which were tied to either the Morgan group, Kuhn-Loeb, or the Rockefellers, to pay for war supplies to the Allies.[24] Morgan left no stone unturned.

To sell Wilson's 180-degree policy reversal to a skeptical American public and to mobilize them to wage war on Germany, the Wilson White House created the most impressive propaganda bureau the world had ever seen.

Propaganda as a weapon

On April 13, 1917 Woodrow Wilson created the Committee on Public Information (CPI) to promote the war domestically and to publicize American war aims abroad. Under the leadership of a journalist crony of Wilson named George Creel, the CPI combined advertising techniques with a sophisticated understanding of human psychology. It marked the first time that a government disseminated propaganda on such a large scale. It was in every sense a precursor of the world depicted by George Orwell in his novel *1984*.

Creel was joined at the CPI by one of the shrewdest propagandists in American history, a young Viennese-born naturalized American named Edward Bernays. Bernays brought with him intimate knowledge of a new branch of human psychology which had not yet been translated into English. He was the nephew and literary agent in American for Austrian psychoanalyst Sigmund Freud.

Using Creel's muckraking journalism and Bernays' Freudian psychology – with its analysis of unconscious needs and drives -- the Government's Committee on Public Information assaulted the unwitting American public with a calculated barrage of lies, jingoistic epithets demonizing Germans, coupled with horrifying images allegedly showing German soldiers bayoneting Belgian babies, and other manufactured atrocities. These images and symbols were fed continuously through the mainstream media in order to whip the American public into a pro-war frenzy against a nation, Kaiser Germany, which posed no actual threat to it.

The CPI became a de facto wartime media censor. Invoking threats of German propaganda lurking within antiwar viewpoints, the CPI implemented "voluntary guidelines" for news media and was instrumental in getting Congress to pass the Espionage Act of 1917 and the Sedition Act of 1918. Radical newspapers, such as the socialist *Appeal to Reason*, were silenced by wartime limitations on dissent.

Creel and Bernays were joined at the CPI by anglophile journalist and close Wilson adviser Walter Lippmann. As a young Harvard graduate, Lippmann had been recruited to be a link between Wall Street interests around Morgan and the British secret society, the Round Table, which had been agitating England to prepare for war against Germany since its founding in 1909. [25]

Lippmann's biweekly column in the New York *Herald Tribune* was syndicated in hundreds of local newspapers across America, making him one of the most influential pro-British voices in the country. His columns were critical to winning the allegiance of the educated middle class, a sector that would otherwise tend to be neutral or against war.

But it was Bernays' unique, perverse genius for fusing mob psychology and mass media techniques to manipulate specific human emotions on a large scale. He had learned these keys to influencing human behavior through the work of his uncle, Sigmund Freud.

Applying those insights on a mass scale, the Committee on Public Information achieved extraordinary results within months, orchestrating the American public into a mass frenzy in favor of war. With Bernays' genius in full play, the Freudian view of human nature was combined with what became Madison Avenue advertising techniques; the results were deployed by the CPI in the service of war. Having examined the variety of ways that information flowed to the population, CPI flooded these channels with psychologically "charged" pro-war propaganda.

The CPI's domestic division was composed of 19 sub-divisions, and each focused on a particular type of propaganda. The CPI Division of News distributed thousands of press releases as a primary conduit for feeding war-related information into local news outlets. CPI later admitted that more than 20,000 newspaper columns every week had been filled with material taken from CPI releases. The CPI also created a Division of Syndicated Features to recruit leading novelists, short story writers, and essayists. Their job was to present the war to ordinary Americans in easy to understand images. They reached some twelve million people every month.[26]

A CPI Division of Civic and Educational Cooperation had Anglophile scholars who churned out pamphlets with titles such as *The German Whisper, German War Practices,* and *Conquest and Kultur.* It was naked propaganda. More respectable thinkers, such as John Dewey and Lippmann, aimed at the more sophisticated public. Every strata of the population was saturated with fine-tuned war propaganda.[27]

The CPI's Division of Pictorial Publicity had the most talented advertising illustrators and cartoonists of the day. Newspapers and magazines eagerly donated advertising space, and it was almost impossible to pick up a periodical without encountering CPI material. Powerful posters, painted in patriotic colors, were plastered on billboards across the country. Powerful cartoon images promoted the sale of Liberty Bonds to the American public. The image of a stern, grandfatherly Uncle Sam reaching out to young men with the slogan, "Uncle Sam Wants You!" was so successful that it has endured as a symbol of American "pop" art, as well as well as an example of war propaganda.

A Division of Films ensured that the war was promoted in the cinema. The CPI created a national volunteer corps called "Four Minute Men" which grew to 75,000 eager volunteers whose job was to appear as authorized representatives of the Government's CPI at the opening of every movie and give a four minute pep talk about supporting the war, buying Liberty Bonds and such. It was phenomenally effective. [28]

In a 1917 editorial *The Motion Picture News* proclaimed that, "every individual at work in this industry wants to do his share" and promised that, "through slides, film leaders and trailers, posters, and newspaper publicity they will spread that propaganda so necessary to the immediate mobilization of the country's great resources." Movies with titles such as *The Kaiser: The Beast of Berlin, Wolves of Kultur,* and *Pershing's Crusaders* flooded American theaters. One motion picture, *To Hell With The Kaiser,* was so popular that Massachusetts riot police were summoned to deal with an angry mob that had been denied admission.[29]

Because propagandists attempted to "do the other fellow's thinking for him," they preferred indirect messages to overt, logical arguments. During the war, the CPI did this by making calculated emotional appeals, by demonizing Germany, by linking the war to the ideals of various social groups, and, when necessary, by outright lying.

Appeal to baser emotions

CPI propaganda consciously appealed to the emotions, not to the mind. It was heavily influenced by Bernays' adaptations from Freud. Emotional agitation was a favorite technique of the CPI strategists who understood that any emotion may be 'drained off' and re-directed into any activity by skillful manipulation. An article published in *Scientific Monthly* just after the war argued that, "the detailed suffering of a little girl and her kitten can motivate our hatred against the Germans, arouse our sympathy for Armenians, make us enthusiastic for the Red Cross, or lead us to give money for a home for cats."

The CPI invented wartime slogans such as "Bleeding Belgium," "The Criminal Kaiser," and "Make the World Safe For Democracy." A typical propaganda poster portrayed an aggressive, bayonet-wielding German soldier above the caption "Beat Back The Hun With Liberty Bonds." In that case, emotions of hate and fear were redirected toward giving money to the war effort.

After the war, in a sociological and psychological analysis of the role of propaganda during the war, University of Chicago's Harold Lasswell noted that the cause of the failure of German propaganda in America was that it emphasized logic over passion. Count von Bernstorff, a German diplomat, made a similar observation from another perspective: "The outstanding characteristic of the average American is rather a great, though superficial, sentimentality." [30]

German press statements completely failed to grasp this fact. Bernays and the CPI had exploited it to the hilt.

Another propaganda technique used by the CPI was absolute demonization of the enemy. As Lasswell pointed out,

> *So great are the psychological resistances to war in modern nations that every war must appear to be a war of defense against a menacing, murderous aggressor. There must be no ambiguity about who the public is to hate.* [31]

CPI pamphlets painted Germans as depraved, brutal aggressors. In one CPI publication, Professor Vernon Kellogg asked, "will it be any wonder if, after the war, the people of the world, when they recognize any human being as a German, will shrink aside so that they may not touch him as he passes, or stoop for stones to drive him from their path?" [32]

A particularly effective strategy for demonizing Germans was the use of atrocity stories. "A handy rule for arousing hate," said Lasswell, "is, if at first they do not enrage, use an atrocity. It has been employed with unvarying success in every conflict known to man." Incredible tales of German barbarism in Belgium and France gave rise to a myth of unique German savagery. German soldiers, the world was told by the CPI propaganda machine, amused themselves by cutting off the hands of Belgian babies. Another oft-repeated tale related how German soldiers amputated the breasts of Belgian women out of sheer viciousness.

In 1927 Lasswell wrote a book length study, *Propaganda Technique in the World War,* analyzing the work of Creel, Lippmann and Bernays in detail. He shared their conviction that in a democracy, the population could not be trusted to act as the elites wished and must be emotionally manipulated to do so.

After the war, Edward Bernays admitted that his colleagues contrived alleged atrocities to provoke a public outcry against Germany. Some of the atrocity stories that were circulated during the war, such as one about a tub full of eyeballs, or the story of a seven-year-old boy who confronted German soldiers with a wooden gun, were actually recycled from made up atrocities used in previous conflicts.

In his work on wartime propaganda, Lasswell claimed atrocity stories would always be popular because the audience can feel self-righteous indignation toward the enemy, but also, at some level, identify with the perpetrators of the crimes. "A young woman, ravished by the enemy," he wrote "yields secret satisfaction to a host of vicarious ravishers on the other side of the border." [33]Such was the depraved view of human nature shared and propagated by Freud, Bernays, Madison Avenue, the war profiteers, Washington's CPI, and Morgan's Wall Street circle.

To make the propaganda effect complete, the Government's CPI made a major issue out of changing such common Germanic words like hamburger into "liberty steak," reminiscent of the Bush Administration's ploy decades later to ostracize France for opposing war in Iraq by changing "french fries" to "freedom fries." Sauerkraut in the American diet became "liberty cabbage" and well-known German chocolate milk became Dutch chocolate milk. German Americans in many parts of the country, although peaceful and patriotic, lived in fear of attacks by mobs or organized bands simply because of their ethnic origin.

The extraordinary techniques of mass manipulation of opinion during World War I greatly assisted the transformation of America into a democracy-by-outward-appearance, ruled deceptively by a plutocratic elite in its own self-interest.

In 1928, Bernays published a remarkably candid book, titled simply, *Propaganda.* In it, he declared, "It was of course the astounding success of propaganda during the war that opened the eyes of the intelligent few... to the possibilities of regimenting the public mind." Speaking of his own efforts with the CPI, Bernays continued,

> *The American government developed a technique which...was new...the manipulators of patriotic opinion made use of the mental clichés and the emotional habits of the public to produce mass reactions against the alleged atrocities, the terror, and the tyranny of the enemy. It was only natural, after the war ended, that intelligent persons should ask themselves whether it was possible to apply a similar technique to the problems of peace.* [34]

It was to prove all too possible.

Bernays went on to establish a new profession he called 'public relations.' In a book he edited after the Second World War, Bernays referred to his work as "the engineering of consent." [35] Madison Avenue advertising and its sophisticated techniques of creating unconscious and compulsive desires to buy specific products, including cigarettes, expensive women's shoes, cosmetics, cars, and whatever a client wanted to sell-- even including political candidates -- was the creation of Bernays. He acquired the title, "the father of spin," a reference to the technique of manipulating reality to desired ends, whether to sell political policies or Ivory soap.[36]

Committee on Public Information drumming up war frenzy in the American population, J.P. Morgan and allied Wall Street financial interests drastically expanded the volume of their lucrative businesses. Wall Street and Morgan-related industries supplied the private financing and war matériel for Britain, France and Italy. Their operations would now be guaranteed by the Full Faith and Credit of the Government of the United States and by the virtually unlimited ability of the newly created Federal Reserve System of banks to guarantee the extraordinary risks being taken by Morgan and the private banking interests of the Money Trust.

The incredible cost of war

After five ghastly years of war, the costs in terms of human life and destruction were immeasurable. Official government statistics indicated that the deaths caused directly by the "war to end all wars" or indirectly resulting from it, totaled between 16,000,000 and 20,000,000, over 7,000,000 of which were military and more than 10,000,000 civilian.

The Commander-in-Chief of the American Expeditionary Forces sent by Wilson to lead the US forces in Europe, General John J. Pershing, was hailed and cheered in a New York ticker-tape confetti parade like an Imperial Caesar returning from a victorious campaign with the rich loot of captured nations.[37] Only in this instance, the rich loot of the captured nations of Europe went not to the generals, but to the House of Morgan and Wall Street investment bankers and banks. Morgan and Wall Street tightly controlled the buying and selling of Liberty Bonds and other debt issued from the new Federal Reserve – the mechanism whereby the Government financed its involvement in the Great European War.

The monetary cost of the war to all the involved nations reached a staggering $186 billion. Of that $186,000,000,000 Germany had spent some $39 billion compared against $123 billion total for the United States and its Allied powers. The cost to the United States alone was a stupendous $22 billion for about two years of active belligerency.[38]

By the time the Peace of Versailles was signed on June 28, 1919, Great Britain and the British Empire -- including India, Canada and the Commonwealth nations -- had spent a total of 11 billion Pound Sterling, or $54 billion, on executing the war against the German and allied Central Powers. To put that number into historical perspective, in the six fiscal years from March 31, 1914 ending March 31, 1920, British Government expenditure actually exceeded the total cumulative expenditure for the previous 225 years, or two and a quarter centuries, prior to 1914.

The British people paid 36% of the war costs in the form of taxes. The other 64% was borrowed, mainly from the United States Government, through the agency of the Federal Reserve. On the eve of the Great War in 1914, British national debt was a mere 711 million pounds Sterling, less than 5% of the total national wealth of the country. By the end of the war, the national debt had ballooned to 8.2 billion pounds, an increase in public debt of 1,150 times in six years.

It was the end of the British Empire as the banking metropolis of the world, much as Thomas Lamont in 1915 had envisioned. England was choking on her war debts. [39] The public debt of the United States expanded by some 2,500% during the war from $1 billion in 1913 to more than $25 billion by the end of 1919. The debt was financed by the sale of Government bonds via the Federal Reserve to the private bond dealing banks led by J. P. Morgan, Kuhn, Loeb and Wall Street, at a stunning profit to the latter. [40]

The problem for J.P. Morgan, Rockefeller and the Wall Street establishment was that the rest of America was not yet ready to grab the mantle of global empire from Great Britain. That would require a little more work, a lot of Yankee ingenuity, as well as another world war, and a greatly expanded propaganda machine.

Most significantly for J.P. Morgan & Co. and Wall Street, the First World War changed the status of the United States, as Lamont had predicted in 1915, from that of a debtor nation to the world's greatest creditor nation, a role filled formerly by England.

During the war the world's market for bankers' acceptance -- a form of short-term bank credit essential for international trade -- moved from London to New York. Banker and former Federal Reserve board Vice Chairman Paul Warburg, architect of the Federal Reserve Act, back at Kuhn, Loeb & Co., had become the most powerful trade acceptance banker in the world. One major aim of the backers of the Federal Reserve—displacing London as world money market—had been achieved.

The gold standard was still the basis of foreign exchange. The small group of international bankers -- now led by New York banks -- who owned the gold, controlled the monetary system of Western nations.

In December 1919, the New York bankers put through Congress an amendment to the Federal Reserve Act of 1913, the so-called Edge Amendment. That small amendment authorized the creation of special financial institutions expressly for "engaging in international or foreign banking or other international or foreign financial operations, including dealing in gold or bullion, and the holding of stock in foreign corporations." Commenting on the amendment, Princeton University economist, Prof. E.W. Kemmerer remarked, "The Federal Reserve is proving to be a great influence in the internationalizing of American trade and American finance." [41]

Kemmerer, who would play a major role in that internationalization of New York banking during the 1920s, knew what he was talking about. That was precisely why J. P. Morgan, Warburg, Rockefeller and the rest of the Wall Street Money Trust had gone to such great lengths to create the privately owned Federal Reserve. How the Federal Reserve would define world politics over the decade following the end of the Great War in 1919 would prove remarkable.

Endnotes:

[1] Carroll Quigley, *The Anglo-American Establishment: From Rhodes to Cliveden* (New York: Books in Focus, 1981), pp. 38-9.

[2] Ibid., pp. 33-34.

[3] Phil Konstantin, *The Boer War South Africa, 1899-1902* (San Diego: The History Ring), accessed July 25, 2008 on www.geocities.com/Athens/Acropo/8141/boerwar.html.

[4] An interesting geopolitical perspective on this rivalry for global dominance is found in Peter J. Taylor, *Britain and the Cold War: 1945 as Geopolitical Transition,* London, Pinter Publishers, 1990, p. 17: "With hindsight we can interpret the two world wars as contests for the British succession between Germany and the USA. The contest was not decided until the end of the Second World War and the Unconditional Surrender of Germany."

[5] Brooks Adams, *The New Empire*, New York, Macmillan, 1902, pp. xi-xxxiii.

[6] Ibid.

[7] Frederick Jackson Turner, *The Significance of the Frontier in American History* (New York: Henry Holt and Co, 1995), pp. 1, 33, 59.

[8] Brooks Adams, op. cit.

[9] F. William Engdahl, *A Century of War: Anglo-American Oil Politics and the New World Order* (London: Pluto Press, 2004), Chapter 4, notably pp. 35-36.

[10] F. William Engdahl, *Oil and the Origins of the Great War*, History Compass, 5/6, (Oxford: Blackwells Publishing Ltd., 2007), pp. 2041-2060, available in draft in www.engdahl.oilgeopolitics.net.

[11] Ferdinand Lundberg, *America's Sixty Families*, (New York: Vanguard Press, 1937), pp. 130.

[12] Ibid. pp. 130-133.

[13] F. William Engdahl, *A Century of War*, pp. 36-37.

[14] Cited in Eustace Mullins, *The Secrets of the Federal Reserve*, (Staunton, Bankers' Research Institute, 1983), p.85.

[15] The Nye Commission, *Report of the Special Committee on Investigation of the Munitions Industry (The Nye Report)*, U.S. Congress, Senate, 74th Congress, 2nd session, February 24, 1936.

[16] [British Ambassador to Washington, Sir Cecil] Spring Rice to [Secretary of State for Foreign Affairs Sir Edward] Grey, 20 Jan 1915, f. 60, FO 800/85, cited in Kathleen Burk, *Britain, America and the Sinews of War 1914-1918* (London: George, Allen & Unwin, 1985), p. 21. Spring Rice had been best man at the wedding of J.P. Morgan, Jr. and was a member of the elite Wall Street-London Pilgrims Society.

[17] The Nye Commission, op. cit.

[18] Thomas W. Lamont, *The Effect of the War on America's Financial Position*, Annals of the American Academy of Political and Social Science, 1915, 60; pp. 106-112.

[19] The Nye Commission, op. cit., pp. 3-13.

[20] Z. A. B. Zeman, *Germany and the Revolution in Russia, 1915-1918: Documents from the Archives of the German Foreign Ministry* (London: Oxford University Press, 1958), p.92, note 3. The German Minister of Foreign Affairs wrote to the German Kaiser in December 1917, "It was not until the Bolsheviks had received from us a steady flow of funds through various channels and under varying labels that they were in a position to be able to build up their main organ Pravda, to conduct energetic propaganda and appreciably to extend the originally narrow base of their party., --Von Kühlmann, minister of foreign affairs, to the kaiser, December 3, 1917, quoted in http://reformed-theology.org/html/books/bolshevik_revolution/chapter_03.htm#6.

[21] F. William Engdahl, op. cit., pp. 40-41.

[22] Walter Hines Page to President Woodrow Wilson, April 5, 1917, cited in Ferdinand Lundberg, op. cit. P.141.

[23] Woodrow Wilson, *Speech to Congress*, April 2, 1917, in Source Records of the Great War, Vol. V, ed. Charles F. Horne, National Alumni, 1923, in www.firstworldwar.com/source/usawardeclaration.htm, accessed August 4, 2008.

[24] Walter Hines Page, op. cit., p.141.

[25] Carroll Quigley, *Tragedy and Hope, A History of the World in Our Time* (New York: Macmillan Co., 1966), p. 539.

[26] Aaron Delwiche, *Propaganda: Wartime Propaganda: World War I, The Committee on Public Information*, accessed in http://www.propagandacritic.com/articles/ww1.cpi.html.

[27] Ibid.

[28] Ibid.

[29] Ibid.

[30] Aaron Delwiche, *Of Fraud and Force Fast Woven—Domestic Propaganda During the First World War*, in www.firstworldwar.com , August 11, 2001, accessed on August 5, 2008.

[31] Harold D. Lasswell, *Propaganda Technique in the World War* (New York: 1927; reprinted MIT Press, 1971), cited in Aaron Delwiche, op. cit.

[32] Ibid.

[33] Cited in Aaron Delwiche, op. cit.

[34] Edward Bernays, *Propaganda* (Brooklyn, NY: IG Publishers, 1928), pp. 54-55.

[35] Edward L. Bernays, ed., *The Engineering of Consent* (Norman, OK: University of Oklahoma Press, 1955), pp. 3-4. Here Bernays defined his view as follows: "Public relations is the attempt, by information, persuasion and adjustment, to engineer public support for an activity, cause, movement or institution."

[36] Larry Tye, *The Father of Spin: Edward L. Bernays and the Birth of Public Relations* (New York: Henry Holt & Co., 1998), pp. 27-31.

[37] Richard J. Beamish and Francis A. March, *America's Part in the World War: A History of the Full Greatness of Our Country's Achievements*, (Philadelphia, The John C. Winston Co., 1919).

[38] Ibid., p. 24.

[39] Harvey E. Fisk, *English Public Finance From the Revolution of 1688*, (New York:, Bankers Trust Company, 1920), pp.1-5. Notably, Bankers Trust, a Morgan bank, did the extensive study of British finances in the early post World War I days.

[40] The New York Times, *World Debts Now $265,000,000,000: World War Caused Increase of $221,000,000,000 Says Bank Statistician*, June 27, 1920.

[41] Cited in Eustace Mullins, op. cit, p. 124.

CHAPTER FIVE

Gold, Conflicting Goals and Rival Empires

'The explosive mine which underlay the economic system of the world was now coming clearly into view.... It was now evident why the European crisis had so long been delayed. They had kited bills A in order to pay B and their internal deficits. I don't know that I ever received a worse shock.'
– President Herbert Hoover on the 1931 crisis

Congress discovers the 'Money Trust'

Impossible to say was whether, had he lived and remained vigorous to the end of the 1920s, Junius Pierpont Morgan would have approved of the policy pursued by the House of Morgan after his death in early 1913. Morgan died before the Federal Reserve opened its doors in 1914. The *Wall Street Journal* described the degree of personal authority commanded by the 75-year old Morgan in February 1912, as follows:

> *The condition that has developed in Wall Street in the past fifteen years is to a considerable extent a personal one, and the authority which centers in the hands of Mr. Morgan, a man seventy-five years of age, is by no means something which can be passed down to his successors. Such men have no successors; and their work is either left undone after they are dead or the world devises other means and other works to take its place.*

Morgan died several months after being called to testify before the Pujo House Banking Committee hearings into allegations of monopoly practices in finance. The media ridiculed his testimony – that an individual's personal character was the most important consideration of credit-worthiness -- and denounced Morgan as head of an all-powerful 'Money Trust.'[1] The accusation was more accurate than either the Congress or most Americans realized.

After Morgan's death in March 1913, on the eve of the Great War, J.P. Morgan & Co. was run by the successor partners, including Henry P. Davison, Willard Straight (who died at the Versailles Peace talks), Thomas W. Lamont, and later, J.P. Morgan, Jr.

The bank continued to link the fate of Wall Street, and the American economy it dominated, to the future of England after the end of the war. Through various financial entanglements, J.P. Morgan & Co. pursued an evolving imperium of American finance that would ultimately displace the prewar role of the City of London as the world's financial superpower. J.P. Morgan & Co., Rockefeller's financial group, and the major investment banks of Wall Street -- such as Kuhn, Loeb and Dillon, Read -- were the leading players in these developments.

The House of Morgan's foreign entanglements after the World War, aided by its control over the newly created Federal Reserve, were highly problematic for the United States, and ultimately for the world.

In ways remarkably analogous to the unfolding global financial crisis of 2007-2008, world credit had been built after 1919 on a pyramid of ever more dubious debts, with the House of Morgan and Wall Street financial houses sitting at the peak of the pyramid. Most of Europe and a large number of developing countries from Bolivia to Poland were linked into the Wall Street credit pyramid. In 1929-31, the domino-style failure of those Morgan-initiated credit links to Europe and beyond turned a manageable American stock market crash into the worst deflation crisis in American history, precipitating a global depression.

The central reason for the collapse of the world economy was little understood and discussed then or in the decades following the Great Depression and the European crisis of 1931. The true origin of the Great Depression of 1931-1938 lay not in an overvalued New York stock market and its subsequent collapse. Rather, the fundamental cause of the global depression and banking crisis of the early 1930s, and also the driver for the stock bubble in the first place, was the misconceived attempt by the House of Morgan and the Wall Street banking establishment to replace the City of London with New York as the heart of world finance. Gold would play the decisive role in this attempt.

There were different views within the New York Money Trust about how to accomplish the *de facto* monetary coup. There was unity, however, on the goal of New York becoming the world's finance center, displacing London in the process.

The Morgan faction owed much of its enormous power within the United States since the 1870s to its intimate links with leading London financial groups, above all, the House of Rothschild. Morgan therefore favored a strategy of alliance, a form of 'special relationship' between a weakened City of London and the emerging power of Wall Street, as the preferred path to an ultimate American Century. J.P. Morgan's ties with the City of London and the British Treasury were so strong, in fact, that his bank remained the British Government's official financial agents in the United States from the 1870s until September 1931, when England left the Gold Standard over the objections of J.P. Morgan & Co. The influential Governor of the New York Federal Reserve Benjamin Strong was strongly tied to Morgan's London alliance strategy. [2]

Others in Wall Street, in particular Dillon, Read & Co. and their influential consultant, Edwin Kemmerer, had a different view. Kemmerer had played the key role in the 1920s in reorganizing the world onto a new, US-dominated Gold Standard. This faction agreed that an emerging, informal American Empire, based on the dominance of US gold reserves and of the banks of Wall Street, should ultimately replace Britain as the leading global power. However, Kemmerer and others in his circle saw little need to be as amiable as the House of Morgan was with the City of London or Britain. In Kemmerer's view Morgan, with its influential London subsidiary, Morgan Grenfell, and with its strong ties into the Bank of England, was perhaps too closely tied to London interests to pursue a truly American strategy.[3]

All major Wall Street factions agreed nonetheless that their future lay in extending highly profitable credits to Europe, Latin America, Japan and the rest of the world, areas that had been the province of City of London bankers for the better part of a century. Those loans, and especially Wall Street underwriting of bonds to the world, earned the New York bankers the very attractive foreign interest rates of 5% and even as high as 8%. The bonds or credits were to be secured by national governments, which had agreed to 'stabilize' their postwar currencies by linking them to a new, US-led Gold Standard. The system of stabilization was a crude, *ad hoc* version of what the New York banks would later institutionalize in the International Monetary Fund and World Bank as the heart of the post-World War II dollar-based system.

In February 1922, during the early phase of the foreign lending bubble, President Warren Harding had called a special White House conference at the urging of his Commerce Secretary Herbert Hoover, who had become alarmed at the dramatic rise in risky foreign loans by large US banks. Present at the White House meeting were President Harding, Treasury Secretary Andrew Mellon, Secretary of State Charles Evans Hughes, Secretary Hoover and leading representatives of the Wall Street bond-issuing houses, including J. P. Morgan, Dillon/Read, Kuhn/Loeb and others. The aim was to discuss the potential dangers to the health of the US economy of such large foreign lending, especially where risks were unknown. The meeting concluded that all proposals for new foreign loans would be submitted to the State Department for its opinion, which in turn would submit same to both Commerce and Treasury secretaries for comment. The State Department would advise on political implications of the proposed new credits for the United States.[4]

Within less than a month, the powerful New York bankers had organized their counter-attack against any US Government meddling in their affairs. They convinced New York Federal Reserve Governor Benjamin Strong to file a vigorous protest with the State Department demanding that the US Government 'take their hands off' Wall Street's lucrative foreign lending. The Money Trust won. Harding and Treasury Secretary Andrew Mellon, a powerful Anglophile banker whose wealth rivaled that of Rockefeller, sided with Wall Street, forcing a retreat, and the agreement became toothless. The foreign lending boom continued at an ever-expanding rate, until the collapse in 1929-1931.[5]

In its major features, Wall Street's foreign bond issuing bubble of the 1920s was the relative equivalent, in terms of risk and inevitability of disaster, to Wall Street's 21st Century "securitization" bubble that caused the greatest financial calamity in history when it collapsed in 2007.

During the creation of the huge financial bubble of the 1920s Wall Street bankers were in firm alliance with US Treasury Secretary Andrew Mellon. Mellon, the longest-serving US Treasury Secretary, oversaw the entire process under several Administrations, from the beginning of the bubble in 1921 to the point when newly elected President Hoover dismissed him in 1932. The troika of the US Treasury, New York Federal Reserve and Wall Street was to remain the heart of American financial power into the next century.

The amount of foreign bonds issued by Wall Street in the decade until the 1929 market crash was about $7,000,000,000, a relatively huge amount equal to nearly 10% of total Gross Domestic Product.6 The war-damaged European economies used more than 90% of these American loans to buy American goods, a boon to major US corporations listed on the New York Stock Exchange. When the buying collapsed after 1929, however, Wall Street's foreign lending boom became a vehicle that severely worsened the US industrial depression.

The New York Fed takes control

After 1914, under the guidance of Morgan's man, Benjamin Strong, the powerful first President of the New York Federal Reserve Bank, US monetary policy and capital flows in the critical years up to 1929-1931 were, in effect, guided by the needs of Wall Street in its drive to displace London as the world's banker. As a crucial part of the process, the banking reserves of the remaining eleven regional Federal Reserve banks were channeled into New York under Strong's influence. Strong had been Vice President of the Morgan-controlled Banker's Trust of New York, and had been JP Morgan's personal emissary to the secret Jekyll Island Georgia bankers meeting in 1910 which drafted the plan for what became the Federal Reserve in 1913. To call Strong a Morgan man was no exaggeration. Through his influence on Strong at the NY Federal Reserve, J.P. Morgan essentially led Wall Street policies and practices during that critical period.

From 1920-1929, the banks centered in New York channeled the wealth created by American industry and agriculture, via Wall Street, into foreign credit markets. Benjamin Strong at the New York Federal Reserve, by far the most powerful of the Federal Reserve banks, focused on encouraging US loans abroad to bring about the creation of a new, US-led, international Gold Standard. Money that did not find its way overseas to Germany or other profitable foreign markets in the 1920s went into the New York stock market, increasingly so after 1925. The remaining eleven regional Federal Reserve banks were left to deal with their own local or regional economic issues.

One consequence of the destructive European War of 1914-1918 had been the unprecedented transfer of Europe's gold reserves out of Europe's central banks and into the vaults of the Federal Reserve, as debt-strapped European belligerents, from England to France to Italy and beyond, were forced to pay for American manufactured war supplies in gold.

By the time the Treaty of Versailles was signed, the United States had become the possessor of the vast bulk of the world's monetary gold, a 400% increase in US gold reserves since the prewar period. Until the 1914 outbreak of war, gold had been the basis of the international monetary system, a system that had been centered in the City of London since the Napoleonic Wars.

By 1920, however, the United States Federal Reserve had accumulated 40% of the world's monetary gold reserves. It had garnered the gold by being able to pay the world's highest price for monetary gold at a time Britain and Continental Europe were burdened with America's severe war reparations and war debt repayment obligations pursuant to Versailles.[7]

Benjamin Strong shaped Federal Reserve policy from Wall Street with the clear priority of re-establishing the international Gold Standard of pre-1914. The centerpiece would be the postwar economic reconstruction of Europe, financed at a handsome return by New York bank loans and Wall Street bond underwritings. The thinking was that if Britain were to join, such a New York-dominated Gold Standard would be credible in terms of the world economy, finance and trade.

The New York Money Trust, however, even Benjamin Strong, viewed the role of Britain and the Bank of England as a distinctly junior or subordinate part of their New York-centered system -- something the City of London and the British establishment were not about to accept.

When the US Treasury demanded, at the Versailles peace talks in 1919, that all Allied nations, particularly Britain, must repay all their billions of dollars of war loans, it confirmed that the US elites were no longer content to play a junior role. In a very real sense, the entire history of British geopolitics in Europe and the rest of the world from 1919 to the outbreak of the Second World War in 1939 was a desperate attempt by the British to avoid being pushed into that subordinate role and to maintain their imperial global hegemony.[8]

The economic and political power of the British Empire had been severely damaged by the war and the huge debts it had necessitated, but the Empire still formed an essential part of the world financial system, essential for any new Gold Standard, even one dominated by New York.

Benjamin Strong was personally an Anglophile. He had spent his annual summer holidays in England and southern France with Montagu Norman, the arch conservative governor of the Bank of England throughout the 1920s. Strong and Norman supported the aims of finance capitalism "to create a world system of financial control in private hands, able to dominate the political system of each country and the economy of the world as a whole."[9] The late American establishment insider, Carroll Quigley, described these aims in detail in his monumental work, *Tragedy and Hope.*

Quigley was a former Princeton and Harvard professor who later taught at Georgetown University and was a major influence on Bill Clinton. During the 1960s, Quigley reportedly was granted privileged access to confidential papers and archives of the New York Council on Foreign Relations to research his book on the history of global economics, on condition that he would not mention the central role of the Rockefeller faction in his book. He remained faithful to that promise, and instead Quigley concentrated his exposé on the role of the J.P. Morgan faction, so greatly weakened from its former power that it never recovered after the Great Depression.[10]

Quigley described the concept behind the Morgan-Strong-Norman plan to return to the Gold Standard of 1914, as follows:

This system was to be controlled in a feudalist fashion by the central banks of the world acting in concert, by secret agreements arrived at in frequent private meetings and conferences....In each country the power of the central bank rested largely on its control of credit and money supply. In the world as a whole the power of the central bankers rested very largely on their control of loans and of gold flows. [11]

The heart of that system in the 1920s was the New York Federal Reserve under Benjamin Strong.

Bank of England Governor Montagu Norman was considered the most powerful central banker from the period of the 1920's to his bizarre death in 1944.

In his later memoirs, Herbert Hoover bitterly attacked Strong, blaming him directly for much of the damage of the Great Depression. In 1941, referring to Strong's direction of Federal Reserve policy, an embittered Hoover wrote, "There are crimes far worse than murder for which men should be reviled and punished." Hoover called Strong, "a mental annex to Europe," a veiled reference to his tight relationship with the Bank of England's Montagu Norman.[12] Hoover had been close friends with Strong in the early 1920s but later broke with him over Strong's policy of unrestricted bank lending to Europe.

Hoover's attacks on Strong were correct, but for the wrong reasons. Hoover either chose to ignore or did not grasp the scale of the geopolitical project that Strong and Wall Street were attempting in terms of creating New York as the center of global capital flows.

Hoover further charged that by shaping New York Fed interest rates to facilitate Britain's return to gold after 1925, Strong had artificially depressed US interest rates at a time when stock speculation fever was getting out of control in 1927, in effect adding fuel to the fire which led to the spectacular 1929 collapse.

Strong hears Europe not 'Main Street'

The Bank of England's Norman, joined by Hjalmar Schacht of the Reichsbank and Charles Rist of the Bank of France, had come to New York during 1925 to urge Strong to lower US Fed discount rates. Their goal was to ease Britain's reentry onto the gold standard and to spur Europe's economic recovery. (In those days US interest rates determined the level of rates across Europe.)

The European recovery was needed for Germany to be able to repay its war reparations, under the Dawes Plan, to France, Britain and Italy. At the same time, France, Britain and Italy needed new dollar loans in order to repay their existing US war loans. The whole edifice of dollar credits that supported Europe's debt pyramid during the 1920's rested on the loans of New York banks, above all from J.P. Morgan & Co., to Europe to refinance short-term credits. The US Government had insisted at Versailles in 1919 that Britain, France and Italy repay its US war loans in dollars. The allies had pleaded unsuccessfully for cancellation of the war debts. Their debts to Washington equaled almost precisely the sum of war reparations the British, French and Italian allied governments had imposed on the defeated German economy at Versailles, by design. The Allied countries therefore needed Germany to repay its Versailles war reparations also in dollars. The entire edifice of the world financial system during the Roaring '20s rested on this absurd and fragile Ponzi pyramid of international loans and debts. [13]

A series of US protective tariffs in the 1920s beginning with the Fordney-McCumber Act of 1922 and ending with the infamous Smoot-Hawley Tariff of

1930, had raised US import barriers to an all-time high. This made it difficult, if not impossible, for European nations to repay their war debts or reparations through the traditional method of building trade surpluses with the US. Europe had no recourse except to borrow even more from US banks.

The Smoot-Hawley Tariff Act of 1930, however, contrary to the prevailing free trade mythology of today, did not cause the world Depression in the 1930s. It was a small aggravating factor in a system that had been built on rotten foundations after 1919. The entire postwar US-created financial edifice had been built on shifting sand. So long as money flowed, it was easy to ignore that basic reality.[14]

During the Great War, Strong had made several trips to London to meet with Bank of England and City banking figures. As powerful head of the New York Federal Reserve, Strong had pushed through a fateful precedent of financing Allied war munitions purchases as early as 1915, despite official US neutrality. Strong personally oversaw these transactions on behalf of J.P. Morgan who served, as noted earlier, as banker to the British and, later, French governments. The role of Benjamin Strong and the New York Fed in discounting their acceptances enabled the war to continue until eventual American entry in 1917.

Strong's role set the precedent that the New York Federal Reserve would take leadership of all international financial dealings of the Fed system and its member banks. Until passage of the Banking Act of 1935, the New York Fed alone directly controlled US international monetary and banking policy. The President of the New York Federal Reserve was essentially in this respect a power unto himself. Only the crisis of the 1930s forced even a cosmetic change in that power.

Bank of England's Gold Strategy

England's return to a gold standard during the 1920s was central to their postwar economic strategy of rebuilding the role of the City of London as world finance center. The gold standard was also the heart of the entire international credit pyramid that built up from 1925 until its ruinous collapse in 1929-1931. More than German reparations payments or Allied war loans, the deeply flawed US-led postwar gold exchange standard, and the shaky position of the Bank of England within it, were the decisive factors in causing the worst global economic deflation in history.

England had fought the bitter Boer War some two decades earlier in order to secure for the Bank of England control of the world's largest known gold reserves in the Witwatersrand. Now, following the prolonged European war, that windfall gain of gold was gone, used up during the costly Great War to purchase vital war matériel from the United States via J.P. Morgan & Co. and the US Government. Along with the depletion of its gold reserves went the City of London's control over world credit, the heart of British geopolitical influence.

In 1919, at the beginning of postwar battles over the terms of Allied war debt, German reparations and other issues, the British government was forced to formally take Sterling off the gold standard and abandon the pre-war dollar parity of $4.86 to the pound as Washington insisted that Britain repay the billions in loans it had taken from the US banks, above all Morgan and later the US Treasury.

The British establishment had naively expected that their American 'cousins' would forget about debt repayment once the war had been won by the Anglo-American-French-Italian allied front. Those illusions evaporated as the US Government, under pressure from Morgan and Wall Street, refused to budge. Since most of its non-Empire trade with America was in chronic deficit, Britain could no longer afford even the illusion it would be able to resume its pre-war role as the center of a world gold standard.

In 1919 the strongest economic power was clearly no longer the British Empire, but rather, the United States which had emerged from the war in a most powerful position – as the creditor to all major European countries. America's gold stocks had multiplied fourfold during the war, giving it the world's largest monetary gold reserves.[15] The process continued up until the great stock market crash of 1929.[16] Britain, by contrast, had massive foreign debts, mostly to the United States. Its currency had sharply depreciated, and its reserves of gold had fallen dangerously low.

The role of gold was a decisive factor in determining which power served as financial center of the world. In 1919 the United States had resumed pegging the dollar to gold, having suspended it for two years when America entered the war in 1917. Unlike Britain, America had no problem to return to the gold standard because of its enormous, accumulated reserves. The United States had the decisive position in creation of a new postwar gold standard, both because of its reserves and its new role in the world's gold market.

South Africa's threat to go it alone

The looming danger for Britain, in addition to its war debts to America, was that South Africa, the world's largest gold producer, would ship its future gold mine production directly to New York, rather than through the City of London, making New York, not London the world's principal gold market. That would rob the Bank of England of its most powerful weapon: control of world gold flows. The financial center of the world would definitively shift from the City of London to New York, with devastating consequences for England's influence in world events.

In March 1919, the London Gold Producers' Committee, a British group that controlled the minting of South African and other gold, wrote a letter to Lord Cunliffe, then Governor of the Bank of England, anticipating dire consequences:

> *Owing to our unfortunate industrial position, the American exchange will remain below the gold parity (with Sterling) for some years, and it is difficult to imagine any conditions arising which would put it above gold parity. Such being the position, it is inconceivable that the South African Gold Producers will not take immediate steps to arrange for the shipment of their commodities to New York, which must for some years be the best market, or that the South African Government will not give them every assistance in doing so. If the stream of gold from South Africa is once diverted to New York, it will not be so easy later to turn it back again, as, if New York becomes the best and freest market for bullion, it will be a powerful influen in establishing New York as the central money market of the world.* [17]

To prevent such a devastating result, the Bank of England and the City of London financial establishment went to extraordinary lengths to exert control over South African government policy. The Bank of England pressured UK shipping companies to reduce freight rates between South Africa and London, in order to penalize the cost of shipping gold to New York. It also set up a close monitor of any increase of US shipping ties to South Africa.

But the most stringent control was accomplished through the direct intervention of the Bank of England, with the help of a friendly government in South Africa. South Africa's Prime Minister in 1919 was Jan Smuts, a member of Britain's Round Table, an inner circle of England's most powerful men. Smuts had spent the war years in London, as a member of Lloyd George's Imperial War Cabinet at the same time he retained his Cabinet post in the government of South Africa. He was an ardent defender of the interests of the Empire, and one of the main architects of the League of Nations concept at Versailles. In short, Smuts was a man who could be trusted to back English interests in the most difficult of situations.[18]

Smuts had become South Africa's Prime Minister in August 1919, just as Britain was forced to abandon the link of Sterling to gold.

In April 1919, the Bank of England drafted an agreement with South African gold mine producers, insuring that all gold produced in South Africa would be sold through the Bank of England, except whatever was needed for local currency. The British Parliament also passed a law in 1920, the Export Control Act, which restricted free export of British gold.

Such dual control of gold flows into and out of London was to the benefit of London's gold banks, among them the Rothschilds -- coincidentally, the largest financial backer of South African gold mining companies. London's objective— to remain off the gold standard while selectively denying control of major gold supplies to New York—was of the highest strategic importance for the future of the British Empire.

The agreement between the Bank of England and the South African Chamber of Mines, signed in July 1919, appeared to give the City of London what it urgently needed: continued exclusive control over South African gold output, and the ability to prevent direct South African gold shipments to New York.

South Africa was the key to London's future strategy of resuming its prewar role at some future date, as the financial Mecca of the world.

A central figure in the effort to re-link South Africa's gold to London was Sir Henry Strakosch, an advisor to the Bank of England and a close intimate of Governor Montagu Norman, as well as Lord Rothschild. Strakosch, a prominent spokesman for City of London banking interests, was also Managing Director of Union Corporation, a leading mining company and major investor in South African gold production. Strakosch was invited by Smuts to advise his government on South Africa's relation with British Pound Sterling.

Strakosch, later Winston Churchill's financial patron in the late 1930s, traveled back and forth in the early 1920s between Smuts in Pretoria and Montagu Norman in London, working to keep the country and its finances firmly in the imperial system.[19] As Strakosch put it, his goal was to have South Africa "march as far as possible in step with Great Britain on the road towards an effective gold standard."[20]

The march of South Africa down London's 'yellow brick road' was abruptly interrupted in 1924, however. South Africa, during World War I, had been forced to link its currency, the Rand, to British Sterling, at a great economic cost to the domestic South Africa economy. By linking the Rand to Sterling and placing an embargo on gold sales other than to the Bank of England, South Africa's largest export earner, gold, suffered. Many mines had become unprofitable. Inflation soared because of the Sterling link, as English inflation increased dramatically after the war. Living standards of ordinary South Africans dropped sharply during the period when the gold standard was abandoned. Strikes of mineworkers demanding higher pay became frequent.

In early 1922, as the cost of living soared and the price of gold fell, mine owners threatened to replace white miners with black miners who would work for lower wages. The predominantly white miners called a general strike throughout Witwatersrand, the gold district. The strike became known as the Rand Revolt and went on for three months. Smuts declared martial law and ordered brutal military repression, resulting in the death of hundreds of mineworkers, and winning Smuts the nickname, "man of blood." Having successfully pitted blacks against whites, the system of Apartheid became a firmly entrenched policy of the South African government, even though opposition inside South Africa to the Sterling-South Africa Pound link became a heated political issue, costing Smuts his re-election in 1924

Under such growing internal pressure, the South African mines consented to hold to their agreement with the Bank of England on embargo of free gold exports only until June 30, 1925, putting a severe time pressure on London to prepare a return to the Sterling Gold Standard.

A return to gold at the pre-war $4.86 parity in 1925 meant a severe deflation of the British economy. It was politically explosive, resulted in soaring unemployment, widespread labor strikes and other consequences. Sterling was at the time trading at a 30% discount or about $3.50 to the South African pound. Delay had been the tactic used to try to keep South Africa in line until the British economy was in a stronger position to return to the prewar gold price. Britain had set her own deadline of 1931 for lifting her restriction on free flow of gold under the Export Control Act. This would give ample time, it was thought, for preparing the way. Ironically, 1931 was to be the year that England left the Gold Standard it had too hastily rejoined in 1925.

Under Smuts' pro-Empire rule, London's delaying tactic had not been that difficult. But national elections in South Africa in June 1924 abruptly changed that. Smuts' pro-London government was defeated, in favor of a coalition of the Labour Party and the National Party headed by Boer nationalist General

J.B.M. Hertzog. Hertzog had campaigned against the country's loss of national economic control and the economic damage caused by Smuts' support of Sterling.

Once in office, one of Hertzog's first acts was to create a commission to advise his government on whether South Africa should break with Sterling and re-establish the South African Pound on an independent gold-backed basis. For the first time, the Bank of England and Strakosch had not been consulted prior to a major South African gold decision. Particularly alarming for London was Hertzog's choice to head his special commission. Instead of choosing someone from England, the new government insisted on someone from the United States, one of America's leading gold and monetary experts, Princeton University professor Edwin Kemmerer.[21]

The 'Money Doctor' and Wall Street's gold scheme

A professor of economics at Princeton University, Kemmerer was an internationally known advocate of the gold standard. His role on behalf of Wall Street and the US Government since he had brought the Philippines onto the Gold Standard in 1903 had earned him the epithet 'The Money Doctor' in international finance circles. He also served, *sub rosa*, as a consultant to the influential Wall Street investment firm, Dillon Read & Co.

Kemmerer was the architect of the Wall Street and New York Federal Reserve scheme to bring, one by one, all the countries of the former British-led gold standard onto a new US-dominated Gold Exchange Standard. Referring to his work advising various countries on their postwar currency stabilization, Kemmerer once admitted,

> *A country that appoints American financial advisers and follows their advice in reorganizing its finances, along what American investors consider to be the most successful modern lines, increases its chances of appealing to the American investor and of obtaining from him capital on favorable terms.* [22]

Kemmerer's stabilization scheme -- using American capital 'on favorable terms' to control the world financial system and displace the prewar role of the City of London -- was the cornerstone of Wall Street's post World War I bid, backed by Washington, to replace London with New York as the financial center of the world. It was audacious, and premature by two decades. It also was the major reason for the Federal Reserve monetary policies that precipitated the 1929 stock market crash and the ensuing domino-default of the entire structure of Wall Street loans to the world, resulting in global depression.

Kemmerer's work had already successfully brought France, Italy, and Belgium onto a new gold currency standard, backed in each case by large syndicated Wall Street loans, primarily from the House of J.P. Morgan. Kemmerer had gone to Germany in 1924 as a member of the Dawes Committee to draft the reorganization of the Reichsbank and stabilize the Reichsmark on the new, US-backed gold standard. In addition, Kemmerer was the key figure in extending the US gold standard to Colombia and Chile by 1925, shifting hegemony over Latin American financial and economic developments from Britain to the United States.

In each case, it was Kemmerer's currency stabilization plan that was implemented. It was disarmingly simple: Kemmerer, through his excellent Wall Street connections for whom he acted as de facto agent, would promise large currency 'stabilization' loans for the given country. In return, the subject country would agree to the condition that their newly stabilized currency be backed by gold. Naturally, the United States, as the world's largest holder of central bank gold reserves, was the power at the center of the new gold diplomacy.23

Kemmerer advises South Africa

Little wonder that alarm bells began to ring, not only at the Bank of England, but also throughout the British establishment. An unanticipated threat to the strategic interests of the British Empire had come from South Africa, where Hertzog, in concert with some very powerful circles in the United States, was playing the vital supporting role. Kemmerer's final report to the Hertzog government stated the problem clearly:

> *Should South Africa decide to tie up definitely with Sterling, hoping that Sterling will return to the gold basis soon, but being prepared to follow Sterling wherever it may go? Or, should she decide to definitely go with gold?*[24]

Kemmerer's answer was to recommend that South Africa go back on the gold standard by July 1, 1925, with or without Britain. In fact, that would mean without Britain because Britain was in no way economically strong enough to resume the pre-war gold standard.

That would mean de facto an American-dominated Gold Standard. Kemmerer argued gold resumption would increase foreign investment in South Africa's economy, control the country's rampant inflation, and benefit the important mining industry -- all of which was true, as London knew only too well.

In January 1925, General J. B. M. Hertzog's National government announced it was implementing Kemmerer's recommendations, in full. In London, this was regarded as a *casus belli*, pulled off by the upstart Americans and holding the gravest implications for future British power. The only problem was that Britain was in no shape to wage war with anyone, least of all the United States.

For well over a century, the ability of the City of London to stand as the center of international finance had depended on controlling the world's physical trade of gold through London. London's N.M. Rothschild & Sons set the world's daily gold price at its bank, and the Bank of England held the bulk of world monetary gold. London had been successful because it had, first, captured the vast bulk of new gold discovered in California and Australia after the 1840s and later, out of the Boer War, it captured South Africa's huge supply from Witwatersrand.

The British economy had undergone a 23-year economic slump, recorded in English economic history as the Great Depression, from 1873 to the mid-1890's, owing to a gold shortage in the Bank of England. The depression had ended only when South Africa's gold potential had been discovered. By 1925, South Africa's gold mines produced fully 50% of the world's gold annually, with the output increasing rapidly each year.

The one and only prospect for Great Britain and the Bank of England to reconstruct its decisive influence in the post-1920 world would be to resume its earlier role manipulating the world's gold bullion supply to its advantage. As in their cricket games, so in gold dealings by the London bullion banks and the Bank of England, the British 'cheated at the edges.' A leading English economist, Paul Einzig, writing in *The Economic Journal* of the Royal Economic Society in March 1931, described the game well:

> *So long as the gold is actually brought to London before it is sold, the Bank of England is at an advantage as compared with other potential buyers, for, in acquiring the gold, the latter have to pay the cost of transport, etc. from London to their centre, while the Bank of England obtains delivery free of charge. Thus, so long as Sterling is at*

par (with gold), the chances are that the gold will find its way into the Bank of England...foreign buyers may be unable to compete with the Bank...Thanks to this advantage, the gold stock of the Bank is in normal conditions replenished out of the newly-produced Rand gold, so that there is no need for raising the exchange by means of high interest rates above gold import point to that end. It would be desirable, therefore, to prevent a change in the system of transport of South African gold.... [25]

Much of the history of the British Empire, and British foreign diplomacy, especially in the period of New Imperialism from the 1850's through the 1920's, traced back to this subtle, little-appreciated manipulation of physical gold production flows into and out of the London bullion market.

Direct shipment of South African gold to New York would have dealt a devastating blow to the plans of the City of London and British financial institutions to rebuild their dominance after Versailles. US intervention into South Africa, via Kemmerer and Hertzog, not only dealt a blow to Great Britain, but also threatened to reshape the entire world credit system on Wall Street's terms.

Churchill tries to block a US Gold Standard

London's response to Wall Street's South African machinations was swift. In late January 1925, Chancellor of the Exchequer, Winston Churchill, whose career had begun in South Africa during the Boer War, issued a memorandum arguing for England's early return to gold, in order to preempt a feared American monetary coup. Bank of England Governor Montagu Norman agreed.

Adding to the sense of urgency in England was the fact that a few months earlier, American bankers, led by Morgan-associate Charles Dawes and aided by Kemmerer, had been able to arrange a stabilization of Germany's currency, following the devastating Weimar hyperinflation of 1922-23. Under the Dawes Plan, as noted earlier, Germany returned to a US-led gold standard, aided by a $100 million loan from J.P. Morgan & Co. to back the new Reichsmark. The United States and Germany now were both tied to the same gold standard, about to be joined by the world's largest gold producer, South Africa.

Britain was sitting squarely on the outside.

Were South Africa to join in an American-centered gold standard, London would be faced with the prospect of being by-passed by the burgeoning world trade. Especially if Germany were to revive Continental European trade, England would be relegated irreversibly to the status of a has-been power. That would leave New York the unchallenged center of world financial power -- a change that the British establishment was not yet ready to accept.

On April 28, 1925 Churchill, as Chancellor of the Exchequer, came before the House of Commons to announce the government's decision, fully supported by the Bank of England, to return to the gold standard. Further, Sterling would be fixed at the same parity level it had on the eve of the Great War in 1914, at $4.86 to the Pound.

The rate had been decided despite the fact that British industrial productivity had declined since 1914, despite the fact that it would price British exports out of desperately needed global markets, and despite the enormous rise in Britain's public debt, inflation, and huge trade deficits, mostly with America. In other words, everything that should determine a nation's proper currency value was ignored. It was a purely political, or more accurately, a geopolitical decision. Its success depended on Montagu Norman's ability to manipulate Benjamin Strong and his friends in New York banking, along with the major central bankers of Europe, to England's advantage.

Churchill and Montagu Norman fixed Sterling at that inflated rate, and rejoined the link to gold in a desperate bid to re-establish the role of the City of London at the center of the world financial system, regardless of the detriment to domestic British industry and the British population. Commenting on his actions, Churchill remarked, "If we had not taken this action, the whole of the rest of the British Empire would have taken it without us, and it would have come to a gold standard, not on the basis of the pound sterling, but of the dollar." [26]

Strong's fatal blunder

What Strong failed to appreciate in 1925 when he decided to follow Montagu Norman's appeal, urging J.P. Morgan and other New York banks to support the return of Sterling to gold, was how effectively Norman and the London banks would pursue their own agenda, while pretending to be the strongest friends and backers of the United States and of the New York Federal Reserve chief. The center of the scheme was the Bank of England and UK Treasury's plan to reshape the emerging new gold standard after 1925.

As already described, the world trade system prior to World War I had been based on an international gold standard that had been more or less self-correcting. International trade rested on market supply-demand principles, with imbalances settled in gold. It was a technical system that, theoretically at least, separated money from the State.

Since England was the preeminent financial center during that period, London dominated the market and the Bank of England had acted as 'Banker to the World.' Other countries, including Germany, France, Italy, all of Britain's colonies and even the United States had maintained large reserves in Pound Sterling with the Bank of England, which held the lion's share of world monetary gold at that time. Confidence in the Bank of England as guarantor of world credit was such that within the British Empire, many of Britain's dominions or colonies did not even have their own national currencies, but rather operated with Sterling held in London.

This was the pre-war system that Montagu Norman, Winston Churchill and leading London bankers were intent on recreating. In 1922 at Genoa in a major postwar international economic conference, the Bank of England managed a diplomatic coup. Over the personal objections of the heads of the New York Fed, the German Reichsbank, the Banque de France and the Bank of Italy, Montagu Norman succeeded in getting the conference to agree to his concept of a new Gold Exchange Standard.[27] Norman had extensive and unique experience with the prewar London gold standard and possessed unequaled international stature as an oracle of central banking.

Under the prewar gold standard, Sterling had been 'as good as gold.' The international market was regulated by inflows or outflows of a country's private as well as public gold reserves, not by its manipulation of foreign exchange levels. A country with chronic inflation would lose gold, forcing it to impose higher interest rates to hold its reserves, resulting in a domestic credit contraction. Holders of its paper currency could always redeem currency in gold on demand. The corrective was more or less automatic.

However, in 1925, Britain could not, and did not, return to the strict pre-war British Gold Standard. The Bank of England no longer held the bulk of world bullion and so Norman and the British Treasury proposed a clever modification of that standard, which also appeared to satisfy the strategic goals of the less experienced bankers dominating New York finance, and of Benjamin Strong in particular. The new standard was called a Gold 'Exchange' Standard.

Under the New York-led Gold Exchange Standard, the United States would act as the ultimate backing for the inflated currencies of Britain, the rest of Europe, and the world. Britain, in particular, would keep its reserves not in gold, as it had before 1914, but mainly in dollars, while the countries of Continental Europe, still struggling with after-effects of the war, would keep their reserves, not in gold, but in Sterling.

This new scheme, in effect, permitted Britain to pyramid its inflated currency, Sterling, and its credit, on top of dollars rather than gold, which it lacked. British client states could pyramid their currencies, in turn, on top of Sterling. It meant in effect, only the United States after 1925 would remain on a strict gold standard, and all others would redeem in national paper currency. [28] That allowed Britain to rebuild its dominant role in Europe and internationally as world banker resting on the implicit or explicit backing of the dollar and US gold. It was a fatally flawed edifice.

The Bank of England's Norman argued that only New York and London central banks should bother to hold monetary gold bullion, while others such as France should be content holding sterling or dollars backed, in turn, by gold. Not surprisingly, Bank of France Governor Emile Moreau, a strong gold advocate, was not happy with Norman's view of an Anglo-American gold world. By 1926 Moreau would restore the balance sheet of the Banque de France and its gold reserves to a level higher than the Bank of England's. That French gold position was later to play a fateful role. [29]

League of Nations key to British plans

At the heart of London's construct for rebuilding its financial role was Britain's domination of the League of Nations bureaucracy. England dominated the powerful Finance Committee of the League. Montagu Norman, in effect, controlled the League's Finance Committee through his two close associates, Sir Henry Strakosch and Sir Otto Niemeyer. British economist, Sir Ralph Hawtrey, from the UK Treasury, also played a key role, calling for a general European adoption of the new Gold Exchange Standard.

Norman and the British used the League to pressure European member states to establish central bank collaboration with the Bank of England, based not on the classical Gold Standard, as noted, but on the Gold Exchange Standard which would permit the countries to continue inflationary and deficit spending, while maintaining a facade of monetary stability. In addition, European countries were pressured to return to gold at highly overvalued parities in order that their exports not unduly threaten British exports. The countries all held their foreign exchange reserves not in gold—they held little—but in Sterling accounts with the Bank of England. The entire edifice was a mirage based on confidence in, above all, the skill of Montagu Norman to orchestrate global, or at least European, monetary harmony.

Using promises of US bank credits together with its political pressure, exercised through control of the League of Nations Finance Committee in Geneva, London devised a system much like that of the IMF after the 1980s. Emile Moreau, Governor of the Bank of France, and bitter opponent of Norman, described the system in his diary in 1928:

> *England having been the first European country to re-establish a stable and secure money had used that advantage to establish a basis for putting Europe under a veritable financial domination. The Financial Committee (of the League of Nations) at Geneva has been the instrument of that policy. The method consists of forcing every country in monetary difficulty to subject itself to the Committee at Geneva, which the British control. The remedies prescribed always involve the installation in the central bank of a foreign supervisor who is British or designated by the Bank of England, and the deposit of a part of the reserve of the central bank at the Bank of England, which serves both to support the pound and to fortify British influence.*

> *To guarantee against possible failure they are careful to secure the cooperation of the Federal Reserve Bank of New York. Moreover, they pass on to America the task of making some of the foreign loans if they seem too heavy, always retaining the political advantage of these operations. England is thus completely or partially entrenched in Austria, Hungary, Belgium, Norway and Italy. She is in the process of entrenching herself in Greece and Portugal. She seeks to get a foothold in Yugoslavia and...in Rumania. The currencies will be divided into two classes. Those of the first class, the dollar and the pound Sterling, based on gold, and those of the second class based on the pound and dollar—with a part of their gold reserves being held by the Bank of England and the Federal Reserve Bank of New York. [30]*

With encouragement from Benjamin Strong, J.P. Morgan & Co. provided the essential dollar loan to back up the British re-entry onto this modified gold standard in 1925. Afterwards, similar Morgan bank credits were extended, always on the suggestion of Montagu Norman and the Geneva Finance

Committee he dominated, and always first endorsed by the New York Federal Reserve's Benjamin Strong. Washington played virtually no role in the process. It was pure Wall Street bankers' diplomacy. Belgium, Poland under the military dictatorship of war hero General Jozef Pilsudski, and Mussolini's Fascist Italy, all came back onto gold at overvalued parities as a result. New York and London bankers increasingly preferred strongarm dictators whom they felt could control trade union protests and guarantee the security of their loan repayment.

Soon after England returned to gold at the inflated $4.86 level, the Bank of England attempted to pursue major deflation of domestic prices and wages, in order to keep exports competitive despite the overvalued Sterling. In reaction to the cuts in wages, there was a General Strike in 1926, growth was sluggish, industrial exports remained depressed and unemployment rose to almost 10%. By 1931 when Britain finally left the Gold Standard, unemployment had reached 22% of the workforce.

The general strike in the protests by trade unions in England made clear that Britain would be able to hold the new gold value of $4.86 only with help from the United States. Strong, who rarely consulted with the Federal Reserve Board in Washington, let alone with other regional Fed presidents, created a significant American monetary inflation and credit expansion in the late 1920s to support the pound at the overvalued parity and with it, to support the British monetary role in Europe. All of this was done in order to hold together the shaky new Gold Exchange Standard. In easing monetary conditions in the US, however, Strong also created the seeds of a stock market and real estate inflation bubble.

Montagu Norman had convinced his friend Benjamin Strong that European recovery and, ultimately, US export strength, depended on the Federal Reserve maintaining artificially low interest rates to encourage gold outflows into Sterling, where interest rates were higher. That in turn would provide the basis for the entire Continental European and colonial gold system and with it, much of world trade, so Norman argued. Artificially low Federal Reserve interest rates fuelled the expanding margin lending trade in Wall Street stocks, in turn fuelling the creation of the unprecedented Wall Street stock rise of the late 1920s. Meanwhile, depressed US interest rate yields, compared with very attractive European rates of typically 6% to 8%, had encouraged American banks to extend increasing sums of short-term credit to the new gold standard countries of Europe and beyond after 1925.

Strong gives markets a 'Coup De Whiskey'

In July 1927, in what would be a fateful shift of US monetary policy, Montagu Norman asked Strong to convene a secret central bank conference on Long Island. There, Strong agreed to a major US Federal Reserve interest rate cut, despite knowing full well that the easy money would immediately stimulate domestic US credit expansion amid an already alarming consumer spending boom.

Morgan banker Benjamin Strong was the powerful President of the New York Federal Reserve whose easy money policies fuelled the 1929 stock market bubble, a side effect of the Morgan plan to create a New York-centered Gold Exchange Standard.

Strong decided to take Montagu Norman's advice to cut US rates and thereby to support the British Pound Sterling despite the objections of the central bank heads of Germany and France. Strong's sole intent was to stabilize the Pound by halting a drain on London gold reserves.

The Chicago Federal Reserve, not closely tied to London or European credits, strongly objected to lowering the Fed's interest rate and refused to cut its rates. The Chicago *Tribune* called for Benjamin Strong's resignation. Strong countered, arguing deceptively that his easy money move was aimed at aiding Midwest farmers. Strong prevailed. He later confided to friends that the unintended side effect of his rate cut would give the stock market 'a little coup de whiskey.' It was more than a little coup. On Wall Street the whiskey started to flow like water.[31]

Strong's 1927 rate cut at the New York Federal Reserve halted the drain of British gold and eased the British Sterling crisis. The London *Banker* magazine later hailed Benjamin Strong for the "energy and skillfulness he has given to the service of England." [32]

Under Montagu Norman's gold exchange architecture, the United States became the sole link, the linchpin of all these countries to gold and so-called 'hard money.' Were the dollar also to inflate, as it did after 1925, the linchpin currency -- the dollar -- would also become unreliable and the entire edifice -- the pyramid of global credit -- would eventually collapse.

This Achilles Heel in the British monetary pyramid was that it made the entire edifice dependent on US credit. This became evident when the credit expansion came to a halt in 1929. Before then, a wide spectrum from American banking and business had hailed what Strong termed a 'New Era' of permanent prosperity and price stabilization, an eerie pre-echo of Alan Greenspan's declaration in 1999 of a New Economy that would no longer undergo cyclical recessions.

The reality was quite different, as the Federal Reserve was forced to resort to inflationary credit expansion to try to stabilize falling prices in Europe by the late 1920s.

Few voices opposed Strong's policies when they appeared to create unbounded prosperity, rising incomes, booming stock prices and economic growth. Among the few critics of Strong's international credit policies, in addition to Commerce Secretary Hoover, were Barton Hepburn, chairman of Rockefeller's Chase National bank, and H. Parker Willis, editor of the *Journal of Commerce* and former aide to Senator Carter Glass. They were joined by several members of the Federal Reserve Board. They were a minority, however. J. P. Morgan & Co., Benjamin Strong, and Treasury Secretary Mellon, along with President Calvin Coolidge, were in control of policy during the 1920s.

For the first several years of the Gold Exchange Standard until early 1927, the flaw was not that evident. It appeared that the economies of Europe were finally recovering, and that gold had been instrumental in that recovery.

Under the new Gold Exchange Standard, credit flowed out of New York to London and into the dollar-starved economies of Continental Europe after 1925. The House of Morgan, Kuhn Loeb & Co., National City Bank and other Wall Street banks, began to underwrite bonds issued by various European states joined to the new Gold Exchange Standard. The underwriting banks in turn sold these new bonds, often at interest rates as much as 3% above comparable US Treasury securities, to ordinary American households seeking financial return and security. For the New York banks it was a pure gold machine.

Much of the credit from New York banks had flowed into Germany after the 1924 Dawes Plan currency stabilization. Within six years, various German municipalities, private companies, port authorities and other entities, had issued bonds underwritten by New York banks and sold to American investors, totaling the staggering sum of more than $2.5 billions. Germany borrowed nearly $4 billion from abroad during this period.

In the period from 1924 to 1931, almost $6 billion in American credit poured into Europe. If U.S. war loans by the Treasury, and the costs of the War itself were added, a total of $40 billion in U.S. funds had gone into Europe in less than 15 years, fully one-fifth of total American GDP in 1914.

The entire edifice, however, was only as stable as its weakest link under the post-1925 Gold Exchange Standard constructed by Montagu Norman and the British Treasury.

By late 1927, two months after he acted to stabilize Sterling and, in the process, add hot air to the growing Wall Street stock bubble, Strong himself began to express serious misgivings about the entire edifice which Montagu Norman and the Bank of England had convinced him, only three years earlier, would revive world trade and secure monetary stability.

Shortly before his death from tuberculosis in 1928, Strong wrote several letters to his friend, Montagu Norman, and to colleagues in the New York Federal Reserve, expressing his growing doubts whether the Gold Exchange Standard which Strong had backed on the urging of Norman, had been the right policy for world monetary stabilization. One letter, written in September 1927, reveals Strong's growing apprehensions about the nature of America's postwar monetary entanglements:

> *Banks of issue [central banks -w.e.] now hold bills and balances in the United States alone exceeding $1,000,000,000, not to mention a sum at least approaching that now held in London, and considerable amounts in other gold standard countries. In fact, as I have written you, I am inclined to the belief that this development has reached a point where instead of serving to fortify the maintenance of a gold standard it may, in fact, be undermining the gold standard because of the duplication of the credit structures in different parts of the world sustained by a few accumulations of gold in the hands of a few countries whose currencies are well established upon gold, such as England and the United States.* [33]

'It all came tumbling down...'

As with the bursting of the US sub-prime mortgage securitization bubble in 2007, the collapse of the New York stock market in October 1929 was but a symptom of a far more serious and fundamental sickness in the system of global finance. The Bank of England's Norman had urged Strong to keep Federal Reserve rates low because that would influence rates across the UK and Continental Europe on which the entire financial stability of postwar Britain was dependant because financially linked, and it would help ward off recession there. The low rates produced an upswing in the New York stock market as easy money, predictably, fuelled a US consumption boom financed primarily by the newly available terms of installment credit.

America's conspicuous consumption during the 'Roaring Twenties' was based on an illusion of rising household wealth for the majority of its citizens. This severely distorted, debt-driven consumption created the nation's illusory wealth -- the Achilles Heel of the economy in 1929. In America, by 1929 fully 60% of all cars and 80% of home radios were bought on installment credit. People bought on credit as most Americans earned a comparatively low income during the 1920s.

A series of Republican tax cuts during the Coolidge Presidency, drafted by the very wealthy Treasury Secretary Andrew Mellon, further shifted income to a tiny minority of corporate owners and those who inherited wealth. The tax cuts benefited the wealthy, helping to concentrate more of a share of rising national income into the upper one-tenth of 1% of very wealthy Americans. Taxes on a person with a million dollar annual income dropped during the 1920's from $600,000 to $200,000 while taxes on the middle class and poorer families increased.

By 1929 as the number and size of giant corporations such as US Steel, General Electric, and RCA Corporation continued to expand, some two-thirds of the industrial wealth had passed from individual ownership to ownership by large, publicly-financed, privately-owned corporations. At the top of the corporate pyramid of control stood the major banks of Wall Street such as J.P. Morgan, Chase Bank, Kuhn, Loeb, Mellon Bank and the like. The very conservative US Supreme Court added to the wealth disparity in 1923 with its decision in *Adkins vs. Children's Hospital*, in which it ruled that minimum wage laws were unconstitutional.[34]

"The rich got richer and the poor got poorer," said a popular Tin Pan Alley song of the 1920s titled, sardonically, *Ain't We Got Fun*.

The combined income of the top one-tenth of 1% of Americans in 1929 was equal to the total combined income for the lowest 42% of the population. Translated into family units, 24,500 wealthy families in America had the same combined income as more than 11,000,000 poor and lower middle-class families. The wealthiest stratum controlled 34% of all savings while 80% of Americans held no savings at all. Behind the façade of American prosperity of the 1920s was an edifice built on debt and illusions of permanent prosperity and rising stock prices. Once the consumer credit carousel stopped in 1929-1931, the consumption boom collapsed, as the majority of Americans simply could not afford to buy on credit any longer. [35]

The rising stock prices attracted investment by more people who could borrow from their bank to buy stock on 'margin,' that is by paying only some 10% of the actual price, the rest being loaned. Margin buying of stocks was predominant in the last phase of the Wall Street stock market mania, as banks lent freely to brokers and other speculators, anticipating repayment from ever-rising stock prices.

When that entire credit pyramid came to a halt in 1929 as the panicked Federal Reserve belatedly raised interest rates in a futile bid to stop the stock bubble, the entire installment consumer credit edifice crashed with it, and soon the real manufacturing economy, as well.[36]

By October 1929 there had built up a record $8 billion of loans on stocks on the New York Stock Exchange, loans that had to be repaid. Most of those loans had gone to buy stocks on margin. Margin buying was encouraged by the big Wall Street banks as their profits were staggering, at least until the music stopped.

The October 1929 New York stock market crash hit seven months into Herbert Hoover's Presidency. No previous President had ever intervened in a market crash, and the conventional view was that such things should be left to self-correct, free of government meddling.

Overcoming objections from Treasury Secretary Andrew Mellon, Hoover announced a ten point plan of action in late 1929, among other things aimed at avoiding bank panics, to prevent widespread bankruptcies and loss of homes, to aid agriculture, relieve distressed unemployed, and preserve the strength of the currency. Government public works projects were accelerated to provide more jobs. Hoover, true to his conservative Republican roots, sought to leverage the potential of government and to support private initiatives, rather than have direct government takeover. By early 1931 the US economic recession showed some signs of stabilizing. It was only a brief pause in the horrendous downslide.

As the foundations of Montagu Norman's fragile European Gold Exchange Standard began to crumble, a new and even more powerful financial tsunami was building which would devastate the world. It was fed by the political decisions of France to 'teach the Germans a lesson.'

France pulls down the Gold Standard

In spring of 1931, the storm in Europe broke the dam. A peculiar form of French 'exceptionalism' played a decisive role in inadvertently toppling the entire world monetary system and tipping the world economy into depression.

In March 1931, Austria, a tiny shard of the prewar Austro-Hungarian Empire with 6 million people, announced it had entered talks with Germany to create a common customs union to boost trade, as depression threatened. Such a union would not even be a technical violation of the Versailles Treaty. It was certainly no threat to world security.

The Government of France reacted swiftly and demanded immediate re-payment of some $300 million in short-term credits owed by Germany and Austria to French banks, to pressure both countries to halt their customs union. The demands triggered a panic flight from the shaky Austrian currency. The weakest link in the Austrian financial system was the Vienna Credit Anstalt Bank. It was also the largest bank in Austria.

The Credit Anstalt of Vienna, with loans in Hungary and across the Danube region, was the creditor to a major part of Austrian industry and real estate, with over fifty percent of all the bank loans in the country. Credit Anstalt collapsed in May 1931 amid a depositors' panic withdrawal run. Frantic efforts by the newly created Basle Bank for International Settlements to provide emergency loans to stabilize Credit Anstalt failed.

The French Government insisted meanwhile, as pre-condition for its Basle loan portion, that Germany and Austria renounce the planned customs union. The customs union itself, as pointed out, did not violate the Versailles Treaty, which only prohibited full annexation of Austria by Germany. [37]

The crisis spread across Austria and into the inter-connected German bank-ing system like a brushfire.

The collapse of the Credit Anstalt led to a depositor panic run on the Darmstaedter-und Nationalbank or Danat-Bank in Germany and created a currency crisis for the Brüning government, as well. At that point, the Bank of England, the US Federal Reserve, the German Reichsbank, and the Bank of

France met to discuss an emergency credit infusion to try to stop the spread of currency panic.

Hoover had won a one-year moratorium on German reparations payments to try to ease pressure on Germany. It took effect June 30, 1931. That move, however, was seen as too little too late and ignited a panic flight of foreign banks out of German assets, as investors feared worse to come. Germans also began flight capital out of the Reichsmark into dollars, Sterling, Francs or gold. In July, the president of Reichsbank Hans Luther went from Paris to Basle to London, warning that Germany's Reichsbank needed an urgent $500 billion loan to avert bankruptcy default. That news spread panic even more. The entire postwar international financial edifice was beginning to crumble. [38]

At that point the French government held the trump card. France had gone through its own currency crises in the early 1920s and had narrowly averted hyperinflation. In 1926, the right-wing government of Raymond Poincaré took office and immediately acted, with the backing of the Bank of France's Moreau, to impose severe budget austerity, tax increases and other moves to stem capital flight and stabilize the Franc, which was still outside the gold system. It announced plans to return to a gold standard at the earliest possible date to further instill confidence. The Franc appreciated 40% in value within weeks of Poincaré's return in 1926 as a result.

In 1928, after two years of building its gold reserves, the Poincaré government and the Bank of France, under Governor Emile Moreau, had announced France would impose what was called the Stabilization Law to facilitate the return of the Franc to the gold standard. But Paris was not about to play by the rules of Montagu Norman and leave the Bank of England to set the international rules of the gold standard to England's advantage.

Unlike Britain which, in order to regain the international role of the City of London, had sacrificed British export competitiveness and British jobs by pegging to the prewar parity of $4.86, the Bank of France rejoined the gold standard at a parity equal to 20% of its prewar level.

That led to a major French export recovery, rising employment, expanded industrial output, huge trade surpluses and, with it, foreign currency reserves with foreign central banks, above all the Bank of England. What was good for France, however, owing to the structure of international debt propped up by the Gold Exchange Standard, was bad for the rest of the world. Gold flowed into the Bank of France and away from London and various Continental European capitals.

In 1927 the Bank of France had demanded that the Bank of England convert some 30 million pounds Stering held by the Bank of France into gold in order to build French central bank gold reserves for joining the gold standard. That French gold accumulation was what led the Bank of England to fatefully call on Benjamin Strong for help to stabilize the pound.

The Bank of France, fearing a return of inflation from holding its reserves in foreign paper currencies such as the Pound, which were free to inflate arbitrarily, had decided to base its reserves on gold alone, in the manner of the pre-1914 gold standard. France went "purist" and rejected the loose paper plus gold reserve standard initiated by Britain and other countries in 1925.[39]

France, again, was odd-man out in terms of central bank policy. Moreau, an extremely conservative banker, was, not without good reason, convinced that the Gold Exchange Standard of Montagu Norman's Bank of England was dangerously flawed. How right he was would soon become clear for the entire world.

Moreau was also determined that France, after years of chaos and instability, return to hard money policies and fiscal prudence. The only problem was that that the Norman-Strong Gold Exchange Standard dominated the world monetary system. That system, and the indebted European economies tied to it, was rotten to the core.

The edifice of the Gold Exchange Standard had been built on an international credit structure centered on New York bank loans which in turn were predicated on the ability of the major European economies to continue borrowing to finance their own economic growth at abnormally low interest rates. Once the interest rates set by the New York Federal Reserve, the heart of the debt pyramid, reversed, the entire edifice of cheap credits began to unravel in domino-style defaults and bankruptcies, first in the weakest economies of Europe, then ultimately within the United States itself as confidence collapsed.

French actions around gold were a mixture of political fears of Germany's resurgence, and fears of a re-eruption of domestic economic chaos, strikes and recession if France were to go back to easy money policies. This led the French government and Bank of France to act alone.

The return to Franc stability in 1926 and the re-pegging to gold at 20% the prewar parity in 1928, led to a repatriation of French capital back into French banks, and new foreign capital inflows, as the economy prospered. By 1931, France reached full employment just as the rest of the world plunged into depression. France was beginning to feel its own independent power in European affairs.

As a result of its policy of converting foreign currency assets into gold for the Bank of France reserves, France became the world's second largest holder of monetary gold by 1931, next to the US Federal Reserve. In just five years, French central bank gold holdings had increased tenfold. By 1931, those two central banks, the Federal Reserve and the Bank of France, controlled fully 75% of the world's monetary gold reserves. The Federal Reserve was severely restricted as to use of its reserves by amendments inserted by Congress into the Federal Reserve Act of 1913, legal limits which were only removed in 1933 and 1935, well after the onset of the Depression.

This left France and the Bank of France in an extraordinarily strong position when the European crisis erupted, a crisis that in many ways had been detonated by French political and financial demands on Germany and Austria.

In July 1931, as Germany pleaded for another $500 million emergency loan from central banks in London, Paris, and New York, France was the decisive player. She used the occasion to announce French willingness to participate in another German rescue, but on condition that the German government disband its 'Steel Helmets' quasi-military force, halt further construction of 'pocket battleships' that had been allowed under Versailles, and also abandon its customs union with Austria. The German Government of Heinrich Bruning rejected the French conditions as humiliating efforts to reduce Germany to economic slavery.

Hoover tries to plug the dike

The crisis now was fully focused on Germany's debt, private and public, which had ballooned since the Reichsmark stabilization created in 1924 by the Dawes Plan. Most American bankers during the 1920's, including J.P. Morgan & Co. and Benjamin Strong, tended to treat Germany as simply another borrower, albeit with slightly higher risk, and not all that different from lending to American railroads, or floating bonds for American companies. They believed that the backing of the world's strongest central bank and its gold would insure against any potential risk from Germany, forgetting it was a sovereign country with its own ideas about debt repayment.

Unlike the American bankers, French bankers tended to view every German loan as a political step in the efforts of German institutions to repudiate Versailles and restore prewar German integrity. The French view was far closer to reality, underscoring the deadly fallacy of Benjamin Strong's decision, almost unilaterally, to link US financial and credit structure to the monetary structure of a post-1917 Europe.

By July 1931, the gold reserves of Germany, Austria, Hungary and most of Eastern European countries had been drained, and most banks had been closed.

President Hoover called personally on the US Treasury Secretary and Federal Reserve to determine how badly American banks were exposed to Europe, in order to determine what steps the US should take. A close friend of Hoover from a major California bank had expressed alarm at the widespread practice of American banks issuing bank acceptances, a form of short-term loans, to German and other European banks. The acceptances were usually 60 or 90 day paper, secured only by bills of lading covering goods shipped, but not yet delivered. Hoover asked the Fed and Treasury for an estimate of how much of such unsecured lending to European banks there was.[40]

The Federal Reserve told the President that they estimated it was a mere $500 million at most, calling it no threat to American banks. Fearing worse, Hoover ordered an independent estimate from his Comptroller of the Currency. Their estimate was an alarming $1.7 billion or more, a sum that threatened the entire, weakly capitalized US banking system if news were to leak out.

When Benjamin Strong, in 1927, had cut New York Federal Reserve interest rates in order to help the Bank of England counter the French gold draw-downs, US loans to Europe had ballooned. European banks had been willing to pay a hefty premium of rates up to 7% or more for desperately needed dollar credits. By July 1931, Hoover was informed by his Comptroller that European banks were by then in default on many of these bank acceptances, which American banks had attempted to keep quiet to avoid further panic.[41]

Hoover sent his Under Secretary of Treasury, Ogden Mills, to London to discreetly inquire about the extent of exposure of British banks to such unsecured bank acceptance paper. The Bank of England had no idea, but two days later gave an initial estimate even more alarming to the stability of the Gold Exchange Standard: English banks were fully exposed with over $2 billion, along with Dutch and Scandinavian banks.

Hoover estimated that German, Austrian and Hungarian banks alone held as much as $5 billion of such short-term bills—all due in 60 to 90 days, a staggering sum. Until that time, no one had the slightest awareness of the total bank exposure.

Bankers, reassured that the credit was ultimately secured by delivery of physical goods, had loaned to individual borrowers. As the flow of trade began to plunge in the spring of 1931, deliveries began to collapse with it -- across Germany, Austria, and Hungary.. The paper based on anticipated commercial trade became worthless, much like the 2007-2008 collapse in value of several trillion dollars worth of securitized bonds after the default on sub-prime and other US home mortgages began to snowball.

The very-short-term debt was over and above the $5 billions of longer-term borrowing that had been undertaken by German industry, municipalities and governments.

In his memoirs, Hoover recounted his reaction on learning the dimension of what was then unraveling within Europe's debt pyramid:

> *The explosive mine which underlay the economic system of the world was now coming clearly into view. It was now evident why the European crisis had so long been delayed. They had kited bills A in order to pay B and their internal deficits. I don't know that I ever received a worse shock. The haunting prospect of wholesale bank failures and the necessity of saying not a word to the American people as to the cause and the danger, lest I precipitate runs on our banks, left me little sleep. The situation was no longer one of helping foreign countries to the indirect benefit of everybody. It was now a question of saving ourselves. [42]*

Unfortunately, it was already a bit late for salvation. At that point, Hoover, over strong objection from Treasury Secretary Mellon, issued a public call for a 'debt standstill' agreement, or moratorium, among all private banks that were holding German and Central European short-term obligations. Mellon, who was in London with Secretary of State Stimson for a conference on the banking crisis, called Hoover to discuss the deteriorating European situation. Mellon urged the President instead to agree to Germany's request for an additional $500 million to hold the line. Hoover replied that this would only bail out the foolish mistakes of private banks, but not solve the larger problem.

Hoover insisted, "The bankers must shoulder the burden of solution, not our taxpayers." Over the strenuous objections of Mellon and Stimson, and the Bank of England, Hoover instead issued his public call for a voluntary bank 'standstill agreement.' The London conference at that point endorsed the Hoover Moratorium, as did the new Bank for International Settlements in Basle, which Hoover asked to oversee the voluntary plan. A group of New York banks told the President they rejected the standstill, pressuring Hoover to agree in the end to a new US Government loan to Germany.

The Bank for International Settlements, when it issued its final report in 1932, reported that the "total amount of international short-term (private) indebtedness which existed at the beginning of 1931, aggregated more than $10 billion." That was twice the amount estimated by Hoover.

The standstill calmed matters only briefly, until September 21, 1931 when the Bank of England defaulted on foreign payments.

The Bank of France had begun on July 24, 1931 to withdraw their sizeable gold deposits from the Bank of England as well as from the New York Federal Reserve. The French withdrawal triggered a crisis of confidence in Sterling.

London banks also held large sums of now insolvent short-term loans to Eastern European and German banks. In August 1931, to try to stop the run on Sterling, the Bank of England raised its interest rates. That only made matters worse, as panic spread.

The British government borrowed some $650 million from US banks to try to stop the panic, only making it worse again. On September 14, sailors of the Atlantic Fleet of the British Royal Navy organized an insurrection against the government in response to pay cuts and worsening conditions of employment in what became known as the Invergordon Mutiny. It threatened the Government's very stability, and a week later, September 21, 1931, the Bank of England officially went off the gold standard, forcing the closing of most securities and commodity markets across Europe.

With disastrous consequences for its own population, however, the Federal Reserve kept its gold discount window open, permitting drain of US Federal Reserve gold abroad, thereby forcing a severe credit crunch in the US domestic economy. The entire edifice of the Roaring '20's consumer credit binge, the new practice of "buying on the installment plan," came crashing down in the process.

Instead of injecting liquidity into the domestic economy to stave off the growing economic contraction, the New York Fed, now under the Governorship of George Harrison after the death of Strong in November 1928, withdrew liquidity from the economy in a vain attempt to hold onto the Gold Exchange Standard, raising Federal Reserve discount rates in the process from 1% to 3% in October, 1931, a staggering differential.

That desperate attempt by Wall Street and the New York Federal Reserve to salvage their gold standard and with it, their dreams of an American financial empire, resulted in the destruction of both, even though they refused to accept the fact. The higher rates of the Federal Reserve pushed the US economy deep into depression and deflation.

It was not because of economic orthodoxy that it held on to the fixed gold standard so long. It was because the powerful forces directing Wall Street, the Money Trust, were determined not to sacrifice their goal of a US-controlled global money power through the Gold Exchange Standard that J. P. Morgan & Co., Benjamin Strong, Dillon, Read, Edwin Kemmerer and the leading financial elites of the United States had built on the ashes of World War One. They had few qualms about plunging the economy of the United States into the most severe depression in American history in their ultimately vain bid to grasp global financial power from England.

In contrast to developments in the United States, after 1931 British Sterling floated free of ties to gold, and a devaluation of some 40% boosted British exports and mitigated the effects of world collapse. In rapid succession, other European countries left the gold standard, except for France. The United States, meanwhile, clung to the deflationary gold parity until April 1933.

The conjuncture of these crises led to an increased role of the Federal government in American economic life. It took the form of Franklin Roosevelt's New Deal, when the first Democratic President since World War I was inaugurated on March 4, 1933. Most of FDR's recovery programs were in reality the continuation or implementation of many of the infrastructure projects that had been initiated under the hapless Hoover.

From the full onset of the Great Depression in 1931 through the peak of war spending in 1944, US government debt rose from 29% of GDP to over 130% of GDP. Simultaneously, the share of public spending in the overall national economy rose from 12% in 1931 to over 45% by 1944.

Benjamin Strong's grand project for making New York and Wall Street the bankers to Europe and to the world had fundamentally distorted the structures of the global financial system and of global trade and economic development, leading to their eventual, inevitable collapse.

It would take six years of domestic economic depression, corporate restructuring and preparation for a new great war in Europe to reverse the setback to Wall Street's bid to displace the British Empire as the world's dominant power. It required knocking out the revitalized German Reich as a future rival to American hegemony once and for all.

The process would be called World War II. In reality it was a continuation of the unresolved geopolitical issues of World War I, a titanic and tragic battle between two powers—Germany and the United States—to become successor to the failing British Empire as world hegemonic power. At least that was how leading elites in the US establishment saw it. It was doubtful whether German elite circles ever seriously entertained the idea of a global imperium, certainly not prior to 1914, and by all evidence, not even during the 1930s. Hitler had too much awe for the power of the British Empire for that. [43]

There could be no doubt, however, that the United States Money Trust did have the idea and intention of creating a global imperium, an informal empire of finance secured by the world's most powerful military. To realize that goal they needed a new World War.

The Federal Reserve was to play a decisive role here as well. The first bid by the powerful New York Banks, backed by their private Federal Reserve of New York, had proved a catastrophic failure that plunged the United States into the worst financial crisis in its history, with chain-reaction bank failures and years of depression. Within less than a decade, Wall Street and the powerful families behind it were ready to make their second and victorious bid for global power.

Endnotes:

[1] United States. Congress. House. Committee on Banking and Currency. *Money trust investigation: Investigation of financial and monetary conditions in the United States under House resolutions, nos. 429 and 504*, Subcommittee of the Committee on Banking and Currency, Washington, Government Printing Office, 1913. http://fraser.stlouisfed.org/publications/montru/.

[2] Kathleen Burk, *Finance, Foreign Policy and the Anglo-American bank: the House of Morgan, 1900-1931*, Historical Research, vol. LXI, no. 145, June 1988, p.210.

[3] Mark Metzler, *Lever of Empire: The International Gold Standard and the Crisis of Liberalism in Prewar Japan* (University of California Press, 2006), pp. 170-171.

[4] Herbert Hoover, *The Memoirs of Herbert Hoover, Volume Two: The Cabinet and the Presidency 1920-1933* (New York: The Macmillan Co., 1952), p. 85.

[5] Ibid., pp. 86-88.

[6] Ibid., p. 90.

[7] Leland Crabbe, *The International Gold Standard and U.S. monetary policy from World War I to the New Deal*, Federal Reserve Bulletin, June 1989.

[8] For background on the Anglo-American rivalry between the wars see, F. William Engdahl, *A Century of War: Anglo-American Oil Politics and the New World Order* (London: Pluto Press, 2004), Chapter 5, pp. 50-64.

[9] Carroll Quigley, *Tragedy and Hope: A History of the World in Our Time* (New York: The MacMillan Company, 1966), p. 324.

[10] According to a first hand report the author has from a former Georgetown student of Quigley's, the man ended his days in fear for his life that he may have revealed too much of the inner motives and workings of the power establishment in his book despite the fact, astonishingly, there is scarcely mention of the central Rockefeller role in the entire 1300 pages of the book.

[11] Ibid.

[12] Herbert Hoover, op. cit., p. 86.

[13] Herbert Hoover, *The Great Depression: 1929-1941*, pp. 6-7.

[14] Paul Alexander Gusmorino III, *Main Causes of the Great Depression*, Gusmorino World, May 13, 1996, accessed in www.gusmorino.com/pag3/greatdepression/.

[15] Russell Ally, *Gold and Empire: The Bank of England and South Africa's Gold Producers 1886-1926* (Witwatersrand University Press, 1994), p. 42.

[16] C. Reinold Noyes, *The Gold Inflation in the United States, 1921-1929*, The American Economic Review, vol. xx, no.2, June, 1930, pp. 181-198.

[17] Russell Ally, op. cit., p. 43.

[18] The following details regarding Smuts, London and the struggle over control of South African gold flows relies on the invaluable research of Professor Ally whose book, drawing on Reserve Bank of South Africa archives and other government documents illuminates the intense three-way political struggle between New York, London and Praetoria to control world monetary gold during the 1920's. The author also greatly benefited from numerous discussions over a period of years regarding the mysterious workings of the gold standard and international central banking with Dr Diederik Goedhuys, formerly Adviser, South African Reserve Bank.

[19] John Charmley, *Churchill—The End of Glory* (London: Sceptre, 1993), p. 336.

[20] Russell Ally, op. cit., p.99.

[21] Ibid.

[22] Paul W. Drake, *The Money Doctor in the Andes – The Kemmerer Missions, 1923 – 1933* (Durham: Duke University Press, 1989), p. 250.

[23] Mark Metzler, op. cit., pp. 170-171.

[24] Russell Ally, op. cit., p. 128.

[25] Paul Einzig, *Recent Changes in the London Gold Market*, The Economic Journal of the Royal Society, March, 1931, p. 62.

[26] Winston Churchill, *April 1925 Budget Statement to Parliament*, cited in Ed Balls, Speech by the Chief Economic Adviser to the Treasury, in www.HM-Treasury.gov.uk/ed_balls_at_2002_cairncross_lecture.htm.

[27] Richard Hemmig Meyer, *Bankers' Diplomacy: Monetary Stabilization in the Twenties* (New York: Columbia University Press, 1970), p. 6, described in detail in endnote 7.

[28] Russell Ally, op. cit., pp.88-89.

[29] James Grant, *Money of the Mind: Borrowing and Lending in America from the Civil War to Michael Milken* (New York: Farrar, Straus and Giroux, 1992), pp. 189-190.

[30] Cited in Kevin Dowd, R.H. Timberlake, *Money and the Nation State* (Edison N.J.: Transaction Books, 1997), p. 135.

[31] James Grant, op. cit., p.192. and Herbert Hoover, *The Great Depression: 1929-1941*, pp. 10-11.

[32] Cited in Murray N. Rothbard and Joseph T. Salerno, *A History of Money and Banking in the United States* (Auburn: Ludwig von Mises Institute, 2005), p.416.

[33] Benjamin Strong to Montagu Norman, cited in James Grant, op. Cit., p.10.

[34] Robert S. McElvaine, *The Great Depression: America, 1929-1941* (New York: Times Books, 1984), pp. 37-41.

[35] Ibid., pp. 38-40.

[36] Ibid.

[37] Charles P. Kindleberger, *The World in Depression: 1929-1939*, (London: Allen Lane, 1973), pp.148-151.

[38] Harold James, *The German Slump: Politics and Economics 1924-1936* (Oxford: Clarendon Press, 1986), pp. 283-285.

[39] Kevin Dowd, op. cit.

[40] Herbert Hoover, *The Great Depression*, p.7.

[41] Ibid.

[42] Ibid.

[43] Fritz Hesse, *Das Spiel um Deutschland* (Munich: Paul List Verlag, 1953), pp. 240-241. Hesse, a senior adviser to Foreign Minister Ribbentrop during the Third Reich in his memoirs lashed out at the German Foreign Ministry and Hitler for not grasping the basic geopolitics of Britain's Halford Mackinder. As Hesse put it, 'For the Anglo-saxons it was completely irrelevant who governed Germany. The simple fact that Germany had become the greatest Continental power was sufficient for the Anglo-saxons and the French to go to war.' (p. 240).

CHAPTER SIX

A New Deal, a Great Depression: Rockefellers take charge

'Why that's just plain stealing, isn't it, Mr. President?'
- Senator Thomas Gore to FDR on the President's 1933 decision to repeal debt repayment in gold

Decline of the House of Morgan

The first attempt at creating New York as the center of world finance under a US-dominated Gold Exchange Standard had collapsed in September 1931 when Great Britain abandoned gold, along with a host of other European nations. The collapse was lawful and entirely predictable, given the fragile international system of bank loans and bond underwriting that had been created by the House of J.P. Morgan & Co. after the Versailles peace conference in 1919.

In 1930, as an agricultural depression in America reached its full force, aggravated by record drought and Dust Bowl conditions fed by decades of extensive farming without crop rotation, 1,345 banks failed, most of them small rural farm banks. The spreading depositor withdrawals in the remaining banks led to a self-feeding spiral of bank closures, credit rationing by remaining banks, and even deeper economic depression leading to yet more bank failures.

By 1931, there were 2,294 more bank closings, almost double the year before. And another 1,453 banks closed their doors in 1932. By that year, a Presidential election year, the crisis had spread from individual banks to entire states. State governors, beginning in Nevada, began to declare state-wide 'bank holidays' to try to halt the panic cash withdrawals, which soon spread to the industrial state of Michigan.

Fearing an inevitable US devaluation of the dollar against gold, a rational move that would stimulate American industrial exports and slow the rising tide of unemployment, foreign central banks and other holders of dollars began to redeem their dollars for gold. That made the ultimate crisis even more certain, reinforcing Federal Reserve resolve to hold onto gold parity at all costs, regardless of its domestic impact.

The New York Federal Reserve raised its discount rate -- the interest rate charged commercial banks on loans from it -- from a low of 1.5% in October 1931 to 3.5% a week later. This was an enormous increase that more than doubled interest costs, but was done in order to respond to the 'gold loss and currency demands' under the rules of the prevailing gold standard.

The higher rates killed any chance of a domestic US bank recovery and further aggravated the domestic crisis which, in turn, fuelled more bank depositors' runs. Between August and November, the US money supply, including circulating currency and bank deposits, dropped 8%, unprecedented in the short history of the Federal Reserve. At the same time, the gold stock of the Federal Reserve, which theoretically should have risen under the attraction of higher US interest rates, fell instead by an alarming 11%.

Between the October 1929 stock market crash and the end of 1932, just three months prior to the inauguration of Franklin Delano Roosevelt in March 1933, America's national wealth had evaporated on a scale never before imagined. National income or GDP fell from some $88 billion to less than half that, or $42 billion, by the end of 1932.[1]

Amid the turmoil of the 1929-1933 New York stock market meltdown, and the failure of the thousands of smaller regional banks across America, a titanic power struggle was taking place within the highest ranks of the New York banking elites over who would emerge strongest from the crisis.

For the first time in United States history, other than during the 1861-1865 Civil War, the public debt of the United States Government dominated the American capital market. In 1930, a few weeks after the October 1929 New York stock market crash, US public debt had stood at just over $16 billion, or a mere 22% of national income. By the end of the Second World War in January 1946, the public debt stood at $278 billion, or 170% of national income. This represented an increase in nominal Federal debt of more than 1,700% in just sixteen years.[2]

The business of US banking shifted dramatically from financing stock margin buying and international loans, to that of financing the rise of an enormous Federal Government debt. Banks became, in effect, government bond traders rather than commercial business lenders. The stock market was not to recover its highs of 1929 for almost four decades.

The longer-term consequence of the Roosevelt era policies was a dramatic shift away from the power of international private banking, especially investment banking as done by J.P. Morgan, Kuhn Loeb, Dillon Read and others. Their ability to earn bountiful profits from underwriting bond issues in Europe or Latin America collapsed in September 1931 when Britain left the Gold Exchange Standard.

With no gold standard to serve as a psychological underpinning for the possible risk of huge international loans, banks were forced to look closely at the actual credit risk of their borrowers. What they saw was scary. The result was that international credit dried up almost overnight. Banks, fearing default, called in existing loans. The cumulative effect contributed to a self-fulfilling cycle of default and deflation worldwide.

J. P. Morgan & Co. was never to recover its previous dominance in New York and international finance after that. From the years in which Morgan & Co. were the exclusive bankers to the UK Treasury during the First World War—cemented by the intimate friendship during the 1920's between Morgan-protégé Benjamin Strong at the NY Federal Reserve, and the Bank of England's Montagu Norman—the House of Morgan had built its growing international influence through deepening and leveraging its ties to the power of the fatally weakened City of London.

During frantic and fruitless efforts by the Bank of England's Norman to keep Britain within the Gold Standard in summer of 1931, the New York Fed's Strong told Norman that Britain's government would have to work out a rescue package with J.P. Morgan & Co, the United States Financial Agent to Her Majesty's government since 1914.

The British Labor government of Ramsay MacDonald was brought down over the refusal of a majority of the Government's Cabinet members to accept the harsh cuts in British unemployment benefits demanded by J.P. Morgan & Co. as a precondition for their loan. Morgan had pledged to organize a syndicate of New York and other banks to raise the sizeable sum of $200 million to save the Pound and, with it, Morgan's gold standard. [3]

In the end, Morgan was too late. On September 19, 1931 MacDonald's government announced that Britain had decided to leave the gold standard entirely. That decision effectively ended J.P. Morgan's strategy of incorporating Great Britain and the City of London as partners in a New York-centered financial imperium.

From that point on, the British Government never again would use J.P. Morgan & Co. as its exclusive Government financial agents in the United States, a role Morgan had played since 1914 to its enormous advantage.[4] This marked the clear decline of the House of Morgan within the American establishment, as well. Sharks are good at smelling blood, especially of their rivals.

The second devastating blow to the primacy of the House of Morgan in New York finance came in June 1933 when the US Congress passed the Glass-Steagall Act, officially named the Banking Act of 1933. As a measure intended to curtail future stock and financial speculation bubbles, the new act prohibited a bank holding company from owning other financial companies, including insurance and investment banks. In addition, it established the Federal Deposit Insurance Corporation for insuring bank deposits.

In 1933 Roosevelt signed the Glass-Steagall Act that insured bank deposits and separated insurance from commercial banking and stock brokerages to avoid concentration of financial power.

The only major New York bank that encouraged Congress to pass the Glass-Steagall Act was Rockefeller's Chase Bank. Chase chairman Winthrop Aldrich was the son of Senator Nelson Aldrich, the same Senator Aldrich of the infamous 'Aldrich Plan' that became the core of the 1913 Federal Reserve Act.

Winthrop Aldrich strenuously lobbied Congress to pass Glass-Steagall, despite the strong opposition from Morgan and other New York banks. Unlike J.P. Morgan, the Chase Bank had become the world's largest deposit bank largely through extending traditional loans to the circle of Rockefeller companies such as Standard Oil. Chase was less dependent than Morgan on the underwriting of international bonds or the speculation in buying and selling of stocks. [5]

The Rockefellers conveniently put the knife in the back of their Morgan rivals when they were weakest. Chase emerged unscathed from the Congressional investigations into bank improprieties by the Senate Banking Committee, and the bank was prominently profiled as a 'friend' of the New Deal, a rarity in a Wall Street milieu in which Franklin Roosevelt was scornfully referred to as a 'traitor to his class' for his speeches attacking Wall Street greed and corruption, calling them 'economic royalists.' Traditional conservative Wall Street bankers regarded Roosevelt's depression relief measures, such as the National Recovery Administration, as a giant step to Bolshevism. [6]

The Glass-Steagall Act, passed amid the national bank panic in the first days of Roosevelt's administration, dealt a devastating blow to the once almighty House of Morgan, a blow from which it never fully recovered. [7] The Rockefeller faction emerged on the ashes of the House of Morgan to dominate US establishment policy as no other.

Gold Crisis and Dollar Debasement

By January 1934, the flawed workings of the US-centered Gold Standard were operating in effect to undermine public confidence in banking. Meanwhile, the Government publicly disclosed which domestic US banks it considered to be in danger and in need of government aid, triggering new panic depositor runs on thousands of smaller, poorly capitalized banks.

Two days after his inauguration as President on March 6, 1933, Roosevelt decreed a four-day national banking holiday. The main aim was to prevent anyone from hoarding or exporting gold or silver. [8] Every bank in the United States was shut down. Neither deposits nor withdrawals were possible, as Federal auditors were sent in to check the accounts of all banks before certifying which were solvent and which must be closed. The President showed his disdain for formal legal procedure and simply invoked the unrelated "Trading with the Enemy Act" of 1917 as his legal basis. Presumably, the foreign holders of gold-backed US dollars were now 'the enemy.'

In March 1933 President Roosevelt closed all banks in a declaration of national emergency and changed the basis of the Gold parity.

Within three days Congress had passed the Emergency Banking Act that validated the President's actions and gave him near *carte blanche* powers to go further. On April 5, 1933 Roosevelt signed an Executive Order declaring it illegal for American citizens to hold or own gold coins, bullion or gold certificates. [9] Violation was punishable by a $10,000 fine or ten years in prison, making owning of gold a felony.

The Federal Government thus had confiscated its own citizens' gold. As gold was universally regarded as the ultimate store of value for a currency or for repayment of debts, it was a massive, forced confiscation by the State of the private wealth of its citizens in return for mere paper promises to pay. The citizenry were powerless to act; they could merely hope for better times amid a deepening depression. Few people understood the complex workings of gold. By confiscating civilian gold holdings the US Government not only restocked its gold vaults at the expense of its citizens, it also cut off any chance citizens could resort to gold for a personal long-term store of value in the middle of the nation's worst economic depression.

Meanwhile, the Government had stopped converting its dollars into gold. On June 5, 1933 Congress formally abandoned the Gold Standard and declared the traditional gold-clause contract -- whereby a creditor, foreign or domestic, could demand repayment in either currency or gold -- to be null and void. Some $100 billion of such contracts, a staggering sum, were then outstanding for everything from mortgage deeds to life insurance policies to railroad bonds. The gold-clause had been an insurance against inflation and a guarantee of sound money repayment. [10]

Not any more. Creditors could no longer demand private debts be repaid in gold coin. Senator Thomas Gore from Oklahoma, when asked his opinion of the gold-clause repeal by Congress, snapped back, "Why that's just plain stealing, isn't it, Mr. President?" London referred a bit more diplomatically to the US Treasury's declaration that it would no longer honor its debts with gold as, "the American default." [11]

Baruch gains, others lose

One person emerged from the financial crisis with vastly larger power and financial resources. He was Bernard Baruch, one of the most politically influential of the Wall Street Money Trust. Baruch was a financier, a political "contributor" of Wall Street money to influence Congress, and an adviser to Presidents from Wilson to Hoover to Roosevelt and even a British Prime Minister, Winston Churchill. His Wall Street fortune had been tied to the railroad millionaire, E. H. Harriman as well as the Rockefellers.[12]

One of the most influential voices demanding rigid adherence to the orthodoxy of the Gold Standard in those days, Baruch had made a fortune before and during the First World War as a stock promoter for the American copper trust headed by the Guggenheim family.

In 1916, prior to US entry into the war, President Wilson had named Baruch to head the Advisory Commission of the Council of National Defense, which later became the War Industries Board. He was thereby made *de facto* wartime czar over US industry for the duration of combat. In that position, as later Congressional investigations documented, Baruch cartelized major sectors of American industry, and helped create huge price-fixing trusts in copper and other industries, enabling immense profits to be made from war production at Government -- that is, at taxpayer -- expense. [13]

Baruch used privileged insider information from his position at the Council of National Defense. In one documented instance, he alerted his business friends in the cartel of copper producers to sell a huge sum of copper, vital for war production, to the US Government at a highly inflated price just two weeks before President Wilson declared war on April 2, 1917.[14] This all took place while Baruch was holding a sensitive position of public trust.

Insider trading and conflicts of interest were never considered a problem by Baruch. After the US entry into the European war in April 1917, when Baruch's obvious conflict of interest was so brazen that it was attacked in the press, Baruch named his old Wall Street crony and business partner Eugene Meyer Jr. to oversee all Government purchases of copper. At the time, Meyer was Chairman of the Government War Finance Corporation. Baruch was later to secure ownership of the politically influential *Washington Post* for his friend Meyer, most likely out of gratitude.

Throughout the Republican presidencies of the 1920's, Baruch had built up his influence, mainly by making large financial contributions to influential Congressional Democrats. He was a power broker without rival in that day, widely known to control the votes of at least 60 Senators and Representatives in Congress, through his money and influence.

Money Trust Wall Street insider Bernard Baruch (R) helped Churchill make a killing on the New York Stock market before the 1929 crash.

At the time of the Wall Street crash, Baruch was considered the most influential Democrat in Hoover's Washington and, with Congress increasingly under Democratic control in the early 1930s, this was a position of enormous power.

After 1930, Republican Herbert Hoover increasingly sought out Baruch for advice on what overtures a Democratic Congress might accept to counter the nation's spreading economic crisis.

Baruch made no secret that he had gained a fortune in the stock market by selling all his stocks at peak prices some weeks before the October 1929 crash, thus giving his public statements the weight of the oracle of Delphi in the crisis of the early 1930s. He didn't say that his close friend, Winston Churchill, had done the same on Baruch's advice. Both Baruch and Churchill, curiously, managed to get out at the stock market peak, just before the Bank of England triggered the events leading to the London market crash in September 1929. Suspicions in certain quarters held that Churchill and Baruch both benefited from their respective insider positions.

In the critical months of 1931 and 1932, Bernard Baruch forged a Congressional consensus of Democrats and Republicans that dominated legislation and political debate. The influential Senate Finance Committee chairman and other powerful legislators were frequent hunting guests at Baruch's South Carolina plantation retreat in the early 1930s.

Baruch thus held an unequalled position of power and influence over Washington economic policy during those critical first few years of the depression. What he did with that influence was to prove decisive to the course of subsequent events.

He urged Senate Democrats not to embark on any course that would provide an alternative to the paralyzed White House, but instead, to come to a consensus with Hoover's Republicans. "The country is in a highly excited condition," he told Senate friends. "What it needs now is rest, not any more changes. Let us not try to rectify too many things now."[15]

Baruch's unique influence blocked any genuine Democratic alternative to the disastrous Hoover laissez faire policy in those critical months. That lack of initiatives or solutions from the Democrats in the 1930s was not unlike the deafening silence of Congressional Democrats more than eight decades later during the 2008 Congressional debate over an unprecedented $700 billion Republican bailout bill for Wall Street.

Baruch argued that the deflation of commodity prices had bottomed out in October 1930 and that, "natural curative forces have set themselves in motion. I do not believe government can do anything to help. Every time government steps in, they make it worse."[16]

He told a group of Democratic Party academic economists at the time that, "business must go through the wringer, and start over again," as though the national economy were a giant washing machine. When one economist present protested that such a laissez faire approach by government risked riots in the streets, Baruch snapped back, "There is always tear gas to take care of that."

He used his influence to vigorously oppose any proposals for government public works spending to ease unemployment, which he contemptuously termed, "job inflation." A front page headline in the November 12, 1931 *New York Times* proclaimed this baseless optimism: "Baruch Sees Nation Rising From Slump." Alongside it ran an article reporting 67,000 unemployed lining up in New York City to register for emergency jobs. Baruch called for raising income taxes to keep the government's budget "balanced and sound" in the crisis, insisting that any vigorous public spending would inflate the dollar. His eye was on the price of gold, not the public welfare.

Through his influence over Congressional Democrats, Baruch succeeded in winning them to the same destructive fiscal deflation as Hoover's Republicans, thus successfully paralyzing any prospect for significant policy initiative as the nation sank deeper into the economic morass. Bernard Baruch was unremitting in his advocacy of continued deflation as national policy during the years of the onset of depression.

The core of Baruch's strategy was to prevent any Congressional attempts to modify the Federal Reserve System and to demand, at all costs, rigid US adherence to the Gold Standard, even after Britain and 24 other nations had abandoned it in late 1931. As Baruch wrote to his close friend, Senator Jimmy Byrnes, "This country cannot go off the gold basis." [17]

Coincidentally, during the entire period when Baruch was urging Congress and the Hoover Administration not to abandon the gold standard, Baruch was also the private business partner of Hoover's Undersecretary of the Treasury Ogden Mills Jr. in an Alaska gold mine. A third partner was Baruch's old crony, Eugene Meyer, Jr., who had just been named by President Hoover to the Federal Reserve Board. [18]

By February 1932, in the midst of the presidential election year, US gold reserves had fallen to alarming lows. More than $1 billion of monetary gold had gone, owing to foreign drains and to private hoarding of gold as the domestic American banking crisis escalated. The Federal Reserve was mandated by law to find another $1.5 billion of gold reserves. The amount of Federal Reserve 'free gold' at that point was down to $433 million, and it was disappearing at the rate of $150 million per week. Baruch redoubled his public and private call to maintain adherence to the gold standard at all costs.

Hoover adamantly affirmed he would do nothing further to "tamper" with the automatic workings of the Gold Standard. Gold continued to leave the vaults of the Federal Reserve, and bank failures mounted ever higher.

An editorial in the *Philadelphia Record* in May 1932 expressed the growing alarm in the nation:

> *Within three months the United States must suspend gold payment. If the Government waits until its hand is forced, it courts disaster. If the Government acts now, it can arrest deflation, end depression, win back prosperity...At the rate gold is going out of the Federal Reserve System, Federal Reserve banks will have to stop their open market transactions within six weeks. They will be pulled up short by dwindling gold reserve--the golden chain which has circumscribed any adequate action to cure the depression...*
>
> *Why can't we fight this depression as we fought the war, when we declared an embargo on gold in 1917, and no one thought anything of it?... President Hoover declared a moratorium on allied debts, but allows the subjects of these debtor nations [i.e. France and Britain-w.e.] to drain our gold and drive us toward destruction. Are we in the grip of some strange obsession, which makes us act irrationally whenever the precious metal is mentioned?*

When it became clear that Democrat Franklin Roosevelt would win the November 1932 presidential elections, Baruch shrewdly shifted his allegiance to Roosevelt, a man he had earlier opposed for the nomination.

At the same time, Baruch began privately hoarding gold bars in a New York bank vault, buying from European suppliers as well as from his own Alaska Juneau Gold Mining Company. Baruch's gold fortune reached an impressive sixty-six gold bars by February 1933, the month before Roosevelt's inauguration, when Baruch abruptly ceased buying gold. It turned out that some members of President-elect Roosevelt's 'Brain Trust' had privately informed Baruch of Roosevelt's gold policy plans.

On April 5 1933, Franklin Delano Roosevelt issued a proclamation calling for the return to the US Treasury of all privately held gold. At the time, Baruch was reportedly "the greatest single individual holder of gold bricks." Later that year, the Roosevelt government announced it was buying all newly mined gold at a price above the market price, a misguided effort to revive commodity prices.

Needless to say, Baruch was a major beneficiary. Baruch kept his friend Winston Churchill closely informed of all these developments.

In any event, dollar convertibility with gold was to hold until the new President, Franklin Delano Roosevelt, in one of his first official acts of office, declared on April 19, 1933 that the United States had suspended convertibility of the dollar under the Gold Standard.

Roosevelt resumed the Gold Standard under the Gold Reserve Act, passed by Congress in January 1934. The act of 1934 represented the first official dollar devaluation against gold since 1900, when President McKinley had signed the Gold Standard Act, fixing the dollar to a value of 25.8 grains of gold.

The Gold Reserve Act of 1934 ended domestic redemption of dollars for gold. The new law nationalized all gold by ordering the Federal Reserve banks to turn over their supply to the US Treasury. In return the banks received gold 'certificates' to be used as reserves against deposits and Federal Reserve notes. The act also authorized the President to devalue the gold dollar so that it would have no more than 60 percent of its existing weight, a huge devaluation and a staggering loss for foreign creditors.

Roosevelt used his powers under the Gold Reserve Act to declare an immediate 59% devaluation of the dollar to a new fixed parity price of $35 per ounce of gold. The dollar was to remain at $35 per fine ounce gold until the fateful dollar crises of the early 1970's. By sharply devaluing the dollar against foreign currencies the Government hoped to give export trade a big boost and with it lift the economy out of depression.

Rockefellers emerge triumphant

The fateful consequence of the decline of the House of Morgan within the banking establishment was that the Rockefeller family and its interests rose to a position of dominance in US economic and political policy never before seen in America.

The Rockefeller group had been more or less in the background during the 1920s in terms of the Morgan group's efforts to build their global dollar power. Rockefeller, meanwhile, had concentrated on building the power of Standard Oil in the Middle East, Latin America, in Europe and elsewhere, and on building an international chemicals and military industry, the predecessor to America's Cold War era military industry complex.[19]

By the late 1930s the powerful Rockefeller dynasty was managed by four brothers, the sons of John D. Rockefeller Jr.—David, Nelson, John D. III and

Laurance Rockefeller. A fifth brother, Winthrop, played a relatively minor role in the political activities of the family empire. The four brothers organized the emerging power of their faction within the highest ranks of the US power establishment around two banks: 1) New York's First National Bank, the bank of the Standard oil empire, headed by James Stillman, and whose Board of Directors included William Rockefeller, brother of John, Jr; and 2) the Chase Bank, the house bank of Standard Oil and by 1933 the largest bank in the world, now under Rockefeller control after the merger with the Rockefellers' Equitable Trust.

While most of Wall Street initially treated Roosevelt's New Deal as anathema and a major step in the direction of economic Bolshevism for the United States, the Rockefeller brothers realized they could use the depression crisis and the emerging role of the state to huge advantage in building their global empire. They had little reason to fear any policies out of Roosevelt's Cabinet. Their own establishment people dominated the President's famous 'Brain Trust,' five men who guided the President's policy decisions, but who had no official positions or titles. They included, in addition to Baruch, A. A. Berle; James Warburg, Wall Street banker (and son of the architect of the Federal Reserve, Paul Warburg); Professor Rexford Guy Tugwell; and Raymond Moley.

The Rockefellers had one of their top men, a former Rockefeller employee, at President Roosevelt's side – FDR confidante Harry Hopkins. He would make certain Roosevelt did what was useful for the vast Rockefeller interests. Hopkins had been financed by the Rockefeller Foundation for more than a decade, when he ran its Organized Social Service. Hopkins soon became Franklin D. Roosevelt's alter ego, even to the point of living in the White House. He became the second most powerful man in America during the war years, dubbed by the press, 'Deputy President.'

In addition, the Rockefellers had close ties to another influential member of FDR's Brain Trust, Columbia University Professor A. A. Berle, Jr. Berle had been on close terms with the Rockefeller family since the early 1920s as a prominent New York lawyer. Berle would later work for the Rockefeller interests after the war as family adviser on Latin America, and co-author of Nelson Rockefeller's 'autobiography.' [20]

Shortly after his reelection to a second term in 1937, Roosevelt, notorious for lack of understanding of economics, accepted the opinion of his Treasury Secretary Henry Morgenthau that the depression was ending, and that the greatest danger was potential inflation from too much government spending.

As a consequence, FDR slashed Federal spending and dramatically reduced the budgets of New Deal agencies such as the Works Progress Administration.

The Federal Reserve duly tightened the money supply, slamming the brakes on consumer spending. The stock market underwent its most severe drop in US history as two million Americans were thrown out of work. The press called it "Roosevelt's Depression." Shortly after the second fall of the economy into depression, FDR turned anew to people like A.A. Berle and to the Rockefeller interests for a strategy to bring America out of the second depression. The Rockefellers were more than ready to help.[21]

In that climate of the depressed stock market the Rockefellers were able to greatly extend their vast web of interlocked industrial and financial holdings as they pulled key corporate assets into their vast industrial empire. In contrast to its impact on most small and mid-sized industries, the New Deal dealt most kindly with the Rockefeller interests and most Fortune 500 corporations close to them, including Rockefeller Standard Oil companies as well as the group of chemical companies linked to them.[22]

Investigative journalist Walter Winchell reported at the time that Harry Hopkins acknowledged his debt to the Rockefellers when he was appointed Secretary of Commerce, by offering the post of Assistant Secretary of Commerce to Nelson Rockefeller, son of John D. Rockefeller, Jr.

According to an account in the Los Angeles *Herald Examiner* of September 7, 1975, Hopkins had brought Nelson Rockefeller into the inner circles of the New Deal in the 1930s. Soon after his appointment, Rockefeller, then in his 30's, became a Roosevelt intimate, spending his holidays with the President at Shangri-la, now Camp David. [23]

A. A. Berle Jr. became Assistant Secretary of State for Latin America in 1938, a position from which he could immensely benefit Rockefeller oil and other business interests from Venezuela to Brazil and beyond.

Baruch, Rockefeller, Big Business and Mussolini

Rockefeller's Wall Street interests, Bernard Baruch, and a powerful circle of big business leaders at the time were determined to reorganize the US economy along the centralized corporatist model of Mussolini's fascist Italy. Of course they were politically astute enough not to say so too loudly.

Baruch and his close friend, Bernard Swope, a director of General Electric and of National City Bank, had initially urged President Hoover in 1931 to "stabilize industry" with what they characterized as an emergency program. The aim was to free big business from the restraints of the Sherman Anti-Trust Act, thus opening the door to major consolidation of corporate power during the depression when cheap stock prices made takeovers easy and cheap for those such as the Rockefeller group who were flush with cash. [24]

Hoover, who was ideologically opposed to state intervention, rejected the Swope Plan and Baruch's ideas. When it became clear that Democrat Franklin Delano Roosevelt (FDR) would oppose Hoover in 1932, Baruch and his Wall Street friends quickly ingratiated themselves into the inner circle of FDR, greasing their entry with ample bundles of cash. [25]

Contrary to carefully planted propaganda in the media portraying FDR as the "hero of the little man" who was ready to "chase the money lenders from the temple," Roosevelt was the scion of a wealthy East Coast family, a distant relative of Teddy Roosevelt, and every bit The Man of Wall Street—especially of Baruch, Rockefeller and their group. [26] According to Roosevelt's Secretary of Labor, Frances Perkins,

> *At the first Cabinet meeting following the inauguration of the President in 1933, the financier and Roosevelt adviser Bernard Baruch and Baruch's friend, General Hugh S. Johnson, later to head the National Recovery Administration, came. They handed out copies of a book by Gentile, the theoretician of Italian fascism, to every Cabinet member and we all read it with great concern.*[27]

The same industrial reorganization under state control that Baruch and Swope had unsuccessfully tried to get Hoover to embrace in 1931 was now embraced by FDR.

In May 1933, during his first weeks in office, FDR proposed to Congress the creation of a National Recovery Administration (NRA). It passed with a minimum of debate amid the depression crisis. Its first head was Hugh S. Johnson, associate of and advisor to Bernard Baruch.

The concept of the NRA was largely drawn from the national military emergency mobilization of industry that Baruch and Johnson had administered during the First World War. Ever since then, Big Business and Wall Street had been salivating over the possibility of getting such power over the economy into their hands once again. The Great Depression would be their chance. Johnson would be their man. Within Roosevelt's Administration, Johnson was open about the fact that he saw Mussolini's Italian Fascist corporatism—the merger of government and corporate power to the one-sided gain of business—as a model for America.[28]

Johnson's NRA organized thousands of businesses under codes drawn up by trade associations and industries, with NRA-approved companies being given the right to display the NRA symbol, the "Blue Eagle."

Guiding policies at NRA was a troika of three extremely powerful industry magnates—Walter C. Teagle, President of Rockefeller's Standard Oil of New Jersey; Gerard Swope, author of the earlier Swope Plan and also President of General Electric; and Louis Kirstein, vice president of Filene & Sons department stores of Boston.[29]

The Rockefeller group, working through Teagle, was able to use its influence over Johnson's NRA to re-centralize the 33 independent companies that had made up the earlier Standard Oil Trust, the combine that the Supreme Court had broken up under the Sherman Anti-Trust Act in 1911.[30] It was only one of a series of moves by the Rockefeller faction as it consolidated its decisive role in United States domestic and foreign policy during the course of the depression and the Roosevelt Presidency.

In 1930 as most banks were struggling to survive, Rockefeller's Chase National Bank was thriving. The bank's head during that time was Winthrop Aldrich, son of Senator Nelson Aldrich of the Jekyll Island secret Federal Reserve meeting of 1910, and brother-in-law of John D. Rockefeller Jr. Chase Bank's most significant acquisition during the first months of the financial crisis in 1930 was the Equitable Trust Company of New York, the largest stockholder of which was John D. Rockefeller Jr. This made the Chase Bank the largest bank in America and indeed the world.[31]

As a result of their dominant position following the decline of the House of Morgan during the depression, the Rockefeller group, in addition to controlling Chase Bank and First City Bank of New York, controlled the largest US oil companies -- Standard Oil of NY (Mobil), Standard oil of New Jersey (ESSO/Exxon), Standard of California (Chevron) and Texaco (The Texas Company).

The Rockefeller group also consolidated a commanding control over the major chemical and defense-related industries, including Allied Chemical, Anaconda Copper, DuPont, Monsanto Chemicals, Olin Industries (Winchester Arms), Shell, Gulf Oil, Union Oil, Dow Chemicals, Celanese, Pittsburgh Plate Glass, Cities Service, Stauffer Chemical, Continental Oil, Union Carbide, American Cyanamid, American Motors, Bendix Electric, and Chrysler. [32] The Rockefellers also bought up large blocks of stock in General Motors, General Electric and IBM, then a new company.

By the end of the 1930s the Rockefeller group's industrial holdings and banks were uniquely poised to reap handsome gains from any future war. They did not have to wait long.

Endnotes:

1 Paul Studenski and H. E. Krooss, *Financial History of the United States* (New York: McGraw-Hill Book Co., 1963), p. 353.

2 Morris H. Hansen, *Statistical Abstract of the United States* (Washington, D.C.: US Department of Commerce, US Government Printing Office, 1946), p. 355.

3 Kathleen Burk, *Finance, Foreign Policy and the Anglo-American Bank: The House of Morgan, 1900-31*, Historical Research, Vol. LXI, no.145, June 1988, pp. 208-210.

4 Ibid., p. 209-210.

5 Peter Collier and David Horowitz, *The Rockefellers: An American Dynasty* (New York: Holt, Rinehart and Winston, 1976, pp. 160-161.

6 Ibid). p. 161-162.

7 Kathleen Burk, op. cit., p. 210.

8 United States Department of the Treasury, *History of the Treasury: Chronology of Events 1900 through 2003*, accessed in www.ustreas.gov/education/history/events/1900-present.shtml.

9 Ibid.

10 James Grant, *Money of the Mind* (New York: Farrar, Straus and Geroux, 1994), pp. 227-230.

11 Ibid., p. 230.

12 Bernard M. Baruch, *My Own Story* (New York: Henry Holt and Co., 1957), pp. 138-39. Baruch related that, "our firm did a large business for Mr. Harriman...."

13 Jordan A. Schwarz, *The Speculator: Bernard M. Baruch in Washington, 1917-1965* (Chapel Hill: University of North Carolina Press, 1981), passim.

14 Ibid., p. 271.

15 Ibid., pp. 270-276.

16 Ibid.. p. 271.

17 Ibid., p. 270-276.

18 Ibid., p. 296.

19 F. William Engdahl, *A Century of War: Anglo-American Oil Politics and the New World Order*, op. cit., see especially Chapter 5.

20 Gerard Colby and Charlotte Dennett, *Thy Will Be Done: The Conquest of the Amazon— Nelson Rockefeller and Evangelism in the Age of Oil* (New York: HarperCollins, 1995), p. 89.

21 Ibid. pp.88-89.

22 Anthony C. Sutton, *Roosevelt und die internationale Hochfinanz* (Tuebingen: Grabert-Verlag, 1990), pp. 149-150.

23 The New York Times, May 20, 1960.

24 Anthony C. Sutton, op. cit., pp. 149-154.

25 Ibid., p.142.

26 Ibid., pp. 142-145.

[27] Frances Perkins, *The Roosevelt I Knew* (New York,: Viking Press, 1946), p. 206., cited in Anthony C. Sutton, op. cit., p.199.

[28] Stanley G. Payne, *A History of Fascism, 1914-1945* (Madison: University of Wisconsin Press, 1995), p. 230, footnote 65.

[29] Anthony C. Sutton, op. cit., p. 153.

[30] Ibid. p. 167.

[31] David Rockefeller, *Memoirs* (New York: Random House, 2002), pp. 124-25.

[32] Gary Allen, *The Rockefeller File*, Chapter Three, accessed in http://www.mega.nu:8080/ampp/gary_allen_rocker/ch1-4.html#ch3.

CHAPTER SEVEN

For an 'American Century': The War & Peace Studies

'If war aims are stated which seem to be solely concerned with Anglo-American imperialism, they will offer little to people in the rest of the world. The interests of other peoples should be stressed. This would have a better propaganda effect.'
- Memo from the Council on Foreign Relations to the US State Department, War & Peace Studies, 1941

Rockefellers' 'Discreet Venture'

J.P. Morgan never found the time or inclination to organize his vast wealth into tax-exempt foundations and to extend his influence far beyond the confines of his bank and corporate holdings. John D. Rockefeller, on the other hand, after a wave of bad publicity surrounding a Colorado coal miners' strike in which his private security guards attacked a miners' tent with machine guns and set it on fire, killing unarmed workers and also 11 children, was convinced of the public relations advantage of such a move.

Rockefeller's principal business adviser, Frederick T. Gates, suggested that he organize his wealth into a tax-exempt foundation after 1913, using tax-free funds, to extend the power and influence of the family in a manner somewhat like an American Medici, absent the cultural refinements but cloaked in the myth of "philanthropy."

The Rockefeller Foundation was incorporated in New York State in 1913, under the direction of Gates, whom Rockefeller called the greatest businessman he ever encountered. Gates would focus the new foundation's activities on programs that would dramatically leverage Rockefeller wealth, but above all, the family's political and social power.

› Under this mantle of philanthropy, the Rockefeller Foundation would re-shape the map of the entire world, beginning in the late 1930s. The programs and mechanisms through which it operated were phenomenally important and little understood, as they were extremely well disguised.

In 1939, with a major funding grant from the Rockefeller Foundation, the New York Council on Foreign Relations (CFR) began what would be a series of long-term studies in collaboration with the US State Department.

The top secret project, called the War & Peace Studies, ran for five years until 1944. The project was headed by Prof. Isaiah Bowman, director of the CFR and an original member of Woodrow Wilson's secret strategic advisers during World War I, a group of academics called "the Inquiry." Bowman, President of Johns Hopkins University and a geographer, called himself America's Haushofer, a reference to Hitler's geo-politician.[1]

Well before the victory of the United States in World War II, it had become obvious to the Rockefellers and to other heads of the largest American corporations and banks that the US domestic market was far too small for their ambitions. As they saw it, America's 'Manifest Destiny,' the unlimited expansion of American power, was to be a worldwide business. A seemingly easy victory in World War I and the gains of the Versailles Treaty in Europe had only whetted their appetite for more.

The Rockefellers had secretly created the highly influential policy group in late 1939, just weeks after Germany invaded Poland, and two full years before Pearl Harbor would bring the US directly into the war.

The task of the secret group was set out by the Rockefellers, who funded it through their Rockefeller Foundation: to shape US post-war economic and political goals, based on the assumption a world war would come, and that the United States would emerge from the ashes of that war as the dominant global power.

The CFR's War and Peace Studies Group carried out all significant postwar planning for the understaffed US State Department. After 1942, most of the group's members were quietly put directly on the State Department payroll in senior positions where they continued implementation of the project from within the Government.

Between November 1939 and late 1942, the Rockefeller Foundation had contributed no less than $350,000 to finance a plan for post-war American economic hegemony via the War & Peace Studies Group. It was an investment that, like most 'philanthropic' investments made by the Rockefellers, would be repaid thousands of times over in later years. It defined the post-war American business empire globally. Their American Century was very much a Rockefeller empire though most Americans were blissfully ignorant of the fact.[2]

In their official authorized history published decades later, the CFR admitted to a remarkable extent what the War & Peace Studies project was all about:

> *More than two years before the Japanese attack on Pearl Harbor, the research staff of the Council on Foreign Relations had started to envision a venture that would dominate the life of the institution for the demanding years ahead. With the memory of the Inquiry in focus, they conceived a role for the Council in the formulation of national policy.*
>
> *On September 12, 1939, as Nazi Germany invaded Poland, [CFR's Hamilton Fish] Armstrong and Mallory entrained to Washington to meet with Assistant Secretary of State George S. Messersmith. At that time the Department of State could command few resources for study, research, policy planning, and initiative; on such matters, the career diplomats on the eve of World War II were scarcely better off than had been their predecessors when America entered World War I.*
>
> *The men from the Council proposed a discreet venture reminiscent of the Inquiry: a program of independent analysis and study that would guide American foreign policy in the coming years of war and the challenging new world that would emerge after. The project became known as the War and Peace Studies.*
>
> *'The matter is strictly confidential,' wrote [Isaiah] Bowman, 'because the whole plan would be "ditched" if it became generally known that the State Department is working in collaboration with any outside group.' The Rockefeller Foundation agreed to fund the project, reluctantly at first, but once convinced of its relevance, with nearly $350,000. Over the coming five years, almost 100 men participated in the War and Peace Studies, divided into four functional topic groups: economic and financial, security and armaments, territorial, and political. These groups met more than 250 times, usually in New York, over dinner and late into the night. They produced 682 memoranda for the State Department, which marked them classified and circulated them among the appropriate government departments.[3]*

The aim of the CFR's secret project was to lay a solid, enduring basis for the final succession of the United States to assume the role held by the British Empire prior to 1914; a 'Pax Americana,' an unchallenged successor to the failing Pax Britannica.

The new, unofficial policymakers were selected from the elite membership of the New York Council on Foreign Relations, which was increasingly dominated by handpicked Rockefeller people.

Unlike the British Empire, which was based on military conquest and direct possession of colonies, their American vision of global domination was based on financial conquest and economic possession. It was a brilliant refinement, one which allowed US corporate giants to veil their interests behind the flag of 'democracy and political rights' for 'oppressed colonial peoples,' support of 'free enterprise' and 'open markets.'

A confidential memo from the Council on Foreign Relations War & Peace Studies group to the US State Department in 1941 stated it clearly:

> *If war aims are stated which seem to be solely concerned with Anglo-American imperialism, they will offer little to people in the rest of the world. The interests of other peoples should be stressed. This would have a better propaganda effect.* [4]

The interests represented in the Council on Foreign Relations task force were anything but democratic. It reflected the interests of the elite handful of American banks and industrial corporations that had developed global interests. The businessmen and their law firms represented in the Council on Foreign Relations were a breed apart from the rest of Americans, an oligarchy to themselves, an aristocracy of power and money.

The minutes of the CFR's War & Peace Studies Security Sub-Committee reveal the parameters of their US post-war foreign policy. Realizing it was doubtful that "...the British Empire as it existed in the past will ever reappear and....the United States may have to take its place...," the US "must cultivate a mental view toward world settlement after this war which will enable us to impose our own terms, amounting....to Pax Americana."

Americans could retain their vitality, the CFR strategists of postwar Pax Americana argued, only by accepting the logic of endless expansionism. In 1942 the Council's director Isaiah Bowman wrote, "The measure of our victory will be the measure of our domination after victory...(The US must secure areas) strategically necessary for world control." [5]

TIME

The Weekly Newsmagazine

JOHNS HOPKINS' BOWMAN

Volume XXVII   Number 12

CFR founder and geopolitical strategist Isaiah Bowman headed the Rockefeller Foundatio'sn secret wartime project, War & Peace Studies, at the Council on Foreign Relations. Time, the magazine of American Century's Henry Luce, made Bowman famous.

Another policy statement of the secret group, Memorandum E-B19, contained the essentials for United States foreign policy after the war, summarizing the "component parts of an integrated policy to achieve military and economic supremacy of the United States...." Such supremacy would be bolstered, they argued, through the postwar "coordination and cooperation of the United States with other countries to secure the limitation of any exercise of sovereignty by foreign nations that constitutes a threat to the minimum world area essential to the security and economic prosperity of the United States and the Western Hemisphere."

A State Department memorandum of April 1944 clarified the philosophy behind the group's concept of Western 'access to resources.' US 'supremacy' in this regard meant:

> *[T]he preservation of the absolute position presently obtaining, and therefore vigilant protection of existing concessions in United States hands coupled with insistence upon the Open Door principle of equal opportunity for the United States companies in new areas.*[6]

The CFR's economic and financial studies had shown how dangerous a unified Europe -- with or without Nazi domination -- would be to the United States. The Council's group inside the US State Department during the War determined that, at a minimum, most of the non-German world was needed for US economic 'elbow room,' for a new American 'Grand Area.'

Hamilton Fish Armstrong pointed out in mid-June 1941 that a unified Europe could not be allowed to develop because it would be so strong that it would seriously threaten this American 'Grand Area.' Europe, organized as a single entity, was considered "fundamentally incompatible with the American economic system."[7]

In its final form, America's plan for a postwar Grand Area consisted of Western Europe, the Far East, the former British Empire (which was being dismantled), the incomparable energy resources of the Middle East (which were then passing into American hands as rivals France and Britain were pushed out), the rest of the Third World and, if possible, the entire globe. The whole of China was also included.

Modesty had no room in their imperial blueprint. The only question unresolved in the minds of the architects of the American Century's foreign policy was whether Stalin would be willing to make the vast Soviet Union part of an American Century or not.

'American Century'

At the beginning of 1941, ten months before the Japanese bombing of Pearl Harbor, Henry Luce, publisher of *Time* and *Life* magazines, and a well-connected member of the policy elite, wrote an editorial in the February 17 issue of *Life* entitled, 'The American Century.'

In his pivotal essay, Luce described the emerging consensus of the Rockefeller establishment around the CFR and the War & Peace Studies group: "Tyrannies," Luce wrote, "may require a large amount of living space; but Freedom requires and will require far greater living space than Tyranny." He openly called for Americans to embrace a new role as the dominant power in the world, despite the fact that the United States had not yet entered the war. Luce wrote,

> *[T]he cure is this: to accept wholeheartedly our duty and our opportunity as the most powerful and vital nation in the world and in consequence to exert upon the world the full impact of our influence, for such purposes as we see fit and by such means as we see fit.[8]*

It was a recruitment call to support the creation an American empire without naming it such. Luce clothed the empire in idealistic, democratic clothes, much as the War & Peace Studies group had done:

> *Throughout the 17th century and the 18th century and the 19th century, this continent teemed with manifold projects and magnificent purposes. Above them all and weaving them all together into the most exciting flag of all the world and of all history was the triumphal purpose of freedom.' He concluded with stirring rhetoric, 'It is in this spirit that all of us are called, each to his own measure of capacity, and each in the widest horizon of his vision, to create the first great American Century. [9]*

Luce, a product of Yale University, housed his publishing empire in the huge Time-Life Building at the newly built Rockefeller Center in New York. His editorial reflected the emerging view of the internationally oriented US business and banking establishment around Rockefeller. They needed unfettered access to global resources and markets after the war, and they saw the chance to get it when, as they foresaw, all other contending powers had been devastated by the war.

The American banking and industrial giants needed new markets to conquer, what the War & Peace Studies group called a 'Grand Area,' a concept remarkably similar to Haushofer's *Lebensraum* for Germany. The CFR's Economic & Financial Group made a survey of world trade in the late 1930s. They proposed linking the entire Western Hemisphere with the Pacific, within a US-dominated bloc premised on the anticipated "military and economic supremacy for the United States." [10] The bloc included what was then, still, the British

Empire. The American Grand Area was to encompass most of the planet outside the sphere of Stalin's Soviet Union that remained, to their irritation, still closed to American capital penetration.

 The world vision of the Rockefeller-financed War and Peace Studies group was unsentimental. Memorandum E-B19 from their Economic and Financial Group to the CFR and State Department stated bluntly,

> *The foremost requirement of the United States in a world in which it proposes to hold unquestionable power is the rapid fulfilment of a programme of complete re-armament... to secure the limitation of any exercise of sovereignty by foreign nations that constitutes a threat to the minimum world area essential for the security and economic prosperity of the United States.*

More than six decades later, in September 2002, the Bush Administration declared almost verbatim the same explicit goals to be US national security policy.

Founding CFR member and leader of the War & Peace Study group, Isaiah Bowman -- known as 'America's Geo-politician' during the Second World War -- had another term for the Grand Area. Bowman called it, in reference to Hitler's term justifying German expansion, "an American economic Lebensraum."[11] The term was later dropped for obvious reasons, and the more neutral-sounding term, 'American Century,' was used instead to describe the Rockefeller group's emerging vision of postwar US imperialism.

 As Bowman and others of the CFR envisioned it, the champions of the new American economic geography would present themselves as the selfless advocates of freedom for colonial peoples and as the enemy of imperialism. They would champion world peace, but through multinational control. Since World War I, when he had worked with Wilson's secret strategy group, The Inquiry, Bowman had been occupied with how to clothe American imperial ambitions in liberal and benevolent-sounding garb.

The American domination of the world after 1945 would be accomplished via a new organization, the United Nations Organization, the "jewel in the crown of the American Lebensraum," It would include the new Bretton Woods institutions of the International Monetary Fund and World Bank, and later, the General Agreement on Tariffs and Trade (GATT). [12]

The CFR group drafted the basic outline for President Roosevelt of what would become the United Nations Organization, and convinced the President to give it his hearty backing. Under the banner of 'free trade' and the opening of closed markets around the world, US big business would advance their agenda, forcing open new untapped markets for cheap raw materials as well as new outlets for selling American manufactured goods after the war.

ɔ Bowman's team drafted more than 600 policy papers for the State Department and the President, covering every conceivable part of the planet, from entire Continents to the smallest islands. It was all based on a presumed US victory in a war that Washington had not yet even officially entered.

Nelson Aldrich Rockefeller was to play a discreet and decisive behind-the-scenes role in defining those private, global interests of the Rockefeller family, and also shrewdly repackaging them as 'America's national interests.' It was Mussolini's "corporatism" headed by the Rockefeller dynasty. ɛ

Third Reich skeletons in the Rockefeller closet

The Rockefeller group within the American power establishment, along with numerous related corporate heads from Henry Ford to the DuPonts, had long been attracted to the European models of Mussolini's corporatist Fascism and even German Nazism. Wall Street and major US industrial circles had been traditionally anti-labor and heavy-handed when it came to granting concessions to the broader population. They were clearly fascinated by the ability of Hitler and Mussolini in the early thirties to discipline organized labor and to smash trade unions and their political parties, whether social democratic or communist.

However, there was a larger geopolitical motive to their fascist sympathies before the war. They, like their cousins in the British Round Table circles, desired a larger war, a war between their two formidable potential Eurasian rivals for hegemony: Russia and Germany. They wanted a war in which both great powers, Stalin's Soviet Union and Hitler's Third Reich would, as one British insider put it, "bleed each other to death."[13] It had little to do with ideology or romantic illusions about the superiority of the Aryan race, despite the fact that until 1939 the Rockefeller Foundation generously funded eugenics research, including live human experiments in Hitler's Third Reich. Their motivation had everything to do with the building of their American Century on the ashes of Europe, which would require decimating both Germany and the Soviet Union. [14]

In 1941, at the onset of the US entry into the war, Standard Oil of New Jersey, later renamed Exxon, was the largest oil company in the world. It controlled 84% of the US petroleum market. Its bank was Chase Bank, and its controlling ownership was held by the Rockefeller family and their tax-free foundations. After the Rockefellers, the next largest stockholder in Standard Oil was I.G. Farben, the enormous petrochemicals trust of Germany, which at the time was a vital part of the German war industry. The Rockefeller–I.G. Farben relationship went back to 1927, around the same time the Rockefeller Foundation began heavily funding German eugenics research at the Kaiser Wilhelm Institutes. [15]

While Nelson Rockefeller was ostensibly combating Nazi economic interests in Latin America as head of the US Government's CIAA (Coordinator of Inter-American Affairs), the Rockefeller family's Standard Oil, through its Chairman Walter C. Teagle, and President William S. Farish, was arranging to ship vital tetraethyl lead gasoline to the German Luftwaffe. Standard Oil's Teagle, Henry Ford and Royal Dutch Shell's Sir Henry Deterding were all openly pro-Third Reich before the war. [16]

Shortly after Hitler's seizure of power in 1933, Teagle had arranged for the Rockefeller family's personal public relations 'spin doctor' Ivy Lee to supply I.G. Farben and the Nazi government in Berlin with intelligence on the American reaction to German rearmament, the Third Reich's treatment of the church, and the organization of the Gestapo. Lee's task then became to shape a pro-German propaganda campaign within the United States to create sympathy for the Third Reich. Lee was paid in cash through an account at the German-controlled Bank for International Settlements (BIS), an institution that had been set up, ironically, by the Owens Plan in 1930 to administer payment of German war reparations from World War I. At the time of the payments to Ivy Lee, the BIS was headed by an American, Gates W. McGarrah, formerly with Rockefeller's Chase Bank in New York and the Federal Reserve. [17]

The Rockefellers' bank, the Chase Bank, played a vital role in arranging the financing of the Rockefellers' various German enterprises. In 1936, as Hitler was occupying the Rheinland, the Schroeder Bank of New York formed a partnership with the Rockefellers called Schroeder, Rockefeller & Co. Investment Bankers. Time magazine referred to the bank at the time as "the economic booster of the Rome-Berlin Axis." [18]

The notable aspect of their new bank were the partners, which included John D. Rockefeller's nephew Avery Rockefeller to represent the family, Baron Bruno von Schroeder of London, and the Baron's cousin, Baron Kurt von Schroeder, head of J.H. Stein Bank of Cologne and director of the Bank for International Settlements in Basle. J.H. Stein Bank had played a key role in the early financing of Hitler as far back as 1931 and served as Hitler's liaison to German Big Industry, *Die Wirtschaft*, through the *Harzburger Front* of leading figures including Hjalmar Schacht, Fritz Thyssen, *Generaloberst* von Seeckt and numerous others who backed Hitler during the early phase of Germany's economic crisis as the potential savior of their power.[19]

Moreover, the New York attorneys who arranged the legal aspects of the Schroeder, Rockefeller bank were two brothers, John Foster Dulles and Allen Dulles, both partners of Rockefeller's law firm, Sullivan & Cromwell. Allen Dulles sat on the board of the new bank as well. Notably, during the war, Allen Dulles joined the US Office of Strategic Services, predecessor to the CIA, and spent the war running intelligence operations, ostensibly against Nazi Germany from Berne, Switzerland.[20]

The affairs of the Schroeder, Rockefeller bank were handled through the Paris branch of Chase Bank, which remained open for business during the entire war, even when Paris was under Nazi occupation during the Vichy regime. The Paris branch of Chase Bank was the nexus for financial dealings not only with Schroeder in New York, but also with the pro-Nazi French Banque Worms, and the French operations of Rockefeller's Standard Oil. Standard Oil directors in France, meanwhile, sat on the board of the Vichy Banque de Paris et des Pays-Bas, which itself linked various German circles with Chase Bank. [21] During the war, Chase Bank also handled the personal banking affairs of Otto Abetz, German Ambassador to Paris.

Following the Japanese attack on Pearl Harbor in December 1941, all branches of American banks still in Paris closed for reasons of hostilities – with one notable exception: Rockefeller's Chase Bank. It was a close relationship between the Rockefellers and Berlin. [22]

The Rockefeller clan was not alone in secret financial and industrial dealings with the Third Reich. They worked with other leaders of the US power establishment, most notably the DuPont chemicals family and the Bush family through Prescott Bush, father of President George Herbert Walker Bush and grandfather of President George W. Bush.

Duponts and Bushes join 'The Project'

During the German Luftwaffe bombing of London, the British Government protested the shipment to Nazi Germany of Standard Oil's tetraethyl lead, a necessary additive to produce high-octane aviation fuel without which the Luftwaffe planes could not fly over England. Standard Oil, DuPont and General Motors had world patent rights to the ethyl additive and in 1938, Standard Oil's chairman Teagle had arranged during a secret meeting in London with I.G. Farben's chairman Hermann Schmitz to 'lend' tons of their tetraethyl lead to

I.G. Farben. Teagle made a similar arrangement to provide the Japanese Air Force with the same chemical additive.

Also involved in Standard Oil's secret agreements with I.G. Farben during the war was the Delaware-based chemical giant DuPont. Through various petrochemical agreements, Standard Oil had effectively brought DuPont into the Rockefeller orbit of companies, and into the agreement to produce tetraethyl lead for Japanese and German planes, as well as for cars. The resulting Ethyl Company was a joint venture between Standard Oil, General Motors and DuPont.[23]

As early as 1919, DuPont executives had broached a proposal on dyestuffs with Carl Bosch, the inventor of synthetic ammonia and future founder of I.G. Farben. Bosch, who saw little advantage in sharing German expertise with the Americans at that time, had rebuffed this bid.

Undaunted, DuPont persisted in its attempts to acquire German technical know-how after I.G. Farben was created in 1925. The following year DuPont officials signed a secret 'gentlemen's agreement' with two Farben subsidiaries, *Dynamit Aktien Gesellschaft* and *Köln Rottweiler*—both major explosives manufacturers—granting each party a first option on new processes and products, such as black powder and safety fuses.

DuPont invested more than $3 million in the German armaments industry in the 1920s, thereby gaining a large lead over its US competitors. In 1933, with Hitler now in power, DuPont officers agreed to sell the Third Reich "military propellants and military explosives," in violation of the Versailles Treaty and a separate peace treaty between the United States and Germany. This was done despite a warning from a DuPont executive in Germany that it was "common knowledge" that I.G. Farben was bankrolling the Nazis.[24]

Reports of DuPont's secret cartel pacts with I.G. Farben and other European firms were aired in the US Senate's munitions hearings in 1934. A parade of DuPont family executives--Lammot, Felix, Pierre, and Iréné--denied the existence of any such arrangements until documents were introduced in evidence that described a cartel pact on explosives with several German firms.

Despite these embarrassing revelations, DuPont cultivated further ties with I.G. Farben during the Nazi years, making available licenses in acrylates and nitrogenous products, and then, in 1938, giving the German chemical manufacturer important processes necessary for the manufacture of buna rubber, an important, newly developed synthetic substance for making tires – all of which were critical for Hitler's war machine.

The exchanges of strategically important industrial know-how continued, even though they violated US neutrality laws and even though President

Roosevelt was warned about them by his ambassador in Berlin, William Dodd. DuPont continued to negotiate trade agreements with I.G. Farben until 1941, when DuPont's board finally voted to sell its stock in the German firm and "suspend" patent exchanges until "the present emergency has passed." The "present emergency" DuPont referred to was the official US declaration of war against Nazi Germany and the Axis powers. [25]

Rockefeller's Standard Oil, meanwhile, had handed over to the Third Reich the secret of synthetic rubber manufacture, its superior acetylene process and its method for producing synthetic gasoline. The gasoline processes kept the Luftwaffe in the air for two and a half years and enabled Hitler to keep his gigantic motorized army in motion. [26]

Right up until German Panzer tanks rolled into the Low Countries and France, British leaders around Neville Chamberlain and Rockefeller's Wall Street circles believed that the Third Reich would turn east, not west, to secure its Lebensraum. The very purpose of Chamberlain's infamous Munich 'appeasement' diplomacy over German claims to Sudetenland in Czechoslovakia was to entice German Lebensraum expansion eastward in the direction of Stalin's Soviet Union. Chamberlain deliberately encouraged this by showing that Britain had no interest in the Sudetenland.

Chamberlain's geopolitical instructions came from the powerful Round Table faction within the British establishment. The Round Table group of Lord Milner had been the catalyst for the propaganda drive to go to a war against Germany before 1914.

By the late 1930s, the same Round Table that propagandized for a war against the German Reich, also beat the drums for accepting a German remilitarization of the Rhineland. Using their house organ, the London *Times,* and their own magazine, *The Round Table*, the same group called for non-intervention into the Spanish Civil War when Germany backed Franco's forces with arms and logistical support.

In January 1935 Lord Lothian, an outspoken Germano-phobe who later became His Majesty's Ambassador to Washington, met with Hitler. Hitler reportedly proposed to Lothian an alliance between England, Germany and the United States that would give Germany a free hand to march East to Russia. Hitler was said to have promised Lothian in return that he would not make Germany a 'world power' or try to compete with the British Navy's control of the seas. [27]

The only way to make sense of the 180 degree flip-flop of British Round Table policies towards Germany in the different periods, and also that of leading Round Table allies in the Council on Foreign Relations, was to understand British geopolitics.

As Sir Halford Mackinder had stated back in 1919 during the Versailles peace talks, the aim of British Balance of Power geopolitics was to *always ally with the weaker of two Continental Eurasian rivals against the stronger*. At the turn of the Century and up until the outbreak of War in August 1914, France was the weaker of her two Continental rivals, Germany the stronger. During the 1930s up to the invasion by the Wehrmacht of the Low Countries, France was the stronger of two British opponents on the Continent.

Strategic miscalculations occurred on both sides. Hitler and his inner circle failed to appreciate the essence of British geopolitical strategy; at the same time, the British Round Table failed to appreciate how deeply Germany had learned the lesson of the First World War—never again for Germany to fight a war on two fronts— a lesson deeply engrained in the Reichswehr General Staff and Nazi leadership. [28]

Rockefeller Circles don't miscalculate

If the British Round table elites, as well as Hitler, had miscalculated their relative power equations, the emerging power circles around the Rockefeller brothers and their War & Peace Studies group at the Council on Foreign Relations did not. They clearly saw that if England were to emerge in any way intact and the "victory" in the war, then the emerging US hegemony would be blocked perhaps for decades or longer. That was clearly something they wanted to avoid. They also knew that Germany, too, must be eliminated as a postwar contender for hegemony.

One way to do so was to insure that Germany was able to prosecute the war with enough fuel, at least at the beginning. It was not a matter of corporate profit for the Standard Oil group or for Rockefeller banking interests. It was about balance of power calculations and the American establishment's own understanding of the lessons of geopolitics.

Isaiah Bowman of the CFR study group well understood the difficulties, for any European land army, of penetrating the Russian heartland. For Germany and Russia to be "played" against each other in a destructive war of attrition, therefore, the Germany Luftwaffe and tank corps would at least have to be assured of adequate fuel. [29]

As early as 1938, some of these entanglements provoked concern. Not surprisingly, however, when the US Government's Securities & Exchange Commission opened an investigation in February 1938 into the role of Standard Oil in the control of American IG, a joint US venture with I.G. Farben, Teagle lied and denied any knowledge of it. Standard Oil also lied to the Government and claimed it had changed its policy of working with German firms and was no longer doing so.

The change was purely cosmetic. German ships continued to carry oil to Tenerife in the Canary Islands, off the coast of Morocco and Spanish Sahara in Northwest Africa, where they refueled and siphoned oil onto German tankers for shipment to Hamburg. Standard Oil merely altered the registration of its entire fleet from Germany to Panama to avoid British search or seizure on suspicion of trading with the enemy. [30]

I.G. Farben, meanwhile, had kept a toehold in the lucrative US market through its 90 percent ownership of the New York-based firm General Aniline and Film Corporation (GAF). This front company controlled $11.5 million of assets in American firms, including Standard Oil and DuPont.

When this was revealed in the press, it caused a stir in Washington and led to seizure of General Aniline's assets under the Trading with the Enemy Act, and to a 1943 indictment of DuPont, along with two other American companies, for engaging in a worldwide conspiracy to control strategically important metals. DuPont was eventually convicted.

DuPont was brought back into court in January 1944 and charged as a co-conspirator in cartel agreements governing explosives. In Germany, the only individuals who knew about this pact were I.G. Farben's Supervisory Board, three or four top I.G. Directors, and the trusted financial advisor who had helped draw up the agreement, Erwin Respondek. [31]

The outbreak of war between Germany and the United States in December 1941 did not affect this pact. As Respondek explained after the war, I.G. Farben "supplied DuPont with information, in the greatest detail, before the war and during the German-American conflict up until January-February 1945, by means of a secure route through Basel." The confidential papers I.G. Farben sent to DuPont--and received from it--were kept "locked in a special safe, to which no one in the company had access other than three or four special directors." [32]

DuPont and I.G. Farben were heavily involved in extremely sensitive war-related research and development. During the First World War, a German chemist by the name of Walter Heldt had perfected a poison gas known as Zyklon B for use as a delousing agent. Production of this gas was now in the hands of the *Deutsche Gesellschaft fuer Schaedlungs-Bekaempfung* (DEGESCH), or the German Society for Pest Control, which was 42.5 percent controlled by I.G. Farben. When the Nazis began to carry out their 'Final Solution' by setting up gas chambers in 1942, DEGESCH provided the Zyklon B.

In 1942 during the war, US Senator Harry S. Truman charged in a Senate investigation that the Rockefeller-I.G. Farben relationship "was approaching treason."[33] CBS News war correspondent Paul Manning reported that on August 10, 1944, the Rockefeller-I.G. Farben partners moved their "flight capital" through affiliated American, German, French, British and Swiss banks. Under protection from the FDR White House, nothing was done to the Rockefeller and DuPont interests beyond minor fines for their violations of the Trading with the Enemy Act.

Another major player in the Rockefeller and Wall Street backing for the Third Reich and a future war against the Soviet Union was Prescott Bush, father of President George Herbert Walker Bush, and father of George Walker Bush. All three were members of Yale University's secret society, Skull & Bones.

The Bush family had collaborated intimately with the powerful Rockefeller group for decades before World War II. Both families made their money in oil and in war industries.

George H. Walker and Samuel Prescott Bush, the grandfathers of George Herbert Walker Bush, were the dynasty's founders during and after World War I.

Walker, a St. Louis financier, made a fortune in war contracts. In 1919, he was hired by railroad heir W. Averell Harriman to be president of the Wall Street-based W.A. Harriman Co. which invested in oil, shipping, aviation and manganese, partly in Russia and Germany, during the 1920s.

Samuel Bush ran an Ohio weapons manufacturing company, Buckeye Steel Castings. In 1917, Samuel Bush was appointed head of the

Thyssen Funds Found in U.S.

NEW YORK—(INS)—Existence of a $3,000,000 fund established here by Fritz Thyssen, German industrialist and original backer of Adolf Hitler was disclosed today in a news story in the New York Journal American.

The story added:

Whether the money is for Thyssen personally, or, perhaps, for some of his high-placed Nazi friends in the event of an "emergency" compelling them to leave Germany, no one knew.

However, it will do neither Thyssen nor any of his Nazi friends any good now, as it has been "frozen" along with the $4,500,000,000 Axis assets now held in this country.

The money exists in funds of the Union Banking corporation, an investment company incorporated and licensed under New York state laws in August, 1924.

Money for its $400,000 capital stock came from Thyssen's bank Voor Handel En Scheepvaart in Rotterdam.

Among members of its board of directors are E. R. Harriman, Ray Morris and Prescott S. Bush, partners in the firm of Brown Brothers Harriman and company, of which W. Averell Harriman is now American minister plenipotentiary to England.

Also a director is H. D. Pennington, Brown Brothers Harriman and Co. manager.

On Jan. 14, 1941, Knight Wooley, another partner in the Harriman company, wrote to State Banking Superintendent William R. White in behalf of Harriman, Morris, Bush and Pennington:

"Should the United States enter the war, they felt they might be under some embarrassment because of their connection with the bank, even though we have no financial interest in the Union Banking corporation, nor do we participate in its earnings."

In July 1942, US Media reported the wartime scandal of Prescott Bush, Averell Harriman, and others in the Rockefeller circle aiding Thyssen and the German war effort.

ammunition, small arms and ordnance section of the federal War Industries Board of Bernard Baruch.[34] Both George Walker and Sam Bush were deeply invested in the creation of what became the US military-industrial complex.

Prescott Bush made his fortune as director of companies involved in US war production throughout World War II. One Bush company, Dresser Industries of Texas, produced the incendiary bombs dropped on Tokyo and made gaseous diffusion pumps for the atomic bomb project. At the same time, his companies were strategically engaged in secretly arming and financing the Third Reich through German steel magnate, Fritz Thyssen.

The Bush family, in addition to long-standing ties with the influential Harriman banking and railroad fortune, enjoyed intimate links to the Rockefellers and their control of the US oil industry.

Bush family ties to John D. Rockefeller and Standard Oil went back 100 years, when Rockefeller had made Sam Bush's Buckeye Steel Castings fabulously successful by convincing railroads that carried their oil to buy heavy equipment from Buckeye Steel. George H. Walker helped rebuild the Soviet oil industry in the 1920s, and Prescott Bush acquired experience in the international oil business as a director of Dresser Industries in Texas, a part of the Harriman family banking holdings and a company with intimate ties to the Rockefeller oil interests. Dresser later became part of Halliburton Corporation, the firm made infamous through Dick Cheney. [35]

In 1931, as a consequence of the reorganization of power on Wall Street after the 1929 stock crash, the investment bank, W.A. Harriman & Co. merged with the British-American investment house, Brown Brothers, to create the investment bank, Brown Bros. Harriman. The senior partners were Averell Harriman and his brother, and Prescott Bush and Thatcher H. Brown. The London branch operated as Brown, Shipley, the bank where Montagu Norman had been a senior partner before heading the Bank of England. [36]

During the 1920s Harriman had become banker in New York for German steel magnate Fritz Thyssen. In 1934, a year into the Third Reich, Prescott Bush, senior partner at Brown Bros., Harriman, was also a director of the German Steel Trust's Union Banking Corporation. In 1926, Wall Street investment banker Clarence Dillon, a close friend of Prescott Bush, had created the German Steel Trust on behalf of Thyssen, and held two seats on the board of the new steel trust. [37]

The Union Banking Corporation, located at W.A. Harriman & Co and interlocked with Thyssen-owned *Bank voor Handel en Scheepvaart* (BHS) in the Netherlands, was set up as a unit of W.A. Harriman & Co. BHS was used as the vehicle to move money back and forth across the Atlantic between the United

States and Thyssen enterprises in Germany. Meanwhile, Prescott Bush and Averell Harriman, at Brown Bros. Harriman, were the managers for Thyssen's financial operations outside Germany.

In 1942, the US Government's Alien Property Custodian Leo T. Crowley signed Vesting Order Number 248, seizing the property of Prescott Bush under the Trading with the Enemy Act. The order was published in obscure government record books and kept out of the news. It explained only that the Union Banking Corporation was run for the "Thyssen family of Germany and/or Hungary...nationals ... of a designated enemy country." [38]

After the war, US Congressional investigators probed the Thyssen companies, Union Banking Corp. and related Nazi enterprises. They reported that Thyssen's huge German steelworks, *Vereinigte Stahlwerke*, had produced the following shares of total German national output during the Third Reich: 50.8% of pig iron; 41.4% of universal plate; 36.0% of heavy plate; 38.5% of Nazi Germany's galvanized sheet; 45.5% of pipes and tubes; 22.1% of wire; 35.0% of explosives. [39] Their role in producing Hitler's war armaments was enormous.

The deep involvement of the Rockefeller, Harriman and Bush families in providing vital strategic and financial support to Hitler's war buildup was, in the final analysis, an integral part of an even more ambitious agenda. Their aim was not to back a victorious Germany, but to create the global war out of which an American Century, more accurately, a Rockefeller Century, would emerge after 1945.

Bush, Rockefeller, Harriman, DuPont and Dillon were all instrumental in providing critical support to the Third Reich in its early years as part of their grand geopolitical game plan -- to bring the great European powers, especially Germany and Russia, to ruin by 'bleeding each other to death,' thereby opening the door to the hegemony of the American Century. That was the real agenda of Rockefeller's War & Peace Studies.

Pretext for War: FDR's 'Pearl Harbor'

When President Roosevelt won re-election to an unprecedented third term in 1940, he had secretly been preparing for war against Germany for months. Not only did FDR provide aid to Churchill through his Lend-Lease program, in violation of the formal US pledge of neutrality, but FDR also played an active role in shaping the events that led Japan to try to destroy the US Pacific naval fleet at Pearl Harbor in December 1941.

Release of classified Congressional records and other documents after the war and the death of Roosevelt demonstrated beyond doubt that the President and his Secretary of War, Henry Stimson, had deliberately incited the Japanese into war. They did so by embargoing Japanese oil supplies and preparing a US military action against Japanese expansion in the Pacific. The documents show that Roosevelt was fully informed days before the bombing of Pearl Harbor of the exact details of the Japanese naval advance, down to the hour of the planned strike.[40] The documents also show that Roosevelt took steps to provoke Japan's assault.

In 1946, at the end of the War, a Joint Committee on the Investigation of the Pearl Harbor Attack of the US Congress, chaired by Senator Alben Barkley of Kentucky, heard a report from the US Army Pearl Harbor Board. It was classified 'Top Secret' and only decades later declassified.[41] The report was a clear indictment of the Roosevelt Administration, President Roosevelt himself and of War Secretary Stimson.

The Japanese attack on Pearl Harbor was deliberately provoked by FDR in December 1941 to bring America to war not with Japan but with Germany, as documents later revealed.

As early as January 25, 1941, US Admiral James Richardson and Admiral Husband E. Kimmel, in a letter that they jointly prepared and dispatched to the US Chief of Naval Operations, warned of a possible Japanese attack at Pearl

Harbor, almost eleven months before it occurred. The letter stated, "Japan may attack without warning, and these attacks may take any form...Japanese attacks may be expected against shipping, outlying positions, or naval units. Surprise raids on Pearl Harbor, or attempts to block the channel are possible."

The report also noted, as background to the Japanese decision to bomb Pearl Harbor, that Roosevelt had "issued an Executive Order on July 26, 1941, freezing Japanese assets in the United States. This order brought under control of the US Government all financial and import and export trade transactions in which Japanese interests were involved. The effect of the order was to bring to virtual cessation trade between the United States and Japan." [42] In Tokyo it was interpreted as an act of war against Japan.

On July 19, five months before the attack at Pearl Harbor, Admiral Kimmel was advised for his information on the substance of an intercepted Japanese dispatch, decoded by US intelligence under their program code-named "Magic." The intercepted message from Canton to Tokyo read in part:

> *The recent general mobilization order expresses Japan's irrevocable resolution to end Anglo-American assistance in thwarting Japan's natural expansion...Immediate object will be to attempt peaceful French Indochina occupation but will crush resistance if offered and set up martial law...Next on our schedule is sending ultimatum to Netherlands Indies. In the seizing of Singapore the Navy will play the principal part...with submarine fleet in Mandates, Hainan and Indochina we kill, crush British American military power and ability to assist in schemes against us.* [43]

Thus fully five months before the attack on Pearl Harbor, the highest levels of the United States Government knew a war was imminent with Japan, based on US intelligence's top secret Magic intercepts which had broken the Japanese Naval and diplomatic encryption codes. On November 7, a month before the attack, US Pacific Fleet commander in chief, Admiral Kimmel received the following dispatch from Admiral Stark in Washington:

> *Things seem to be moving steadily towards a crisis in the Pacific. Just when it will break, no one can tell. The principle reaction I have to it all is what I have written you before...A month may see, literally, most anything.* [44]

Then, on November 28, 1941, Kimmel got an updated dispatch from Stark in Washington stating in part,

> *[N]egotiations with Japan appear to be terminated to all practical purposes...Japanese future action unpredictable but hostile action possible at any moment. If hostilities cannot repeat not be avoided the United States desires that Japan commit the first overt act.* [45]

After receiving this warning, Admiral Kimmel was ordered by Washington not to institute long-range reconnaissance from Pearl Harbor against possible air attacks.[46] Following instructions from Stimson's War Department, between November 28th and December 5th, Kimmel ordered the two US aircraft carriers, USS Enterprise and USS Lexington, together with six heavy cruisers and fourteen destroyers, to leave Pearl Harbor for Midway and Wake Island -- placing the most modern strategic ships of the Pacific Fleet conveniently far from the site of the Japanese attack on December 7th. Washington deliberately withheld vital intelligence from Kimmel that would have indicated days in advance that the Japanese goal was Pearl Harbor. He was given the distinct impression the likely target would be the Philippines or islands nearby. As the Senate inquiry further noted,

> *Admiral Newton received no information concerning the increasing danger of our relations with Japan. He was given no special orders and regarded his departure from Hawaii as a mission with no special significance other than to proceed to Midway for the purpose of flying off the Lexington a squadron of planes for the reinforcement of the island.*

> *In consequence, no special orders were given for the arming of planes or making preparation for war apart from ordinary routine...no change was made in the condition of readiness in port [Pearl Harbor-w.e.] except that a Coast Guard patrol was started off Pearl Harbor and they began sweeping the harbor channel and approaches... A squadron of patrol planes from Pearl Harbor was ordered to replace the squadron which went from Midway to Wake. This squadron of patrol planes left Pearl Harbor on November 30.* [47]

Thus, the defense of Pearl Harbor was further jeopardized. As the official Senate inquiry then noted, "Nothing was done, however, to detect an approaching, hostile force coming from the north and northwest, recognized as the most dangerous sector, and it is into the justification for this non-action that we shall inquire." [48]

As the inquiry noted, it was Washington's responsibility to give Admiral Kimmel its best estimate of where the enemy's major strategic effort would come from. It was Admiral Kimmel's responsibility as commander in chief of the Pacific Fleet to be prepared for the worst contingency, and "when he was warned of war and ordered to execute a defensive deployment it was necessarily in contemplation that such action would be against all possible dangers with which the Hawaiian situation was fraught." [49]

Deliberate steps had been taken, however, to insure that Pearl Harbor would be defenceless in the event of such a Japanese attack. As the US Army Pearl Harbor Board investigation revealed:

> *The situation on December 7 can be summed up as follows: No distant reconnaissance was being conducted by the Navy; the usual four or five PBY's were out; the anti-aircraft artillery was not out on its usual Sunday maneuvers with the Fleet air arm, the naval carriers with their planes were at a distance from Oahu on that Sunday; the aircraft were on the ground, were parked, both Army and Navy, closely adjacent to one another; the Fleet was in the harbor with the exception of Task Forces 9 and 12, which included some cruisers, destroyers, and the two carriers Lexington and Enterprise.*
>
> *Ammunition for the Army was, with the exception of that near the fixed antiaircraft guns, in ordnance storehouses, and the two combat divisions as well as the anti-aircraft artillery were in their permanent quarters and not in battle positions. Everything was concentrated in close confines by reason of anti-sabotage Alert No. 1. This made of them easy targets for an air attack. In short everything that was done made the situation perfect for an air attack and the Japanese took full advantage of it. [50]*

The attacks on Pearl Harbor and on the US Army Air Force bomber fleet by Japan in 1941 resulted in 2,403 American dead, 1,178 wounded, the loss of 18 battleships and 188 airplanes. As a final warning, on November 26, two weeks before the attack, Roosevelt had been urgently and personally alerted to an imminent attack on Pearl Harbor by none other than Winston Churchill. Roosevelt responded by stripping the fleet at Pearl Harbor of air defenses, a measure bound to insure Japanese success. [51]

Churchill's November 26, 1941 message to Roosevelt is the only document in their correspondence that has to this day never been made public, on grounds of 'national security.' Churchill reportedly explicitly warned FDR of an imminent attack on Pearl Harbor to come on "December 8," the actual date Tokyo time, of the December 7 Japanese attack, according to the memoirs of Churchill's Washington Ambassador, Lord Halifax.

Roosevelt and his advisers thus incited the Japanese attack on the US Naval base at Hawaii in order to mobilize unwitting American citizens into a war to establish the American Century. It was to be the vehicle for actualizing the postwar agenda of the Rockefeller War & Peace Studies plan. Historians, indeed everyone, called it the Second World War.

Washington's 'Black Magic'

As the Senate report detailed, the War and Navy Departments had secretly broken the Japanese diplomatic codes. Through the so-called Magic Project, the exploitation of intercepted and decoded messages between Japan and her diplomatic establishments, a wealth of intelligence was made available to Washington concerning the intentions of the Japanese. Magic intelligence was regarded as pre-eminently confidential and was strictly limited to just a few eyes to safeguard the fact that the codes had been broken.

Roosevelt did not even inform Churchill, whose own intelligence services at Cheltenham had also broken the Japanese codes under its own top-secret project, code-named Ultra. Of course, Churchill likewise chose not to inform Roosevelt of his Ultra secret although, as noted, he apparently did try to warn Roosevelt about the impending attack.

Distribution of the English texts of the intercepted Japanese messages was limited in the US to Secretary of War Stimson, his Chief of Staff, the Chief of the War Plans Division, and the Chief of the Military Intelligence Division; the Secretary of Navy, the Chief of Naval Operations, the Chief of the War Plans Division, and the Director of Naval Intelligence, the State Department, and the President's naval aide who was responsible for direct confidential transmittal to the President. [52]

On December 6, a Magic intercept was translated and sent to the War Department, and to Admiral Breadall, the President's naval aide at the White House, between 9:30 and 10:00 p. m., with orders that the intercept be given to the President at the earliest possible moment. Commander Schulz delivered the message to the President who, along with Harry Hopkins, read its contents.

Delivery was then made to Secretary Knox and to Admiral Wilkinson, both of whom presumably read the dispatch.

The intercept contained a communiqué between Tokyo and the Japanese Ambassador to Washington. It indicated that a dramatic event was to occur at 13:00 Washington time December 7 -- at dawn, Pearl Harbor time. That event was the Japanese bombing of the US naval fleet at Pearl Harbor,.

Admiral Kimmel subsequently testified that,

> *Had I learned these vital facts and the 'ships in harbor' messages on November 28th, it is my present conviction that I would have rejected the Navy Department's suggestion to send carriers to Wake and Midway. I would have ordered the third carrier, the Saratoga, back from the West Coast. I would have gone to sea with the Fleet and endeavored to keep it in an intercepting position at sea. This would have permitted the disposal of the striking power of the Fleet to meet an attack in the Hawaiian area.*[53]

Kimmel instead was made the scapegoat for allowing Pearl Harbor to be attacked and he was forced to resign.

The devastating attack on Pearl Harbor gave Roosevelt the cause to wage the war he so urgently sought. It was the war needed and encouraged by the War & Peace Studies group to create a new American empire, Luce's American Century.

Even after Congress declared war against Germany, Japan, and the Axis powers in December 1941, however, powerful circles within the Roosevelt Administration and around the Rockefeller faction in US industry continued their illegal collusion with leading German military industries, a story of treason that was duly buried in the postwar history accounts.

Simultaneously, in addition to their activities in Germany and Europe during the war, Nelson Rockefeller was to play a strategic role in securing the vast resources and political alliances of Latin America for the emerging American postwar empire.

For the Rockefellers and other forward-looking architects of US policy, global power after World War II would no longer be measured in terms of military control over colonial territories. The British and European style empires had proved far too costly and inefficient. Instead, American power would be defined directly in economic terms. It would be based largely on what one Harvard proponent, Joseph Nye, later called 'soft power.' A soft power backed by the world's most powerful military machine and its dominant financial power. [54]

Rockefellers build a Latin American business empire

As the War drew to an end in 1945, no group epitomized the global outlook of American big business more than the Rockefeller family, whose fortune had been built on a vast global network of oil and banking. The family—above all, brothers Nelson, John D. III, Laurance and David—viewed the victorious end of the War as a golden opportunity to dominate global policies to their advantage as never before.

Precisely what Isaiah Bowman and his War & Peace Studies colleagues in the US establishment had in mind with their notion of an American 'Grand Area' and 'free market' development soon became clear. Nelson Rockefeller, in particular, wasted no time in taking advantage of the new economic possibilities World War II had opened up to his family, particularly for Latin American business development.

During the War itself, Nelson had promoted the vast Rockefeller family interests throughout Latin America, from his position as a senior US Government intelligence analyst -- Coordinator of Inter-American Affairs (CIAA) -- nominally on behalf of the Roosevelt White House. From that strategic position, Nelson could funnel US Government support to Rockefeller family business allies from Brazil to Peru, Mexico, Venezuela and even Argentina. Under the guise of combating Nazi infiltration of the Americas and of promoting 'American democracy,' he was carefully laying the basis for post-war American business expansion, above all that of the Rockefeller interests. [55]

Nelson had been named by President Roosevelt as CIAA director in August 1940, in a clear violation of US official neutrality by engaging in active espionage abroad. To conceal that delicate point, the CIAA was given a cover façade as an organization promoting "American culture" in Latin America.

Nelson Rockefeller's role in Latin America during the War was to coordinate US intelligence and covert operations in the days before the creation of the CIA. He was the direct liaison between President Franklin Roosevelt and British Prime Minister Winston Churchill's personal intelligence head for the Americas, Sir William Stephenson, who directed a front company called British Security Coordination or BSC.

Notably, Stephenson's clandestine headquarters for his covert activity was in room 3603 in Rockefeller Center, in New York City, not far from Nelson's own office. It was no coincidence. Rockefeller and Stephenson coordinated closely on mutual intelligence operations in the Americas, at the same time Rockefeller was organizing to grab the choice British assets in the region. [56]

Rockefeller brought with him to Washington a team he selected from family business connections, including Joseph Rovensky from Chase Bank, and Will Clayton, a Texas cotton magnate from the agricultural commodity firm Anderson Clayton.[57] Nelson's assistant, John McClintock, ran the vast United Fruit plantations across Central America after the war, on whose behalf the CIA later conveniently orchestrated a coup in Guatemala in 1954.

During the war, Nelson Rockefeller's work laid the basis for the family's vast expansion of interests in the 1950s. He shaped a US-Latin American defense concept that was to tie South America's military elite to US policies during the Cold War, often through ruthless military dictators who benefited from the backing of the Rockefeller family and who were assured favorable treatment by Rockefeller business interests. Nelson called the cooperative Latin military dictators he backed, "the New Military." Such politico-military-commercial alliances would become the model for NATO several years later. [58]

Nelson Rockefeller had been a leading figure in US corporate investment in Latin America since the 1930s when he was a director of Standard Oil's Venezuelan subsidiary, Creole Petroleum. In 1938, he had tried, and failed, to negotiate a settlement with Mexico's President Lazaro Cardenas for Standard Oil in Mexico. Cardenas had nationalized Standard Oil, leading to bitter US-Mexico relations.[59]

In the 1940s, Rockefeller had set up the Mexican American Development Corp. and was a personal investor in Mexican industries after the war. He encouraged his brother David to set up Chase Bank's Latin American division. [60]

During the War, as head of Roosevelt's CIAA, Nelson organized a network of journalists and of major newspaper owners throughout the region. He did this by threatening neutral Latin American newspaper publishers with a cut-off of newsprint paper stock from Canada. Soon Rockefeller boasted of controlling 1,200 newspaper publishers by this tactic of threatening their supplies of newsprint paper that had to be carried on US ships.[61] Rockefeller's media staff then saturated Latin America with news stories friendly to US and especially Rockefeller business interests in the region.

During the entire period that Nelson Rockefeller was serving the US Government as coordinator of US intelligence in Latin America, the Rockefeller banking and Standard Oil interests were actively providing vital raw materials and financing to Hitler's Third Reich. Right up to the US declaration of war in December 1941, Standard Oil worked overtime to supply vital oil to the German military. A British blockade along the Atlantic seaboard stopped the illegal Standard oil tankers bound for Europe. At that point, Standard Oil's President, William Farish, arranged to ship the oil to Russia and from there, via Trans

Siberian Railroad, to Berlin and also to French Vichy North Africa, notably Casablanca.[62]

The Rockefeller oil from their South American oil fields was supplemented by an agreement between I.G. Farben and Standard Oil through which Standard leased its oilfields in Rumania to the German I.G. Farben industrial trust.

For its part, I.G. Farben financed the creation of General Ian Antonescu's Rumanian Iron Guard to police the oil pipelines. As noted above, to assure delivery of Rockefeller's South American oil to the Axis powers -- including Mussolini's Italy – and to avoid being seized, Standard Oil changed the registration of its tankers from Germany to Panama. To top it off, Standard's Farish won an official promise of "immunity from seizure" from US Navy Under-Secretary James Forrestal, a Rockefeller insider. Forrestal, it turns out, also sat on the board of Standard Oil-I.G. Farben, General Analine and Film, as Vice President. [63]

The oil shipments to Axis powers via Rockefeller outposts in Brazil, as well as Tenerife in the Canary Islands, continued illegally, even after Pearl Harbor, despite Farish's assurances to the agencies of the US Government that he had stopped them. Farish at the time also sat on the US Government's War Petroleum Board.[64]

While the Rockefeller group actively secured its own private, postwar Latin American *Lebensraum* through the actions of Nelson Rockefeller's CIAA, the Rockefellers' German industry partners were busy with their own version of an economic *Lebensraum*.

Endnotes:

[1] Neil Smith, *American Empire: Roosevelt's Geographer and the Prelude to Globalization* (Berkeley: University of California Press, 2003), pp. 325-326.

[2] Peter Grose, *Continuing the Inquiry: The Council on Foreign Relations from 1921 to 1996* (New York: Council on Foreign Relations Press, 1996), pp. 23-26.

[3] Ibid., pp. 25-26.

[4] New York Council on Foreign Relations, *Memo from the Council on Foreign Relations to the US State Department*, War & Peace Studies, 1941, accessed in www.worldproutassembly.org/archives/2008/11/the_nature_of_e.html.

[5] Isaiah Bowman, cited in Michio Kaku and Daniel Axelrod *To Win a Nuclear War: The Pentagon's Secret War Plans* (Boston: South end Press, 1987), pp. 63, 64.

[6] Neil Smith, op. cit.

[7] Hamilton Fish Armstrong, quoted in Laurence H. Shoup, William Minter, *Imperial Brain Trust: The Council on Foreign Relations and United States Foreign Policy*, (New York, Monthly Review Press, 1977), p. 137.

[8] Henry Luce, *The American Century*, Life, February 17, 1941.

[9] Ibid.

[10] Handbook, The New York Council on Foreign Relations, *Studies of American Interests in the War and the Peace*, New York, 1939-1942, cited in Neil Smith, op. cit., pp. 325-328.

[11] Neil Smith, *op. cit.*, p. 287.

[12] Ibid., pp. 374-375.

[13] Sir David Stirling, founder of the British elite force, SAS, in private remarks cited in F. William Engdahl, *A Century of War*, op. cit., pp. 80-84.

[14] F. William Engdahl, *Seeds of Destruction: The Hidden Agenda of Genetic Manipulation*, Montreal, Global Research Publishing, 2007, pp. 74-84.

[15] Charles Higham, *Trading with the Enemy: An Exposé of the Nazi-American Money Plot, 1933-1947* (New York: Delacorte, 1983), pp. 53-54.

[16] On March 25, 1942, US Assistant Attorney General Thurman Arnold announced that William Stamps Farish of Standard Oil had pleaded 'no contest' to charges of criminal conspiracy with the Nazis. When George H.W. Bush was elected US Vice President in 1980, Bush's personal wealth was put into a 'blind trust' administered by William Stamps Farish III, grandson of the Standard Oil chief. As President, Bush named old family friend, Douglas Dillon of Dillon Read as his Treasury Secretary.

[17] Charles Higham, op. cit., pp. 53-55.

[18] Ibid., p. 43.

[19] James E. & Suzanne Pool, *Hitlers Wegbereiter zur Macht* (Bern: Scherz Verlag, 1979), pp. 250-252.

[20] Ibid,, p. 43.

[21] Ibid.

[22] Ibid., pp. 46-47.

[23] John K. Winkler, *The DuPont Dynasty*, Kessinger Publishing, 2005, pp. 275-277.

[24] John V. H. Dippel, *Two against Hitler: Stealing the Nazis' Best-Kept Secrets* (New York: Praeger Publishers, 1992), pp. 80-86.

[25] Ibid., p. 86.

[26] Charles Higham, op. cit., p. 55. See also, Art Preis, *America's Sixty Families and the Nazis: The Role of the US-Nazi Cartel Agreements*, Fourth International, Vol.3 No.6, June 1942, pp.165-170.

[27] Carroll Quigley, *The Anglo-American Establishment: From Rhodes to Cliveden* (New York: Books in Focus, 1981), pp. 270-271.

[28] A. L. Rowse, *Appeasement: A Study in Political Decline* (New York: W.W. Norton & Co., 1961), pp. 30-75. Significant is the documentation that the very same members of the British Round Table circle around Lord Lothian, wartime Ambassador to Washington, who in 1914 led the drum roll for a war against Germany, in 1938 were doing the same to back German military acquisitions. Both were merely part of a larger geopolitics of destroying Continental rivals. The Rockefeller group in the United States coordinated closely with the Round Table for their own purposes. See also, Carroll Quigley, op. cit., pp. 628-629 for a discussion of the strategic considerations of Chamberlain at Munich in 1938 to appease in order to fuel the German 'Drive to the East.'

[29] Neil Smith, op. cit., p. 420.

[30] Charles Higham, op. cit., pp. 56-57.

[31] Ibid., p.85.

[32] Ibid., pp.85-86.

[33] Ibid., pp. 67-69.

[34] Kevin Phillips, *Bush Family Values: War, Wealth, Oil*, February 8, 2004, The Los Angeles Times.

[35] Ibid.

[36] Sir Henry Clay, *Lord Norman* (London: MacMillan & Co., 1957), pp. 18, 57, 70-71.

* [37] Robert Sobel, *The Life and Times of Dillon Read* (New York: Dutton-Penguin, 1991), pp. 92-111.

[38] Office of Alien Property Custodian, Vesting Order Number 248. Signed by Leo T. Crowley, Alien Property Custodian, executed October 20, 1942; F.R. Doc. 42-11568; Filed, November 6, 1942. 7 Fed. Reg. 9097 (November 7, 1942). The *New York City Directory of Directors* 1930s-40s, lists Prescott Bush

as a director of Union Banking Corp. from 1934 through 1943.

[39] United States Senate, *Elimination of German Resources for War,'* Hearings Before a Subcommittee of the Committee on Military Affairs, 79th Congress; Part 5, Testimony of Treasury Department, July 2, 1945. Page 507; The Thyssen organization, including Union Banking Corporation, detailed in pp. 727-731.

[40] Robert B. Stinnett, *Day of Deceit: The Truth about FDR and Pearl Harbor* (New York: The Free Press, 2000), pp. 301-307, Stinnett reproduces a declassified document, dated March 5, 1941, from Admiral Thomas Hart, commander-in-chief of the US Asiatic Fleet disclosing that the British unit in Singapore had broken the Japanese code. The message was deleted from the record and not made available to Congress in the investigations of 1945 or 1995. The note states that the US code breaking solution would be delivered to Manila on March 26, 1941 - that is, nine months before the attack on Pearl Harbor. There were only thirty-six Americans cleared to read these Top Secret Japanese diplomatic and military intercepts. The list began with President Roosevelt.

[41] Alben W. Barkley, Senator, et al, *Investigation of the Pearl Harbor Attack,* Report of the Joint Committee on the Investigation of the Pearl Harbor Attack, 79th Congress, 2nd Session, US Senate, Document No. 244, US Government Printing Office, July, 1946.

[42] Ibid., p. 19.

[43] Ibid., pp. 92-93.

[44] Ibid.

[45] Ibid., p. 97.

[46] Ibid., p. 105.

[47] Ibid, p. 105-106.

[48] Ibid. p. 107.

[49] Ibid., p.108, 114.

[50] Ibid., p. 75, footnote 3.

[51] Ibid., pp. 75-79.

[52] Ibid, pp. 179-180.

[53] Ibid. p. 232.

[54] Joseph S. Nye Jr, *Propaganda Isn't the Way: Soft Power,* The International Herald Tribune, January 10, 2003. Nye defines what he coined as 'soft power': "Soft power is the ability to get what you want by attracting and persuading others to adopt your goals. It differs from hard power, the ability to use the carrots and sticks of economic and military might to make others follow your will. Both hard and soft powers are important...but attraction is much cheaper than coercion, and an asset that needs to be nourished."

[55] Kramer, Paul, *Nelson Rockefeller and British Security Coordination*, Journal of Contemporary History, Vol. 16, 1981, pp. 77-81.

[56] William Stevenson, *A Man Called Intrepid* (New York: Ballantine Books, 1976), pp. 308-311.

[57] Gerard Colby and Charlotte Dennett, *Thy Will Be Done: The Conquest of the Amazon-Nelson Rockefeller and Evangelism in the Age of Oil* (New York: HarperCollins, 1995), pp. 115-116.

[58] Thomas O'Brien, *Making the Americas: U.S. Business People and Latin Americans from the Age of Revolutions to the Era of Globalization,* History Compass 2, LA 067, 2004, pp. 14-15.

[59] Gerard Colby, op. cit., p.116.

[60] Los Angeles Times, *Mexico 75 Years Later, Today's Zapatistas Still Fight the Rockefeller Legacy,* May 14, 1995.

[61] William Stevenson, op. cit., p. 309.

[62] Charles Higham, op. cit., pp.58-59.

[63] Ibid.

[64] Ibid., pp.67-69.

CHAPTER EIGHT

War and Conflicting Geopolitical Agendas

'Who rules East Europe commands the Heartland; who rules the Heartland commands the World Island; who rules the World Island commands the entire World.'
  – Sir Halford Mackinder, in 1919 [1]

Ignored lessons of British geopolitics

The policy makers from the Council on Foreign Relations (CFR) and the internationalists around the Rockefeller group engaged in seemingly paradoxical and contradictory policies. They were simultaneously financing and staffing the CFR War & Peace Studies—intended to be a detailed blueprint for a postwar US global domination, an American Century—while at the same time they were going to extraordinary lengths supporting the Third Reich's war buildup, accruing huge profits from the sales to their 'enemy' that soared far beyond anything normal. It appeared that Rockefellers' Standard Oil and allied companies like Dow Chemical and DuPont went to extraordinary lengths to support Hitler's war machine.

The resolution to the paradox lay in appreciating American geopolitical strategy as formulated by people like Isaiah Bowman of the CFR and Yale University's geopolitical strategist, Nicholas Spykman. They had developed a uniquely American synthesis of Halford Mackinder's British geopolitics – identifying the most vital, 'pivotal' nations needed for the support of an American postwar global domination, an American Empire.

For the influential US elites grouped around the CFR, war was merely an instrument through which to extend their financial power in the postwar world and create an American imperium, one displacing not only the British Empire, but also the German Reich and any other potential European competitor. They understood quite well, as Yale's Spykman put it, that wars enabled the conquering and subjugating of new markets, and that what the world called 'peace' was but a 'temporary armistice' or ceasefire in the continual war process, until prospects for looting a given area had reached relative limits and a new war of conquest became necessary.[2]

In 1938, with great geopolitical prescience, Spykman wrote,

> *Unless the dreams of European Confederation should materialize, it may well be that fifty years from now the quadrumvirate of world powers will be China, India, the United States and the USSR.* [3]

That was how Spykman, Bowman and others around the Rockefeller dynasty understood international politics. The minutes of the CFR War & Peace Studies' Security Sub-Committee of the Advisory Committee of the Post-War Foreign Policy set the likely parameters of US post-war foreign policy long before the US formally entered the war: "...the British Empire as it existed in the past will ever reappear and...the United States may have to take its place... The US must cultivate a mental view toward world settlement after this war which will enable us to impose our own terms , amounting... to Pax Americana." [4] *Time's* Henry Luce would call it the American Century.

In many ways, the influential British Round Table circles failed to appreciate German fundamental geopolitical requirements, but the Germans as well, particularly Hitler, appeared to misunderstand fundamental British geopolitics.

Contradictory geopolitical strategies

The tragedy that became World War II was a titanic clash of mutually contradictory geopolitical strategies for world domination.

The British had their traditional geopolitical strategy of dividing Continental Europe and of controlling the seas. Churchill's unprecedented decision to ally with the United States, the stronger of its major adversaries, against Germany, the weaker adversary, was based on a calculation that such an alliance was the only possible means of preserving the British Empire as a dominant global power.

It marked the first time in the history of British Balance of Power diplomacy that she had sought an alliance with the stronger foe against the weaker. It was also fraught with risk. Churchill and his allies in and around the Round Table were, however, realists. They realized the Empire as such was at an end and that it could project its power only indirectly through a 'special relationship' with Washington.

The emerging 'special relationship' between Churchill and Roosevelt how-ever, was made more complicated by the fact that the United States could emerge as the dominant global power.

American leading circles around the Rockefellers and Wall Street had re-solved among themselves that *all* potential European rivals for power would have to grind themselves down in a mutual slaughter. The goal of these Ameri-can elites was to eliminate, above all, the prospect of a German Reich that would fill the power vacuum in Central Europe left by the collapse of France and its allies.

In Washington FDR carried on a secret correspondence with Churchill well before US entry into the war in December 1941. Churchill, for his part, being a shrewd champion of British Imperial interests, tried to play on his American ties to the President to gain as much as possible for England in the run up to open warfare on the Continent.

The internal opposition to Hitler within German big industry and finance, as well as leading circles in the military high command, had their own geopo-litical agenda -- an *economic* imperialism rather than a military imperialism. They had their eyes on a 'penetration pacifique' to the east of Europe, *Drang nach Osten*, including at a certain point even the possibility of a peaceful alliance with the Soviet Union. Hitler, on the other hand, had a geopolitical strategy of *Lebensraum* that called for brutal military subjugation of the Slavs, rather than big industry's attempt to gain the same territory through economic means instead of through war.[5] The end game for both factions within the Third Reich was in effect the same—German domination of Eurasia, her *Lebensraum*.

The United States meanwhile developed its future war strategy within the internationalist circles around FDR, Rockefeller, Prescott Bush and the Council on Foreign Relations. Their geopolitical agenda, quite separate from Great Britain's, was to 'support' and use Hitler in order to destroy Germany once and for all, eliminating the potential of a resurgent German challenge to their version of an 'American *Lebensraum*.'

The goal of these circles in the United States was to realize a global Ameri-can supremacy built on the war-ravaged ashes of Germany, of Britain and of Stalin's Russia. The Rockefellers and their crowd were no more 'pro-German' than they were 'pro-British.'

They were pro-American Century, and above all, pro-Rockefeller in an al-most monarchical sense.

They formed tactical alliances with Nazi Germany one moment, and with Russia and Britain the next. These were simply matters of expediency—tactics in pursuit of their strategic end goal: global American hegemony, their American Manifest Destiny, their *Lebensraum* or Grand Area.

Hitler's military 'mistake'

Fritz Hesse, Ribbentrop's expert adviser on England within the German Foreign Office, believed that Hitler's principal strategic military flaw was his fatal miscalculation of British geopolitical axioms. Hesse was in an unusually good position to understand British elite thinking as well as German. He had lived in England for years and served as press attache at the German Embassy in London from 1935-39. After 1939 he was called to become a special adviser on British affairs at Hitler's headquarters until the end of the war.

Hesse wrote in his memoirs after the war that Hitler had failed to realize why Churchill refused even to consider a deal with Germany over dividing the world, even at a time when the survival of Great Britain itself did not appear all that certain. The kind of 'deal' Hitler had written about years earlier in *Mein Kampf* [6] would allow both empires—the British and German—to divide up the world, without America.

What Hitler and his inner circle apparently did not grasp was the fact that no matter who ruled Germany, once Germany threatened to dominate the Eurasian land area, she would pose an ultimate threat to British supremacy and from Britain's perspective, therefore, would have to be ultimately crushed.

Hitler's decision in May 1940 to order a three-day cease fire just as his *Wehrmacht* had boldly and brilliantly driven British, Canadian, Polish and French allied forces to the sea at Dunkirk in France, astonished Hitler's military command every bit as much as it did Churchill. [7] The reason was simple, according to Hesse: Hitler wanted to give the British the chance to cut a deal before the German war machine launched its fateful war against the Soviet Union. It was an ill-conceived attempt to try to avoid another devastating two-front war as in 1914.

In an extraordinary gesture towards England, Hitler allowed the escape of 338,000 allied troops over the Channel to England. That "miracle of Dunkirk" as British propaganda dubbed it for the British population, was in reality no miracle.

Equally naive as geopolitical strategists, however, were Hitler's high-level German internal opposition circles. Fritz Hesse was an intimate of most of the leading anti-Hitler factions as they turned to him to facilitate their own contacts in England.

Hesse realized that Hitler's opposition within the German establishment—inside the German Foreign Ministry, the *Wehrmacht* General Staff, and leaders of German banking and industry—were unwilling to grasp the importance of British geopolitical axioms. [8] The British could not accept any strong, economically dynamic Germany, least of all one whose leadership appeared to be more "respectable" to the world at large than Hitler. Their failure to realize that simple fact doomed the efforts of those forces within Germany to execute a coup against Hitler. They assumed their efforts would be supported from England. The opposite was the case.

Chamberlain's time is over

British Prime Minister Neville Chamberlain's infamous Munich 'appeasement' agreement in September 1938 was a last calculated attempt by England to entice Germany eastwards rather than westwards. The Four Power conference in Munich—with Hitler of Germany, Chamberlain of Britain, Daladier of France and Mussolini of Italy—was ostensibly to decide the fate of Sudetenland, a region bordering Germany and containing a large German-speaking population. Sudetenland was then part of Czechoslovakia and Hitler threatened to annex it by force. The talks in Munich excluded both Czechoslovakia and the Soviet Union, therefore making an 'agreement' possible.

Chamberlain and France's Edouard Daladier agreed that Germany could have the Sudetenland. In return, Hitler promised not to make any further territorial demands in Europe, signing the infamous Munich Agreement that transferred the Sudetenland to Germany.

When Eduard Benes, Czechoslovakia's head of state, protested the decision, Chamberlain told him that Britain would be unwilling to go to war over the issue of the Sudetenland.

The Munich Agreement was popular in Britain because it appeared to have prevented a war with Germany.

Then in March 1939, the German *Wehrmacht*, its Army, took the rest of Czechoslovakia by point of bayonet. At that point, at the highest level, British policy shifted swiftly from appeasant to preparation for a war against Germany, with Churchill as 'anti-German' Prime Minister, a man chosen partly for his ability to cultivate his American ties.

As Churchill took residence at Ten Downing Street in May 1940, the German *Wehrmacht* had already occupied Poland, the greatest part of Czechoslovakia, Austria, Denmark, Norway, Belgium, Holland, Luxembourg, and most of France.

Hitler was in a strategic military alliance with Italy. He had cooperative relations with Franco's neutral Spain.

In addition, Germany soon had a strategic agreement with Stalin's Soviet Union on the division of the rest of Continental Europe, the Molotov-Ribbentrop Non-Aggression Pact of August 1939—the so-called Hitler-Stalin Pact. That left Germany's eastern flank protected, at least for the time being, to free the *Wehrmacht* forces to launch an attack on Great Britain. The German General Staff was determined never again to face a two-front war as it had in 1914.

From Hitler's perspective, his pact with Stalin was a cynical matter of buying time before his ultimate final military assault on the Soviet Union. For Stalin, it was an equally cynical and pragmatic pact to buy time to rearm and prepare Russia for that looming conflict. For Britain, it was a geopolitical setback, however temporary.

England found herself completely isolated and cut off from any Continental allies who might have been able to do the bulk of the fighting against a German foe. There was no candidate to do battle in alliance with Britain, such as France had done during the Great War in 1914. Churchill also knew that the United States was far from ready to commit its young men to die for yet another European war.

Why, then, did Winston Churchill, when he came to power as British Prime Minister in May 1940, do nothing to support the German anti-Hitler opposition? Churchill had been, after all, the most outspoken opponent in Britain of Chamberlain's appeasement policy. Such support from Britain's new Prime Minister to the nascent Hitler opposition at that early stage of the war in Europe could have decisively weakened, if not entirely defused, Hitler's military threat to Western Europe, and most directly to England herself by engulfing the German Reich in damaging internal power struggles.

Churchill knew very well the importance of the German opposition. Even before he had come into Chamberlain's War Government in September 1939 as First Lord of the Admiralty, Churchill had been aware of the seriousness and the extent of the high-level forces inside Germany trying to avoid a new war. Had Churchill aggressively and secretly attempted to support the Hitler opposition either covertly or otherwise, he might have seriously weakened the inevitable assault on England. In fact, the opposite was Churchill's policy.

Churchill had met the most senior representatives within the elite ranks of that Hitler opposition, including Ewalt von Kleist-Schmenzin, the Pomeranian *Junker* aristocrat who was cousin and collaborator of General Erwin von Kleist.

Churchill had invited von Kleist to his Chartwell estate south of London as early as the summer of 1938 to discuss the German situation. One year later, in

August 1939, on the eve of Hitler's invasion of Poland, Churchill also had held a meeting in London, arranged by the head of German Military Counter-intelligence, Admiral Wilhelm Canaris, with von Kleist's close friend in the Hitler opposition, Fabian von Schlabrendorff. Churchill knew just how senior and how influential the institutional opposition to Hitler was. [9]

Churchill's cold calculation

Why the British Prime Minister refused to support or even to encourage that anti-Hitler opposition was one of the major paradoxes of the war.

It was a paradox only for those ignorant of the axioms of British geopolitics. Chamberlain and Churchill agreed on the most fundamental strategic point: British geopolitical interests were threatened as much, if not more, by Hitler's opposition within the German military, the civil service bureaucracy, and industry, as they were from Hitler himself. That was simply because a Germany under an opposition government would have averted a destructive war and emerged as the dominant economic power on the European Continent as Churchill reasoned.

As German Foreign Minister Ribbentrop's British advisor, Fritz Hesse had argued, so long as Germany threatened to dominate the Eurasian landmass, Germany remained the prime strategic opponent for British geopolitics. Preventing such a Eurasian domination by any Continental power, whether achieved through military or economic means, had been basic British geopoliti-cal balance of power doctrine since well before the time of Sir Halford Mackind-er's 1904 elaboration of his "Heartland" thesis.[10]

As Churchill and the British High Command saw it, the German opposi-tion within the *Wehrmacht* and within big industry-- such as Krupp, Thyssen, and the German banks led by Deutsche Bank -- represented for England merely a softer version of the same geopolitical reality: a German domination of the Central European *Lebensraum* through their economic 'penetration pacifique.'

From the perspective of British circles around Churchill, a 'good Germany' dominating the Eurasian economic space was far more a threat to British imperial power than a Nazi Germany. British geopolitics was never sentimental. As Lord Palmerston had declared a century or so earlier in a debate in the British Parliament, "We have no eternal allies, and we have no perpetual enemies. Our interests are eternal and perpetual, and those interests it is our duty to follow. Britain has no friends, only interests." [11]

The German Foreign Ministry's Fritz Hesse was familiar with Mackinder's geopolitical ideas and even cited Mackinder to back his argument. He had understood the driving motives of both Anglo-Saxon and American geopolitics as outlined by Mackinder.

Hesse noted that the utter lack of such understanding by the Continental European powers, above all by Germany, over the previous century had caused wars by miscalculation. The fact was that neither Britain, nor later America, would allow *any* European Continental power to dominate the Eurasian Continent. Full stop.

As Mackinder had put it in his 1919 essay,

> *Who rules East Europe commands the Heartland; who rules the Heartland commands the World Island; who rules the world island commands the entire world.* [12]

British policy—to prevent a German domination of the Eurasian Heartland landmass via its construction of the Baghdad-Berlin rail link with Ottoman Turkey—dictated its precipitating the European Great War in August 1914. In 1939, the same policy, outlined in Mackinder's geopolitical axioms, guided England's fateful decision to go to war against Hitler's Germany.

Third Reich's Grossraum Mitteleuropa

The pivotal figures of the later Hitler opposition came from the highest ranks of the same conservative families and institutions that had offered Hitler the Chancellery in January 1933. They had backed Hitler at that time as the only figure able to realize their own agenda for recovering or rolling back the losses of Versailles, and establishing Germany at the heart of their planned New European Order.

Everything in Germany's foreign, military and economic policy since Versailles had been oriented to the goal of a revived German power. After 1930, the strategy for achieving this goal centered on establishing hegemony in *Mitteleuropa*—Central Europe -- from Poland and Czechoslovakia to Romania, Bulgaria, the Balkans, Greece, and Turkey.

Following their devastating 1918 defeat in the First World War, leading circles of Germany—the high-level *Reichswehr* military command, influential *Junker* agrarian nobility of the large Prussian landed estates, influential mandarins of the German *Beamtentum* or civil service, and key industry and banking leaders—indeed, all major pillars of Germany's permanent institutional power, had reached a consensus on a long-term, secret strategy. They were determined to regain Germany's destined role as an economic and political Great Power in world affairs.

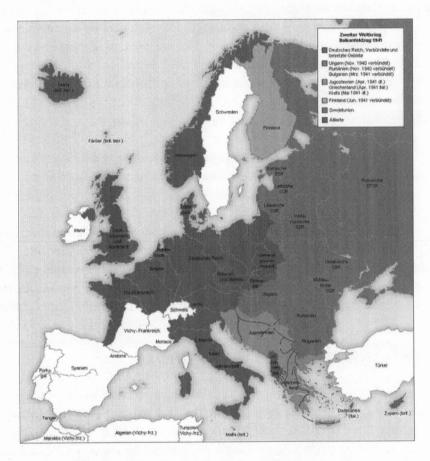

For British Geopolitics a German dominated Mitteleuropa
was intolerable, regardless of who was Chancellor.

Reichspresident von Hindenburg had summed it up in remarks to an audience of German youth at one point during the 1920s: "*Was deutsch war, muss wieder deutsch werden*" – "What was German once, must again be German."

MWT and 'Penetration Pacifique'

Carl Duisberg of I.G. Farben, the chemicals cartel that enjoyed strategic agreements with Rockefeller's Standard Oil, as well as DuPont and other leading US companies, had outlined the German industry elites' strategic economic aims in 1931, two years before Hitler took office.

Duisberg had declared that Germany must create, "a closed, self-contained economic bloc from Bordeaux to Odessa, as the backbone of Europe." He spoke not only as head of the I.G. Farben chemicals trust, but also as chairman of the powerful *Reichsverband der Deutschen Industrie* (Imperial Association of German Industry).

Duisberg's economic bloc from Bordeaux to Odessa would be a German-dominated region straddling the heart of Europe, or what the Hitler Nazi Party propaganda called German *Lebensraum*. Such an economic domain was indispensable if Germany were to be able to launch a competitive challenge to the other rival world powers, most especially to Britain, France, and, ultimately, to the most formidable rival economic power in the world, the United States of America.

To create that *Mitteleuropa* economic domain to Germany's east and southeast, leading industry figures used the little-known private lobby organization known as the MWT, *Mitteleuropaeischen Wirtschaftstag* or Central European Economic Council, noted earlier. The financial backers of MWT included the largest German industrial groups. In addition to Krupp and the steel cartel, it included Duisberg's I.G. Farben, as well as the Ruhr coal mining syndicate, the potash cartel, the large East Prussian Junker agriculture interests, the German Machinery Building Association, and the powerful RDI, the Imperial Association of German Industry. Dresdner Bank board director Carl Goetz and Deutsche Bank's Hermann Abs also played prominent roles in the MWT.

Through the MWT, Krupp, I.G. Farben and others played a commanding role in the buildup of the war economy, especially after 1934.[13] Their secret agreements with Rockefellers' Standard Oil, Chase Bank, DuPont and other major US industries were intended to allow Germany to produce its own synthetic rubber and synthetic gasoline for the coming war. "Economic autarky," as it was called, was vital to their plans.

I.G. Farben and the Third Reich would spend staggering sums for the construction of the special *Leunawerk* facility, at the time Europe's largest chemical facility, to produce the synthetic gasoline. [14]

During the Nazi years of the 1930s Hjalmar Schacht worked closely with the MWT when Schacht was Economics Minister and Reichsbank President, to advance the economic expansion agenda of the MWT. It was a well-oiled machine they had constructed.

In October 1932, months before Hitler took the Chancellor's office, the MWT, in a project developed with the Foreign Ministry and the *Reichswehr*, had organized a secret mission to Rome to meet Italian fascist dictator Benito

Mussolini. The purpose of the visit was to present Mussolini a confidential Memorandum proposing a joint German-Italian carving up of *Mitteleuropa,* all of Central Europe, via economic penetration.

The unofficial MWT Memorandum outlined an Italian sphere of economic interest in Southeast Europe, ceding to Mussolini a major part of Rumania, as well as Serbia, Bulgaria, Albania and Greece. Germany would take Poland and Czechoslovakia as her principle sphere of interest, as well as re-establishing and expanding the 1931 Customs Union with Austria, which Austria had been forced to annul under enormous French pressure. That would give Germany direct access to the Hungarian economy. [15]

The MWT plan proposed that Hungary, Croatia-Slovenia and the Transylvanian part of Rumania would enter into preferential tariff and trade agreements with Germany and Italy. Yugoslavia would be dismembered with the help of German and Italian money, with Slovenia and Croatia going to Germany's economic domain, and Serbia to Mussolini.

In its internal discussions, the MWT was clear that the proposed German-Italian division of *Mitteleuropa* would later be entirely German-dominated. The economically and militarily weaker Italians were to be gradually pushed into the background by more adroit German firms as the MWT industry barons envisioned it.

German industry seduces France

The division proposed to Mussolini was naturally a direct challenge to France, which had supported what was called the 'Little Entente' alliance of Czechoslovakia, Yugoslavia and Rumania, as part of France's continuing attempt to contain any and all German expansionist threats.

An internal memo from the MWT representative of Deutsche Bank in the early 1930s stated that the goal of the MWT was, "to develop and nurture the relationship to the Donau countries; to disrupt the dependence of each country with France; to create cooperative relations with Germany through practical, purely economic definition of their problems." The memo stressed that all this would only be possible if Germany gained political as well as economic influence over the space of *Mitteleuropa.* [16]

Since 1921 France, acting through the League of Nations, had built up the dominant financial and economic ties with Czechoslovakia, Rumania and Yugoslavia, through credits and financial flows organized by the large French steel industry's *Banque de l'Union Parisienne.* [17]

The economic goal of the MWT in the early 1930's was to entice the Balkans and neighboring countries of Central Europe into full economic dependence on Germany.

Within Germany, MWT policy had the politically important backing in the *Reichstag* or Parliament of the large *Junker* landowners whose interests would be protected with high import tariffs on grain, part of the quid pro quo for their political backing of MWT's *Mitteleuropa* industrial project.[18] Under the MWT plan, German small family farmers would be sacrificed in return for a protective tariff and subsidy to the large grain-producing *Junker* nobility.

By 1935, Krupp and I.G. Farben were able to buy a controlling majority of stock in select copper, zinc and bauxite mines in Yugoslavia, their purchases hidden via a Belgian shell company. The *Reichswehr* also asked I.G. Farben to establish large agriculture enterprises in Rumania, Bulgaria and Hungary, to make Germany essentially self sufficient in the important animal feed grains in the event of a future war.

I.G. Farben was also commissioned to work with Dresdner Bank to secure the large oil fields of Rumania, then being operated by Rockefeller's Standard Oil. These fields were essential for a future Germany at war, as she was completely dependent on oil imports. [19]

At the same time as German trade began displacing existing French trade relations in Eastern Europe, the Ruhr steel and coal cartel interests of the MWT pursued a policy of 'reasonableness' with the French iron and steel industry, which culminated in a politically significant series of trade agreements.

Most notable was a July 1937 Franco-German treaty, signed by Schacht as Economics Minister on behalf of the Third Reich, in which German coking coal would become the major source of coal for the French steel industry. In return, the French cartel of steel companies (*Comite des Forges*) agreed to export French iron ore to German steel companies, in effect binding the fate of French heavy industry to the German.

The *Comite des Forges* became the center of a powerful pro-German industrial faction inside France, increasingly isolating the anti-Hitler *Paribas* industrial group which had argued instead for closer ties with the Soviet Union in an effort to contain Germany. Andre Francois-Poncet, France's Ambassador to Berlin until 1938, had personal ties to the French steel industry. He openly represented the interests of the *Comite des Forges* in seeking closer economic cooperation with German steel. For that reason, Francois-Poncet was known in Berlin as Hitler's favorite ambassador.

Further cartel price-fixing agreements between the French and German steel industries helped to stabilize the French steel industry during the world economic depression. Similar agreements between I.G. Farben and French chemical companies were also concluded and later expanded.

Earlier, in September 1931, French Prime Minister Pierre Laval and his business partner, chemical industrialist Albert Buisson, had been invited to Berlin where they negotiated a cartel agreement with I.G. Farben. They also established a *Comite Franco-Allemand*, an alliance of leading French and German industrialists, to encourage French investment in German industry in return for German patent rights.

Thus, step-by-step during the critical pre-war period of 1936-1939, French heavy industry had been enmeshed in a policy of economic collaboration with their German industry counterparts. And step-by-step, a powerful axis of pro-German sentiment and shared interests built up within French industrial groups during the late 1930s.

By early 1939, in the wake of the Munich appeasement talks, French Foreign Minister Georges Bonnet, supported by France's biggest industries, had consolidated this process into an official foreign policy of industrial cooperation with Germany, replacing the prior policy of military containment. The large French industrial groups owned four large Paris dailies and heavily financed ten more, giving them significant power in shaping public opinion in favor of their pro-German economic strategy. [20]

In all important respects, after 1936, the French arm of the MWT and Karl Duisberg's 'economic space' in Central Europe were advancing to fruition just as hoped. Indeed, France's extensive industrial agreements with German industry during the late 1930s played a decisive role in building a large appeasement faction inside France around Laval and Petain, which resisted any "fight to the bitter end" with Germany in May 1940.

The only component of Duisberg and Krupp's 'peaceful penetration' strategy that was not making progress was with Stalin's Soviet Union. In the mid-1930s, Stalin regarded Nazi Germany as the Soviet Union's major strategic threat.

Stalin, as it turned out, was justified in his view. Despite the MWT and its 'peaceful penetration' policy, the German Reich had secretly been preparing since 1935 for the necessity of taking the Soviet Union by war. [21]

A Eurasian economic space

Despite impressive progress on most major fronts, the largest obstacle to the MWT's consolidation of its strategy for peaceful economic penetration in eastern and southeastern Europe was increasingly centered on one man, *Der*

Fuehrer. Hitler, whom big industry and finance had initially backed and put into the Chancellery to realize their agenda of restoring or rolling back the losses of Versailles, had become obsessed with a war to the death to destroy Bolshevism and the "inferior Slavic race," as he had stated more than a decade before in *Mein Kampf.*

As early as October 1935, months before German troops had marched into the Rhineland, Hitler had convened his so-called inner cabinet to discuss preparations needed for launching a war against the Soviet Union by the Spring of 1939. This was a full year earlier than his February 1934 timetable, which had called for a Russian war by 1940.

Present at that October 1935 meeting and at subsequent planning sessions, in addition to Hitler, were Hitler's deputy, Rudolf Hess; Admiral Erich Raeder of the Navy; Minister of War General Werner von Blomberg; Hermann Goering for the Air Force; Konstantin von Neurath as Foreign Minister; Count Schwerin von Krosigk as Finance Minister; and Hjalmar Schacht in his new dual role not only as Reichsbank President, but also as Reich Economics Minister.

In Cabinet discussions, Schacht argued for the agenda of banking and large industry, as embodied in the MWT policy of peaceful penetration. Arguing forcefully against a direct military occupation of central and Eastern Europe, Schacht tried to convince Hitler of Germany's lack of in-depth economic preparation for what would become a full-scale war, a war likely involving France and the Entente powers against Germany. Chief of the General Staff General Ludwig Beck also argued that the military lacked in-depth readiness for war.

Schacht fought against Goering's, and ultimately, Hitler's demands for huge deficit financing of military spending, insisting it threatened new inflation and would destabilize the entire economy.

Above all, as Schacht and his industry backers at the MWT knew, the best prospect for their strategy of economic domination of Central Europe and other eastern lands of Continental Europe lay in Germany's pursuing Carl Duisberg's original strategy of a *penetration pacifique* -- economic domination of neighboring lands, without a forced military occupation of the conquered territories.

When Hitler demanded in November 1935 that Germany prepare to launch full-scale war against Russia by 1939, Beck and his General Staff, in concert with the MWT circles of industry, drew up a list of four essential preconditions for the success of such a war. [22]

The prerequisite was that Germany must first have established a firm economic domination of the *Mitteleuropa* region. That, they argued, must be done not through military conquest and occupation, which would overextend the

Wehrmacht. Rather it must be accomplished through economic, political and other controls, which would guarantee the raw materials, agriculture products, energy, transport, post and administrative infrastructure necessary to support a major war with the Soviet Union. In effect, they demanded that their MWT *Mitteleuropa* agenda be made Third Reich State policy. Krupp, I.G. Farben and the steel cartel stood behind the General Staff on that crucial point.

The second pre-condition of the General Staff was that the Polish military, if it were to be used as a future German ally against Russia, must be brought up to German battle standards and discipline. This, they suggested, should be done through a Polish-German Mutual Defense Treaty, something previously proposed by Germany in late 1934 and rejected by Poland.

The third condition was that Hitler create a mutual alliance with Japan against Russia, in which Japan would agree simultaneously to invade Siberia in Russia's Far East, as German forces struck at Russia's western borders.

Finally, the General Staff demanded assurance of England's strict neutrality in any such German strike eastwards in order to avoid a repeat of a catastrophic two-front war as in 1914.

The demands were carefully formulated in order to try to preserve the core strategy of the MWT, while Beck, Schacht and others tried to steer Hitler into a course of gaining his demands on Austria, Sudetenland, and later Poland by threat of military force, but short of actual war.

By late 1936, Hitler had appointed Hermann Goering to administer the new Four-Year Plan that aimed to prepare Germany for war by building economic self-sufficiency or autarky in fuels, rubber and other necessities.

An unexpected geopolitical shift

After Hitler lost patience with Polish Foreign Minister Josef Beck, he had decided to accept Stalin's shrewd proposal for a Soviet-German dismemberment of Poland. On August 23 1939 in Moscow the Molotov-Ribbentrop Non-Aggression Pact was signed, resulting in the military occupation and dismemberment of Poland.

The German military non-aggression pact with the Soviet Union was accompanied by a far-reaching German-Soviet Trade and Credit Agreement that gave the USSR an immediate credit line to purchase up to 200 million *Reichsmarks* of industrial goods from Germany in return for vital oil and industrial raw materials from Russia.

The Agreement explicitly mandated "construction of factories, delivery of every kind of machine and machine tool, equipment for building a naptha industry, essential for high octane gasoline, and a Soviet chemicals industry, equipment for an electro-technical industry, ships, vehicles, transport equipment, measuring instruments, laboratory equipment...." The 200 million Reichsmark credit for the initial Russian purchases of German industrial equipment would come from the *Deutsche Golddiskontbank*, 'Dego.'

The trade and credit agreement with Stalin opened Germany's prospects, at least theoretically, for a far-reaching German economic *penetration pacifique* of the vast Soviet Union itself. Baron von Weizsaecker's Foreign Ministry was jubilant about the economic accords with Moscow. In a memorandum for Ribbentrop, Hitler and the cabinet, he wrote,

> *Both countries will economically enrich themselves in a most natural way: The Soviet Union, the land of inexhaustible riches of raw materials, the land of great, long-term investment planning, which into the far-distant future, has need of the highest quality manufactured goods. Germany, the country with the most specialized and highest quality industry, which is able, in respect to the current partly developed state of industrialization of the Soviet Union, to deliver the required factories and equipment to their industrial sector. Germany is as well capable, without limits, to deliver this Soviet production...* [23]

Germany's goal of economic domination of the vast Eurasian landmass appeared suddenly within reach by the summer of 1940. That was not what London desired and it most certainly was not what the emerging power constellation around FDR and the Rockefeller interests in America's Establishment desired.

"Neue Ordnung" in Europe

Under the Hitler-Stalin pact, Russia was becoming the raw materials supplier and industrial export outlet for the German economy. The MWT was working with Hermann Abs at Deutsche Bank to develop the blueprint for Hitler's proposed *Neue Ordnung*, a New Order in Europe—a German-dominated Europe from Bordeaux to Odessa, and perhaps well beyond.

On July 25, 1940, Schacht's successor at the Economics Ministry, Walther Funk, announced Hitler's "New Order for Europe," promising an end to economic crises, unemployment and social chaos for the countries now within the sphere of Hitler's Germany. The promise was a calculated contrast to the economic chaos and depression of liberal economic orthodoxy.

In 1941 on the eve of the invasion of Russia, Goering appointed Karl Blessing to join Funk, Hermann Abs of Deutsche Bank and I.G. Farben's Carl Krauch, on the board of the state-controlled *Kontinentale Oel*, one of the companies secretly working with Rockefeller's Standard Oil through front companies to secure vital petroleum supplies for Germany's military effort, especially in Rumania. [24]

Hitler's *Neue Ordnung* was intended to be a single European economic sphere, a European unified market. Economic relations between Germany and the nations of Eastern Europe, as well as the parts of Western Europe under the hegemony of Hitler's Reich, were to be fixed in national currencies that would in turn be pegged to the Reichsmark, much like America's postwar Bretton Woods system and the dollar.

Berlin was to become the financial center of the New European Order. Eventually all national exchange rates of New Europe were to be fixed to the Reichsmark, and maintained through rigid price controls by the various governments. Gold was to be rejected in favor of the peg to the Reichsmark – similar to the role of the US dollar after leaving the gold exchange standard in August 1971.

In explaining the currency system for the New European Order, Funk declared:

> *We shall never pursue a currency policy which makes us in any way dependent on gold, because we cannot tie ourselves to a medium of exchange, the value of which we are not in a position to determine.* [25]

Ultimately, the idea envisioned a four-power pact among Germany, Mussolini's Italy, Japan and Russia that would establish joint economic control over the entire Eurasian landmass stretching between the Atlantic and Pacific Oceans.

Such a consolidated concentration of power over Eurasia was precisely what Mackinder had warned British elites to prevent at all costs, and precisely what their American cousins in and around the Rockefellers' Council on Foreign Relations would not allow. British secret intelligence services, as well as British diplomacy, began an intensive courtship of Stalin in hopes of winning him away from the pact with Hitler. The efforts had nothing to do with pro-Soviet sentiments; Churchill by personal disposition was more at home with the Germans. It had to do with calculations of British Balance of Power. Britain would seek a deal with the weaker of its two foes, Russia, and try to use her against the stronger. It came to be called World War II.

Central to the New European Order was the role of the Third Reich's large Berlin banks, most of all Deutsche Bank and Dresdner Bank. Within the directorate of Deutsche Bank, Germany's most powerful bank, Hermann Abs was the person responsible for all foreign banking matters. Abs had joined the management board of Deutsche Bank in 1937, recommended by fellow banker, Economics Minister Schacht.

Under the New European Order, the German banking model—direct ownership of key industry groups—was to be exported to the occupied parts of the New Europe, especially in the east. Deutsche Bank gained control of a major part of occupied Czechoslovakian banking by its purchase of the *Boehmische Union-Bank*, and of Austrian banking and industry through takeover of the large Vienna *Creditanstalt-Bankverein*. Dresdner Bank took over the *Laenderbank Wien* in Vienna, and the important *Boehmische Escompte Bank* in Prague.

German banks' control of the largest Austrian and Czechoslovakian banks greatly boosted the MWT strategy of economic development of trade with Southeastern Europe. Through Creditanstalt, Deutsche Bank extended its banking interests into the former Habsburg Empire—Zagreb, Budapest, Lvov and Belgrade. Through control of the Prague banks, German banks controlled or gained valuable footholds in Bratislava, Belgrade, Sofia and Bucharest. The banks in those countries—Yugoslavia, Hungary, Czechoslovakia, Bulgaria, Rumania and Poland---controlled the most important agriculture and industrial firms of those regions. Explaining the German policy of banking consolidation in the east, the Reich Economics Ministry declared it was, "necessary in order to secure the sources of the raw materials so essential for our economic welfare." [26]

Operation Barbarossa begins

The expansive economic development of the Reich's big banks, major industry and the MWT in building the New Order for Europe began to run amok after November 12, 1940 when Soviet Foreign Minister V.M. Molotov visited Berlin. Molotov angrily confronted Hitler with allegations of German violations of the Molotov-Ribbentrop agreements of 1939, notably in Finland and Rumania.

In October, only days before Molotov's trip to Berlin, Rumanian dictator Ion Antonescu had allowed the German Wehrmacht to occupy his country to secure the invaluable strategic oil resources of the Ploesti complex for the Third Reich war machine. That did not go down well with Stalin who saw it as a direct threat.

At the Berlin talks with Hitler, Molotov forcefully restated Soviet demands on Finland and on the Balkans, with emphasis on Rumania, as a Soviet sphere of interest. In addition, Stalin demanded control of the Dardanelles, a move that threatened Germany's alliance with Mussolini's Italy.

Shortly after that confrontation with Molotov, Hitler resolved to exclude the Soviet Union from a planned Four-Power Pact with Italy and Japan. On December 18, 1940 Hitler ordered his military High Command to prepare for a full-scale war of destruction against the Soviet Union, under the code-name *Operation Barbarossa*, reviving the plans of 1935. [27]

FDR's geopolitical game

At that point Roosevelt and the circles around Rockefeller's War & Peace Studies at the Council on Foreign Relations were certain that they would emerge the victors in the most costly war in history. They began a careful propaganda campaign to prepare public opinion to come into a war against Hitler's Germany. The reason for the US entering the European war, at least from the perspective of Rockefellers and their allies on Wall Street and in big industry, had nothing to do with Hitler's policies of "final solution" against Jews or other atrocities of the Third Reich.

Rather, the growing propaganda campaign to win American hearts to another war in Europe had to do with the need to destroy the most serious rival to a postwar American Century—the German Reich.

The US plan, as Stalin feared, was to delay launching the Anglo-American Second Front against Hitler long enough to let Russia and Germany bleed each other to death. *Operation Barbarossa* lasted from June through the brutally cold winter of December 1941. It involved the deployment of over 4.5 million German and Axis troops in the invasion of the Soviet Union. *Barbarossa* was the largest military operation in human history in terms of manpower, area traversed and human casualties.

At that juncture, the entire strategy and influence of von Wilmowsky's MWT collapsed. Their network within the industries and institutions of the Third Reich redefined their activities in what came to be known after the war as *Der Widerstand,* or The Resistance.

The curious ebbs and flows of their active opposition to Hitler's war agenda after 1939 – including the attempt on Hitler of July 20, 1944 by Colonel Claus von Stauffenberg --could be understood perhaps only from the perspective of the parallel ebbs and flows of the Middle European and Eurasian agenda of the German financial and industrial circles around Schacht, Krupp, General Thomas and von Wilmowsky's *Mitteleuropaeische Wirtschaftstag*.

As England's Prime Minister Churchill saw it, through the ice cold lens of British geopolitics, the Resistance to Hitler inside Germany was Churchill's more dangerous German opponent.

Churchill had been reading an inside account of the MWT's agenda of economic imperialism written by Alfred Sohn-Rethel, who had left Germany in 1936 as the Gestapo became suspicious of his activities. From exile in France, Sohn-Rethel wrote detailed accounts of his experiences in the middle of the German industrialists at the MWT and he sent his writings to Wickham Steed, the influential Foreign Editor of the Round Table-owned London *Times* and an intimate friend of Winston Churchill.[28]

By September 1945, the Tripartite Axis powers—Germany, Japan and Italy—had all been defeated. The cost of that victory in human terms had been staggering. The war had involved the mobilization of over 100 million military personnel, making it the most widespread war in history. In a state of 'total war,' the major belligerents had placed their entire economic, industrial, and scientific capabilities at the service of the war effort, blurring the distinction between civilian and military resources. Over 70 million people, the majority of them civilians, had been killed, making it the deadliest conflict in human history.

At war's end, the United States of America, its landmass and infrastructure intact, stood as the unchallenged global power. Its industry had been upgraded with the most advanced technology then available, with taxpayer dollars, for the wartime production of planes, tanks, munitions, bombs and other explosives.

Roosevelt's New Deal and its vast public infrastructure projects—from the Hoover and Colorado dams to the Tennessee Valley Authority—provided abundant, cheap electricity to American aluminum and munitions factories and other war plants. Its chemical companies -- from DuPont to Dow Chemical and Hercules Powder -- had grown into giant multinational corporations. And out of it all, one group had managed to emerge at the pinnacle of American power: by 1945, the four Rockefeller brothers were standing at the heart of an emerging global colossus called the American Century.

America's wealthiest and most powerful circles around the Council on Foreign Relations and Wall Street had created their new global "Open Door" or, in the words of the CFR's Isaiah Bowman, "America's Grand Area." They were now ready to march through, victorious in a complex geopolitical play that had successfully shaped the American Century of Rockefeller and friends, and their vast industrial allies.

Cynically, the same industrialists and CFR policy makers who had secretly been active in aiding the war preparations of the Third Reich became, after the war, America's leading proponents of 'spreading democracy' and 'the American free enterprise system' around the world. It was nothing personal, merely business as usual for them. It was the birth of the American Century.

Endnotes:

[1] Halford J. Mackinder, *Democratic Ideals and Reality*, 1919, Henry Holt & Co., p. 150.

[2] Nicholas J. Spykman, *Geography and Foreign Policy: I*, The American Political Science Review, Vol. XXXII, No. 1, February, 1938, pp. 28-50.

[3] Ibid., p. 39.

[4] Quoted in Michio Kaku and Daniel Axelrod, *To Win a Nuclear War: The Pentagon's Secret War Plans*, (South end Press, Boston, 1987) p.p. 63,64

[5] Alfred Sohn-Rethel, *Industrie und Nationalsozialismus: Aufzeichnungen aus dem 'Mitteleuropaeischen Wirtschaftstag* (Berlin: Verlag Klaus Wagenbach, 1992), pp. 102-110.

[6] Adolf Hitler, *Mein Kampf*, New York, Reynal & Hitchcock, 1941 (original German 1923), pp. 182-183. In the 1923 writing from his prison cell, Hitler stated "If one wanted land and soil in Europe, then by and large this could only have been done at Russia's expense, and then the New Reich would again have to start marching along the road of the knights of the orders of former times to give, with the help of the German sword, the soil to the plow and the daily bread to the nation. For such a policy however, there was only one single ally in Europe: England."

[7] B. H. Liddel Hart, *History of the Second World War* (New York: G.P. Putnam, 1970), p. 46.

[8] Fritz Hesse, *Das Spiel um Deutschland* (Munich: Paul List Verlag, 1953), p. 240. In a footnote referencing Mackinder's 1919 work, Hesse noted, "The pre-existing conception of the British and the Americans I find especially clear in the book of Sir Halford Mackinder, *Democratic Ideals and Reality* (1919). Its lessons about the Heartland as well as the lessons of Admiral Mahan have led to a complete misunderstanding on the part of the Continental Powers, without which one cannot understand the political strategy of the English or the Americans. It was for these reasons that the Anglo-Saxons for reasons of her own security must destroy Germany." (fn., p. 240.)

[9] The discussions between German opposition leaders and Churchill are documented, among other places in Schlabrendorff, Fabian von, *The Secret War Against Hitler* (Boulder: Westview Press, 1994).

[10] Ibid. p. 240.

[11] Henry Temple, 3rd Viscount Palmerston, Speech to the House of Commons, Hansard (1 March 1848).

[12] Fritz Hesse, op. cit.

[13] Ibid., p. 105.

[14] Ibid., pp. 86-87.

[15] Ibid., pp. 69-70.

[16] The Deutsche Bank memo on the aims of MWT can be found in ZStA, Potsdam, Deutsche Bank AG, nr. 21 838, Bl.131. (cf. *DDR Lexikon zur Parteigeschichte*, Band 3, p. 370, Leipzig 1985).

[17] Alfred Sohn-Rethel, op. cit., p. 81-82.

[18] The 'feudalization of industry' in late 19th Century Germany has been described in Helmut Boehme, *Deutschlands Weg zur Grossmacht* (Cologne: Kiepenhheuer & Witsch, 1972). See also, Otto-Ernst Schueddekopf, *Die deutsche Innenpolitik im letzten Jahrhundert und der konservative Gedanke* (Braunschweig: Verlag Albert Limbach, 1951); and Klaus Epstein, *Vom Kaiserreich zum Dritten Reich* (Berlin: Ullstein Verlag, 1972). A detailed account of the Junker-industry symbiosis at the turn of the Century is found in Kurt Gossweiler, *Grossbanken, Industriemonopole, Staat* (Berlin: Deutscher Verlag der Wissenschaft, 1971).

[19] Ibid., p. 105.

[20] The role of major German industry and banking circles of the *Langnamverein* and *Reichsverband der Deutschen Industrie*, through the *Mitteleuropaeische Wirtschaftstag* (MWT) is found in the memoirs of MWT former director, the Krupp representative, Tilo Freiherr von Wilmowsky, *Rueckblickend moechte ich sagen...* (Oldenburg: Gerhard Stalling Verlag, 1961). See also, a useful account by one who worked with von Wilmowsky and Fritz Hesse in the Deutschen Orient-Verein within the MWT is Alfred Sohn-Rethel, *Industrie und Nationalsozialismus: Aufzeichnungen aus dem 'Mitteleuropaeischen Wirtschaftstag* (Berlin: Verlag Klaus Wagenbach, 1992). A published doctoral dissertation by Axel Schildt, *Militaerdiktatur mit Massenbasis?: Die Querfrontkonzeption der Reichswehrfuehrung um General von Schleicher am Ende der Weimarer Republik* (Frankfurt am Main: Campus Verlag, 1981), also has details on the relation of the MWT industry group in the end of the 1920's and early 1930's. John R. Gillingham, *Industry & Politics in the Third Reich* (New York: Columbia University Press, 1985), details the role of the Ruhr coal and steel industry and the agreements with French industry. A declassified US Government document, *Report on the Banque Nationale pour le Commerce et l'Industrie: Laval's Bank* by Alexander Sacks, Antitrust Division, Department of Justice, 225 Broadway, New York to Fowler Hamilton, Esq., Chief, Enemy Branch, OEWA, Board of Economic Warfare, Washington, D.C., dated April 21, 1943, contains the details of the role of Laval and Albert Buisson of Rhone-Poulenc in 1931 with I.G. Farben and German industry.

[21] Alfred Sohn-Rethel, *Industrie und Nationalsozialismus: Aufzeichnungen aus dem 'Mitteleuropaeischen Wirtschaftstag* (Berlin: Verlag Klaus Wagenbach, 1992), pp. 103-110.

[22] Ibid.

[23] The German Foreign Office memorandum of 20 August 1939 is reproduced in full in Hass, Gerhard, *23.August 1939: Der Hitler-Stalin Pakt, Dokumentation* (Berlin: Dietz Verlag, 1990).

[24] Peter Hampe and Albrecht Ritschl, *Neue Ergebnisse zum NS-Aufschwung: Jahrbuch für Wirtschaftsgeschichte*, Akademie Verlag, 2003, p. 196.

[25] Walther Funk, cited in Patricia Harvey, "*The Economic Structure of Hitler's Europe: The Planning of the New Order in 1940*," in Royal Institute of International Affairs' Survey of International Affairs: 1939-1946: Hitler's Europe, Oxford, 1954.

[26] Cited in Board of Governors of the Federal Reserve Internal Memorandum, *German Banking Penetration in Continental Europe* (Washington: September 1944).

[27] Text of the Credit Agreement between German Reich and Soviet Union dated 19 August 1939 can be found in *Akten zur Deutschen Auswaertigen Politik 1918-1945, aus dem Archiv des deutschen Auswaertigen Amtes* (Baden-Baden: Imprimerie Nationale, 1956). The German Foreign Office memorandum of 20 August 1939 is reproduced in full in Hass, Gerhard, *23.August 1939: Der Hitler-Stalin Pakt, Dokumentation* (Berlin: Dietz Verlag, 1990).

On the role of Hermann Abs' Deutsche Bank and other large Berlin banks in extending German influence into the Balkans and Eastern Europe in the period after 1936, a declassified internal Memorandum to the Board of Governors of the Federal Reserve System, Washington, *German Banking Penetration in Continental Europe* (Washington: September 1944), has valuable details, especially regarding the importance of Deutsche Bank acquisitions in Czechoslovakia and Austria after 1938. Patricia Harvey, op.cit. provides details of the Funk speeches on the New Order. Lothar Gall, et al, "Die Deutsche Bank: 1870-1995" (Munich: Verlag C.H. Beck, 1995) details Abs' central role in trying to create the economic and banking framework for *Die Neue Ordnung* after 1940. The fateful November 1940 clash between Molotov and Hitler is detailed in many sources, though a useful eyewitness account is that of the Third Reich Finance Minister, von Krosigk, Lutz Graf Schwerin, *Memoiren*, (Stuttgart: Seewald Verlag, 1977)

[28] Alfred Sohn-Rethel, op. cit., p. 23.

CHAPTER NINE

The End of Pax Britannica

'Tyrannies may require a large amount of living space; but Freedom requires and will require far greater living space than Tyranny.'
 – Henry Luce on the American Century, 1941 [1]

Putting the British Empire in her place

One of the most significant outcomes of the Second World War was the relative demise of the political power that had dominated the world for 150 years—The British Empire. Viewed in larger geopolitical terms, the two world wars from 1914 through 1945 could best be understood in the words of one British geopolitical historian as, "contests for the British succession between Germany and the USA. This contest was not decided until the end of the Second World War and the unconditional surrender of Germany." [2]

The US establishment and its Washington representatives lost no time in implementing America's imperial succession. Even before war's end, Washington made clear to Churchill that there would be no respect for traditional spheres of influence in the postwar world, specifically no more British domination of Middle East oil politics, no sharing of atomic bomb secrets, and no more unfettered Lend-Lease aid to Britain. In fact, as soon as he became President, Harry Truman drove a severe bargain in return for postwar US financial aid to its former ally.

During the 1930s, the British had created its own economic bloc, the Sterling Area, along with a system of trade called Imperial Preference that favored the nations of the British Empire. London's Sterling Area--its colonies and Commonwealth member countries, including Canada, Australia and South Africa--had been created after Britain abandoned gold in 1931 and it had shielded the British economy from the worst extremes of economic depression.[3] Churchill did not intend to surrender that protection after the war. He forced Roosevelt to water down the Atlantic Charter's 'free access' clause before agreeing to it.

From Washington's perspective, however, Imperial Preference and the Sterling Area were crass British efforts to shut out US goods. For their part, the powers of Wall Street and corporate America were determined to force open access to the protected British Empire in the postwar world of Bretton Woods. The combined value of British and US trade was well over half of all the world's trade in goods. Quite simply, for Washington to 'open' global markets would mean busting up the British Sterling Preference Area, by hook or by crook. The increasingly powerful members of the Council on Foreign Relations and their backers in Washington intended the postwar world to be the American Century, just as the previous era had been a British Century, a Pax Britannica. [4]

The Sun rises on the American Century...

American petroleum interests emerged from the Second World War vastly more powerful than before the war. A major factor was that its British and French oil rivals had been devastated and strategically weakened through the war. Washington did not hesitate to take advantage of their weakness.

After the war, Rockefeller's corporate and banking interests were positioned to dominate the energy supplies of their new American imperium. Their hand-picked War & Peace Studies people were effectively running US State Department policy. Meanwhile David Rockefeller's Chase Bank—which had continued to operate in Nazi-occupied Paris throughout the pro-German Vichy regime—had managed the funds and financial transactions of I.G. Farben and other Third Reich clients throughout the war. Nelson Rockefeller was firmly in control of Franklin Delano Roosevelt's Latin American 'Good Neighbor' policy, a reworked version of the Monroe Doctrine extending US influence over the Americas, opening vast new markets for Rockefeller-dominated oil companies, mining companies and other interests.

Augmenting this already formidable and unprecedented monopoly, President Roosevelt granted one more favor to the emerging Rockefeller imperium—exclusive rights for Rockefeller oil companies to the staggering oil treasures of the Kingdom of Saudi Arabia. It was to prove a fateful act that would determine the course of US Middle East policy over the next several decades.

In 1941 when the United States Government was still officially neutral, Congress had passed the Lend-Lease Act. Under its terms, US aid was to be given to countries whose fate the President felt was vital to US defense -- for the sake of 'national security' Despite the fact that Saudi Arabia in 1943 was in no way immediately vital to US national security, the rules were bent to grease the path for the Rockefeller oil majors to take over the vast untapped oil riches of the desert Kingdom.

Harold L. Ickes was the go-between. Ickes was another member of FDR's inner circle who was also intimate friends of the Rockefeller family. Since the 1930s Ickes had been a frequent guest at the private Rockefeller family compound at Pocantico Hills in New York State, a privilege accorded to very few.[5]

Ickes was FDR's Secretary of the Interior for thirteen years and from 1941, he was Petroleum Coordinator for National Defense. (He also served the President as powerful head of the New Deal's Public Works Administration, directing billions of taxpayer dollars to private industry during the depression.)

Rockefeller's Standard Oil group and their Saudi Arabian-based ARAMCO oil corporation, through the intervention of Ickes, convinced Roosevelt in 1943 to agree to give generous US Lend-Lease aid to Saudi Arabia, which would involve the US government there for the first time.

The arrangement would create a US Government shield for the private interests of ARAMCO, the Arabian-American Oil Company, a consortium of the major Rockefeller oil companies, led by Standard Oil of California (Chevron), which had been struggling since the early 1930s to get control of the Saudi oil riches. [6]

In December 1942 the US State Department wrote in a memorandum to the White House, "It is our strong belief that the development of Saudi Arabian petroleum resources should be viewed in the light of the broad national interest."[7] The "national interest" in this case had been defined for FDR by the Rockefellers and their man Ickes—getting an exclusive US mandate to exploit Saudi oil riches, and shutting out their British rivals.

In February 1943, when he announced wartime special Lend-Lease aid to the Saudi Kingdom, FDR proclaimed Saudi Arabia as "vital to the defense of the United States." How that was the case, he did not bother to explain. Lend-Lease aid was the foot in the door for ARAMCO to grab exclusive Saudi oil rights.

London was furious with Roosevelt's decision to pour millions of dollars of US aid into the Saudi Kingdom, but Britain was financially helpless to enter a bidding war with their Washington ally. Britain's economy was itself dependent on US emergency Lend-Lease aid. [8]

The US State Department had come late to Saudi Arabia. London had long since taken for granted that the Saudi region was part of Britain's control of the Middle East, ever since the days of World War I and the exploits of British intelligence agent T.E. Lawrence, 'Lawrence of Arabia.' It was not until 1942 that Washington opened even a small legation, not yet even an embassy, in Riyadh.

On his return from the Three Powers Yalta Conference in 1945, FDR had arranged a secret meeting with Saudi King Abdul Aziz aboard the President's ship.

When the destroyer USS Murphy pulled into the Saudi port of Jeddah in February 1945, it was the first time a US ship had ever docked in the Kingdom. Abdul Aziz and his entourage boarded and sailed to the Great Bitter Lake in the Suez Canal, where the King transferred to the USS Quincy to meet the President of the United States on February 14. It was Abdul Aziz's first meeting with a foreign leader. [9]

During their discussion, Roosevelt was careful not to smoke or drink in the presence of the Saudi monarch, in order not to offend the King's strict religious sensibilities.

During their talk, the King expressed his concerns about the prospect of a large influx of European Jewish refugees into Palestine, then a British League of Nations mandate territory. FDR promised that he would do nothing to assist the Jews against the Arabs and would make no move hostile to the Arab people.

Abdul Aziz reportedly left the talks with FDR delighted at the "understanding" the American President showed for the Arab point of view on the Palestine question. FDR had also sealed their "friendship" by giving the Saudi King a duplicate of Roosevelt's own wheelchair and a DC3 aircraft as gifts. The King was reportedly delighted. [10]

Three days later, Churchill, furious at FDR's secret Saudi diplomacy, requested a similar meeting with the King. The British Prime Minister, a legendary drinker and cigar smoker, told His Excellency before their talks that in Churchill's world it was considered a "sacred rite" to smoke and to drink alcohol. The King was apparently not amused. Churchill refused to make any concessions to the Arab views on Palestine, and in response to luxurious jewel-studded gifts from the King, Churchill sent him an inexpensive box of herbal scents.

On April 5, 1945 Roosevelt formalized his pledge to the Saudi King in a letter, stating that the promises had been issued in FDR's "capacity as Chief of the Executive Branch of this Government." [11] He had secured for the US companies of ARAMCO exclusive rights to exploit Saudi oil riches.

One week later Roosevelt was dead.

Josef Stalin, who loathed Churchill, wrote a confidential letter to Eleanor Roosevelt, FDR's widow, offering to send Stalin's personal doctor to conduct an independent autopsy, informing the First Lady of his conviction that Churchill had had FDR poisoned. She declined the offer.

FDR had lived just long enough to secure the greatest prize for the Rockefeller global oil imperium—exclusive rights for their ARAMCO partners to all of Saudi Arabia's oil riches. That prize would define US foreign policy into the next century. It was the first time American national security had been officially linked with the fate of the desert kingdom on the Persian Gulf. It would not be the last time US 'national interests' would be linked to Middle East oil supplies.

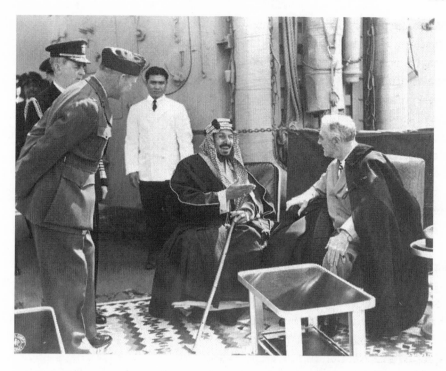

In 1945 just before his death, FDR managed to woo Saudi Arabia's King Abdul Aziz (Ibn Saud) and his oil away from the British.

The move to incorporate Saudi oil riches into the official spectrum of America's national interests in the 1940s was all the more remarkable since the United States at the time was entirely self-sufficient in oil and required no imports. When the world's largest oilfield was discovered at Ghawar in Saudi Arabia in 1948, it added a major lever to America's oil supremacy over the world economy.

Oil was becoming the essential energy resource, the basis of postwar global economic growth. The US Rockefeller oil majors would hold a tight grip on that power in the new postwar world of the American Century.

...and the Sun sets on the British Empire

Six years of a world war spanning the entire globe had left more than 55 million dead in its wake by 1945. No power had lost more of its citizens than Stalin's Soviet Union, where at least 26 million had perished.

Washington was well aware who had lost what. However, the prime concern in Washington D.C. was who had won -- i.e., how to manage the emerging

American hegemony. In 1945 the United States political establishment, under the banner of 'freedom' and 'democracy,' 'colonial liberation' and 'American free enterprise,' was poised to dominate world events to a degree that not even the British Empire had been able to do.

Following the Versailles Peace Conference of 1919, the British Empire had achieved its largest geographical reach, a dominion covering one quarter of the entire surface of the world. It was truly the Empire 'upon which the sun never set.' A mere thirty years later, by 1949, the British Empire was disintegrating in every region, as demands for colonial independence were escalating against the oppressive mother country. The British Empire was in the throes of the largest upheaval of perhaps any Kingdom in history.

American foreign policy shrewdly encouraged the anti-colonial ambitions for freedom and independence within the British Empire, stopping just short of supporting genuine de-colonization in those countries after independence.

Following a mutiny of the Indian Royal Navy in February 1946 over issues of pay and conditions, Britain's Labor Prime Minister Clement Atlee appointed Viscount Mountbatten of Burma to be the last Viceroy of India; his job was to arrange the withdrawal of British colonial forces and government administration. Within five months of his arrival in India, by August 15, 1947, Mountbatten's 'arrangement' consisted of partitioning the vast Indian subcontinent into a bizarre quilt of East and West Pakistan with predominantly Muslim populations, separated by a Hindu-dominated India.

Within a few short years, Britain had ceded formal colonial control over large parts of her empire in Africa, the Pacific, and bordering the Mediterranean. It was not done out of benevolence, or any sudden sympathy for the principle of self-determination of subject peoples. It was driven rather by necessity, by Britain's financial ruin, and by the severe demands of Washington who dictated a reshaping of postwar power relations in the late 1940s and early 1950s.

As Churchill feared, Washington had indeed fought World War II in order to "preside over the dismantling of the British Empire," the only power which in the late 1940s could potentially challenge American hegemony. Britain could be an ally but, in the earlier words of Henry Adams, American imperialist philosopher and descendent of two US Presidents, only as "a Britain that was part of the American System." [12]

As a consequence of the War, the trading mechanisms of the Empire that had formed the foundation of British financial power had been shattered. Vast overseas investments had long since been sold to pay Britain's war costs. The UK National Debt had soared to unprecedented heights. Domestically, England's factories, infrastructure and equipment were rotted and worn out. The electricity supply was no longer reliable, England's housing stock was dilapidated, the population exhausted. By the end of the war, British export trade had sunk to a mere 31% of its 1938 pre-war level.

The final blow to Britain's ambition to hold onto the shards of global Empire came abruptly on September 2, 1945, less than four weeks after Truman dropped two atomic bombs on Japan at the end of the Pacific war, when Washington unexpectedly cancelled British Lend-Lease aid. Since the program had been initiated by the US Congress in March 1941, nine months before the US officially entered the war, the US had supplied the United Kingdom with some $31 billion in war material and other essential aid. That was the equivalent of more than $420 billion in 2007 dollars. For their part the British government had fully expected that this aid would not only continue for a time after the war, but would also include debt forgiveness and a generous interest-free dollar loan to allow the postwar British economy to get back on its feet.

Large quantities of essential goods had already arrived in Britain or were in transit when Washington suddenly and unexpectedly terminated Lend-Lease on 2 September. Britain needed the equipment in the immediate post war period. Instead, Washington offered a $4 billion loan at 2% interest with strings attached. This, in effect, ended Britain's preferential trade with its Commonwealth member countries and severely weakened Britain's economic and trade role in the postwar world. [13]

Britain was dependent on the postwar financial support of the United States and its Wall Street financial elite. For its part, America's policy makers from the East Coast Establishment, as they were coming to be known, realized that if the United States was going to dominate the postwar world, it would need the vast worldwide expertise and cooperation of the City of London. After 1945 Britain would be permitted to exert global influence but only indirectly, through developing and deepening a 'special relationship' with the United States, as its distinctly junior partner in what was now already being called, by some observers, the American Century or Pax Americana.

The financial and monetary pillar of postwar American hegemony, however, depended on an equally powerful American military role to guarantee American dominance in the world after 1945. After all, what was to prevent other nations from forming new alliances to challenge the American Century? What would prevent the former allies of 1945, for example, from becoming deadly adversaries a decade or two later?

Washington delivered an answer to those questions only four weeks before she cancelled British Lend-Lease aid. The United States had secretly developed the most terrifying weapon in the history of warfare. Moreover, the political elites of the United States would demonstrate to the entire world that they were mad enough to use that awesome weapon on their adversaries.

Endnotes:

[1] Henry Luce, *The American Century*, Life, February 7, 1941. Reprinted in *The Ambiguous Legacy*, M. J. Hogan, ed. (Cambridge: Cambridge University Press, 1999).

[2] Peter J. Taylor, *Britain and the Cold War: 1945 as Geopolitical Transition*, (London: Pinter Publishers, 1990), p. 17.

[3] M.W. Kirby, *The Decline of British Economic Power Since 1870*, (London: Allen & Unwin, 1981), pp. 91-94.

[4] Geir Lundestad, *Empire by Invitation? The United States and Western Europe, 1945-1952*, Journal of Peace Research, Vol. 23, No. 3 (Sept. 1986), pp. 263-277.

[5] Peter Collier & David Horowitz, *The Rockefellers: An American Dynasty* (New York: Holt, Rinehart and Winston, 1976), pp. 156-157.

[6] Robert Lacey, *The Kingdom: Arabia and the House of Saud* (New York: Avon Books, 1981), p. 262-263.

[7] Robert Lacey, op. cit., p. 263.

[8] Ibid. pp. 266-267.

[9] Ibid., pp. 262-271.

[10] Ibid., p. 272.

[11] Ibid., p. 274.

[12] Henry Adams, *The Education of Henry Adams: An Autobiography* (New York: Time Books, 1964), p. 143. Adams was a descendent of President John Adams, framer of the Constitution, and of President John Quincy Adams, and of Brooks Adams, Teddy Roosevelt's adviser and advocate of American empire. Henry Adams wrote of himself in the year 1898 as the US began the first imperial war, the Spanish-American War which gained her the Philippines, Cuba and Puerto Rico, '*He carried every scene of it, in a century and a half since the Stamp Act, quite alive in his mind—all the interminable disputes of his disputatious ancestors as far back as the year 1750—as well as his own significance in the Civil War, **every step in which had the object of bringing England into an American system.**'* (author's emphasis).

[13] Leo T. Crowley, *Lend Lease*, in Walter Yust, ed. 10 Eventful Years... (Chicago, E.B. Inc.,1947) 1:520, 2, pp. 858-860.

CHAPTER TEN

Washington Drops the A-Bomb

It seems to be the most terrible thing ever discovered, but it can be made the most useful... This is the greatest thing in history."
- President Truman on his order to use the Atomic bomb on Japan in August 1945 [1]

A new US monopoly on power

In the summer of 1945 President Harry Truman signed the order to drop a terrifying new bomb on Japanese cities.

No other act of the war underscored the brutal new message of postwar American power more than Washington's use of two atomic bombs, one on August 6 on Hiroshima and on August 9 on Nagasaki, Japan. Although the United States had previously dropped leaflets warning civilians of air raids on twelve other Japanese cities where conventional bombing raids were to take place, residents of Hiroshima were given no notice of the atomic bomb.

Each of the two bombs, the only two the US had been able by then to produce from its supplies of enriched fissionable Uranium-235 and Plutonium-239, was more devastating than any bomb in the history of warfare. And they were to go down in history as the only use of nuclear weapons in warfare by any nation in the world.

The bomb dropped on Hiroshima had more than two thousand times the explosive power of the British 'Grand Slam' which had been the largest bomb ever yet used in the history of warfare. A mere 8 kilograms of Pu-239 in a single bomb over the Japanese city of Nagasaki had wreaked carnage that was unprecedented in war. The bomb was deliberately exploded some 2,000 feet in the air above Hiroshima to give the world the most convincing evidence of the new weapon's staggering power. At a range of some 500 meters from Ground Zero, objects became incandescent in heat that soared above one million degrees.

The two bombs had killed as many as 140,000 people in Hiroshima and 80,000 in Nagasaki by the end of 1945, with roughly half of those deaths occurring on the days of the bombings. Among those, perhaps 20% died from injuries or the combined effects of flash burns, trauma, and radiation burns, compounded by illness, malnutrition and radiation sickness.

American government officials deliberately tried to downplay and deny the deadly effects of the bomb's nuclear fallout and the ongoing deaths, diseases and destruction from radiation. In reality, as official Japanese research later documented, countless thousands of Japanese suffered birth deformities, higher incidences of cancer, permanent hair loss, purple skin blotches, leukaemia or cancer of the blood. Added to these physical injuries and chronic illnesses was the unimaginable trauma suffered by survivors.

The US Occupation Authority deliberately hid reports of the radiation deaths and sicknesses. They prohibited filming in Hiroshima and Nagasaki and "ordered anyone who had shot any footage to submit it to American headquarters." One official film project, undertaken by the US military's Strategic Bombing Survey, shot thousands of feet of black and white footage in order to preserve a record of the bomb's effects. When the raw footage arrived in the US, however, it was classified "Top Secret," locked in a vault and never shown to the American public.[2]

When Roosevelt suddenly died in April 1945, his Vice President, Harry Truman, a poorly prepared former Senator from Missouri, succeeded him as President. One of Truman's first acts as President, as his military chiefs of staff briefed him on the existence of the A-Bomb, was to approve dropping the bomb on Japan.

In fact, Truman had already secretly authorized the use of the bombs, and approved the selected target cities by the time he met in Potsdam, Germany with Stalin and Churchill during July and August 1945. This would be Truman's only meeting with his future adversary in the Cold War.

The dropping of the A-bomb on Japan has been surrounded by controversy. Truman claimed he acted in order to force Japan to surrender and to prevent a longer war with further loss of American lives in an allegedly necessary invasion. To careful observers of events, Truman's argument was not very convincing.

Hitler's Germany had surrendered to the Allied Forces in May 1945, a month after Truman became President. Japan was by then isolated, economically on its knees and *de facto* a defeated power. Its exhausted troops were deserting in droves. According to military experts, an effective naval blockade of Japan by US and Allied warships would have been sufficient to force the Japanese Emperor to surrender, even on the harsh terms demanded by Washington and with no further loss of lives.

In point of fact, subsequently declassified documents revealed that the Japanese had already notified the Americans prior to their arrival at Potsdam that Japan would surrender on condition of being permitted to retain their Emperor. Truman, it turned out, was well aware that Japan wanted to surrender; he was also aware that the A-bomb had been successfully tested in New Mexico on July 16.

Given that the Japanese Emperor was the linchpin of Japanese society and would have been essential to postwar American occupation of Japan anyway, Truman's stubborn insistence at Potsdam on Japan's unconditional surrender has been interpreted as a deliberate ploy to allow time, and create a cover justification, for dropping the atomic bombs on Japan. The timing, and subsequently declassified documents, lend credence to this view. Truman's insistence on unconditional surrender was the only way to thwart the Japanese bid to surrender, and to create the fiction that the atomic weapons were necessary to end the war.[3]

After Washington unleashed its terrifying new atomic weapon, Truman insisted he had acted on advice of his military in order to "save the lives of 100,000 American boys." In reality, it was to make clear to the world, above all to Russia's Stalin, that American power was awesome and unimaginably brutal. The purpose of dropping the atomic bombs on Hiroshima and Nagasaki had been not for terrorizing Japan into surrender—they were already on their knees—but for overwhelming the Soviet Union with a convincing demonstration of American military power. The dropping of the bomb in a real sense was the first shot in what would come to be called the Cold War between the Soviet Union and the USA.

In his private diary dated July 25 1945, Truman wrote a revealing entry, speaking of his decision to order the bomb to be used against Japan: "It is certainly a good thing for the world that Hitler's crowd or Stalin's did not discover this atomic bomb. It seems to be the most terrible thing ever discovered, but it can be made the most useful."[4] Privately, on receiving a detailed military briefing of the effects of the bomb, Truman reportedly exploded in childish joy, shouting, "This is the greatest thing in history." This was indeed a most curious way to describe this "most terrible" weapon.

During July 1945, US Secretary of State James Byrnes advised Truman to refuse any surrender from the Japanese that might end the war. The reason was that the atomic bomb had just been successfully tested in Alamogordo, New Mexico. Japan's conditional request to retain the Emperor provided Truman with the "out" that he needed to publicly justify his decision to use the terrifying new bomb.

The real target of the atomic devastation of Hiroshima and Nagasaki was Moscow. On hearing the report of the successful first test of the bomb at Alamogordo, US Secretary of War Henry L. Stimson expressed his joy. Using terminology from card-playing, he wrote in his diary that the combination of America's overwhelming postwar economic strength, together with its monopoly on the atomic bomb, would give the US a "royal straight flush and we mustn't be a fool about the way we play it." Truman told Stimson he agreed that the "cards were in American hands," and that he, Truman, meant to "play them as American cards." [5]

In 1945 the United States possessed a monopoly on the industrial and scientific capacity, as well as the material resources needed to produce atomic bombs.

As military historian Hanson Baldwin described the new strategic power reality, the willingness of America to use the bomb had definitively ended America's claim to moral leadership in the world. It did open the way to another kind of leadership however, a system of perpetual international conflict called the 'Cold War.'

The Manhattan Project, America's Top Secret project to build the A-bomb, was headed by Army General Leslie R. Groves. Groves used his unique role as the military person on top of this secret and awesome new weapon to influence US foreign policy. Against the advice of several Truman advisors who believed many other nations could soon develop their own bomb and their own uranium fuel, Groves insisted the US could hold its unique atomic monopoly for years.

In his briefings to Truman, Groves falsely claimed that only two countries, Sweden and Russia, were in a position to challenge the American and British joint control of areas believed to contain 97% of the world's high-grade uranium ore needed to build atomic bombs. Groves further wrongly claimed that "Russian resources of raw materials are far inferior" to those controlled by the United States. Groves set out to convince Truman that it would take the Russians as much as 20 years or more to build a single atomic bomb. [6]

Groves also deliberately withheld from the US President a petition signed in late July 1945 by seventy of the leading US scientists working on the bomb, urging that Truman not drop the bomb on Japan "unless the terms which will be imposed upon Japan have been made public and Japan, knowing these terms, has refused to surrender." [7] Japan was not told beforehand of the nuclear weapon's power and Truman was not told of the petition from his leading scientists until days after the bombs had fallen on Japan.

General Groves saw the monopoly of atomic weapons and the industrial economic advantage of the United States as the keys to an American domination of the world after 1945. He openly called for using the bomb as a "diplomatic bargaining point to lead to the opening up of the world...," a message that implied, "trade with us on our terms or we obliterate you from the face of the earth." In a 1946 Memorandum for the US Congress, Groves stated, "If there are to be atomic weapons in the world, we must have the best, the biggest and the most." This was the military version of an American Century, projecting its power under a radioactive mushroom cloud.[8]

During the Truman Administration's post-Hiroshima Cabinet debates about the consequences of having used the Atomic Bomb on Japanese civilians, Vice President Henry A. Wallace and Secretary of War Henry Stimson advocated a policy of friendly cooperation with Russia to ensure peace, rather than a policy of military confrontation. Secretary of State Jimmy Byrnes, the Manhattan Project's General Groves, as well as Navy Secretary James Forrestal all called for secrecy and military monopoly of the new weapon. In his personal diary, Wallace described the debate only weeks after the bombs had been dropped on Japan:

September 21, 1945 --

At the cabinet meeting the one subject up for discussion was the atomic bomb and the peacetime development of atomic energy. The President asked Secretary Stimson to open the meeting, which he did in an unusually fine and comprehensive statement. He said that all of the scientists with whom the War Department worked were convinced that there was no possible way of holding the scientific secret of the atomic bomb and that, therefore, they felt there should be free interchange of scientific information between different members of the United Nations.

He said that the scientists told him that the bombs thus far dropped were utilizing only a very small fraction of the power of the atom and that future bombs would be infinitely more destructive - perhaps being as greatly advanced over the present bombs as the present bombs are over the bombs which existed prior to 1945. He said some of them were afraid they would be so powerful as to ignite the atmosphere and put an end to the world. He said he recognized that any interchange of scientific information with the other United Nations would bring into the foreground the problem of Russia. He then entered into a long defense of Russia, saying that throughout

our history Russia had been our friend – that we had nothing that
Russia wanted and that Russia had nothing that we wanted. He
said our relationship with Russia during recent months had been
improving...

The President then called on (Treasury Secretary) Fred Vinson, who
disagreed with Secretary Stimson and expressed great distrust of
other nations. Secretary Stimson had said it was conceivable that
some of the other nations could learn the secret of the atomic bomb
without any help from us within three years, and almost certainly
within five years. Vinson rather questioned this statement. Tom
Clark took very much the same attitude as Secretary Vinson. Secre-
tary Forrestal took the most extreme attitude of all. He had a memo-
randum which had been prepared by his admirals, which he read. It
was a warlike, big-Navy, isolationist approach.... [9]

Some days later, Truman told the press he had decided to exclude both wartime allies, the British as well as the Russians, from any sharing of atomic
secrets. The military and its allies in industry had convinced the President.

To further underscore the new postwar power relationship, in November
1945 Truman told British Prime Minister Clement Atlee that Washington would
refuse a requested $6 billion interest-free loan to help rebuild Britain's war-torn
economy. The forced dissolution of Britain's Sterling Preference Area was the
target.

Truman would only make a $3.75 billion loan at 2%. In addition, Truman
made clear that Washington intended to jealously guard its atomic monopoly.
Truman backed out of wartime cooperation with Canada and Britain on atomic
energy, having already violated the 1943 Quebec Agreement which had stipulated that the US and Britain would not only consult before deciding to use the
bomb, but not use it without the express consent of the other. Washington was
bent on monopolizing atomic weapons, even with respect to its closest allies.

Vice President Wallace privately expressed his dismay. He wrote a prophetic
warning to Truman,

The nature of science and the present state of knowledge in other
countries are such that there is no possible way of preventing other
nations from repeating what we have done or surpassing it within
five or six years...The world will be divided into two camps with the

*non-Anglo-Saxon world eventually superior in population, re-
sources, and scientific knowledge.* [10]

Perhaps Wallace did not realize that this was precisely the aim.

The bombing of Japan failed to produce any signs of fear or softness on the part of Stalin's Russia. Stalin had a network of informants inside the US Government in very high positions. They kept Moscow apprised of the status of the US bomb project and some also secretly provided Soviet scientists with the blueprints needed to produce atomic weapons.[11]

Russia shocked the United States and much of the world when it exploded its own atomic bomb in 1949, a mere four years later. The nuclear confrontation of the Cold War had begun.

A postwar American *Lebensraum*

The driving force behind the entire War & Peace Studies of the Rockefellers' Council on Foreign Relations, the motive for Roosevelt to bring the United States into war, the entire war mobilization and public indebtedness that the war effort required in the United States, all were aimed at one postwar objective: the creation of a vast captive global market or economic space for the United States, an American *Lebensraum* as the CFR's Isaiah Bowman termed it, a truly "American Century."

America was to be an empire in much the same way that Great Britain had been an Empire after 1815, with one significant difference. America's economic imperialism would disguise itself under the rhetorical cover of 'spreading free enterprise,' and supporting 'national self-determination' and 'democracy.' The term 'empire' was to be scrupulously avoided.

Its architects in the State Department, the White House and foreign policy establishment created the clever deception that theirs was not an empire, as they insisted it did not seek to militarily occupy other nations. At least, that was the argument. It was every bit an empire, albeit a less visible one, based on the role of the United States in international finance, with the dollar as the pillar of the postwar system, backed up by overwhelming military superiority.

The deception was astonishingly successful, in part because the US establishment realized the value of giving abundant local spoils to the wealthy and often corrupt national elites in foreign markets they wished to conquer. The system that evolved after 1945 was one of a single, overwhelming global power, the United States, and a growing number of de facto vassal states whose wealthy elites were in one way or another dependent for their existence on the 'good graces' of Washington and the Pentagon. The 'good graces' usually included US-trained secret police forces, death squads, and timely coups.

The American Century was to be an informal empire of dependent "client states" rather than occupied colonies, deemed by them to be an outmoded and inefficient model of domination.

American history over the previous century, as described in earlier chapters, had been driven by an increasingly powerful cartel of financial elites and the large industrial trusts they controlled. Their interests, rather than the interests of the nation and the population as a whole, defined the strategic priorities of that powerful cartel. Their overwhelming control of the national media allowed their propaganda experts to portray their interests as 'America's interests.' Most Americans, wanting to think the best of their country, bought the propaganda.

The philosophers of American expansionism such as Frederick Jackson Turner and Brooks Adams asserted that America had a God-given 'Manifest Destiny' to constantly expand its frontiers, that the plunder of other countries was a matter of 'Divine Right.'

That, in any case was the mystical or romantic formulation of the increasingly concentrated monopoly economy that the Money Trust had created since the dawn of their Federal Reserve in 1913. It was the pseudo-religious justification for constantly needing to conquer new markets to survive.

Their economic model was that of the British East India Company or, more accurately, of the Barbary pirates, looting and plundering to exhaustion one region after the next to prop up their empire, leaving behind as little of value as possible. For the Rockefellers, the most prominent proponent of the Manifest Destiny idea in the postwar period, the entire world was considered their 'frontier.' [12] By portraying their mission after 1948 as a Cold War fought by 'American democracy' against 'Godless Communism' they gave the cause of advancing American interests a messianic religious cover that was astonishingly effective for decades.

"...those markets are abroad"

In 1944 Assistant Secretary of State Dean Acheson told a Congressional committee studying the issue of the postwar economy, "...no group...has ever believed our domestic markets could absorb our entire production under our present system. Therefore you find you must look to other markets and those markets are abroad." [13] That brief statement defined the outlook of the US business and banking establishment looking to emerge as the dominant economic power of the postwar era.

Acheson was called by some the "architect of the Cold War." [14] He drafted the Truman Doctrine, as well as the document creating the NATO alliance, and convinced Truman to embark on an undeclared war in Korea in 1950. Acheson played a key role in the creation of the Bretton Woods agreements including the idea for the International Monetary Fund and the World Bank later in 1944, to advance that US search for 'markets abroad.'

By 1945 the foreign policy circles of Washington and the Council on Foreign Relations could say they had made a giant advance in their agenda, having reached a consensus on the commitment to global expansionism. Their only problem, as they saw it, was that eventually they must destroy or seriously cripple the two large expanses of territory which had been sealed off, at least temporarily, from their economic expansion—namely, the Soviet Union and later the Peoples' Republic of China—if they were to dominate the economies and markets of the world.

During his work with the War & Peace Studies project for the Rockefellers and the Council on Foreign Relations, Isaiah Bowman convinced the aging father of British geopolitics, Sir Halford Mackinder, to author a strategic piece for the CFR journal *Foreign Affairs* on his idea for a postwar geopolitical order. The essay, *The Round World and the Winning of the Peace*, appeared in July 1943, almost a year before the Allied invasion of Normandy.

In his essay, Mackinder outlined his vision for a US-dominated postwar order. He reiterated his initial 1904 definition of 'the Heartland' as the most formidable opponent of continued Anglo-American supremacy after the war. He defined 'the Heartland' as essentially the area covered by the USSR. Mackinder planted the geopolitical seed for what became the Cold War:

> *The conclusion is unavoidable that if the Soviet Union emerges from this war as conqueror of Germany, she must rank as the greatest land Power on the globe. Moreover she will be the power in the strategically strongest defensive position. The Heartland is the greatest natural fortress on earth.* [15]

Bowman and his US foreign policy colleagues obviously took that lesson to heart, but with one important, critical difference: Mackinder had envisioned Russia as an ally in an Anglo-American postwar containment of Germany. The US elites around Bowman had to find an adversary whose very existence would provide the rationale for one power—the United States of America, together with a core of allied powers in NATO---to shape the 'free world' on its terms.

Soon after FDR's death, the US foreign policy establishment moved in tandem with Churchill to define their wartime ally, the Soviet Union, as their prime enemy and 'The' threat to world peace. Initially, operating from the perspective of classic British Balance of Power tactics, Churchill assumed, even before the end of the war, that Germany would have to be recruited as England's ally against the stronger Soviet Union. The calculation had nothing to do with ideology, but rather with pure geopolitical power calculus whereby Britain would ally itself with the weaker of its two rivals for Eurasian hegemony, against the stronger one. Few observers understood this at the time, nor were they intended to understand.

On April 15, 1945, a few days after the death of Franklin Delano Roosevelt, and only days before the German surrender, a group of senior foreign policy advisors met behind closed doors at the State Department in Washington. Among the fifteen powerful men present were John J. McCloy, then Assistant Secretary of War, the president of General Motors, a major defense contractor, and several other hand picked establishment insiders.

The men discussed how to turn America's military focus from Germany to the Soviet Union in the face of the overwhelming sentiment among ordinary Americans that the war had been won with the help of the Soviet Union and that a return to peacetime would reflect this. They discussed how to achieve a radical shift in US opinion, turning it against America's wartime ally, Russia. They concluded that such a dramatic shift would require provoking Stalin into some aggressive act that would appear to the world as a breach of trust and a threat to peace. [16]

Washington prepares a strategic shift

In 1946, as the ashes from the war against Nazi Germany were still smoldering, a faction within the US State Department, including George F. Kennan, began agitating in Washington for a hard line against Moscow.

In February 1946 the US Treasury in Washington asked the US Embassy in Moscow to explain why Moscow was not supporting the new Bretton Woods organizations, the International Monetary Fund and World Bank. Kennan, then Minister Counselor in the Moscow Embassy wrote what came to be known as the "Long Telegram," a five-part road map of his personal views of Soviet policy. Kennan insisted that the USSR saw itself at perpetual war with capitalism and that while Soviet power was "impervious to the logic of reason, it was highly sensitive to the logic of force." [17]

Kennan, serving then under US Ambassador and Wall Street investment banker, Averell Harriman, worked with Defense Secretary James Forrestal and a small handful of hawkish US policymakers to shift US policy perceptions of the Soviet Union, and American public opinion, as well. They had to replace the reality of an exhausted wartime ally who had done the lion's share of the fighting and dying in the war to defeat Hitler's Germany, with the image of an implacable enemy determined to destroy American capitalism and somehow bent on taking over the world.

The result in September 1946 was a Top Secret report to the President, developed by Kennan and an inter-departmental team from the Departments of State, War, Justice, Joint Chiefs of Staff and the Central Intelligence Agency, titled *American Relations with the Soviet Union*. The report was considered so sensitive by President Truman that its existence remained secret until 1968.

The report called for the first time for a US policy of "restraining and confining" the Soviet Union. It was to be the US strategy document for a Cold War. The report, dubbed the Clifford-Elsey Report for its two prime authors, began with a stark picture: "The gravest problem facing the United States today is that of American relations with the Soviet Union. The solution of that problem may determine whether or not there will be a third World War." The authors continued, "Soviet leaders appear to be conducting their nation on a course of aggrandizement designed to lead to eventual world domination by the USSR." [18]

For anyone inside the USSR at the time, such an assessment seemed far from plausible. Since the 1920s it had been clear to any careful student of Stalin's foreign policy that security of borders and not world revolution was the utmost priority. Stalin had repeatedly shown willingness before the War to enter into pacts with non-communist regimes in return for assurances of security or non-aggression. There was even less likelihood after the devastation of the World War that that policy would abruptly shift into an adventuresome one of pursuing world revolution and domination.

Perhaps sensing the sharp mood change in official Washington from one of wartime 'friendship' to one of emerging adversary, that same month, September 1946, the Soviet Ambassador to Washington had sent a telegram to Moscow in which he described Washington policy as being in the control of powerful industrialists who were building up US military capability "to prepare the conditions for winning world supremacy in a new war." [19]

The Soviet Union, unlike the United States, had suffered horrendous damage during the war. Russia's industry was completely gutted, its labor force severely depleted by war losses. Stalin was determined to replenish and rebuild the war-ravaged Soviet heartland as quickly as possible, using captured German industrial materials to do it. He fully backed Roosevelt's Morgenthau Plan for occupied Germany, viewing it as essential to guarantee no future invasion from a rearmed Germany, as well as providing Russia with vitally needed plant and equipment taken from occupied Germany.

The Morgenthau Plan, drawn up by FDR's Treasury Secretary Henry Morgenthau, called for "converting Germany into a country primarily agricultural and pastoral in its character." Its major industry and mining regions were to be declared international zones or given to neighboring nations, and all heavy industry was to be dismantled or otherwise destroyed. As a commentary in Henry Luce's Time magazine characterized the plan, "German steel production was to be reduced from over 20,000,000 tons a year to 5,800,000. German heavy industry was to be cut to approximately one-half of its 1938 level. The manufacture of synthetic gasoline, rubber, ball bearings, radio transmitters, heavy machine tools and many other war-important products was banned altogether. But manufacturers of ceramics, glass and bicycles would be encouraged to surpass prewar records. Germany would not be starved, but it would be reduced to its 1932 standard of life." [20]

On September 6, 1946, Secretary of State and anti-Soviet hardliner James Byrnes delivered a speech in Germany repudiating the Morgenthau Plan of Roosevelt, suggesting a major shift in US policy towards Germany.

In the speech, Byrnes warned the Soviets that the US intended to maintain a military presence in Europe indefinitely.[21] Byrnes admitted a month later: "The nub of our program was to win the German people...it was a battle between us and Russia over minds."

In March 1946, a few weeks after Kennan's "Long Telegram," former British Prime Minister Winston Churchill, who had been secretly lobbying Washington to launch an offensive against the Soviet Union since at least 1943, delivered his famous "Iron Curtain" speech in Fulton, Missouri, calling for an Anglo-American alliance against the Soviets, whom he accused of establishing an "iron curtain" from "Stettin in the Baltic to Trieste in the Adriatic."

As seen in Moscow, the speech was a call for the West to begin a war with the USSR, as it called for an Anglo-American alliance against the Soviets.

The policy circles in Washington around Kennan -- Clark Clifford, Dean Acheson, and James Forrestal -- realized that creating a hostile Soviet Union on Western Europe's eastern borders would create an economic space in Western Europe, Japan and much of Asia, Africa and South America that could be dominated by the United States.

The vast region of Western Europe would become dependent on American military security. Moreover, as their economies had been devastated by the war, the countries of Western Europe as well as Japan would automatically become a captive market for American industrial exports under Bretton Woods and Washington's call for a system of 'free and open trade.' That was to be the realization of the CFR War & Peace Studies strategy for their undeclared postwar American empire.

The decision by Washington to use the devastating power of the atomic bomb on Japan was a signal event that was intended among other things to declare to the world the dawn of the American Century and to open the way for a postwar dollar imperium, a Pax Americana on American rules. No debate was to be tolerated. The Cold War was born to underpin that economic imperium, the American Century. Bretton Woods and the unique role of the US dollar as 'key currency' would become the basis of a new American global empire, the American Century.

So long as the weakened nations of Western Europe had to depend on a US military security umbrella in a prolonged Cold War with the Soviet Union and later the Peoples' Republic of China, Washington could virtually dictate vital economic conditions of that alliance. It did, and the Bretton Woods System was the cornerstone of that economic domination.

Endnotes:

[1] Harry S. Truman, quoted in Robert H. Ferrell, *Off the Record: The Private Papers of Harry S. Truman* (New York: Harper and Row, 1980), pp. 55-56.

[2] Robert Jay Lifton and Greg Mitchell, *Hiroshima in America: A Half Century of Denial* (New York: Avon Books, 1995), p. 57-58.

[3] Gar Alperovitz, *The Decision to Use the Atomic Bomb* (New York: Alfred A. Knopf, 1995), pp. 232-248.

[4] Harry S. Truman, op. cit.

[5] Gregg Herken, *The Winning Weapon: The Atomic Bomb in he Cold War"* (New York: Alfred A. Knopf, 1980). Herken provides extensive details of the background debates around President Truman's decision to drop the bomb on Hiroshima. Clear is that Japan was not the primary target, but rather the Soviet Union and the need to demonstrate to Stalin that Washington was prepared to dominate the postwar world. Stalin fully understood the message and Soviet spies inside the United States had already obtained the crucial scientific information needed to produce the first Soviet nuclear weapon, laying the foundation for four decades of so-called Cold War.

[6] Ibid.

[7] John Rutherford and Jim Popkin, NBC News, *Secret documents released in Rosenberg spy case*, September 11, 2008. accessed in http://deepbackground.msnbc.msn.com/archive/2008/09/11/1380081.aspx..

[8] US Joint Chiefs of Staff Records, August 24, 1945, Air Force Series 7-18-45, *Effects of Foreseeable New Developments*. Here General Groves states he knew 'the bomb would be developed too late for use against Germany.' Many believed the real reason Japan was chosen had to do with the fact that Truman and US military planners considered the Japanese to be non-white. Others argue it was to show Stalin that the US was capable of any act.

[9] Henry A. Wallace, *The Price of Vision: The Diary of Henry A. Wallace*, 1942-1946 (Boston: Houghton-Mifflin Co., 1973).

[10] Ibid.

[11] John Rutherford and Jim Popkin, NBC News, *Secret documents released in Rosenberg spy case*, September 11, 2008. accessed in http://deepbackground.msnbc.msn.com/archive/2008/09/11/1380081.aspx.

[12] Frederick Jackson Turner had expressed the philosophy most explicitly. Turner's main concept was that America's uniqueness was the product of an expanding frontier. He defined American historical existence as perpetual geopolitical expansion toward new frontiers in the West. "The existence of an area of free land, its continuous recession, and the advance of American settlement westward explains the American development." The "universal disposition of the Americans, an expanding people, is to enlarge their dominion." For Turner, American history was a history of "continually advancing frontier line...The frontier is the line of most rapid and effective Americanization...Movement has been its dominant, and ...the American energy will continually demand a wider field for its exercise."

As historian William Appleman Williams stated, the unique American imperialist *Weltanschauung* was contained in the thesis of Brooks Adams that America's uniqueness could be preserved only by a foreign policy of expansionism. Adams' contribution was to project Turner's explanation of American past into the future. "Taken together, the ideas of Turner and Adams supplied American empire builders with an overview and explanation of the world, and a reasonably specific program of action from 1893 to 1953," Williams explained. "Expansion was the catechism by this young messiah [Turner] of America's uniqueness and omnipotence...Turner gave Americans a nationalistic world view that eased their doubts...and justified their aggressiveness." Turner, looking at the American past, saw in the final conquest of the West, the realization of Manifest Destiny in the Western Hemisphere. Adams saw the coming new frontier - the whole world. Fully in that tradition, it is notable that the name of President John Kennedy's guiding idea was called the New Frontier. Brooks Adams' global vision was inevitably to lead to a one world empire—the American World Empire, not some plurality of *Grossraüme* or Pan-regions, as envisioned by Carl Schmitt or Haushofer. See Frederick Jackson Turner, *The Significance of the Frontier in American History*, (New York: Henry Holt and Co, 1995). See also, Brooks Adams, *The Law of Civilization and Decay* (New York: The Macmillan Co., 1896). Franklin Delano Roosevelt and the leading elites of the early 20th Century were all steeped in the ideas of Turner and Brooks Adams. A fascinating cultural and historical analysis of this drive to external new frontiers inherent in the American elites since the Civil War can be found in the remarkable work of the 19th and early 20th Century German writer, Oswald Spengler, *The Decline of the West, Vol.1: Form and Actuality* (London: George Allen & Unwin, 1926), especially Chapter 4, *The Problem of World History: The Idea of Destiny and the Principle of Causality*. For Spengler, the drive of a given culture for extending its 'civilization' ever more broadly rather than deepening its cultural basis was a typical manifestation of an empire in terminal decline, regardless whether Rome, Britain or America.

[13] Michael Tanzer, *The Sick Society: An economic examination* (New York: Holt Rinehart & Winston, 1971), p. 77.

[14] Randall Bennett Woods, *The Good Shepherd*, Reviews in American History, Volume 35, Number 2, June 2007, pp. 284-288.

[15] Sir Halford J. Mackinder, *The Round World and the Winning of the Peace*, Foreign Affairs, Vol. 21, No. 4, July 1943, p. 601.

[16] Mansur Khan, *Die geheime Geschichte der amerikanischen Kriege* (Tuebinen: Grabert-Verlag, 2003), pp. 237-238.

[17] George F. Kennan, reprinted in U.S. Department of State, *Foreign Relations of the United States: Eastern Europe; the Soviet Union*, vol. VI, 1946 (Washington, DC: GPO, 1969), 696-709.

[18] Clark M. Clifford, et al, *Draft of Introduction to Clifford-Elsey Report*, Harry S. Truman Administration File, Elsey Papers, accessed in http://www.trumanlibrary.org/whistlestop/study_collections/coldwar/documents/index .php?pagenumber=1&documentdate=0000-00-00&documentid=8-8&studycollectionid=coldwar.

[19] Andrew Kydd, *Trust and Mistrust in International Relations* (Princeton: Princeton University Press, 2005), p. 107.

[20] *Germany: Cost of Defeat*, Time, April 8, 1946, accessed in http://www.time.com/time/magazine/article/0,9171,852764,00.html.

[21] John L. Gaddis, *The Cold War: A New History* (London: Penguin Press, 2005), p. 30.

CHAPTER ELEVEN

Creating the Bretton Woods Dollar System

We, my dear Crossman, are Greeks in this American Empire. You will find the Americans much as the Greeks found the Romans—great big, vulgar, bustling people, more vigorous than we are and more idle, with more unspoiled virtues but also more corrupt.

- – Harold Macmillan, wartime adviser to Churchill, on the reality of the postwar Anglo-American relationship [1]

An American Dollar Standard

As war erupted in Europe in September 1939 with Hitler's and Stalin's dismemberment of Poland, European gold was flooding into the United States. In 1935 US official gold reserves had been valued at just over $9 billion. By 1940 after the onset of war in Europe, they had risen to $20 billion. As desperate European countries sought to finance their war effort, their gold went to the United States to purchase essential goods. By the time of the June 1944 convening of the international monetary conference at Bretton Woods, the United States controlled fully 70% of the world's monetary gold, an impressive advantage.[2] That 70% did not even include calculating the captured gold of the defeated Axis powers of Germany or Japan, where exact facts and data were buried in layers of deception and rumor.

By 1945 the United States Federal Reserve controlled the overwhelming share of the world's monetary gold.

The major Wall Street financial powers intended to use their advantage to the full in creating their postwar American Century. The American dollar, under the postwar system constructed by Washington and Wall Street banks, would be the mechanism for US control of global money and credit.

Beginning as early as 1941, calculating that Hitler's march against the Soviet Union would destroy Germany, US policy circles began laying the basis for their postwar economic hegemony. They would be remarkably effective in maintaining that hegemony for the first two decades after the end of the war.

The centerpiece of US economic strategy for shaping its dominance of the postwar world was called the Bretton Woods Agreements -- the promotion of an American-defined 'free trade' and of the US dollar as the sole currency of that world trade.

World War II had caused enormous destruction of infrastructure, industry and populations throughout the Eurasian landmass from the Atlantic to Vladivistock. The only major industrial power in the world to emerge intact—indeed, greatly strengthened from an economic perspective—was the United States.

At the Mount Washington Hotel in New Hampshire, US negotiators hammered out details of the postwar US monetary hegemony called the Bretton Woods Treaty of 1944.

As the world's greatest industrial power, physically unscathed by the war, the United States stood to gain enormously from opening the entire world to unfettered trade. The US industrial sector would have a global market for its exports, and it would have unrestricted access to vital raw materials from countries that were former colonies of Britain, France and the other European powers. Little wonder that 'free trade' assumed the dimension of religious dogma in postwar Washington.

'Free trade' involved lowering tariffs and removing national protections that hindered the flow of goods, especially US exports, into global markets, or removed barriers to US import of cheap raw materials from former or existing European colonial territories in Africa or Asia.

As the British well understood, 'free trade' or a 'level playing field' was the rallying cry of the strongest, most advanced economies, seeking to open up less developed markets for their goods. A century earlier, in 1846 with the repeal of their Corn Laws, Britain had been in a similar position to demand that the rest of the world open its borders to a British version of 'free trade.' Now, in 1945, the tables had turned. Washington's vision of free trade meant economic ruin for much of what remained of British industry.

The European economies, devastated by almost six years of war, had little choice but to agree with the US vision of postwar international economic management. Even Great Britain, which saw itself as at least an equal of the United States at the bargaining table, was forced to take a bitter lesson in humility before harsh US demands.

The final agreement for a postwar New World Order in monetary and economic affairs was reached following months of bitter infighting, especially between British and US negotiators. US negotiators, led by the Treasury's Harry Dexter White, pushed through a system different from all previous gold standard currency exchanges that had existed before.

Under the 19th Century British Gold Standard, and even in the New York version after 1919 until the British left in 1931, each national currency was backed by a given reserve of national monetary gold. If a country suffered an imbalance in its foreign trade, in theory, it would automatically be corrected by the workings of the gold standard as the country would lose or gain gold depending on whether it had a trade deficit or surplus. Under the new rules of the Bretton Woods, Washington imposed a system where only one currency— the US dollar—would be backed by gold. All other currencies were fixed in value in relation to the dollar.

It was a coup for the United States and for the Wall Street banks behind the Bretton Woods negotiations. The dollar became the world's reserve currency, required by all trading nations to conduct trade with one another after 1945. The US dollar, not gold, under the Bretton Woods Gold Exchange Standard, became at one and the same time a 'world currency' or more accurately, *The* world currency. Yet, as pointed out, the US Treasury also had unlimited power to create dollars, and it did so. Because its currency, the dollar, was the world reserve currency, the world was more or less forced to accept the inflated dollars. No other country enjoyed that enormous advantage.

The fateful Bretton Woods signing

The final agreement was signed by representatives of 29 nations in December 1945 at the Mount Washington Hotel in Bretton Woods, New Hampshire. It was a crowning moment for the members of the Council on Foreign Relations' War & Peace Studies project—their dream of postwar economic empire had been successfully achieved. Their institution, the International Monetary Fund, would now be able to reorganize much of the world under the sovereignty of the dollar.

American hegemony over the world financial and trading system was central to the Bretton Woods agreement. The crucial terms had already been hammered out in a series of private negotiations beginning in 1943 between Britain's Lord Keynes, Advisor to the UK Treasury, and Harry Dexter White, US Assistant Secretary of the Treasury under Secretary Henry Morgenthau. [3]

The Bretton Woods talks, which began in June 1944, were intended as the first institutional component of a new postwar United Nations organization (UN) that would replace the British-dominated League of Nations. The UN, unlike the League, was to be a US-dominated agency, under a concept created by the authors of the War & Peace Studies to advance the US agenda in the postwar world.[4] The Rockefeller brothers who financed the studies even donated the land for construction of UN headquarters in Manhattan. The resulting rise in adjacent land values, as foreign diplomats descended on Manhattan, more than made up in gain for their original generosity.

One of the reasons the US version of Bretton Woods prevailed over the alternative British version argued by John Maynard Keynes for the British Government, was the simple fact that the US was the most powerful country at the table, ultimately able to impose its will on the others. At the time, a senior official at the Bank of England described Bretton Woods as, "the greatest blow to Britain next to the war." [5] It demonstrated the dramatic shift in financial power from the UK to the USA.

The Bank of England, as well as influential Round Table members such as Leo Amery and Churchill's old ally, Lord Beaverbrook, correctly saw the US proposal for the International Monetary Fund as a device intended to make the US dollar the primary currency of world finance and trade, a shift that would come at the expense of the vital role of the City of London as well as undermining the British Sterling Area and Imperial Preference trade links. [6]

In order to secure the desired US version of the Bretton Woods agreement, however, Washington urgently required the bloc of votes that were represented by the nations of Latin America. Here Nelson Rockefeller, Roosevelt's wartime intelligence coordinator for Latin America, played a key role in manipulating the votes with deals using his far-reaching influence in Latin America.

Nelson buys some UN votes

The Yalta agreement signed by the US, Great Britain and the Soviet Union in 1945, had stipulated that only those countries that had formally declared war on Germany could be founding members of the postwar United Nations organization. To be one of the select UN founding members suggested a better 'seat at the Big Table' in terms of trade privileges especially with the large and booming United States market, something most Latin American countries were desperate to have.

In order to insure it had enough votes in forming the UN to assure its Bretton Woods agreement, Nelson Rockefeller personally organized a 'packing' of the votes in favor of the US plan by securing the votes of all 14 nations of the Pan American Union, seven of which, including Argentina, had been neutral countries during the war.

Nelson Rockefeller, having just been named by the President as Assistant Secretary for Latin America, gave the nations of Latin America an ultimatum that unless they formally declared war on the Axis Powers by February 1945, they would not be allowed to participate in the creation of the new United Nations Organization, nor to share in the postwar trade bonanza it promised.

That formal declaration of war against the Axis powers was necessary to comply with the just-agreed Three Power Yalta agreements.

Only Argentina remained neutral, but its vote was also needed to counter the balance of British votes. Rockefeller persuaded the ailing FDR to authorize inviting Argentina to join the UN as a founding member, even though it violated the Yalta agreements with Britain and the USSR that only nations that had declared war on Germany could be founding members. The gesture was meaningless in military terms, as the war was already over in a practical sense.

It was a ploy by Nelson Rockefeller to pack the votes against the British who used Britain's dominions and commonwealth countries to beef up her votes. Stalin was furious at the obvious move by Washington to control the voting members in a way that allowed Washington to dominate the key decision making bodies of the new United Nations. [7] It confirmed Stalin's apprehensions that Washington was using the UN, as well as its new IMF and World Bank organizations, as disguised tools for an American economic postwar imperium. His fears were well justified.

The Bretton Woods Dollar System

The Bretton Woods System was to be built around the three pillars: an International Monetary Fund, whose member countries would contribute to an emergency reserve available in times of balance of payment distress; a World Bank, or International Bank for Reconstruction and Development, which would provide loans to member governments for large public projects; and, somewhat later, a General Agreement on Tariffs and Trade, designed to manage 'free trade' through multinational tariff reduction talks.

Each member country would be assigned a quota, an amount to pay into a common IMF fund, in currency and gold. According to its share of the overall IMF quota, each would have a proportionate voting right in the Board of Governors. It was a US-dominated game from the outset. The US, as the strongest economy with the largest gold reserves, ended up with some 27% of total votes; the UK had 13%; by contrast and France had a meager 5%. Thus the new IMF was an American instrument to shape their form of postwar world economic development. [8]

In the end, over the objections of the British, Washington got its way in terms of voting rights, rules and other vital aspects of the new institutions, the IMF and World Bank. The US Treasury would de facto control the new IMF. Voting rights were proportional to a country's IMF contribution. The US, as the strongest economic power among the initial 29 founding nations, was by far the largest contributor, gaining the largest bloc of votes in the board.

Under the bylaws of the new IMF the US was in a position to block any decision it opposed by virtue of its vote share. By virtue of its large vote, Washington would also be able to control the decisive IMF Executive Board, directing overall policy to the wishes of the US Treasury and Wall Street. To make the US control of the rules of the new postwar monetary game clear, IMF headquarters were located in Washington, close to the US Treasury. Small wonder that Stalin decided not to join the IMF after 1945.

Dollar Standard replaces gold

Very few people, other than a handful of international monetary experts, grasped how skillfully the United States negotiators at Bretton Woods had structured an institutional base for a postwar dollar imperium. Bretton Woods changed the international currency system in a way that was congenial for the United States and an improvement, from their perspective, over the earlier gold standard. The new agreement required all member countries to fix the value of their currencies not to a weight of gold, but to the US dollar. The supply of US dollars in the world would, conveniently, be determined by Washington—the US Treasury and the Federal Reserve.

In 1945 it was argued—as the British had said about the pound sterling a century before—that the dollar was 'as good as gold.' Within two decades that axiom of international financial stability was to prove a tragic delusion. In 1945, however, it was the reality. European countries were starved for dollar credits to rebuild their ravaged infrastructures. Their currencies were not convertible and their economies were in ruins.

The New York Federal Reserve Bank, the private institution controlled by the Wall Street Money Trust since its creation in 1913, was the heart of the system that would now control the majority of the non-communist world's monetary gold.

For the US, the Bretton Woods currency system had unique and obvious advantages. In practice, since the principal reserve currency would be the US dollar, other countries would have to peg their currencies to the dollar, and—once their free currency convertibility was restored—they would buy and sell those dollars to keep their market exchange rates within plus or minus 1% of their initial 1945 value in relation to that US dollar, as required by IMF rules.

The US dollar thereby took over the role that gold had played under the gold standard in the international financial system before the war. In practice it meant that world trade was almost exclusively transacted in dollars, a decisive advantage for the US, who had unlimited power to print new dollars, unfettered by having to hold gold reserves against new dollar issue. Never had the British in the height of their financial power had such one-sided power over world money as Washington and Wall Street enjoyed after 1945.

The two pillars of American power

The unchallenged role of the US dollar as the world's reserve currency was one of two fundamental pillars of American power after the war. The second pillar was the unchallenged role of the United States as military superpower, a superiority that not even the Soviet Union during the Cold War was able to successfully challenge. The military pillar was obvious to all. Not so obvious was the dollar pillar, especially in the days after World War II.

The nations of Western Europe involved in World War II were deeply in debt after the war. They had been forced to finance their war efforts, especially

Britain, as well as numerous exile regimes in London, to transfer large amounts of their gold reserves into the United States, a fact that contributed to the supremacy of the United States as the 'leader of the Free World' after 1945. The exact details of the transfer of billions of dollars in foreign central bank gold to the New York Federal Reserve during the war remain buried in secrecy to the present. [9]

Under the Bretton Woods system, after 1945 each member country's national currency would be pegged to the US dollar. The US dollar was in turn set at an official rate of $35 per fine ounce of gold, the rate set by President Roosevelt in 1934 during the depths of the Great Depression and before the major inflationary effects of a world war. The dollar had inflated enormously during the war years, but was still fixed at $35 per fine ounce of gold, a rate greatly advantageous to the dollar and to Wall Street international banks. Fewer dollars bought more gold.

The distinction from the earlier Gold Exchange system created by J.P. Morgan and Wall Street between 1919-1934 was the fact that this time the United States had no rival, either politically or militarily, for world hegemony. Washington and Wall Street could literally dictate the terms. They did just that.

While the role of the dollar as reserve currency gave US capital an advantage over potential rivals such as British Sterling, the German Mark or French Franc during the postwar period, more importantly, it allowed the US Treasury and Federal Reserve the uncontrolled power to issue virtually unlimited dollars for international lending, regardless of gold backing, as the dollar and not gold was the world reserve commodity.

Because of the unique role of the American dollar as world reserve currency, the United States was able to finance its growing military expenses abroad by issuing new dollars rather than increasing its own gold reserves. To get gold was not easy in a world where gold was sought by most other central banks, but dollars could be created by the US Treasury more or less at will.

Washington's unique advantage after 1945 was having the US dollar as 'key currency' or the cornerstone of world money flows and trade settlement. If the US Government was forced to run a deficit to finance costs of its expanding network of military bases abroad, in effect, outposts of a new informal empire, disguised as defense against Communist expansionism, it could simply issue debt in the form of US Treasury bonds.

Foreign central banks holding surplus trade dollar accumulations had little recourse but to invest their surplus trade dollars in US Treasury debt, in effect financing the US military expansion globally. As the deficits grew, the relation of the dollar supply to a fixed reserve of gold diverged dramatically. In effect the

US, as the 'key currency' country, was able to export its inflation onto its trading partners in the form of de facto devalued dollars.

Under previous Gold Standard systems -- both the interwar years as well as the pre-1914 British Gold Standard -- each nation fixed its own currency to gold. Gold was the bedrock of stability, not the Pound Sterling, the dollar or any other single currency. Given its strong position in 1945, for the first time in history, one nation, the United States, was able to impose not gold but its own national currency on the world as the 'dollar standard.' Moreover, the supply of those dollars was a question of political will and not of physical supply, as with gold. As Soviet economists rightly pointed out, no other country had such a luxury.[10]

Initially, the IMF and World Bank played only a small role as a slightly modified strategy of geopolitics took shape under the Truman Administration after the death of FDR in April 1945.

The initial idea of Isaiah Bowman's War & Peace Studies group at the Council on Foreign Relations was that the US would ally with Russia and the other Allied nations after the war to prevent a re-emergence of a strong Germany. China as well as Russia would be an American ally against a potential resurgence of Japan.

However, Truman was influenced by former Moscow Ambassador and Wall Street banker Averell Harriman and by Secretary of State Dean Acheson, both of whom urged stronger opposition to Stalin's activity in Eastern Europe, even though Truman thereby violated the agreements reached at Yalta on division of postwar Europe among the three major war powers—Russia, Britain and the USA.

In February 1945 Roosevelt, Churchill and Stalin had met at Yalta on the Black Sea to discuss the postwar occupation of Germany. Among the agreements signed by the three was an explicit recognition of the fact the Soviet Red Army had liberated Poland and would play a key role in a new Polish government. The three agreed to move the Polish eastern boundary westward to the 1919 Curzon Line and to restore western Byelorussia and the western Ukraine to the Soviet Union. Germany would be 'temporarily' divided into three zones of occupation, with France invited to become a fourth occupying power.

Stalin, for his part, promised at Yalta that the Soviet Union would enter the war against Japan after the fighting ended in Europe. Stalin's terms for this were accepted by Roosevelt and Churchill, as follows: the southern Sakhalin and adjacent islands to be returned to the Soviet Union; Darien to be internationalized; Port Arthur to be leased as a naval base to the Soviet Union; Chinese-Soviet companies to operate the Chinese Eastern and the South Manchurian railroads; Outer Mongolia to remain independent of China; and the Kurile

Islands to be handed over to the Soviet Union. China would be sovereign in Manchuria.

The man in charge of working out the details of Yalta for Roosevelt was then-US Ambassador to Moscow, Averell Harriman, the man whose investment bank had had extensive wartime involvement with the Nazi Reich.

FDR's grandiose plans for using the United Nations to extend the American *Lebensraum* were put on hold by Truman, who preferred that Washington would pursue the same goals bilaterally instead. Rather than build on their wartime cooperation with the Soviet Union in defeating Nazi Germany, the United States would team up with Britain against their wartime ally. By rolling back the Yalta agreements, Washington could be assured Stalin would react aggressively to defend what he saw as Russia's vital security interests in Eastern Europe by force if necessary. Such was the trap set for Stalin by Churchill and later by Washington. Stalin took the bait.

Churchill had come to Truman's home state of Missouri in 1946 to deliver his famous 'Iron Curtain' speech in the small town of Fulton, proclaiming that a new division of Europe was underway. Since at least 1943 Churchill and the British Round Table circles near him calculated they needed to create a new conflict with the Soviets in order to make Britain indispensable to the inexperienced Washington as the 'mediator' between the Soviets and the United States.

Early in 1945, before the German surrender, Churchill had ordered captured German divisions to be maintained intact, along with their weapons, for possible further deployment against the Soviet Red Army. This was an extraordinary and unprecedented procedure. The plan was vetoed on military grounds by General Eisenhower and the White House. It revealed however that the British were already preparing the ground for the next phase in their 'Balance of Power' world.[11] Washington and London were already secretly back-stabbing their ally Russia.

By 1945 Churchill had realized that Britain would have to put up a hard fight with Washington to maintain even a semblance of its pre-war power. Truman made clear very early in his Administration that such would be the case.

When Truman unexpectedly canceled Lend-Lease aid to Britain just after the Japanese surrender in August 1945, and demanded repayment of Britain's war credits, Washington signaled the new postwar order. By war's end Britain's gold and dollar reserves were down to less than $1,500 millions and her short term debt stood at a staggering $12 billion. England's non-war related industry was in desolate condition. Coal production had fallen dramatically; electricity blackouts were common. Millions of returning soldiers had to be reintegrated into a tattered civilian economy.

If Churchill and the British could lure Truman into a new confrontation with Russia, there was a chance that Britain would become indispensable to Washington and at least preserve a semblance of its former Great Power standing. That at least was the logic in London.[12]

Canceling Lend-Lease was clearly hostile to London, particularly as Truman made an exception in continuing Lend-Lease aid to China at the same time.[13] The cancellation of US credits and supplies to Britain was consistent with the CFR's strategy of maintaining the weakened position of America's one potential economic rival for the postwar era—Great Britain—especially its Sterling Preference agreements with its dominions and vast number of colonies around the world. The architects of the American Century had no intention of dealing with anyone, not even its old ally Great Britain, as an equal.

Roosevelt and the Rockefellers clearly had not gone to war in order to save the British Empire. Exactly the opposite. Roosevelt and Truman both knew that Britain would have to be brought to her knees before she would agree to be junior partner in an Anglo-American 'Special Relationship.' As Britain's Harold Macmillan, wartime emissary of Winston Churchill, expressed the new reality to Richard Crossman, a prominent British Social Democrat,

We, my dear Crossman, are Greeks in this American Empire. You will find the Americans much as the Greeks found the Romans— great big, vulgar, bustling people, more vigorous than we are and more idle, with more unspoiled virtues but also more corrupt. We must run Allied Forces Headquarters as the Greek slaves ran the operations of the Emperor Claudius. [14]

Churchill's April 1946 Iron Curtain speech in Fulton Missouri marked the turning point in swinging Washington behind England's confrontationist policy towards Stalin and the Soviet Union. The Anglo-American postwar 'special relationship' was not to be a marriage of equals no matter how much London wished. But at least they were still in the game as they saw it, even if it was an American game.

That American 'game' was to use its military and economic power to create a new economic imperium using the manufactured threat of Soviet spread of communism as the new global threat replacing Hitler's armies.

Endnotes:

[1] Harold Macmillan, quoted in Christopher Hitchens, *Blood, Class and Nostalgia: Anglo-American Ironies* (New York: Farrar, Straus & Giroux, 1990), p. 23.

[2] Phillip Cagan, *Determinants of Change in the Stock of Money: 1875-1960* (New York: Columbia University Press, 1965), p. 341.

[3] In a curious footnote to the history of Bretton Woods, following the opening of secret Soviet archives after 1991, it was confirmed that White, as later US intelligence circles suspected, had indeed been a member of the Silvermaster Soviet spy ring within the US Government. On reports of his possible Soviet role, Truman rescinded his nomination as first Director General of the new International Monetary Fund, without explanation.

White had played a role in formulating the notorious Morgenthau Plan for the deindustrialization of postwar Germany, a plan which makes more sense as a Soviet rather than US goal, though Roosevelt, a fervent Germanophobe, heartily backed the idea until his death. The plan, under US military directive JCS (Joint Chiefs of Staff) 1067, would allow the Western occupation powers and the Soviet Union dismember German industrial plant and turn the nation into a 'pastoral' food supplier. In March 1945 just days before his death, when Roosevelt was warned that the JCS was not workable, unless he were ready to eliminate 25 million Germans, his response was 'Let them have soup kitchens! Let their economy sink!' Asked if he wanted the German people to starve, he replied, 'Why not?' FDR also reportedly told Morgenthau, 'We have got to be tough with the Germans and I mean the German people not just the Nazis. We either have to castrate the German people or you have got to treat them in such a manner so they can't just go on reproducing people who want to continue the way they have in the past.' On May 10, 1945, following the death of FDR, Truman signed the JCS 1067. It remained in effect for two brutal years, despite the strong protest of Churchill and others. See Michael R. Beschloss, *The Conquerors: Roosevelt, Truman and the Destruction of Hitler's Germany, 1941-1945*, p. 196 for the FDR quote. See Allen Weinstein & Alexander Vassiliev, *The Haunted Wood*, 1999, Random House, New York, p. 90 for the details of Harry Dexter White's KGB activities as revealed in declassified Soviet archives after the end of the Cold War.

[4] Neil Smith, *American Empire: Roosevelt's Geographer and the Prelude to Globalization* (Berkeley: University of California Press, 2003), p. xii.

[5] Cited in Gideon Rachman, *The Bretton Woods Sequel will Flop*, London Financial Times, November 10, 2008.

[6] M.W. Kirby, op. cit., pp. 91-92.

[7] Peter Collier & David Horowitz, *The Rockefellers: An American Dynasty* (New York: Holt Rinehart & Winston, 1976), pp. 234-235.

[8] Victor Argy, *The Postwar International Monetary Crisis* (London: George Allen & Unwin, 1981), p. 24.

[9] A. Stadnichenko, *Monetary Crisis of Capitalism*, (Moscow: Progress Publishers, 1975), pp. 88-101.

[10] Ibid, pp. 100-103.

[11] Fraser J. Harbutt, *The Iron Curtain: Churchill, America and the Origins of the Cold War* (Oxford: Oxford University Press, 1986), pp. 101-149.

[12] Sir Richard Clarke, *Anglo-American Economic Collaboration 1942-1949* (Oxford: Clarendon Press, 1982), pp. 21-26.

[13] Richard N. Gardner, *Sterling-Dollar Diplomacy* (Oxford: Clarendon Press, 1956), pp. 184-186.

[14] Harold Macmillan, op. cit.

CHAPTER TWELVE

A National Security State is Born

A more rapid build-up of political, economic, and military strength... is the only course which is consistent with progress toward achieving our fundamental purpose. The frustration of the Kremlin design requires the free world to develop a successfully functioning political and economic system and a vigorous political offensive against the Soviet Union. These, in turn, require an adequate military shield under which they can develop.

   –   Paul Nitze, principal author NSC 68[1]

Marshall Plan: Dawn of the American Century

By 1947 Washington was prepared to bring Western Europe into its economic fold, and to isolate the Soviets. They proposed a bilateral US Marshall Plan for reconstruction of Europe as the vehicle for the new strategy.

The most powerful figures in US industry, New York banking, and international policy—most of them linked to the Rockefeller group—were clear as to what their postwar agenda was about.

In 1946 Leo D. Welch, then Treasurer of Standard Oil Company, called for Washington "...to set forth the political, military, territorial and economic requirements of the United States in its potential leadership of the non-German world area, including the United Kingdom itself, as well as the Western hemisphere and the Far East."

Welch continued his call, using American business vernacular:

> As the largest source of capital, and the biggest contributor to the global mechanism, we must set the pace and assume the responsibility of the majority stockholder in this corporation known as the world...nor is this for a given term of office. This is a permanent obligation.[2]

In 1948, George F. Kennan, wrote a confidential internal State Department memo. It outlined the postwar agenda of the US power establishment very succinctly:

> ...[W]e have about 50% of the world's wealth but only 6.3% of its population.... In this situation, we cannot fail to be the object of envy and resentment. Our real task in the coming period is to devise a pattern of relationships which will permit us to maintain this position of disparity without positive detriment to our national security. To do so, we will have to dispense with all sentimentality and day-dreaming; and our attention will have to be concentrated everywhere on our immediate national objectives. We need not deceive ourselves that we can afford today the luxury of altruism and world-benefaction. [3]

Kennan, architect of the Cold War 'containment' policy, outlined the real nature of post-war US policies. Kennan was coldly honest and realistic about the true postwar goal of the US elite: it was US domination of the world, or at least as much of it as it could seize and hold onto in 1948. That was the CFR's proposed Grand Area.

In July 1947 Secretary of State George Marshall unveiled the plan for the economic reconstruction of Europe that was designed to entrench the domination of US industry, big oil and finance in postwar Europe—the Marshall Plan or, officially, the European Recovery Program, ERP.

The US drafters of the Marshall Plan, including George Kennan, deliberately offered US aid to the Soviet Union for their postwar reconstruction, but they made it conditional on Stalin's allocating large volumes of Soviet raw materials for Western Europe as well as opening its socialist economy to the capitalist west. These and other unacceptable conditions predictably led to Soviet rejection of the aid, leaving the US to dominate Western Europe economically, without having to make any pretense of cooperating with the Soviets.[4]

The terms of Marshall aid were drafted to include massive transfers of US industrial products to Europe, a practical way to penetrate the markets of postwar Western Europe to a degree not possible before the war. Above all, the aid involved selling oil from the reserves of the Rockefellers' Standard Oil empire. According to a US Senate inquiry, the single largest expenditure for countries receiving Marshall Plan aid was for the purchase of American oil -- oil supplied by the Rockefeller Standard Oil companies at highly inflated prices - paid for in US dollars.[5]

By the end of the war, the Rockefeller-dominated US oil industry had become every bit as international as its British counterpart. Its main resources were in Venezuela, the Middle East and other far away places. Big Oil, nicknamed the "Five Sisters," included five giant companies—Standard Oil of New Jersey (Exxon), Socony-Vacuum Oil (Mobil), Standard Oil of California (Chevron), Texaco, and the Mellon family's Gulf Oil. They quickly took decisive control of Europe's postwar petroleum markets.

The ravages of war had severely hurt European economies dependent on coal as their primary energy source. Germany had lost her eastern coal reserves to the Soviet zone, and coal output in the war-torn west was only 40% of prewar levels. British coal output was 20% below the level of 1938. The oil of Eastern Europe, behind what Churchill had called the 'Iron Curtain,' was inaccessible to the west. By 1947, therefore, half of all Western Europe's oil was being supplied by the five big American companies.

The American oil majors didn't hesitate to take advantage of this remarkable monopoly.

Despite Congressional inquiry and mid-level bureaucratic protest at the obvious misuse of Marshall Plan funds, the American oil majors forced Europe to pay inflated prices. The Rockefeller oil companies, for example, more than doubled the price they charged European customers between 1945 and 1948, going from $1.05/barrel to $2.22/barrel. Though the oil was supplied from the inexpensive Middle East reserves of the US companies -- where extraction costs were typically less than 25 cents a barrel -- the freight rates were calculated in a deliberately complex formula, tied to freight rates between the Caribbean and Europe, resulting in a far higher cost.

Even within European markets, there were staggering cost differences among the countries. Greece was forced to pay $8.30/ton for fuel oil, the same fuel oil for which Britain paid only $3.95/ton. Further, the US companies, with support from Washington, refused to allow Marshall Plan dollars to be used to build indigenous European refining capacity, further tightening the lock-grip of American Big Oil on postwar Europe. [6]

The Marshall reconstruction plan was established on July 12, 1947 and continued beyond the Korean war to 1953, during which time Washington had advanced some $13 billion in economic and technical investments to help the recovery of European countries. The aid was given with heavy strings attached, even extending into the entertainment industry. For example, in return for its receipt of American financial assistance, France was required to show American films, to the detriment of the French film industry. Washington well understood the value of Hollywood as a propaganda vehicle to promote the 'American way of life' as well as American products.

The Marshall Plan also opened the way for large US corporations to invest in the industries of Western Europe at bargain prices as European currencies were heavily depreciated in dollar terms after 1945 under the parities set under initial IMF rules in relation to the dollar.

Initially, Marshall Plan aid was used primarily for the purchase of consumer goods from the United States, such as food and fuel, and later for industrial goods for reconstruction. After the start of the Korean War in 1950, an increasing amount of the aid was spent on rebuilding the militaries of Western Europe, under the creation of a new Atlantic defense organization, NATO, mostly with military equipment made in America. US arms exports were to become a strategic priority of US postwar export policy.

NATO Cold War—America's *Lebensraum*

Greece became the unlikely staging ground for the first direct confrontation of the Cold War – instigated not by the United States, but by Britain. Since 1946, internal Greek politics had been marked by a power struggle between the conservative government of Konstantinos Tsaldaris and the KKE, the Greek communist party. Churchill initiated support to the conservatives and Truman's hawkish Secretary of State Dean Acheson urged Truman to back up the British.

However, prior to this, in an October 1944 Moscow conference between Churchill and Stalin, the Soviet and British leaders had agreed on the postwar division of southeastern Europe into respective Soviet and British spheres of interest. Under their agreement, the Soviet Union and Great Britain worked out respective percentages of 'influence' that each would have in Romania, Bulgaria, Greece, Hungary and Yugoslavia. Initially, Churchill proposed that Great Britain should have 90 percent control in Greece, and the Soviet Union would have 90 percent influence in Romania, while in Hungary and Yugoslavia, Churchill suggested that they should have 50 percent each.

Their two foreign ministers, Anthony Eden and Vyacheslav Molotov, negotiated about the percentage shares on October 10 and 11. The result of those discussions was that the percentages of Soviet influence in Bulgaria and Hungary were amended from 90 percent and 75 percent respectively to 80 percent. More significantly, apart from that, no other countries were mentioned, leaving Greece within Britain's sphere. Stalin kept to his promise in Greece;

Great Britain supported the Greek government forces in the civil war, and the Soviet Union did not assist the communist partisans. [7]

Despite that fact – of Soviet non-intervention -- Acheson convinced President Truman that a bold declaration of support for 'freedom' in Greece was urgently necessary, even though Greece at the time was not considered a strategic priority for US interests in Europe, and even though there was no Soviet involvement or threat of involvement.

Truman proclaimed what came to be called the Truman Doctrine in an address to the US Congress on March 12, 1947, amid the crisis of the Greek Civil War. He declared, "I believe that it must be the policy of the United States to support free peoples who are resisting attempted subjugation by armed minorities or by outside pressures." The "outside pressures" were not identified.

Truman insisted that if Greece and Turkey did not receive the aid that they needed, they would inevitably fall to Soviet-led Communism with consequences throughout the region, an argument that would be repeated two decades later in Vietnam, when it was termed 'the domino effect'-- a prediction of dire consequences that never materialized in that region either.

Surprisingly, Truman was supported at the time by Senator Arthur H. Vandenberg, the influential head of the Senate Foreign Relations Committee and previously leader of Senate isolationists. Vandenberg convinced the Republican-controlled Congress in March 1947 to endorse the Truman Doctrine "at the urging of the United Kingdom." British intelligence had quietly wooed and won over Vandenberg, traditionally one of her most ardent and influential Congressional foes. [8]

Thus, less than a year after his famous Fulton Missouri Iron Curtain speech, Churchill was successfully pulling Truman into his Cold War strategy against the Soviet Union. The Council on Foreign Relations had been urging the same policy for months, but for quite different motives -- establishment of their American *Lebensraum* in Europe once it was clear that Stalin would not open Russia's doors to American economic penetration.

The Truman Doctrine, which ably served the Washington *Lebensraum* agenda, aimed at replacing the British Empire with the United States as the economic and military guarantor of Greece and Turkey. It was a radical reorientation of US foreign policy. As one historian noted, "For the first time in its history, the United States had chosen to intervene in a period of general peace in the affairs of people outside of North and South America." [9]

The ground for the interventionist Truman Doctrine had been laid in a sensational Council on Foreign Relations essay appearing in their *Foreign Affairs* magazine under the signature, 'Mr. X.' The article was adapted from what was called a "long telegram from Moscow" written by George Kennan, the State Department's assistant to Ambassador Harriman in Moscow.

In February 1946, Washington asked the US Embassy in Moscow why the Soviets were not supporting the newly created World Bank and the International Monetary Fund. In reply, Kennan wrote his "Long Telegram" in response, outlining his opinions and the views of the Soviets, and sent it to Secretary of Defense James Forrestal, a close Rockefeller ally within the Truman Administration who brought it to the attention of the Council on Foreign Relations to help push the policy shift to a hostile stance towards Moscow.

Kennan argued among other things that while Soviet power was impervious to the logic of reason, it was highly sensitive to the logic of force. He argued that the Stalinist state perceived the world as divided between irreconcilable forces of communism and capitalism. It was the birth of US 'containment' of the Soviet Union as policy, and laid the propaganda basis for more than forty years of US Cold War containment policy towards Russia. In reality containment of the Soviet Union served the useful purpose for the US power establishment and their military industry of creating a permanent national security state with what later were revealed as fictional images of an aggressive, threatening Soviet Union. [10]

US foreign policy was being significantly shifted from an alliance with the Soviet Union against the German threat to one of gradual alliance with a postwar humiliated Germany against the alleged Soviet threat. It was classical British "Balance of Power" machinations—only done in an American style.

The Greek crisis, however, was not sufficient to achieve the kind of American economic restructuring which the powerful banking and industry circles of the establishment needed. Nor were a Soviet Berlin blockade, or even a communist takeover of the government of Czechoslovakia in February 1948 sufficient, although they had spurred the isolationist US Congress to vote for financial aid to Western Europe via the Marshall Plan, and soon led to US support of NATO. It took a major shock to convince a reluctant war-weary American citizenry that a new state of war, a more or less permanent "cold war" was required for their security.

Not even the victory of the Communist Party of China under Mao Zedong in the Chinese Civil War which ended in 1949 with the defeat of the Kuomintang (KMT) and the corrupt despot, Chiang Kai-shek, which had led to the proclamation of the People's Republic of China, was sufficient to galvanize domestic US support for the levels of military spending which the powerful defense industries were hoping for.

For the Rockefeller faction and their allies in American finance and industry, the mere fact that state socialism in the Soviet Union and China now effectively removed more than one-fifth of the planet's land mass and untold treasures of raw materials and resources as well as potential markets from their grip was sufficient grounds to declare them the new "enemy image." Their problem was how to sell it to a skeptical American population, how to sufficiently mobilize fear and anxiety in the American public to justify financing a permanent war state directed against the new "absolute evil, Godless Communist Totalitarianism."

NSC 68 and a phantom 'enemy image'

Leading circles in and around the Truman Administration concluded by late 1949 that the only means to mobilize a sense of sacrifice from the American population for vastly larger military spending—spending they saw as needed to secure their new global *Lebensraum*—would be a new war. The ideal war would be one that could be managed, and one that posed no direct threat to the United States or the still-fragile Western Europe.

By 1948 the US economy faced a dramatic postwar recession as contracts for the war industry fell dramatically and no civilian spending of a comparable scale filled the economic deficit. Between 1948 and 1950 official US unemployment rose by an alarming 130%. The national index of production, which stood at a peak of 212 in the height of the war mobilization effort, had dropped to 170 by 1948 and as low as 156 by 1949. By the first quarter of 1950 capital investment had dropped an alarming 11% from a year earlier. Beginning 1947 US exports registered a decline, dropping from March 1949 to March 1950 by some 25%.

For various reasons, Korea was chosen as the ideal place to stage a limited war designed to mobilize popular support for a permanent national security state. The goal was the enormous expansion of military industry on a permanent basis -- what financier and Truman adviser Bernard Baruch labeled a "Cold War."[11]

In late 1948 Washington announced plans for the creation of a new Atlantic military alliance with its Marshall Plan partners, in return for permanent US bases in western European countries. The legal instrument to create a North Atlantic Treaty Organization, NATO, was signed in April 1949, with Belgium, Luxembourg, the Netherlands, France and Britain joining Washington.

Within months, the Korean War would galvanize NATO members to accept an active, permanent military defense organization in Western Europe under the control of Washington, with headquarters in Brussels. A war weary Europe was drawn into Washington's Cold War strategy via a military alliance; both the strategy and the alliance would endure well beyond the collapse of the Soviet Union some four decades later.

The first military commander of NATO, Britain's Lord Ishmay, announced that the purpose of NATO was "to keep the Russians out, the Americans in, and the Germans down."[12] This would be modified during the Korean War when Washington turned to the German steel industry for weapons production. Germany by the early 1950s was being integrated into the new US geopolitics of the Cold War. NATO was to serve as the major military pillar of an American Century.

In 1949, a year after the creation of NATO, a top secret group within the US State Department convened to formulate a new US strategic policy. Their report, "NSC 68: United States Objectives and Programs for National Security," argued for a US military buildup to confront what it claimed was an enemy "unlike previous aspirants to hegemony... animated by a new fanatic faith, antithetical to our own."

The group, chaired by former Wall Street banker Paul Nitze, argued that the Soviet Union and the United States existed in a polarized world in which the Soviet Union wished to "impose its absolute authority over the rest of the world." [13]

The top secret document argued that this would be a war of ideas in which "the idea of freedom under a government of laws, and the idea of slavery under the grim oligarchy of the Kremlin" were pitted against each other. The US as "the center of power in the free world" should build an international community in which American society would "survive and flourish" while pursuing a policy of containment. The document drew heavily from Kennan's earlier 'Mr. X' paper, but emphasized a military rather than political response to the alleged Soviet global threat.[14]

NSC 68 painted a hair-raising and quite unreal picture of Soviet military intentions in 1950, a time when the USSR was not yet even recovered from the devastations of the Second World War in which more than 26 million of her people had perished and major cities had been reduced to rubble. After the war, the Soviet Union had, in fact, dramatically demobilized her army in order to have enough manpower to rebuild the country. The reality of a devastated and drastically weakened Soviet Union played little role in the team's report. They simply conjured an alarming threat analysis:

> Should a major war occur in 1950 the Soviet Union and its satellites are considered by the Joint Chiefs of Staff to be in a sufficiently advanced state of preparation immediately to undertake and carry out the following campaigns.

*a. To overrun Western Europe, with the possible exception of the
Iberian and Scandinavian Peninsulas; to drive toward the oil-
bearing areas of the Near and Middle East; and to consolidate
Communist gains in the Far East;*

*b. To launch air attacks against the British Isles and air and sea at-
tacks against the lines of communications of the Western Powers in
the Atlantic and the Pacific;*

*c. To attack selected targets with atomic weapons, now including
the likelihood of such attacks against targets in Alaska, Canada,
and the United States. Alternatively, this capability, coupled with
other actions open to the Soviet Union, might deny the United
Kingdom as an effective base of operations for allied forces. It also
should be possible for the Soviet Union to prevent any allied 'Normandy' type amphibious operations intended to force a re-entry
into the continent of Europe.* [15]

· The 1950 Nitze report recommended a clear course of action, short of a
preemptive nuclear war, against the Soviet Union. It concluded:

*A more rapid build-up of political, economic, and military strength
and thereby of confidence in the free world than is now contem-
plated is the only course which is consistent with progress toward
achieving our fundamental purpose. The frustration of the Kremlin
design requires the free world to develop a successfully functioning
political and economic system and a vigorous political offensive
against the Soviet Union. These, in turn, require an adequate military shield under which they can develop.* [16]

The initial response to Nitze's NSC 68 recommendations was hardly positive. Truman, concerned at the budget costs, sent the paper back for estimates of
its cost. Congress regarded it as unnecessarily alarmist. Willard Thorp, Assistant
Secretary of State under Truman for Economic Affairs, disagreed with the
alarming picture of Soviet military readiness for war. Thorp questioned its
contention that the "USSR is steadily reducing the discrepancy between its
overall economic strength and that of the United States." He argued, "I do not
feel that this position is demonstrated, but rather the reverse... The actual gap is
widening in our favor." As for Soviet military investment, Thorp was skeptical

that the USSR was committing such a large portion of its GDP: "I suspect a larger portion of Soviet investment went into housing." [17]

William Schaub of the Bureau of the Budget was also critical, arguing that "in every arena"—Air Force, Army, Navy, the stockpiling of atomic bombs, the economy -- the US was far superior to the Soviet Union. Even George Kennan disagreed with the document, particularly its call for massive rearmament. As one consultant to the Nitze report noted, "the government was going to need assistance in getting public support for the national effort which would be called for." [18]

Following proclamation of the Truman Doctrine, a creation of Secretary of State Dean Acheson, the Administration's propaganda apparatus tried to drum up popular support for their Cold War against the 'evil, Godless' communists in the Soviet Union. They believed that they could win popular voter support for huge increases in Federal defense spending by "scaring the hell out of America," as one of Truman's advisors put it --perhaps by engendering a "war scare to deceive the nation." [19]

In his memoirs, Dean Acheson admitted, "the task of a public officer seeking to explain or gain support for a major policy is not that of the writer of a doctoral thesis. Qualification must give way to simplicity of statement, nicety and nuance to bluntness, almost brutality, in carrying home the point." [20] Third Reich Propaganda Minister Josef Goebbels couldn't have stated it better.

The circles around Acheson, Harriman, key Pentagon military figures such as General Douglas MacArthur, and the Rockefellers set about to manufacture just such "real and continuing crises."

Korea gives the excuse

The first 'crisis' began two months after Nitze's report had been distributed to carefully selected members of the Administration. The crisis was located in the US client dictatorship of South Korea's Syngman Rhee, a man who had been restored to power by Washington to take control of the South Korean government after living 33 years in the United States.

A war to 'defend' South Korea had many attractions. First it would indirectly implicate the Soviet Union as the main supporter of the North Korean regime of communist Kim il Sung. Second, the Rockefellers and the Dulles brothers and their business associates had poured huge investments into South Korea. Following the defeat of Japan, the US and Soviet Union had agreed to divide the country temporarily at the 38th Parallel until order could be restored. The division into two countries had been arbitrary and jerry rigged from the start.

Truman and his advisers manipulated events to declare a UN 'police action' in Korea to create a permanent Cold War with the USSR and China in 1950. The mentally unstable General Douglas MacArthur wanted to use Korea to declare war on China.

On June 25, 1950 the world received the shocking report from South Korea that the North Korean Army had launched a major invasion of the south. The reports were initially conflicting however. American historian John Gunther, then traveling in Japan with General MacArthur, provided this first-hand account of an aide to the US General excitedly reporting a telephone call from Seoul: "The south Koreans have attacked the north!" [21]

Also casting suspicion on the Washington version of events was that the US called an extraordinary meeting of the UN Security Council when the Soviets were staging a temporary protest boycott. This meant that Moscow was not there to veto a UN Security Council resolution authorizing UN 'peacekeeping forces' (in reality US troops under the command of Douglas MacArthur) to "stop the north Korean aggression." Conveniently left out of official statements by the US Embassy and Washington was also the fact that the South Korean Air Force, two days *before* the June 25 response by North Korea in the south, had repeatedly bombed targets in the North and South Korean troops had marched into and occupied Haeju in the North.

Contrary to these facts, Washington's entire argument for the 'UN' intervention -- technically termed a 'UN police action'-- was that the communist north had initiated a massive unprovoked invasion of the south, a line that was repeated throughout the coming months and for years thereafter in all US official propaganda statements.

General MacArthur, for his part, had demanded of Truman that US forces under his command use the pretext of the Korean conflict to launch a direct military attack on China itself, one using nuclear weapons. US Defense Secretary Louis Johnson was also convinced that an immediate war against Mao's regime before they could consolidate power would be easier than a war he considered "inevitable" later on. MacArthur agreed.

MacArthur, US Chief of Joint Chiefs of Staff General Omar Bradley, Defense Secretary Johnson and Rockefeller lawyer and State Department consultant, John Foster Dulles, all wanted to use Korea as a stepping stone for a direct war not just against China, but ultimately against the Soviet Union itself in Asia.[22]

They were overruled in Washington by Harriman, Acheson and others who understood that the purpose of the war was not to 'win' in the sense of conquering China and the Soviets. Rather, Korea's war was a matter of US geopolitical grand strategy to shift the pieces on the Asian chess board and mobilize Cold War fears within NATO and the US population, in order to provide the pretext for creating an enormous, permanent US national security state. Once the 'war' began, Congress passed NSC 68 quickly. Dean Acheson later remarked: "Korea... created the stimulus which made action."[23] The Korean War led most Americans to conclude that the Soviet Union was indeed bent on world domination. It was the needed catalyst to justify mobilization of the nation's significant resources to counter the perceived threat.

US war propaganda in the media played up the major US investment stake in Korea, reporting, accurately, that US banks and firms had invested the impressively large sum of more than $ 1,250,000,000 into south Korea. The Rockefeller-controlled National City Bank was a major investor and Rockefeller attorney John Foster Dulles sat on the board of the bank's *New Corea Company* in Seoul.[24]

The Korean War served the agenda of the Washington Cold War faction masterfully. The US Defense budget soared 400% from less than $13 billion at the start of the war to more than $60 billion by war's end in 1953. US puppet regimes under Chiang Kai-shek in Taiwan and Syngman Rhee in South Korea, and a US Military Government in Japan under Douglas MacArthur, would provide the basis for America's Cold War presence in East Asia. Under MacArthur's occupation, assisted by a young New York banker named John D. Rockefeller, III, Japan's industry was allowed to reorganize into giant conglomerate groups to provide a 'bulwark against communism' in Asia.

With an annual budget of $60 billion the Defense Department became the world's largest contractor, issuing billions of dollars of orders to US and select European and Japanese industry for defense 'preparedness.' Germany was permitted to begin rebuilding the Ruhr steel industry as a result of the war in Korea. The military industrial complex grew to gargantuan dimensions during the 1950s. The Cold War was on in high style and Standard Oil was a huge benefactor, providing fuel to the air force, tanks, jeeps, destroyers and other vehicles of the Pentagon. In the domestic US economy, politicians quickly realized that they could get almost any program passed by Congress if they argued 'US national security' and 'defense against totalitarian Godless communism.'

In 1953, the war and national security anxiety of the American public had been raised to such a fever pitch that retired wartime General Eisenhower was elected President. It was the Rockefellers initially who had convinced Eisenhower to run and who organized Wall Street money behind his campaign. After the 1952 Republican convention, isolationist Senator Robert Taft, who had been passed over by the Rockefellers, declared bitterly, "Every Republican candidate for President since 1936 has been nominated by the Chase Bank."[25]

It was not surprising that the Rockefeller interests played a major role in Eisenhower's cabinet choices. The new President named as his CIA chief, Allen Dulles, former President of Rockefellers' Council on Foreign Relations.[26] Allen Dulles and his brother John Foster as earlier noted,[27] were both attorneys for the Rockefeller interests and had been instrumental in various business deals between Standard Oil, the Rockefellers' Chase Bank and I.G. Farben during the Third Reich. After the war, Allen Dulles had served as station chief in Berne Switzerland for the Office of Strategic Services, predecessor to the CIA. OSS head, William J. Donovan, had set up his initial headquarters in Room 3603 of the Rockefeller Center.

To add to the Rockefeller/CFR domination of Eisenhower's Cold War foreign policy team, the President named John Foster Dulles to the vital post of Secretary of State. John Foster Dulles, as partner of the Wall Street law firm, Sullivan & Cromwell, had represented Rockefellers' Standard Oil and also sat as a Trustee of the Rockefeller Foundation. [28]

In addition to dominating the two largest banks in New York -- Chase Bank and National City Bank of New York -- Rockefeller controlled the largest oil companies in the world, the Standard Oil group, and numerous strategic military industries, chemical companies, and agribusiness firms. In addition to controlling the CFR and now, through the Dulles brothers, the Central Intelligence Agency and State Department, Nelson Rockefeller himself was named in 1954 as Eisenhower's Special Assistant on Cold War Strategy, responsible to the President for oversight of CIA covert operations, and development of various strategic policy positions. [29]

CIA coups against phantom communists

As one of his first operations, Dulles authorized the CIA in 1953 to manufacture a coup against the enormously popular and democratically elected Prime

Minister of Iran, Mohammed Mossadegh who had nationalized the operations of British Petroleum (Anglo-Persian Oil Company) when they refused to pay a higher royalty fee for their control of Iran's oil. After the US-backed Shah of Iran was returned to power and installed a brutal dictatorship, control over Iran's oil shifted from British Petroleum to the Rockefeller Standard Oil companies. [30]

Soon thereafter, Allen Dulles' CIA quickly moved to topple the democratically elected government of President Jacobo Arbenez in Guatemala in 1954, claiming that it threatened American business interests and was "communist-influenced." In actual fact, the 'business' was the Rockefeller and Dulles-linked United Fruit Company. Arbenez was a nationalist trying to implement mild land reform to give peasants land at the expense of the large foreign banana plantations.

During the war, in 1944, the people of Guatemala overthrew an oppressive right-wing dictator Jorge Ubico and the country held its first true elections in history, electing Dr. Juan Jose Arevalo Bermej President. A new constitution based on the US Constitution was adopted. Arevalo was an educator who built over 6,000 schools in Guatemala and emphasized education and health care.

At the time in Guatemala had been in the firm grip of giant wealthy landowners with just over 2% of the population owning over 70 % of the land. The most powerful landowner was the American-owned United Fruit Company. For 90% of the mostly Indian population they were forced to eke out a dismal survival on only 10% of the country's land while most of the land owned by the large latifundistas lay idle.

In 1951 in a second free election Arevalo was succeeded by Jacobo Arbenz who continued Arevalo's reform process. Arbenz proposed to redistribute part of the unused land and make it available for the landless Indian majority to farm. United Fruit was the largest holder of unused land in Guatemala, holding an incredible 42% of all land in the country, and some 95% of it standing idle, and paying virtually no taxes in Guatemala.

Reacting to the nationalization threat, United Fruit mobilized its friends in the Eisenhower Administration, not least the Dulles brothers. Allen Dulles was head of the CIA and brother John Foster, Secretary of State. The two Dulles brothers launched a black propaganda campaign falsely alleging that Guatemala under Arbenz had become a "Soviet satellite." [31]

The US State Department and United Fruit embarked on a major public relations campaign to convince the American people and the rest of the US government that Guatemala was a Soviet "satellite." The ties between United Fruit and the Dulles brothers went back to the days John Foster Dulles' old law firm, Sullivan and Cromwell, had long represented the company. Allen Dulles, had served on United Fruit's board of trustees. Ed Whitman, the company's top public relations officer, was the husband of President Eisenhower's private secretary Ann Whitman.

In a propaganda bid that rivaled Woodrow Wilson's World War I propaganda effort, Ed Whitman produced a film, "Why the Kremlin Hates Bananas," that pictured United Fruit fighting in the front trenches of the cold war. The firm's success in linking the taking of its lands to the evil of international communism was later described by one company official as "the Disney version of the episode." United Fruit paid all expenses for US journalists to fly to Guatemala to learn United Fruit's side of the crisis, and soon the nation's leading press including the *New York Times* were running with the communist version of Guatelmalan events that had been spoon fed them by United Fruit's Whitman.[32]

In 1954 Dulles' Central Intelligence Agency orchestrated a coup, code-named *"Operation PBSUCCESS,"* with an invading force of only 150 men under the command of Castillo Armas, whom Washington installed as "their" dictator. United Fruit was left untouched. The propaganda credibility of the Cold War was significantly enhanced. [33]

Highways, too, against the 'Soviet threat'

Even domestically the Rockefeller interests were turning the Cold War climate to their decided advantage. President Eisenhower's largest public investment program was the National Interstate and Defense Highways Act (Public Law 84-627). The law was enacted on June 29, 1956. Congress appropriated $25 billion for the construction of 41,000 miles (66,000 km) of interstate highways over a 20-year period. It was the largest public works project in American history to that point. The national highway infrastructure laid the foundation for the postwar automobile and truck transport age. Detroit's General Motors and Rockefellers' Standard Oil companies were the primary beneficiaries.

National railway infrastructure was deliberately neglected in favor of truck and passenger car transport. The American public was, meanwhile, being told that all of this was in their interests, as the highways should supposedly speed the exit from cities in event of a Soviet nuclear attack, or so Americans were told. As Eisenhower's Defense Secretary and former chairman of General Motors Charles Wilson stated in a famous remark in 1955, "What's good for General Motors is good for America."

By 1957 however, despite or more accurately, because of, the creation of the American National Security State and the Cold War, major fault lines in the postwar US Bretton Woods dollar system were beginning to appear. The US economy had entered a severe recession. The economies of Western Europe were emerging as economic powerhouses, none more than the Federal Republic of Germany that had rebuilt its industry with state-of-the art technology for steel and other sectors.

US corporations for their part had been neglecting their domestic industrial infrastructure in favor of buying finished companies with the strong dollar in Europe and Latin America, Africa and around the world. The once mighty US Federal Reserve gold stocks -- which had been the world's largest just a decade earlier -- were being slowly drained as foreign central banks redeemed dollar trade surpluses for gold to build their own gold stocks.

Endnotes

[1] Paul Nitze et al, *NSC 68: United States Objectives and Programs for National Security, A Report to the President Pursuant to the President's Directive of January 31, 1950*, dated April 14, 1950, reprinted in Naval War College Review, Vol. XXVII (May-June, 1975), pp. 51-108.

[2] Quoted in, Michael Tanzer, op. cit., *p. 78.*

[3] George Kennan, *Policy Planning Study 23 (PPS/23): 'Review of Current Trends in U.S. Foreign Policy,'* Published in Foreign Relations of the United States, 1948, Volume I, pp. 509-529, marked 'Top Secret' but later declassified.

[4] William Appleman Williams, op. cit., p. 208.

[5] US Senate Select Committee on Small Business, ECA and MSA Relations with International Oil Companies Concerning Petroleum Prices, 82nd Congress, 2nd Session, 1952.

[6] David S. Painter, *Oil and the Marshall Plan*, Business History Review, no. 58, Autumn 1984, pp.359-383.

[7] P. M. H. Bell, *The World Since 1945: An International History* (Oxford: Hodder Arnold, 2001).

[8] For details of British intelligence operations using a British mata hari, Evelyn Paterson, to sway the influential Senate isolationist Vandenberg in a British-friendly direction, see Thomas E. Mahl, *Desperate Deception: British Covert Operations in the United States, 1939-1944* (London: Brassey's, 1998), pp. 150-154.

[9] Stephen Ambrose, cited in Reza Zia-Ebrahimi, *Which episode did more to consolidate the Cold War consensus: the Truman Doctrine speech of March 1947 or the Czech crisis of February-March 1948?*, January 2007, accessed in http://www.zia-ebrahimi.com/truman.html.

[10] George F. Kennan ('Mr. X'), *The Sources of Soviet Conduct*, Foreign Affairs, vol. 25, no. 4, July 1947, pp. 566-582. The article was written by George F. Kennan, the Deputy Chief of Mission of the United States to the USSR, from 1944 to 1946, under ambassador W. Averell Harriman.

[11] John Lewis Gaddis, *The Cold War: A New History*, (New York:Penguin Press, 2005), p. 54.

[12] Quoted in Reynolds, *The Origins of the Cold War in Europe*, International perspectives, p. 13.

[13] Paul Nitze et al, op. cit, pp. 51-108.

[14] Ibid.

[15] Ibid. *V. Soviet Intentions and Capabilities: C. Military*

[16] Ibid., IX. *Possible Courses of Action: D. The Remaining Course of Action—A Rapid Buildup of Political, Economic, and Military Strength in the Free World.*

[17] Willard Thorp, cited in *NSC Summary*, accessed in http://www.bookrags.com/research/nsc-68-aaw-04/.

[18] *FRUS, 1950*, 1: 170-72, 191, 225-26. See also, NSC-68, pp. 43, 54.

[19] See John Lewis Gaddis, *The United States and the Origins of the Cold War*, (New York: Columbia University Press, 1972); Richard M. Freeland, *The Truman Doctrine and the Origins of McCarthyism*, (New York: NYU Press, 1989); Frank Kofsky, *Harry S. Truman and the War Scare of 1948: A Successful Campaign to Deceive the Nation*, (New York: Palgrave Macmillan, 1995).

[20] Dean Acheson, *Present at the Creation: My Years in the State Department*, (New York: W.W. Norton, 1969) pp. 374-375.

[21] John Gunther, *The Riddle of MacArthur* (London: Hamish, 1951), p. 150.

[22] Mansur Khan, op. cit., p.245.

[23] Dean Acheson, quoted in Princeton Seminars, October 10, 1950, reel 2, track 2, p. 15, *Acheson Papers*, Truman Library, Independence, Missouri.

[24] Ibid., pp. 241-242.

[25] Ibid., pp. 270-271.

[26] New York Council on Foreign Relations, *Officers & Directors*, 1947.

[27] See Chapter 7.

[28] Peter Collier & David Horowitz, op. cit., pp. 240-241.

[29] Ibid, pp. 272-276.

[30] William Blum, *Killing Hope: US Military and CIA Interventions since World War II* (Maine: Common Courage Press, 2004), pp. 64-82.

[31] P. Landmeier, *Banana Republic: The United Fruit Company*, 1997, accessed in http://www.mayaparadise.com/ufc1e.htm. See also Kate Doyle and Peter Kornbluh, National Security Archive Electronic Briefing Book No. 4, *CIA and Assassinations: The Guatemala 1954 Documents*, for the partly declassified CIA documents on the 1954 coup, accessed in http://www.gwu.edu/~nsarchiv/NSAEBB/NSAEBB4/index.html.

[32] Walter Le Feber, *Inevitable Revolutions: The United States in Central America*, (New York, W. W. Norton, 1993), p.120-121.

[33] Ibid.

CHAPTER THIRTEEN

The Dollar Standard takes on the World

The United States must cultivate a mental view toward world settlement after this war which will enable us to impose our own terms, amounting to perhaps a Pax Americana.
- US Department of State internal memo, 1942[1]

A new Gold Standard for a new World Order

By the outbreak of the Korean War in 1950, the extent of America's new *Lebensraum* included complete economic domination of Hawaii, the Philippines, Liberia, Saudi Arabia, Greece, Turkey and Israel. The US *de facto* controlled Japan and West Germany by military occupation, and held significant and growing economic control over Argentina, Spain, Egypt, Thailand and Yugoslavia.

In Western Europe, with assistance from the newly created CIA, the United States controlled the governments and key industrial and financial groups in Belgium, Norway and Italy. It had strong political and economic influence over Holland, Sweden, and France.

Washington dominated the economy of its southern neighbor, Mexico, as well as its neighbor to the north, Canada. The US had a 'special relationship' with Great Britain, and maintained a strong and growing presence in key British Commonwealth countries, including Australia, New Zealand and South Africa. In addition, the United States was expanding its presence in most of the oil-rich Middle East and the former Dutch colony Indonesia.[2]

With its Truman Doctrine—nominally developed to justify intervention in civil war crises in Greece and Turkey—Washington unilaterally proclaimed the right to intervene in any country in the world to ensure governments meeting its approval.

Few, if any, nations were in a position to confront or contravene Washington. Creation of the North Atlantic Treaty Organization had enabled the United States, under the banner of 'fighting the Soviet communist threat to the free world,' to establish in peacetime a network of permanent military bases—navy, air force and army—stretching across Western Europe from Norway to Turkey, from Greece to Spain. Claiming dire threats to 'security,' the US also established its military bases on every other continent from Africa to South America to Asia. The world that was not under the direct political control of the Soviet Union or the Peoples' Republic of China became *de facto* a grand American sphere of influence, its postwar *Lebensraum*.

One influential geopolitical thinker of the postwar American Century, sometimes referred to as 'the first Cold Warrior,' was James Burnham, one of Wild Bill Donovan's operatives in the pre-CIA Office of Strategic Services (OSS). After the war, Burnham co-founded the arch-conservative *National Review*, and in 1947 he wrote a major paean to America's new world power, titled modestly, *The Struggle for the World*. The book was adapted from a Top Secret OSS memo Burnham had prepared for the US Delegation to Yalta on the Soviet geopolitical strategy in 1944. Burnham described in the most positive terms what he called, "an American Empire which will be, if not literally worldwide in formal boundaries, capable of exercising decisive world control."[3] Burnham's vision and recommendations were stark and stunningly unequivocal:

> *The United States cannot within the allotted time win the leadership of a viable world political order merely by appeals to rational conviction...Power must be there, with the known readiness to use it, whether in the indirect form of paralyzing economic sanctions, or in the direct explosion of bombs. As the ultimate reserve in the power series there would be the monopoly control of atomic weapons.* [4]

The American Century was to be a 'no nonsense' enterprise. As Burnham put it, "Independence and freedom are, after all, abstractions."[5]

Within that American-controlled economic space, encompassing more than 560 million people, lay a vast potential market beyond even the enormous expanse of the prewar British Empire. The United States, a mere five years into its postwar ambitions, held extraordinary power over much of the world in an informal economic empire. It had done so by using the mechanisms of the Bretton Woods institutions, the IMF and World Bank, through its control of broad western European economic policy via the Marshall Plan and the Paris-based Organization for Economic Cooperation and Development (OECD), through the role of the dollar as the world reserve currency and the heart of world finance, and above all, through the Money Trusts New York banks and their allied civil servants in Washington.

Dismantling the rival British Empire

Germany, America's former wartime rival in the bitter contest to replace the British Empire as global hegemon, lay prostrate, divided into east and west after 1945. With Germany no longer posing any potential threat, the initial postwar aim of Washington and Wall Street would be to dismember Great Britain, their debilitated but still formidable potential rival. They did a thorough job of it, all the while praising their 'friendship' and their Anglo-American 'special relationship.'

Taking a leaf from the Don Corleone Mafia book of etiquette, Washington's policy towards her closest wartime ally was a variation of 'kick 'em while they're down.' During the Atlantic Charter meeting between Roosevelt and Churchill in 1941, according to the eyewitness account of FDR's son, Elliott Roosevelt, Churchill snapped out in frustration at the US President, "Mr. President, I believe you are trying to do away with the British Empire. Every idea you entertain about the structure of the post-war world demonstrates it. But, in spite of that, in spite of that, we know that you constitute our only hope." [6] As usual, Churchill was right in grasping the geopolitical power equation of Washington's intentions.

The abrupt ending of US Lend-Lease aid to Britain in 1945 led the way for London's hard negotiations with Washington for an economic recovery loan. It finally got the loan, but with heavy conditions. Washington demanded as a *quid pro quo* for the dollars, the agreement that Britain and its Commonwealth nations would apply 'non-discrimination' in trade.

That meant Britain's wartime efforts to create its own economic space with its former colonies from South Africa to Canada to Australia, the so-called 'Imperial Preference,' to reduce her dollar dependence, would not be permitted to continue.[7] Washington knew well where the Achilles Heel of Britain's postwar economy lay and they went directly for it.

The relative positions of the United States and Britain had reversed during the war. In terms of private foreign investments, the US total was more than three times British foreign investments by 1949. The United States, specifically a handful of banks in New York, had become "banker to the world," displacing the role of the city of London.

When US Government overseas investment was added, the role of the United States by 1950 was not only three times larger than that of Britain, it also exceeded the foreign investment of all other industrial nations combined. The United States had left Britain hopelessly behind. As the administrator of the postwar dollar standard of Bretton Woods, New York banks and Washington were coordinated in maximizing the leverage of their new financial power. They had the dollars that the rest of the world desperately needed.

US Marshall Plan aid to Europe was an instrument of US economic strategy

Using the new Truman Doctrine, the United States also moved in on Britain's traditional dominance of the oil-rich countries of the Middle East through the supply of US arms for 'defense protection' against what it argued was a "threat of communist takeover."

Under the conditions of the Marshall Plan, certain former European colonies, primarily in Africa, were designated to supply the United States with an adequate supply of strategic raw materials 'for defense.' In 1949 a severe dollar shortage crisis developed in Europe as European economies desperately bid for hard dollars to finance urgently needed imports. Washington exploited the crisis to pressure Britain into devaluing the Pound, further weakening Britain's ability to use her Imperial Preference to avoid subjugating its economy to the dictates of the dollar. [8]

NATO opens new markets

With the signing of the Atlantic Pact creating NATO in April 1949, Washington had a new argument for its economic interventions. In place of the rationale of 'European recovery' under the Marshall Plan, now the US could conduct far more extensive economic intervention into the affairs of its European NATO 'partners' in the name of 'military preparedness,' 'strategic planning' and 'unification of command,' all to wage what was being called the 'Cold War.'

The US imposed heavy restrictions on East West trade with the communist world that largely affected traditional trade patterns of Western Europe, not the USA. Those restrictions hit Britain especially hard. Moreover, backed by American capital during the Korean war, the West German economy was rapidly built up to become yet another rival to British industrial exports. As a result of all these pressures, in 1951 Britain's dollar deficit in its balance of payments reached a new postwar crisis level. [9]

By 1951 US capital investment in Canada, nominally a member of the British Commonwealth, had risen from $4 billion in 1939 at the start of the war to over $9 billion, vastly exceeding the amount of British capital invested in Canada, which had fallen to $1.6 billion by 1948.[10] US capital investment followed a similar pattern in other British colonies or former colonies, including India, Australia and New Zealand.

Most geopolitically significant were American incursions into the traditional British sphere of influence in the oil-rich Middle East. In addition to FDR's 1945 coup over Churchill securing the oil wealth of the Kingdom of Saudi Arabia for the Rockefeller Standard Oil group, US intelligence was delighted to take advantage of the confrontation between Britain's Anglo-Iranian Oil Company and Iran's Nationalist Prime Minister Mossadegh. The US eventually mounted a coup to thwart both Iran's nationalization of its own oil, and British supremacy in Iran's oil fields, as well.

In October 1951 Iran's Prime Minister Mossadegh ordered the British to leave as he declared before the UN General Assembly that Iran's oil resources belonged to the Iranian people. US intelligence began planning its coup to come in and take over the vast oil riches held by the British. In November 1952 Dwight Eisenhower was elected US President and a US-dominated coup went forward.

Meanwhile, in British Northern Rhodesia --, named after British Round Table founder, Cecil Rhodes -- American capital had won control of the rich Rhodesian copper belt in 1952 through its control of Rhodesian American Metal Company.

In South Africa, the Rockefeller group, acting through a merger of the two banking groups, Lazard Freres and Ladenburg, Thalman & Co., moved in to take control of more than one hundred South African industrial and mining companies. J.P. Morgan & Co. combined with the powerful South African Anglo-American Corporation of the Oppenheimer family to dominate gold and metals mining. Henry Luce's Time magazine called the venture, "the first big beach-head of American capital in South Africa." During the same period, New York's giant Kennecott Copper Corporation invested in two major new South African gold mines, while Newmont Mining Co. of Delaware moved took over the assets of previously German-owned mining and railway companies in South-west Africa.[11]

Perhaps no part of Africa's mineral wealth was more valuable to the emerging American Grand Area or *Lebensraum* than the huge uranium reserves of the Belgian Congo, where Rockefeller interests led by Chase Manhattan Bank were able to buy a controlling minority share in Tanganyika Concessions that controlled the Belgian Union Minière du Haut Katanga in April 1950. At the time, it was estimated that the Katanga region in the southeast Congo contained more than 50% of the world's known cobalt reserves and 60% of its known uranium, vital for building the United States' nuclear arsenal amid the unfolding Korean War and the ensuing US-Soviet Cold War. [12]

Cracks in the postwar American edifice

The golden days of US domination of the 'free' world's monetary and economic affairs did not last much more than a decade before cracks in the flawed foundation of its Bretton Woods edifice began to appear. The 1957 Eisenhower recession was the first warning sign of trouble in the dollar world. In effect, 1957 signaled the ageing of the post-1938 US war industry—steel, aluminum plants, machine tool industry and the like—that had been built during the war some twenty years earlier.

Meanwhile, by the end of the 1950s most Western Europe countries, especially West Germany and, to a less extent, France and Italy, were emerging as vital competitors with modern manufacturing plants and equipment. Not only did Western European not need a' large volume of US industrial imports to rebuild their economies, but by 1957 they had begun to export once more in direct competition with US companies.

The largest corporations in US industry and finance had looked abroad to reap the fruits of the strong dollar rather than invest in domestic renewal. The successful launch of the Soviet Union's Sputnik space satellite in October 1957 ahead of any similar feat by the US drove home the point that America was slipping technologically behind the rest of the industrial world.

During the Korean War, the United States began to cheat significantly on the rules behind its Bretton Woods Gold Exchange Standard. To cover its massive and growing war expenditures, Washington opted for 'guns *and* butter.' Washington covered its growing foreign liabilities not with gold, as the rules required, but rather by issuing special Federal Reserve notes and short-term US Treasury bills. Once they realized the rest of the world continued to accept the Reserve notes as though they were 'as good as gold,' the US financial powers decided to continue expanding the supply of paper dollars flowing into the rest of the world without expanding its gold reserves in proportion.[13] In effect, without making any public fanfare, Washington was slowly debasing its own currency in relation to the rest of its trading partners, above all in relation to Western Europe.

Beginning with the Kennedy era, after 1961 the United States began to run significant trade deficits. That was a clear signal for foreign central banks to redeem their trade surplus dollars for US Federal Reserve gold before the problems worsened. US industrialists had all but stopped significant new investment in American domestic manufacturing plants and equipment. Instead, they began investing their surplus dollars in state-of-the art industrial plants in Western Europe where the dollar was still strong and exchange rates were fixed by Bretton Woods.

JFK sounds the alarm

In 1949 on the eve of the Korean War, the gold reserves of the United States had exceeded the total of US liabilities to foreign states by an overwhelming $18 billion. By October 1960 the situation had dramatically reversed. The foreign liabilities of the United States exceeded the total value of its gold reserves by $800 million. During the same time period, the foreign direct investment and holdings of US long-term corporate assets abroad increased from $27 billion in 1949 to more than $62 billion by 1960, an increase of almost 250%.[14]

It was only a matter of time before the rest of the world realized that the US dollar was no longer as good as gold, and that if they wanted any gold for their mounting dollar surpluses they had better be first in line to demand it at the Gold Discount Window of the New York Federal Reserve. It meant that *THE* creditor nation of the entire postwar Bretton Woods system, the United States, was unable to repay its short-term liabilities in gold.

The gap between US liabilities to foreign central banks -- above all, to the German *Bundesbank*, the Bank of France, and the Bank of Japan -- widened into a chasm in the 1960s. It was a colossal boon to US corporations operating abroad. In his first State of the Union message to Congress in January 1961,President John F. Kennedy acknowledged the disturbing condition of the internal US economy:

> *We take office in the wake of seven months of recession, three and one-half years of slack, seven years of diminished economic growth, and nine years of falling farm income....*
>
> *Business bankruptcies have reached their highest level since the Great Depression. Since 1951 farm income has been squeezed down by 25 percent. Save for a brief period in 1958, insured unemployment is at the highest peak in our history. Of some five and one-half million Americans who are without jobs, more than one million have been searching for work for more than four months....*
>
> *Nearly one-eighth of those who are without jobs live almost without hope in nearly one hundred especially depressed and troubled areas. The rest include new school graduates unable to use their talents, farmers forced to give up their part-time jobs which helped balance their family budgets, skilled and unskilled workers laid off in such important industries as metals, machinery, automobiles and apparel.*[15]

Kennedy went on to describe the alarming state of the US international financial and monetary situation:

> *Since 1958...this overall deficit in our balance of payments increased by nearly $11 billion in the 3 years - and holders of dollars abroad converted them to gold in such a quantity as to cause a total outflow of nearly $5 billion of gold from our reserve. The 1959 deficit was caused in large part by the failure of our exports to penetrate foreign markets the result both of restrictions on our goods and our own uncompetitive prices. The 1960 deficit, on the other hand, was more the result of an increase in private capital outflow seeking new opportunity, and a far higher return or speculative advantage abroad.*[16]

And most of that capital flight out of the United States remained abroad, reinvested, rather than repatriated.

To defend the dollar, Washington called on Germany and other European NATO members to increase "their share of the defense burden." In 1962 Washington upped the pressure on Western Europe to remove tariff and other trade barriers to US imports in an effort to reduce the trade imbalances, especially pressuring the European Economic Community's Common Agriculture Policy, the heart of the EEC agreement between France and Germany. None of this had much effect.

JFK outfoxes the Fed

As President, Kennedy earned many powerful enemies during his few months in office, from the head of US Steel, to CIA chief Allen Dulles and the Pentagon. Perhaps no one opposed Kennedy more strongly, however, than the powerful bankers of Wall Street. David Rockefeller, head of Chase Manhattan Bank and emerging as the heir to the power of the Rockefeller dynasty, openly attacked Kennedy's economic policy in an article in Henry Luce's *Life* magazine in July 1962. Rockefeller accused Kennedy of trying to keep interest rates too low, and instead called for "fiscal responsibility," which translated into higher interest rates and larger profits for Wall Street Government bond traders like Chase Manhattan. Kennedy for his part was concerned with getting the economy out of a seven- year recession. [17]

Shortly before he was assassinated, JFK issued United States Notes, interest free and independent of the Federal Reserve. At the top it says, United States Note, not Federal Reserve Note. The Notes were immediately recalled by his successor.

Five months before his assassination by what was decades later revealed to have been a CIA hit team,[18] Kennedy issued an all-but unknown proclamation which may have cost him his life.

Much as Abraham Lincoln did when he avoided dependence on London bank loans to finance the Civil War and instead issued interest-free US Treasury notes, Greenbacks, to finance the war, President Kennedy issued Executive Order 11110 on June 4, 1963. Kennedy's EO 11110, which did not require a vote of Congress, mandated the US Treasury "to issue silver certificates against any silver bullion, silver, or standard silver dollars in the Treasury."[19]

JOHN F. KENNEDY
LIBRARY AND MUSEUM

Executive Order 11110

AMENDMENT OF EXECUTIVE ORDER NO. 10289 AS AMENDED, RELATING TO THE PERFORMANCE OF CERTAIN FUNCTIONS AFFECTING THE DEPARTMENT OF THE TREASURY

By virtue of the authority vested in me by section 301 of title 3 of the United States Code, it is ordered as follows:

SECTION 1. Executive Order No. 10289 of September 19, 1951, as amended, is hereby further amended --

(a) By adding at the end of paragraph 1 thereof the following subparagraph (j):

"(j) The authority vested in the President by paragraph (b) of section 43 of the Act of May 12, 1933, as amended (31 U.S.C. 821 (b)), to issue silver certificates against any silver bullion, silver, or standard silver dollars in the Treasury not then held for redemption of any outstanding silver certificates, to prescribe the denominations of such silver certificates, and to coin standard silver dollars and subsidiary silver currency for their redemption," and

(b) By revoking subparagraphs (b) and (c) of paragraph 2 thereof.

SEC. 2. The amendment made by this Order shall not affect any act done, or any right accruing or accrued or any suit or proceeding had or commenced in any civil or criminal cause prior to the date of this Order but all such liabilities shall continue and may be enforced as if said amendments had not been made.

JOHN F. KENNEDY

A Copy of John Kennedy's Fateful EO 11110 challenging the power of the Federal Reserve

This meant that for every ounce of silver in the US Treasury's vault, the government could introduce new money into circulation. In all, Kennedy brought nearly $4.3 billion in US notes into circulation in $2 and $5 denominations. The $10 and $20 United States Notes were just in the process of being printed by the Treasury Department when Kennedy was assassinated. They were never circulated. It was the first time since Lincoln that a President had issued interest free money and the first time a President had challenged the sole money power of the private Federal Reserve.

At the time of Kennedy's Presidency, William McChesney Martin was Chairman of the Federal Reserve. When Martin left Washington in 1970 as the longest-serving Federal Reserve head, he became a director of the Rockefeller Brothers Fund and their Rockefeller Family Fund, as well. [20] The Fed and the Rockefellers were one small, close family.

After JFK's death, EO11110 was put into abeyance, no more silver certificates were issued and those that had been issued were removed from circulation. [21] The very existence of EO11110 was hidden from the public, and forgotten or ignored by most historians.

The London Gold Pool leaks

The US gold drain continued despite these measures and in late 1961 Washington convinced Britain and the European central banks to establish an international Gold Pool, to be based at the Bank of England, in a joint effort to prevent any panic run on gold reserves of any member country. Calls by foreign central banks to obtain gold for their surplus dollars would henceforth be paid 50% by the US Federal Reserve, and 50% by Britain, Germany, France, Italy, Belgium, Netherlands and Switzerland combined. The result was to reduce demands for gold by the major European central banks but it did nothing to reduce demands for gold by private investors.

By October 1962 US dollar direct private investments abroad – the American investments in foreign manufacturing plants and so on, as noted earlier -- exceeded $35 billion, most of it going into Western Europe, Canada and Latin America. Despite an attempt by the US Congress to slow US capital flight to Europe and abroad through passage of an Interest Equalization Tax in September 1964, a loophole exempting investment into Canada permitted the flight of dollars abroad to continue unabated.[22] Those foreign-held dollars became the basis of a growing threat to the US gold reserves as dollar holders calculated that the dollar could only depreciate in terms of gold and so they moved to cash in while they still could.

The dollar support operations held only until November 1967 when the weak link in the Bretton Woods chain, the British Pound, broke. Britain had become the second pillar of the postwar Bretton Woods system, with former British colonies in Africa, Asia and elsewhere depositing their foreign exchange reserves in British Sterling at London's banks for convenience.

Despite the weakness of the British industrial economy—its technology was obsolescent compared with West Germany or France—its role as financial intermediary had helped to make the City of London the world's second most important capital center after New York, where central bank gold and dollar reserves were based. The British bankers had been simply trying to resume the role London had played before the war.

It didn't quit work. British banks, like their New York cousins, preferred to invest abroad to the detriment of domestic British industry, further weakening Britain's trade and payments balance, gradually threatening the parity of the pound sterling against the dollar that had been fixed since the 1949 devaluation. Returns on capital invested in European industries ran between 12-14%, more than double that of internal US or UK industrial investment.

By the mid-1960s, after Britain was forced to draw on two large IMF loans to try to stabilize sterling, foreign sterling holders, fearing the inevitable, began serious withdrawals from British banks and they converted sterling into gold or other currencies, worsening the pressures on sterling. Because private financial speculators were prohibited from selling sterling and buying gold, they bought dollars with the sterling instead, creating an illusion of dollar strength. In reality the Pound was the weak link in the entire postwar Bretton Woods dollar system. Were the Pound to devalue, it would immediately focus attention on the underlying vulnerability of the US dollar.

A French fly in the British soup

In February 1965, as Lyndon Johnson opted to substantially increase the US commitment to a war in Vietnam, a further drain on the US balance of Payments, French President Charles de Gaulle gave a speech sharply criticizing the international monetary system and the US refusal to devalue the dollar against gold in order to realign the gold exchange with the reality of the day.

De Gaulle quite rightly accused US policymakers of essentially exporting US inflation to Europe, thereby allowing it to finance both the Vietnam War and domestic programs—Johnson's so-called 'guns and butter' program—simply by printing more dollars, but dollars not backed by more gold. De Gaulle, over British and American objections, called for a return to a real gold standard that would force countries to adapt their economic policy to correct growing deficits in their balance of payments. [23]

The gold drain in Britain and in the US worsened. In March 1965, at the urging of New York and other financial circles, Congress passed a law abolishing the Monetary Act of 1945 under which the Federal Reserve System was required to hold, in gold backing or security, 25% of total reserves not only for Federal

Reserve notes in circulation but also for deposits of member Federal Reserve banks. The Federal Reserve gold stocks were being drained down to nearly the 25% threshold. The US position as the bastion of the postwar Gold Exchange Standard of Bretton Woods had dramatically deteriorated by the middle 1960s.

In 1949 the United States held an official gold reserve stock of some $23 billion against $41 billion in total Federal Reserve deposits and notes in circulation, constuting a gold cover of an impressive 57%. By the beginning of 1965 the gold reserves had declined to $15 billion while deposits and notes in circulation had risen to $55 billion, a gold cover of merely 27%.

The only fly in the monetary soup of repealing the mandatory 25% US gold cover was the fact that Bretton Woods had established the US dollar not merely as a national currency, but as the basis of the entire world payments system.[24] The entire trading world accepted US dollars in lieu of gold based on the notion that the dollar was firmly backed by gold should they ever need to have it.

By the late 1960s France, Germany, Italy, Belgium, Netherlands and Switzerland were all steadily accumulating gold as a result of their positive trade balances. France's call for a significant devaluation in the dollar was attacked sharply from Wall Street and the Federal Reserve as "giving unjustified advantage" to countries that were accumulating gold reserves. They never bothered to explain what was "unjustified" under Bretton Woods about countries wanting to redeem their surplus dollars for gold rather than keep inflated paper dollars.

In reality dollar devaluation would weaken the role of the dollar and of US multinational banks and corporations in the world economy, something the Money Trust was loathe to even consider. De Gaulle's economic adviser, Jacques Rueff, explained the French position in a June 5, 1969 article in the *Wall Street Journal*. He pointed out that "The gold price was fixed at the present level in 1934 by President Roosevelt. Since then, all prices in the United States have more than doubled." [25] Rueff argued that economic logic would require a 100% devaluation of the dollar to gold in order to correct the disequilibrium.

By 1967 Britain was forced to support the pound by borrowing foreign currencies, a signal that the end of the fixed exchange rate was near. The growing private international demand for gold instead of sterling or dollars accelerated in 1967, forcing increased interventions from the Bank of England's London Gold Pool.

Under a law passed by Parliament in January 1967, France had imposed full convertibility of the Franc based on a Franc backed by more than 80% gold reserves. It was an attempt by the French to force the question of urgently needed international monetary reform. In the summer of 1967 France withdrew from participating in the Gold Pool, no longer wishing to use her gold in a futile effort to support the dollar. The result was a continuing fall in the foreign exchange rate of the pound and a rise in the market price of privately held gold. The run on gold was on.

Speculators, betting on a sure thing, rushed to convert their pounds into dollars or other currencies that they then used to buy gold in all possible markets from Frankfurt to Zurich to Paris to Pretoria. As the private market price for gold climbed in relation to the fixed Bretton Woods price, the very stability of the dollar as the anchor of the entire world payments system came under pressure.

In a drama not unlike the crisis of the pound against gold in 1931, emergency sterling stabilization loans were unable to stem the pressure on sterling. A consortium of gold-rich Swiss banks led by Union Bank of Switzerland provided a loan of $104 million to Britain in October 1967. The IMF as well as major European countries rejected the idea of further support for sterling. The UK Government was in the process of negotiating an additional $1 to $3 billion private Swiss bank loan when, on November 18, 1967, Labor Prime Minister Harold Wilson announced a devaluation of the pound against gold by 14% and its new parity to the dollar was fixed at $2.40 to a pound. This was far smaller than the 30% devaluation of 1949, but it was significant enough in the changed world of the late 1960s to focus pressures on the heart of the global monetary system, the US dollar.[26]

The US avenges France

In retaliation for what it saw as intolerable French interference in the US monetary system, Washington, backed by Wall Street banks, launched a full-scale economic attack on France and the French franc for her role as main proponent of monetary reform. In order to discredit the French idea of monetary reform, the Wall Street banks and Washington decided to undermine the monetary and financial stability of France. By early 1968 it amounted to a full-scale currency war. None of it was openly declared. Rather it was done behind the scenes, but it was clear to all major market participants that the US banks were behind the ensuing run on the Franc and French gold reserves.

The run was triggered by New York banks abruptly pulling their deposits out of French banks and buying German Marks instead. That was a major blow. Washington pressured West German banks to follow suit, claiming a general lack of confidence in French monetary policy, not an exercise in American financial warfare. Washington restricted French imports to the US and advised Americans not to travel to France for holidays. American companies that had invested in France began quietly to withdraw their capital from France, putting further pressure on the Franc.[27]

Then, with a timing that could hardly have been coincidental, a little-known radical left anarchist sect, the Situationist International, suddenly burst onto the French new left scene, receiving prominent coverage from Anglo-American mainstream media such as the London *Economist*. They emerged seemingly out of nowhere and were portrayed as leaders of the student government at Nanterre University and as influential in the Sorbonne student movement.

Wall Street and the City of London exploited the much-publicized May 1968 University of Paris student uprisings. Despite evidence of a widespread and politically diverse student movement around the Sorbonne, the media made young radicals like Situationist hanger-on Daniel Cohn-Bendit into an overnight 'Che Guevara' of the French and German left. Cohn-Bendit had been part of a group that organized a strike of 12,000 students in November of 1967 as a protest against overcrowding. In the preceding 10 years the student population of France had risen from 170,000 to 514,000. The total area covered by university premises had doubled since 1962, but the student numbers had almost tripled. Facilities were desperately inadequate and overcrowding was a serious issue. That was the background or the social tinder. It didn't take much to light the spark.[28]

US economic warfare against De Gaulle in 1968 helped set stage for May student strikes that ultimately forced de Gaulle to resign a year later.

De Gaulle had been weakened and his popular support severely damaged by the financial crisis and by the police brutality against the students and their supporters in May 1968, events which agencies of US intelligence, acting on the student scene, at the very least encouraged.[29] One year later, in April 1969, De Gaulle resigned from office.

The circles running the financial attack on the Franc artfully spread the rumor that the German Mark was about to be revalued upwards against the Franc, further fuelling panic selling of French currency and the drain on French gold. When the upheaval of student protests subsided, the result of the financial crisis became clear; there had been a devastating drain on French reserves and a deterioration of her international financial ability to be a threat to the dollar.

Between March 1968 and March 1969, French foreign exchange reserves had fallen by 80% as the Bank of France tried in vain to defend the Franc parity to the dollar. By August 1969, France was forced to devalue its currency by 12%. By October, West German monetary authorities were forced to up-value the German Mark by 8%, opening the gap between the two strongest economies of the European Community 20% wider.

Germany was in no position to back the French demand for reform of the monetary order, or to resist pressure from US banks to join their attack on the Franc for fear of losing US troops, or so Washington hinted. Germany perceived itself as in no position to face the Soviet Union without US military troop presence as ultimate guarantee of a US nuclear umbrella.

Through the financial attack on De Gaulle's regime, Wall Street and the Federal Reserve had won a small margin of time before attention would again turn to the vulnerability of the dollar. The respite did not last long before the attacks on the dollar resumed.

Endnotes:

[1] Advisory Committee on Postwar Foreign Policy, Security Subcommittee, Minutes S-3, 6 May 1942, *Notter File*, Box 77, Record Group 59, Records of the Department of State, National Archives, Washington D.C.

[2] Victor Perlo, *American Imperialism* (New York: International Publishers, 1951).

[3] James Burnham, *The Struggle for the World* (New York: John Day & Co., 1947), pp. 188, 193-195.

[4] Ibid., pp. 193-195.

[5] Ibid., p. 201.

[6] Elliott Roosevelt, *As He Saw It* (New York: Duell, Sloan and Pearce,1946), p. 41.

[7] R. Palme Dutt, *The Crisis of Britain and the British Empire* (London: Lawrence & Wishart, 1953), p. 166.

[8] Ibid., pp. 166-167.

[9] Ibid. p. 168.

[10] Ibid., p. 170.

[11] Ibid., p. 174.

[12] For background on the Rockefeller role in the Congo through to independence in the early 1960's, see Paul David Collins, *Conquest by Convergence: The Case Against Elite Convergence*. 2003, accessed in http://www.conspiracyarchive.com/NWO/Elite_Convergence.htm.

[13] A. Stadnichenko, Monetary Crisis of Capitalism (Moscow: Progress Publishers, 1975), pp. 126-127.

[14] Robert Triffin, *The Dollar in Crisis*, (New Haven, Yale University Press,1961), pp. 228-229.

[15] John F. Kennedy, *Annual Message to the Congress on the State of the Union*, January 30, 1961, accessed in http://www.jfklink.com/speeches/jfk/publicpapers/1961/jfk11_1961.html.

[16] Ibid.

[17] Donald Gibson, *Battling Wall Street: The Kennedy Presidency* (New York: Sheridan Square Press, 1994), pp. 73-75.

[18] Wim Dankbaar, *Files on JFK: Interviews with confessed assassin James E. Files* (Victoria, BC: Trafford Publishing, 2005), pp. 43-108. Files, sitting in US Federal Prison in Joliet Illinois made a recorded confession that he had been part of a CIA 'hit team' that was led by CIA officer, David Atlee Phillips, with the mission to assassinate JFK and leave Lee Harvey Oswald to take the blame as a 'lone assassin.'

[19] John F. Kennedy, *Executive Order 11110: Amendment of Executive Order No. 10289, as Amended, Relating to the Performance of Certain Functions Affecting the Department of the Treasury*, June 4, 1963. Reprinted in *The Final Call*, Vol. 15, No.6, January 17, 1996, accessed in http://www.john-f-kennedy.net/executiveorder11110.htm.

[20] Peter Collier and David Horowitz, *The Rockefellers: An American Dynasty*, (New York: Holt, Rinehart & Winston, 1976), p. 560.

[21] Anthony Wayne, *John F. Kennedy vs the Federal Reserve*, accessed in http://www.john-f-kennedy.net/thefederalreserve.htm.

[22] Lyndon B. Johnson, President, *Executive Order 11198 – Imposition of Interest Equalization Tax on Certain Commercial Bank Loans*, February 10, 1965, accessed in http://www.presidency.ucsb.edu/ws/index.php?pid=60529.

[23] Ibid., p.156.

[24] The United States Federal Reserve System, *Consolidated Position of the Federal Reserve Banks,* Federal Reserve Bulletin, Table 15, February 1965, p. 230.

[25] Jacques Rueff, *The Wall Street Journal*, June 9, 1969.

[26] Aaran Hamilton, *Beyond the Sterling Devaluation: The Gold Crisis of March 1968*, Contemporary European History, vol. 17, no.1 (2008), pp. 73–95.

[27] A. Stadnichenko, op. cit., pp. 204-211.

[28] Rene Vienet, *Enragés and Situationists in the Occupations Movement*, 1968, in Situationist International Online Archive, accessed on http://www.cddc.vt.edu/sionline/si/enrages.html.

[29] Council for Maintaining the Occupation, Report on the Occupation of the Sorbonne, Paris, 19 May 1968, accessed in Situationist International texts, http://www.cddc.vt.edu/sionline/si/occupation.html.

CHAPTER FOURTEEN

Nixon walks away from Bretton Woods

You've shown how the United States has run rings around Britain and every other empire-building nation in history. We've pulled off the greatest rip-off ever achieved.
- Herman Kahn of Hudson Institute in 1971 when informed how US payments deficits could be used to exploit other countries [1]

1971: Beginning of the endgame

The early 1970s were a watershed in policy for the American establishment. Dramatic measures were needed to ensure the continued domination of the United States as global economic and financial superpower. It was not at all obvious how they would do it. Soon enough however, the powers that dominated Wall Street developed a strategy.

With Lyndon Johnson's war in South-East Asia escalating, along with its costs, international banks and central banks accelerated their selling of dollars and buying of gold. By 1968 the Federal US budget deficit, fed by exploding costs of the war, reached an unprecedented height of $30 billion. Gold reserves continued to fall precariously close to the legal floor of 25% allowed by law under the Bretton Woods treaty. Political disarray within Johnson's Administration increased the financial flight as Defense Secretary Robert McNamara, widely viewed as the architect of a "no-win war" strategy, handed in his resignation.

The Vietnam War strategy had been deliberately designed by Defense Secretary Robert McNamara, National Security Adviser McGeorge Bundy, along with Pentagon planners and key advisers around Lyndon Johnson, to be a "no-win war" from the onset, in order to ensure a prolonged buildup of the military sector of the US economy. The American voter, Washington reasoned, would accept large costs for a new war against an alleged 'encroachment of Godless communism' in Vietnam, despite the gaping US budget deficits, as long as this produced local jobs in defense plants.

Under the US-dictated Bretton Woods rules, by inflating the dollar through huge spending deficits at home, Washington could, in effect, force Europe and other trading partners to 'swallow' US war costs in the form of cheapened dollars. So long as the United States refused to devalue the dollar against gold to reflect the deterioration of US economic performance since 1944, Europe had to pay the cost by accepting dollars at the same ratio as it had some 20 years before despite a huge inflation over that period.

To finance the enormous deficits of his Great Society program as well as the Vietnam buildup during the 1960s, Johnson, fearful of losing votes if he raised taxes, simply printed dollars by selling more US Treasury bonds to finance the deficits. In the early 1960s, the US federal budget deficit averaged approximately $3 billion annually. It hit an alarming $9 billion in 1967 as the war costs soared, and by 1968 it reached a staggering $25 billion.

The European central banks began to accumulate large dollar accounts during this period, which they used as official reserves, the so-called Eurodollar accumulation abroad. Ironically, Washington in 1961 had requested that US allies in Europe and Japan, the Group of Ten countries, should ease the drain on US gold reserves by retaining their growing dollar reserves instead of redeeming the dollars for American gold, as mandated under the terms of Bretton Woods.

The European central banks in turn earned interest on these dollars by investing in US government treasury bonds. The net effect was that the European central banks thereby in effect 'financed' the huge US budget deficits of the 1960s Vietnam War they so opposed.[2]

'Hot Money' in offshore Eurodollar markets

Beginning in the late 1950s the major New York banks had greatly increased their power and influence through a series of bank mergers. Rockefeller's Chase National Bank had merged with the Bank of Manhattan to form Chase Manhattan Bank, headed by John J. McCloy, Rockefeller's attorney and a Rockefeller Foundation Trustee as well as Chairman of the New York Council on Foreign Relations. McCloy had recently returned to New York after serving as US High Commissioner in Germany. The National City Bank of New York took over the First National Bank of New York to form City Bank of New York, later Citibank, under the chairmanship of James Stillman Rockefeller.

Other large New York banks, including Chemical bank, Manufacturers Hanover Trust and Bankers Trust, underwent similar mergers and consolidations. According to a 1961 US Department of Justice report, the five largest New York banks, dominated by the two Rockefeller banks, controlled 75% of all deposits in the nation's largest city, the world's international financial center. [3]

The remarkable concentration of money power into those few New York banks by the 1960s would prove decisive in determining international political and financial developments for the ensuing four decades into the 21st Century and the financial securitization crisis of 2007.

To facilitate this extraordinary concentration of financial power, the US Government exempted banks from US anti-trust laws prohibiting undue concentration or cartelization.[4]

By the 1960s these newly consolidated and enormously influential New York banks moved to create a new offshore market for dollars outside the United States -- the new 'Eurodollar' market, a name for dollars held abroad in Europe.

During the late 1960s the New York banks, led by Chase Manhattan and Citibank, began to develop a use for the billions of dollars accumulating overseas in London and Continental European banks. Through astute lobbying by the New York banks, loans made by foreign branches of American banks to foreign residents had been declared exempt from the new 1964 US Interest Equalization Tax designed to curb US bank lending abroad and to stop the dollar drain. The exemption of course meant that the dollar drain continued unabated.

As a result, US banks scrambled to establish branches in London and other appropriate centers. Once again, the City of London, despite the weakness of the British economy, had maneuvered to become a centerpiece of world finance and banking through development of the vast new and unregulated dollar banking and lending market with its center in London. [5]

The increasing efforts of Washington to persuade overseas dollar holders not to redeem dollars for gold led to a growing volume of dollars more or less permanently overseas, mostly in Western Europe or London. London's sagging fortunes began once more to brighten as the City of London, the banking district, began to corner the market in expatriate US dollars. The Bank of England and London banker Sir Siegmund Warburg, founder of the influential British merchant bank, S.G. Warburg & Co., were at the heart of the growing Eurodollar offshore money market. With the assistance of his friends in Washington, especially Undersecretary of State George Ball, Warburg had cleverly lured the dollars into what was to become the largest concentration of dollar credit outside of the US itself.

The resulting London Eurodollar market was also 'offshore,' meaning it was outside the jurisdiction of US national laws or central bank supervision.

New York banks and Wall Street brokerage houses set up offices in London to manage the blossoming new Eurodollar casino, far away from the eyes of US tax authorities. The international branches of the large New York banks got cheap funds from the Eurodollar market as well as large multinational corporations. Washington during the early 1960's willingly allowed the floodgates to be opened wide to a flight of the dollar from American shores into the new 'hot money' Eurodollar market.

Buyers of these new Eurodollar bonds, called Eurobonds, were anonymous persons, cynically called 'Belgian dentists' by the London and Swiss and New York bankers running this new game. These Eurobonds were 'bearer' bonds meaning no buyers' names were registered anywhere, so they were a favorite for investors looking for tax avoidance, or even for drug kingpins or other unsavory characters wanting to launder illegal profits. What better way to hold onto your black earnings than in Eurodollar bonds, with interest paid by General Motors or the Italian Autostrada Corporation? An astute analyst of the Eurodollar process noted, "the Eurodollar market was the most important financial phenomenon of the 1960s, for it was here that the financial earthquake of the early 1970s originated." [6]

A major turning point in the relation of the major New York banks to their rapidly growing accumulation of Eurodollars took place in 1966. Like most major new turns of postwar US financial policy, it began with the Rockefellers' Chase Manhattan Bank.

Chase moves on Lebanon

A confidential internal memo was circulated within the bank in 1966 on the subject of the disadvantages that American, i.e. New York, banks had in capturing the lucrative international market for 'flight capital.' The memo pointed to the advantages enjoyed by Swiss banks that dominated the lucrative market in managing and profiting from the hidden fortunes of dictators like Marcos in the Philippines, Saudi princes, drug barons and the like. The memo proposed that Chase open up a foreign entity to capture a major share of the booming offshore flight capital, or 'hot money,' for itself. Citibank had already begun such lucrative 'hot money' banking activity in connection with Bernie Cornfeld, the fraud artist and founder of Investor Overseas Services.[7]

The Chase internal memo identified Beirut, Lebanon as the model location. Beirut was dominated by one bank, Intra Bank, and its affiliated Casino du Liban, the world's largest gambling and money laundering enterprise at the time, exceeding even Las Vegas. [8]

Lebanon's Intra Bank became insolvent under suspicious circumstances in 1966. At a time when the bank needed to borrow to cover stock and gold trading losses, the King of Saudi Arabia, rarely known to make bold decisions without first checking with Washington, abruptly withdrew his substantial deposits. Then Chase Manhattan Bank initiated a freeze on Intra Bank's deposits in New York as hostage to outstanding loans. The Beirut bank was forced to stop payments on October 14, 1966. Its depositors transferred their funds to the Beirut branch of Chase Manhattan for "safety."

Lebanon's Casino du Liban was target of Rockefeller's Chase Bank
in 1966 for its offshore hot money potential.

Chase then sent an intermediary, Roger Tamraz, an ambitious Lebanese-born man who at the time was a young executive with Wall Street's Kidder Peabody & Co. Tamraz successfully re-floated the large Lebanese bank. The bank had been founded in Beirut in 1951 and owned Beirut Port Authority, Middle East Airlines, as well as Casino du Liban. The collapse of the bank had brought the Lebanese economy to a halt and sent shockwaves throughout the Middle East. It was the world's largest bank catastrophe since World War II. [9]

Chase Manhattan's venture into Lebanese offshore hot money' banking marked the onset of a major shift by the powerful New York money center banks away from government regulators and tax obligations. The profits were staggering. Because they were offshore and were de facto permitted by US authorities, they were completely uncontrolled.

That foray into offshore banking marked a sea change in New York banking practice that would explode in importance during the next three decades and beyond. Chase Manhattan, Citibank and other major US money center banks were to launder hundreds of billions of dollars of illicit hot money, no questions asked, whether the funds originated from US-friendly dictators like the Philippines' Ferdinand Marcos, Iran's Shah Reza Pahlavi, Mexico's Raúl Salinas de Gortari, or Juárez drug cartel money being transferred to Uruguay and Argentina, or from countless other controversial and politically sensitive transactions. [10]

It was clearly only a matter of time before the foundational structure of the postwar Bretton Woods system cracked.

The crack finally occurred on August 15, 1971 when President Richard Nixon announced to the world that he had ordered the Gold Discount Window of the New York Federal Reserve to be permanently shut. Foreign holders of dollars had without warning been robbed of their right to gold by the unilateral act of the US President, and in violation of a treaty obligation of the United States.

Nixon's dollar coup

In August 1971, Nixon was acting on the advice of a small circle of Rockefeller-linked advisers, including Secretary of State Henry Kissinger, a life-long appendage of the Rockefeller interests, and budget adviser George Shultz, later Secretary of State and chairman of the vast Bechtel construction giant. The small circle also included Jack F. Bennett of the Treasury who went on to become a director of Rockefeller's Exxon Oil Co., and Treasury Under Secretary for International Monetary Affairs and former Chase Manhattan Bank executive, Paul Volcker, a life-long enabler of Rockefeller interests. Volcker went on eight years later, at the urging of David Rockefeller, to become Jimmy Carter's nominee to head the Federal Reserve. [11]

Nixon's unilateral action on gold convertibility was reluctantly accepted in international talks that December in Washington, by the leading European governments, Japan and a few others. They saw little choice as the dollar was the pillar of the world financial system. The talks resulted in a temporary compromise known as the Smithsonian Agreement, which Nixon called "the most significant monetary agreement in the history of the world."

The US had formally devalued the dollar, but not anywhere near the amount Europe felt was needed to reestablish global equilibrium. They devalued by a mere 8% against gold, placing gold at $38/fine ounce instead of the long-standing $35. The agreement also officially permitted a range of currency value fluctuation of 2.25 percent instead of the original one percent of the IMF Bretton Woods rules. The French had called for a gold price of $70.

By declaring to world dollar holders that their paper would no longer be redeemed for gold, however, Nixon set into motion a series of events that would rock the world. Within weeks, confidence in the Smithsonian agreement had also begun to collapse.

Gold itself has little intrinsic value. It has certain industrial uses and is attractive as jewelry. But historically, because of its scarcity, it has served as a recognized standard or store of value against which different nations have fixed the terms of their trade and therefore their currencies. When Nixon decided no longer to honor US currency obligations in gold, he opened the floodgates to a worldwide Las Vegas-style speculation binge of a dimension never before experienced in history.

Instead of calibrating long-term economic affairs to fixed standards of exchange, after August 1971 world trade was simply another arena of speculation about which direction various currencies would fluctuate. The United States was now free to create as many dollars as it wished, no longer bound by need to back the new dollars with gold. So long as the rest of the world would take the US paper dollars, the game proceeded. So long as the United States remained the Western world's major military power, the world swallowed the inflated US dollars. It saw little choice during the Cold War. Should US-linked countries occasionally forget, they would be rudely reminded by Washington or its Wall Street emissaries.

As a consequence, the total volume of US dollars in world circulation ballooned over the next 20 years. From a rather steady level that had persisted from 1950 through to the end of the 1960s, the volume of dollars expanded exponentially after 1971, increasing by more than 2500% by the end of the 1990s. That printing of dollars was the source of an escalating global inflation. For the New York bankers, their control of the expanding dollar market was a source of vast power and profit. [12]

The suspension of gold redemption and the resulting international 'floating exchange rates' of the early 1970s solved nothing in terms of the basic problems of the US economy. It only bought some time for the US financial powers to decide their next moves. By 1972, massive capital flows again left the dollar for better returns in Japan and Europe. Then on February 12, 1973 Nixon finally announced a second devaluation of the dollar, of 10 percent against gold, officially pricing gold where it remains as of 2009, at $42.22 per ounce.

The devaluation did little to stem dollar selling. However, in May 1973 on a resort island outside Stockholm, a highly secret meeting took place that gave the dollar a new lease on life, a lease at the expense of world industrial growth.

Wall Street and Washington power elites around Secretary of State Henry Kissinger decided to impose a dramatic shock on the world economy in order to rescue the falling dollar as *the* asset of world trade and finance, and restore it as a pillar of the American economic imperial strategy.

Saltsjoebaden: the Bilderberg plot

The design behind Nixon's August 15, 1971 dollar strategy did not clearly emerge until October 1973, and even then, few people other than a handful of insiders grasped the connection. The New York financial establishment used Nixon's August 1971 de-monetization of the dollar to buy time, while policy insiders prepared a bold new monetarist design, a 'paradigm shift' as some preferred to call it. Certain influential voices in the American financial establishment had devised a strategy to rebuild a strong dollar, and once again to assert and expand their relative political power in the world, just when it had seemed that they were in decisive rout.

In May 1973, with the dramatic fall of the dollar still vivid, a group of 84 of the world's top financial and political insiders met at the secluded island resort of the Swedish Wallenberg banking family, at Saltsjoebaden, Sweden. This gathering later came to be known as Prince Bernhard's Bilderberg Group. At the meeting, the group heard an American participant outline a 'scenario' for an imminent 400% increase in OPEC petroleum revenues. The purpose of the secret Saltsjoebaden meeting was not to prevent the expected oil price shock, but rather to plan how to manage the about-to-be-created flood of oil dollars, a process US Secretary of State Kissinger later called "recycling the petro-dollar flows." [13]

Bilderberg annual meetings had been initiated in utmost secrecy in May1954 by an elite trans-Atlantic establishment group which included David

Rockefeller, George Ball, Dr. Joseph Retinger, Holland's Prince Bernhard, and George C. McGhee, then a diplomat with the US State Department and later a senior executive of Rockefeller's Mobil Oil.

Named for the place of their first gathering, the Hotel de Bilderberg near Arnheim in the Netherlands, the annual Bilderberg meetings gathered top elites of Europe and America for secret deliberations and policy discussions. Consensus was then "shaped" and carefully propagandized in subsequent press comments and media coverage, but never with reference to the secret Bilderberg meetings themselves. The Bilderberg process was one of the most effective vehicles of postwar Anglo-American policy-shaping. [14]

At the 1973 meeting, the American speaker was Walter Levy, a consultant to the Rockefeller Standard Oil companies, Levy explained to the Bilderberg meeting on Atlantic-Japanese Energy Policy what was to happen. After projecting that future world oil needs would be supplied by a small number of Middle East oil-producing countries, Levy declared prophetically that,

The cost of these oil imports would rise tremendously, with difficult implications for the balance of payments of consuming countries. Serious problems would be caused by unprecedented foreign exchange accumulations of countries such as Saudi Arabia and Abu Dhabi.

The speaker added,

> *A complete change was underway in the political, strategic and power relationships between the oil producing, importing and home countries of international oil companies and national oil companies of producing and importing countries.* [15]

He then projected an OPEC Middle East oil revenue rise, which would translate into just over 400 %, the same level Kissinger was soon to demand from the Shah of Iran.

In May 1972, a year before the Bilderberg Saltsjoebaden talks, the Shah had met with Kissinger and President Nixon in Teheran. Nixon and Kissinger promised the Shah he could buy any US military equipment he wanted from the US defense arsenal except nuclear weapons, and he would be permitted to do it without US Congressional OK.

In order to finance the huge purchases, the Shah would need vastly higher oil revenues. Chase Manhattan Bank, of course, was Iran's bank, the Shah's personal bank, National Iranian Oil Company's bank, the Pahlavi family bank, and the Pahlavi Foundation's bank. The entire financial empire of the Pahlavi regime was a Rockefeller operation from top to bottom. [16]

It was to take just a year after the May 1972 meeting between Kissinger, Nixon and the Shah before Wall Street's strategy emerged, laid out for the elite powerbrokers of Europe and the United States at the Bilderberg meeting at Saltsjoebaden.

A Swedish winter in May

Present at Saltsjoebaden for the May 1973 gathering were, of course, David Rockefeller of Chase Manhattan Bank, by then the acknowledged 'chairman of the board' of the American establishment; close Rockefeller ally, Robert O. Anderson of Atlantic Richfield Oil Co.; Lord Greenhill, chairman of British Petroleum; Sir Eric Roll of S.G. Warburg, co-creator of Eurobonds; George Ball of Lehman Brothers investment bank, the man who some ten years earlier as Assistant Secretary of State, had advised Siegmund Warburg of London's S. G. Warburg & Co. to develop London's Eurodollar market; Zbigniew Brzezinski, the new Executive Director of David Rockefeller's private Trilateral Commission and soon to be President Carter's National Security Adviser; Italy's Gianni Agnelli, a close Rockefeller business associate and head of the Fiat auto empire; and Germany's Otto Wolff von Amerongen, one of the most influential German postwar business figures and the first German to be named a director of Rockefeller's Exxon Oil Co. Henry Kissinger had also been invited to the gathering.

The powerful Bilderberg elite group that met in Sweden in May 1973 had evidently decided to launch a colossal assault *against* industrial growth in the world, in order to tilt the balance of power back to the advantage of American Wall Street financial interests, and specifically to support the vulnerable dollar, the heart of their global financial and economic power. In order to do this, they would use their most valuable strategic weapon—their control of the world's oil flows.

The Bilderberg policy was put into effect six months later in October 1973 when US diplomacy was deployed to trigger a global oil embargo, shockingly enough, in order to force the intended dramatic increase in world oil prices. Since 1945, world oil trade had by international custom been priced in dollars because American oil companies dominated the postwar market. A sharp and sudden increase in the world price of oil, therefore, meant an equally dramatic increase in world demand for US dollars to pay for that necessary oil. In addition to making Exxon, Mobil Oil and the other Rockefeller companies into the largest corporations in the world, it would make their banks—Chase Manhattan, Citibank and a handful of others—into the world's largest banks.

The Rockefeller-dominated American financial establishment had resolved to use their oil power in a manner no one could imagine possible. The very outrageousness of their scheme was to their advantage. No one could conceive that such a thing could possibly be deliberate. It was. [17]

Kissinger's Yom Kippur 'Oil Shokku'

On October 6, 1973, Egypt and Syria invaded Israel, igniting what became known as the 'Yom Kippur' war. The Yom Kippur war was not the simple result of miscalculation, blunder, or an Arab decision to launch a military strike against the state of Israel. The entire series of events leading up to the outbreak of the October war had been secretly orchestrated by Washington and London, using powerful 'back door' diplomatic channels developed by Nixon's National Security Adviser, Henry Kissinger.

Nixon National Security Adviser Kissinger worked with Israel's US Ambassador Dinitz (top left) to incite 1973 OPEC oil embargo to save the dollar.

Kissinger effectively controlled the Israeli policy response through his intimate connection with Israel's Washington ambassador, Simcha Dinitz. Kissinger had also cultivated channels to the Egyptian and Syrian side. His method was simply to misrepresent to each party the critical elements of the other's position, ensuring the outbreak of war and the subsequent Arab oil embargo.

King Faisal of Saudi Arabia had repeatedly made clear to Kissinger and Washington that the consequence of the US continuing its one-sided delivery of US military supplies to Israel would be an OPEC embargo on oil supplies to the United States.[18] Faisal did not make the threat to his American friends lightly.

US intelligence reports, including intercepted communications from Arab officials, confirmed their buildup for war. Kissinger, who was by then Nixon's intelligence czar, reportedly suppressed the reports.

The war brought about the very oil price shock discussed at the Bilderberg deliberations of the previous May in Saltsjoebaden, some six months before outbreak of the war.

OPEC and the Arab oil-producing nations would be the scapegoats for the coming rage of the world over the resulting oil embargo to the United States and Europe and an ensuing huge increase in oil prices, while the Anglo-American interests that were actually responsible, stood quietly in the background, ready to reap the windfall.[19]

In mid-October 1973 the German Government of Chancellor Willy Brandt told the US Ambassador to Bonn that Germany was neutral in the Middle East conflict and would not permit the US to re-supply Israel from German NATO military bases. On October 30, 1973 Nixon sent Chancellor Brandt a sharply worded protest note, reportedly drafted by Kissinger:

> *We recognize that the Europeans are more dependent upon Arab oil than we, but we disagree that your vulnerability is decreased by dis-associating yourselves from us on a matter of this importance...You note that this crisis was not a case of common responsibility for the Alliance, and that military supplies for Israel were for purposes which are not part of alliance responsibility. I do not believe we can draw such a fine line....* [20]

Washington would not permit Germany to declare its neutrality in the Middle East conflict. But, significantly, Britain was allowed to clearly state its neutrality, thus avoiding the impact of the Arab oil embargo. London had maneuvered itself skillfully around an international crisis it had been instrumental in precipitating. Britain was clearly an insider in matters related to Anglo-American oil control. Germany, as a major European industrial exporter and oil importer had the potential to disrupt that very significant game. For that reason, Nixon and Kissinger made clear to Brandt who ran Germany -- and it wasn't the German Chancellor.

In December 1973, as the dust was settling from the Yom Kippur War, the Saudi King sent his most trusted emissary, his oil minister Sheikh Zaki Yamani, to the Shah in Teheran to ask the Shah why Iran was demanding that such an extraordinarily high price be formalized at the upcoming OPEC ministers meeting. The price demanded by the Shah would raise OPEC prices, on average, a staggering and unprecedented 400% from the level before the crisis. When Yamani asked the Shah on behalf of his King, the Shah replied, "Tell your majesty that if he wants the answer to this question he must go to Washington and ask Henry Kissinger." [21]

One enormous consequence of the ensuing 400% rise in OPEC oil prices was that the risky North Sea investments of hundreds of millions of dollars by British Petroleum, Royal Dutch Shell and other Anglo-American petroleum concerns could produce oil at a profit. It was a curious fact of the time that the profitability of the new North Sea oil fields was not at all secure until after Kissinger's oil shock. At pre-1973 world oil prices, the North Sea projects would have gone bankrupt before the first oil could flow.

By October 16, 1973 the Organization of Petroleum Exporting Countries, following a meeting on oil price in Vienna, had already raised their price by a whopping 70%, from $3.01/barrel to $5.11. That same day, the members of the Arab OPEC countries, citing US support for Israel in the Middle East war, declared an embargo on all oil sales to the United States and the Netherlands-- the location of the primary oil port of Western Europe.

Saudi Arabia, Kuwait, Iraq, Libya, Abu Dhabi, Qatar and Algeria announced on October 17, 1973 that they would cut their production below the September level by 5% for October and an additional 5%, per month, "until Israeli withdrawal is completed from the whole Arab territories occupied in June 1967 and the legal rights of the Palestinian people are restored." The resulting massive shortages produced the world's first 'oil shock,' or as the Japanese termed it, 'Oil Shokku.' Notably, David Rockefeller's good friend, the Shah of Iran was absent from the OPEC embargo producers. In effect, the Shah, dependent on US arms and other support, had agreed to "boycott the boycott" and to supply whatever the US and Britain needed.[22]

Significantly, the oil crisis hit full force just as the President of the United States was becoming personally embroiled in the 'Watergate affair,' leaving Henry Kissinger as *de facto* President, running US foreign policy during the crisis in late 1973.

The US Treasury 'arrangement' with Saudi Arabia on dollar pricing of oil was finalized in a February 1975 memo from Treasury's Under Secretary for Monetary Affairs Jack F. Bennett to Secretary of State Kissinger. Under the terms of the agreement, the huge new Saudi oil revenue windfall would be channeled largely into financing the US government deficits. David Mulford, a Wall Street investment banker, was sent to Saudi Arabia to become the principal 'investment adviser' to SAMA, to guide Saudi petrodollar investments to the correct banks, primarily US banks in London and New York.

The Bilderberg scheme was operating fully as planned. The Eurodollar market that had been built up over the previous several years was to play a decisive role in the offshore petrodollar 'recycling' strategy. [23] Subsequently, Rockefeller's Chase Manhattan Bank estimated that between 1974 and the end of 1978 the oil producing countries of OPEC generated a surplus from oil exports of $185 billion, more than three-fourths of which passed through Western financial institutions, the lion's share through Chase and allied banks in New York and London, and from thereon as loans to the Third World.[24] That was a staggering sum of dollar flows.

Kissinger, already firmly in control of key US intelligence estimates as Nixon's all-powerful National Security Adviser, had secured control of US foreign policy as well, having persuaded Nixon to name him Secretary of State in 1973 just prior to the October Yom Kippur war. Kissinger retained both titles and positions simultaneously, something not done by anyone before or since. No other single person during the last months of the Nixon presidency wielded as much absolute power as did Henry Kissinger.

Following a meeting in Teheran on January 1, 1974, a second oil price increase of more than 100% was added, bringing OPEC benchmark prices to $11.65. This was done allegedly on the demand of the Shah of Iran, who had been secretly ordered to do so by Henry Kissinger. The Shah knew he owed his return to power in 1953 to the CIA and to Washington's backing. As noted, back in 1972 he had sealed his fate by making a secret weapons for oil deal with Nixon that would run Iran's national revenues, as well as the Pahlavi's, through Rockefeller's Chase Manhattan Bank.[25] Kissinger's own State Department had not been informed of Kissinger's secret machinations with the Shah. [26]

From 1949 until the end of 1970, Middle East crude oil prices had averaged approximately $1.90/barrel. They had risen to $3.01 in early 1973, the time of the fateful Saltsjoebaden meeting of the Bilderberg group who discussed the imminent 400% future rise in OPEC's price. By January 1974 that 400% increase was a *fait accompli.*

After Nixon had eliminated the gold exchange mechanism in August 1971, the offshore Eurodollar market exploded to a size that began to dwarf the domestic US banking market. Then, by the mid-1970s, in the wake of the 400% OPEC oil price rise, the Eurodollar market reached an estimated $1.3 trillion pool of 'hot money.' Interestingly, by the end of the 1980s, the volume of international narcotics revenues alone -- which had to be laundered through such offshore 'hot money' banks -- exceeded an estimated $1 trillion a year. The big New York and London banks made sure they got the lion's share of drug money.

The London Eurodollar banking market became the centerpiece of the huge Petrodollar recycling operation, lending OPEC oil revenue deposits from banks 'offshore' in London, to Argentina, Brazil, Poland, Yugoslavia, Africa and other oil importing nations that were starved for dollars with which to import the more expensive OPEC oil after 1974.

The Money Trust's counter-revolution

As indicated, by the early 1970s the US economy was anything but robust. The August 1971 decision to unilaterally tear up the Bretton Woods Treaty and end dollar-gold convertibility was, in effect, the beginning of the end of the American Century, a system that had been based in 1944 on the world's strongest economy and its soundest currency.

The dollar system, in its new incarnation as a paper or fiat currency, went through several phases after August 1971. The first phase, described earlier, could be called the 'petrodollar' currency phase in which the strength of the dollar rested on the 400% rise in oil on the world market priced in dollars, and on the highly profitable recycling of those petrodollars through the US and UK and a select handful of other international banks in the City of London, the offshore haven for Eurodollars. That phase lasted until about the end of the 1970s.

The second phase of the post-1971 dollar system was sustained on the Volcker interest rate coup of October 1979 and lasted until approximately 1989 when the fall of the Berlin Wall opened a vast new domain for dollarization and asset looting by Wall Street banks. That opening, combined with the colossal economic growth of China as a member of the WTO, opened the world economy to a drastic lowering of wages across the board, most dramatically in the industrial countries.

In 1997 yet another phase in the post-1971 dollar system was initiated with a politically-driven hedge fund attack on the vulnerable currencies of the high-growth 'Tiger' economies of east Asia, beginning with Thailand, the Philippines, Indonesia and spreading to South Korea. That phase was in large part responsible for a massive inflow of Asian central bank dollars into the US dollar to build dollar reserves as defense against a possible new speculative attack. The inflow of hundreds of billions of dollars of Asian capital after 1998 fuelled the US IT stock market bubble of 1999-2002.

The final phase of the dollar system after August 1971 was the Alan Greenspan Revolution in finance, which he launched after the collapse of the IT stock market bubble in 2001-2002, By his strong support of the revolution in finance, mortgage and other assets as security to issue new bonds, Greenspan helped engineer the 'securitization revolution' which ended with the collapse of his real estate securitization bubble in 2007.

David's Trilateral scheme

However, the year 1973 and the resulting oil shock marked the most pivotal turning point in the overall strategy of the powerful American establishment around David Rockefeller and his brothers.

The decision of the powerful circles around the Rockefellers and the Anglo-American oil cartel and allied bankers to engineer a major shock to global oil prices during the October 1973 Yom Kippur war would buy several more years of life for the dollar as the foundation of the global economic and trading system, but it was a precarious foundation. Even bolder actions were needed to secure the financial dominance of the giant banks and multinationals around the Council on Foreign Relations and the Rockefellers.

In 1973 David Rockefeller was Chairman of the Council on Foreign Relations and head of the family's Chase Manhattan Bank. He believed it was necessary to broaden the political base of American influence by creating a new international organization that would be private and by-invitation-only, like their Bilderberg meetings. But, unlike Bilderberg, which was restricted to American and European decision-makers, Rockefeller's new organization would have three poles—North America, Europe and Japan -- with which to bring the emerging vast Asian market under their control. It was aptly named the Trilateral Commission.

With Japan emerging as the economic wonder of Asia, it was felt that the Japanese markets and goals had to be brought into closer coordination with the strategic goals of the New York power circles.

Membership in the elite Trilateral Commission was more or less taken from David Rockefeller's Rolodex. Founding members included primarily influential business associates of the vast international Rockefeller interests or politicians close to, British merchant banker and Eurodollar creator, Lord Roll of Ipsden Italian FIAT chief Gianni Agnelli, and Royal Dutch Shell's John Loudon. Rockefeller chose his close friend, geopolitical strategist Zbigniew Brzezinski, to be the first Executive Director. The list also included Wall Street bankers, Alan Greenspan and Chase Manhattan's Paul Volcker and a then-obscure Governor of Georgia named Jimmy Carter. [27]

Indicative of its concerns, a Trilateral Commission Task Force Report, presented at their 1975 meeting in Kyoto, Japan, was called *An Outline for Remaking World Trade and Finance*. It stated:

> *Close Trilateral cooperation in keeping the peace, in managing the world economy, and in fostering economic development and in alleviating world poverty, will improve the chances of a smooth and peaceful evolution of the global system.*[28]

Another Trilateral Commission document read:

> *The overriding goal is to make the world safe for interdependence by protecting the benefits which it provides for each country against external and internal threats which will constantly emerge from those willing to pay a price for more national autonomy. This may sometimes require slowing the pace at which interdependence proceeds...More frequently however, it will **call for checking the intrusion of national government into the international exchange of both economic and non-economic goods**. (emphasis added, w.e.).* [29]

The Rockefeller's Trilateral agenda was, overall, the agenda of the US establishment that had been announced the same year by David Rockefeller's brother, John D. III, in a book modestly titled, *The Second American Revolution*.

In 1973, John D. Rockefeller III had published the family's landmark policy declaration in preparation for the American Revolution's Bi-Centennial in 1976. In the book, the elite of the Money Trust declared their 'Second American Revolution,' appropriately published by the Council on Foreign Relations, chaired by David Rockefeller.

John D. Rockefeller's book called for a radical reduction in the powers of government, for expanded 'privatization' of functions long performed by the state, "moving as many government functions and responsibilities toward the private sector as possible." It was a clear call for abandonment of New Deal Keynesian policies—at least the use of the state to correct imbalances in social distribution of jobs and income that had existed since the 1930s. [30]

Rockefeller's 1973 call served as the signal for launching a national media propaganda campaign against alleged Government inefficiency, incompetence, and obstruction, using the inevitable bureaucratic inefficiencies of social services as a smoke screen to end all oversight and regulation of banking and large commercial transactions. The book used carefully selected examples that every citizen could recognize to build support for essentially destroying the traditional and necessary role of the state in regulating commerce and the pubic welfare, to the advantage of the pure and unfettered profit-maximization of private companies and banks financing those companies. It was a Darwinian world they unleashed where the fittest were the biggest and naturally the ones with the clout to destroy their competitors.

The 'Trilateral President'

In 1976, the Rockefeller agenda for a 'second American revolution' made a significant advance: David Rockefeller's protégé at the Trilateral Commission, Georgia peanut farmer turned Governor, Jimmy Carter, won an upset election against incumbent Gerald Ford who had taken over when Nixon was driven from office by the Watergate scandals. Carter promptly went on to staff his key cabinet positions with 26 members of Rockefeller's Trilateral Commission, including Vice President Walter Mondale, Secretary of State Cyrus Vance, Defense Secretary Harold Brown, and Treasury Secretary Michael Blumenthal.

As President, Carter's entire foreign policy, much of his election strategy, and some of his domestic policy came directly from Rockefeller's Trilateral Commission. The architect of Carter's foreign policy from 1975 was his National Security Adviser Zbigniew Brzezinski who had resigned as Trilateral Commission Executive Director in order to take the post. Brzezinski wrote Carter's major speeches during the campaign, and crafted Carter's foreign policy with assists fromTrilateralists Vance, Brown and Blumenthal. The watchword for Carter's foreign policy from 1975 on was "clear it with Brzezinski." Carter would ask when given a memorandum on foreign policy, "has Brzezinski seen this...?"[31]

The predominance of so many Trilateral Commission members in the Carter Administration led some media to refer to it as the Trilateral Presidency. It
more accurately should have been called the David Rockefeller Presidency. It
was Carter who began the Rockefeller group's long process of Government
deregulation and privatization that his successor, Ronald Reagan, would make
the centerpiece of his Presidency.

Reportedly it was after Gerald Ford, on advice of his then White House Chief
of Staff, Donald Rumsfeld, had decided to drop Vice President Nelson Rockefeller as his 1976 running mate, that David Rockefeller introduced Democrat
Jimmy Carter to Trilateral Commission members at their meeting in Kyoto,
Japan, referring to him as, "the next President." [32]

Clawing back New Deal concessions

The deepening US economic crisis of the 1970s was the motivation for the
Rockefellers and other US establishment leaders to come up with radical new
strategies. The US was faced with stagnation or even decline of its market
strength and corresponding profit share globally and within the United States,
still the world's largest market for goods and services. By 1975 the share of total
wealth held by the wealthiest 1% of American households had fallen to its lowest
since 1922, measured in terms of the combined housing, stocks, bonds, cash and
other durable wealth.[33]

Their dramatic manipulation of world oil prices had been responsible for
triggering the most serious postwar global recession. By 1975 it was clear that
the world economy, in the wake of the declining profit rate, had entered what
economists termed a 'structural crisis.' It included diminished growth rates,
falling per capita productivity, a wave of unemployment, and cumulative high
inflation.

From this crises emerged a new social vision or political philosophy called
"neoliberalism," appearing first within the countries at the center of the industrial world—beginning with the United Kingdom and the United States—and
then gradually exporting to the "periphery," or the so-called emerging markets
of the developing world.

Neoliberalism had little to do with Keynesian 'liberal' economics. The neoliberal revolution that was launched in the mid-1970s was a project of the US
establishment and their British counterparts. Specifically, it was a concoction of
the Rockefeller brothers, based on the radical free market dogma of Milton
Friedman, a member of the arch-conservative Mont Pelerin Society and then

Professor of Economics at the University of Chicago, an institution founded decades earlier with Rockefeller Standard Oil money. Neoliberalism could more accurately have been called neo-feudalism.

Echoing John D. Rockefeller's 1973 manifesto, Friedman's neoliberalism, enshrined in his popular book, *Free to Choose*, called for untrammeled free markets and free trade, and attacked trade unions as a "throwback to a pre-industrial period." [34]

The neoliberal revolution was, in essence, a globalized version of John D. Rockefeller's Second American Revolution. The International Chamber of Commerce in Paris approved heartily of the global neoliberal mandate "to break down barriers to international trade and investment so that all countries can benefit from improved living standards through increased trade and investment flows." [35] It was the initial phase of what two decades later would be called "globalization."

The powerful circles around the Rockefellers within the US financial establishment called explicitly for a global restructuring to their benefit, including:

> *new discipline of labor and management to the benefit of lenders and shareholders; the diminished intervention of the state concerning development and welfare; the dramatic growth of financial institutions; the implementation of new relationships between the financial and non-financial sectors to the benefit of the former; a new legal stand in favor of mergers and acquisitions; the strengthening of central banks and the targeting of their activity toward price stability, and the new determination to drain the resources of the periphery toward the center.* [36]

The predominant feature of the new neoliberalism was not just its structural arrangements, but the creation of mechanisms to extend the dollar's reach to the rest of the planet, the globalization of the dollar and of US finance behind it. The destructive process of market liberalization spread with devastating speed and efficiency, assisted by creation of new multinational institutions such as the World Trade Organization and massive trade pressures from Washington and its free market allies, especially Britain.

Milton Friedman's dogma of monetarism was the theoretical expression of the new revolution, or more accurately, counter-revolution. The decisive year in the economic counter-revolution was 1979 when David Rockefeller got President Carter to name his protege, Paul Volcker, to become Chairman of the Federal Reserve. In October 1979 Volcker imposed the most radical monetarist policy in the history of the Federal Reserve as he allowed interest rates to soar by more than 300% into the 20% range, and held them high until the resulting inevitable Third World debt crisis erupted by August 1982, prompting him to reverse the rate policy.

The year 1979 was what some economists called the year of the neoliberal Coup. [37] Rockefellers, Volcker and their wealthy allies in the Wall Street Money Trust had been able to use the issue of runaway inflation -- an inflation for which their own 1973 Bilderberg oil pricing decision had been initially responsible -- to justify a monetary 'shock therapy' that allegedly would 'squeeze inflation out of the system,' as Volcker liked to phrase it.

In reality the high interest policy was imposed by the wealthiest members of the establishment as part of their long-term strategy of clawing back the concessions forced from them during the Great Depression in terms of the creation of the Keynesian social welfare state, social security, and Government support for labor union organization.

The 'Post-Industrial' world of Wall Street

Confronted with stagnating domestic markets, declining abolute profits and the need to invest huge sums in order to bring their domestic US industries up to world standards, the Rockefeller circles opted instead to walk away from renewing their domestic US economic base, leaving it to become what their think-tanks called a 'post-industrial society.'

Volcker's interest rate policy led to 'real'-- that is, corrected-for-inflation -- interest rates of 6-8%, a staggering windfall boon for wealthy bond holders, the center of the financial system. It also created a recession and with it, a rising wave of unemployment in Europe and in the United States, which created the conditions for a new crackdown on labor implemented by both Reagan and Thantcher in the early 1980s, dramatically weakening the influence of trade unions on wage levels for decades to come.

The 1970s were a transition decade for the development of the American Century. As was noted, by the late 1960s, chronic deficits of the balance of trade appeared for the first time in the United States since World War II, related to the on-going postwar economic recovery by Europe and Japan. Surplus dollars were accumulating in the rest of the world and, thus, the threat of conversion of those foreign dollar earnings into gold was increasing. The dollar had to be devalued with respect to gold and other major currencies. The United States put an end to the convertibility of the dollar in 1971, introducing floating exchange rates.

By 1973 with the regime of floating exchange rates confirmed as permanent, Washington and its allies in London, and through the Bilderberg conference of May 1973, decided on the drastic, oil price inflation to support the falling dollar. By 1979, boosted by the Volcker Federal Reserve coup, they were able to reap staggering profits on their bond and other assets amid a rising dollar.

After 1980 when Republican Ronald Reagan took office, the US implemented this deliberate deficit policy with a vengeance. Reagan's tenure initiated what became the most dramatic and permanent trade and budget deficits in US history.

In hammering out its position in the multinational negotiations in 1973 to make floating exchange rates a permanent fact, Washington made clear it would use its military dominance within NATO and in Asia to extract maximum concessions from its trading partners. In its bilateral negotiations with South Korea in 1973, the US demanded terms that made it "obligatory for South Korean exporters to the American market to import a certain amount of raw materials from the United States." [38]

By 1973 the US trade position with respect to its major allies in Western Europe and Japan was taking form. The terms of the 'grand bargain' would be that the US would open its borders to almost unlimited Japanese or European imports of products such as cars, steel, and later, electronics. In return, the foreign countries would agree to purchase US defense equipment, US agricultural products and US aircraft for its national airlines.

But the most far-reaching aspect of the new regime implemented after 1973 by Washington and adhered to by every Administration since then was the idea that, because of the unique role of the dollar as world foreign exchange reserve under a floating-rate exchange regimen -- and the fact that the dollar could no longer be redeemed for gold -- foreign nations that built up a surplus of dollars exporting to the United States, especially Japan and Germany, would be forced to reinvest those dollar trade surpluses in US Government debt, in order to earn interest and hold them in a safe repository.

Washington, leaving nothing to chance, made certain in its bilateral trade negotiations with countries such as Japan or Germany to make clear that they should invest their dollar trade surpluses in US Treasury bonds or bills. [39]

That began the perverse dependency of the exporting world on the US as 'importer of last resort.' The United States, led by Wall Street banks that held the monopoly on buying and selling US Treasury debt, would emerge as the world's greatest capital market during the 1980s, as US deficits exploded and its internal industry went into malign neglect as a result of the decision. Wall Street bond brokers reaped the gains. Ronald Reagan's Presidency was chosen by the establishment to implement this 'greatest rip-off.'

Endnotes:

[1] Michael Hudson, *Super Imperialism: The Origins and Fundamentals of US World Dominance* (Lonson: Pluto Press, 2003), p. xiii. Hudson's account is part of his brilliant expose of postwar US financial manipulations that used staggering levels of US Treasury debt combined with chronic trade deficits to do what no other country could, by virtue of the fact the dollar was world reserve currency and the rest of the world was dependent on US military security. They had little choice but to buy hundreds of billions of dollars of US Treasury debt with its surplus trade dollars, in effect, as Hudson had pointed out to Kahn, forcing those countries to finance US wars and other exploits that were to the disadvantage of those nations buying the US debt. The decoupling of the dollar from gold in August 1971 was the critical step making that possible, athough as Hudson points out, at first the policy circles in Washington and Wall Street did not realize it. The entire book is available online.

[2] See F. William Engdahl, *A Century of War: Anglo-American Oil Politics and the New World Order* (London: Pluto Press, 2004), p. 114.

[3] Marcello De Cecco, *International Financial Markets and US Domestic Policy Since 1945*, International Affairs. July 1976, London, pp. 381-399.

[4] F. William Engdahl, op. Cit., p. 386.

[5] Marcello de Cecco, op. cit.

[6] Ibid. p. 398.

[7] R.T. Naylor, *Hot Money and the Politics of Debt* (London: Unwin Paperbacks, 1988), p. 33.

[8] Ibid. pp. 33-35.

[9] Naharnet, *Roger Tamraz Arrested in Morocco*, Jan 29, 2009, Lebanese Forces Official Website, accessed in http://www.lebanese-forces.org/regional/Roger-Tamraz-Arrested-in-Morocco1002728.shtml.

[10] Raúl Salinas de Gortari [brother of former Mexican President Carlos Salinas de Gortari] was alleged to have laundered up to $130 million in drug money through Citibank and various Swiss banks during the time his brother was President of Mexico. Raul Salinas was later convicted of murder and sentenced to prison. See *Citibanker for Salinas had been Star U.S. witness*, Money Laundering Alert, April 1996, accessed in http://www.pbs.org/wgbh/pages/frontline/shows/mexico/family/citibankaffair.html.

[11] Ibid, pp. 127-128.

[12] Richard Duncan, *The Dollar Crisis* (Singapore: John Wiley & Sons-Asia, 2003), p., Figure 1.1.

[13] See David E. Spiro, *The Hidden Hand of American Hegemony: Petrodollar Recycling and International Markets*, (Ithaca: Cornell University Press, 1999), p.147 ff.

[14] Ibid, Anonymous, *Saltsjoebaden Conference*, Bilderberg meetings, 11-13 May 1973. Robert D Murphy prepared the agenda for the 1973 Bilderberg meeting. Significantly, Murphy was the man who in 1922, as US Consul in Munich, had sought a meeting with then unknown Adolf Hitler and sent back favorable recommendations to his superiors in Washington. Murphy later shaped US occupation policy in postwar Germany as Political Adviser.

[15] *Saltsjoebaden Conference*, Bilderberg meetings, 11-13 May 1973. The author obtained an original copy of the official discussion from this meeting. The normally confidential document was bought in a Paris used bookstore and it bore the signature of Bilderberg insider, Shepard Stone. Walter Levy, who delivered the Saltsjoebaden energy report at the meeting, was intimately tied to the fortunes of big oil. In 1948 as oil economist for the

Marshall Plan Economic Co-operation Administration, Levy had tried to block a government inquiry into allegations that the oil companies were overcharging.

[16] Mark Hulbert, *Interlock: The Untold Story of American banks, oil interests, the Shah's money, debts and the astounding connections between them* (New York: Richardson & Snyder, 1982), pp. 71-87.

[17] See footnote 9, below.

[18] Robert Lacey, *The Kingdom: Arabia and the House of Saud* (New York: Avon Books, 1981), pp. 398-399.

[19] Matti Golan, *The Secret Conversations of Henry Kissinger: Step-by-step diplomacy in the Middle East* (New York: Bantam Books Inc., 1976).

[20] Henry A. Kissinger, *Years of Upheaval* (Boston: Little, Brown & Co., 1982).

[21] The account of this extraordinary exchange between His Excellency Sheikh Zaki Yamani and the Shah was relayed to the author in a personal discussion between the author and Sheikh Yamani in London in September 2000. Sheikh Yamani had been, in 1974, Saudi Oil Minister and spokesman for OPEC during the embargo.

[22] Mark Hulbert, op. Cit.

[23] Jack Bennett, *Memorandum*, reproduced in International Currency Review, Vol. 20, no. 6. January 1991. London. p. 45.

[24] Ann Crittenden, *Managing OPEC's Money*, The New York Times, June 24, 1979.

[25] Sheikh Zaki Yamani, in a September 2000 private conversation with the author, cited above.

[26] James Akins, interview regarding his tenure as Director of Fuels & Energy Office of US State Department at that time, later Ambassador to Saudi Arabia.

[27] For more on the Trilateral Commission founding and members see F. William Engdahl, op. cit, Appendix I, p. 285.

[28] The Trilateral Commission, *An Outline for Remaking World Trade and Finance* (New York University Press, 1975).

[29] C. Fred Bergsten, *Interdependence and the Reform of International Institutions*, International Organization, Vol. 30, No. 2 (Spring, 1976), pp. 361-372.

[30] John D. Rockefeller III, *The Second American Revolution*, 1973, Harper & Row, New York, pp. 103-112.

[31] Lawrence H. Shoup, *Jimmy Carter and the Trilateralists: Presidential Roots*, excerpted from the book, *Trilateralism*, edited by Holly Sklar (Boston: South End Press, 1980), accessed in http://www.thirdworldtraveler.com/Trilateralism/JimmyCarter_Trilat.html.

[32] Cyrus Vance, from a private discussion relayed in 1975 to the author in New York.

[33] Gérard Duménil and Dominique Lévy, *The Neoliberal (Counter) Revolution*, contained in *Neoliberalism: A Critical Reader*, edited by Alfredo Saad-Filho and Deborah Johnston (London: Pluto Press, 2004).

[34] Milton Friedman, *Free to Choose* (New York: Penguin Books, 1979), p. 271.

[35] International Chamber of Commerce, *Policy and Business Practices*, accessed on ICC official website, http://www.iccwbo.org/policy/trade/.

[36] Gérard Duménil and Dominique Lévy, op. cit.

[37] Ibid.

[38] Ibid., p. 369.

[39] Ibid., p. 363.

CHAPTER FIFTEEN

A Reagan Revolution for the Money Class

'They've done more to dismantle American industry than any other group in history. And yet they go around saying everything is great. It's like the Wizard of Oz.'
- US oilman Robert O. Anderson on Volcker and Reagan[1]

Paul Volcker's monetarist coup d'etat

If the oil shocks of 1973 triggered the polarization of American society into a minority of increasingly wealthy, against a vast majority whose living standards were slowly sinking, monetary shock therapy accelerated the process to its ultimate conclusion. Initiated by Paul Volcker on October 6, 1979, it signified a coup **d'état** by the monied class in the United States.

The monetary shock therapy that Volcker imposed on the United States had been developed and already implemented several months earlier in Britain by Prime Minister Margaret Thatcher. Volcker and his close circle of Wall Street banking friends, including the Morgan Guaranty Trust Company, merely imposed Thatcher's monetary shock model onto US conditions. The goal of both was the same—to dramatically roll back the redistribution of wealth and income in their respective countries in favor of the wealthiest 5%, or even fewer.

In early May 1979 Margaret Thatcher won election in Britain by campaigning on a platform of "squeezing inflation out of the economy." Thatcher, and her inner circle of Adam Smith 'free market' ideologues, promoted a fraud, insisting that government deficit spending, and not the 140 percent increase in the price of oil since the fall of Iran's Shah, was the chief cause of Britain's 18% rate of price inflation.

According to Thatcher's advisers, inflated prices could be lowered simply by cutting the supply of 'surplus money,' thereby inducing an economic recession. Since the major source of surplus money, she argued, was from chronic government budget deficits, therefore government expenditure must be savagely cut, in order to reduce 'monetary inflation.' The Bank of England simultaneously restricted credit to the economy by a policy of high interest rates, as their part of the remedy. It was identical in every respect to the Rockefellers' Second American Revolution, only it was called instead, the 'Thatcher Revolution.'

In June 1979, only one month after Thatcher took office, Thatcher's Chancellor of the Exchequer, Sir Geoffrey Howe, raised Base Rates for the banks a staggering five percentage points—from 12% up to 17%--within a matter of twelve weeks. This amounted to an unprecedented 42% increase in the cost of borrowing for both industry and homeowners. Never in modern history had a major industrialized nation undergone such a shock in such a brief period, outside the context of a wartime economic emergency.

The Bank of England simultaneously began to cut the money supply, to ensure that interest rates remained high. Unable to pay borrowing costs, businesses went bankrupt; families were unable to buy new homes; long-term investment into power plants, subways, railroads, and other infrastructure ground to a halt as a consequence of Thatcher's monetarist revolution.

Thatcher also imposed draconian labor policies, forcing militant British miners to cave in after brutal months of strike, which earned her the epithet 'The Iron Lady.' Unemployment in Britain doubled, rising from 1.5 million when she was elected, to a level of 3 million by the end of her first eighteen months in office. That was part of the bankers' strategy: calculating that unemployed workers who are desperate will work for less to get any decent job. Thatcher targeted labor unions, claiming they were obstacles to the success of the monetarist 'revolution,' and blaming them for creating the enemy—inflation.

Meanwhile, Thatcher accommodated the big City banks by removing exchange controls, so that instead of capital being invested in rebuilding Britain's rotted aging industrial base, funds flowed out to speculative real estate in Hong Kong or lucrative loans to Latin America. [2]

Beginning in Britain, then in the United States, and from the Anglo-American world radiating outward, the shock waves from the radical monetarism of Thatcher and Rockefeller protégé Paul Volcker spread like a virulent parasite after 1979. Country after country buckled under demands to cut government spending, lower taxes, deregulate industry and break the power of organized labor. Interest rates rose around the world to levels never before imagined in peacetime.

*Paul Volcker, the Rockefeller choice to head the Federal Reserve
in 1979 to create the coup d'etat of the Money Trust.*

In the United States, Volcker's monetary shock policy by early 1980 had driven US interest rates up to an astonishing 20% nominal level. The economics of this drastic interest rate regime were soon obvious. For any industrial investment to be profitable at 20% or even 17% interest rate levels would mean that any enterprise that normally required more than four to five years to complete, was simply not possible. Interest charges on the construction alone would prohibit this.

Destroying savings banks

Volcker's shock medicine was imposed on a desperate President Carter, who in March 1980 willingly signed an extraordinary piece of legislation, the "Depository Institutions Deregulation and Monetary Control Act of 1980."

This law was the first in a series of moves imposed by the major New York banks, led by David Rockefeller's Chase Manhattan, on the US and world economy over the ensuing period.

The act empowered Volcker's Federal Reserve to impose reserve requirements on banks, including Savings & Loan banks, even if they were not in the Federal Reserve System, ensuring that Volcker's credit choke succeeded in cutting the flow of credit sufficiently. In addition, the new law phased out all legal ceilings on interest rates which banks could charge customers under what the Federal Reserve called 'Regulation Q,' as well as repealing all state laws which had set interest rate limits, the so-called anti-usury laws.[3]

Regulation Q, a part of the 1933 Glass-Steagall Banking Act, prohibited banks from paying interest on their demand deposit accounts. The rule encouraged savings banks where interest was allowed on long-term deposits. The large New York and other money center banks had long since circumvented Regulation Q by money market funds and other substitutes. The Savings & Loan banks had no such option and had strict ceilings on savings accounts, making them less attractive to customers than the rival money market funds of the big banks. Repeal of Regulation Q, while sounding logical, actually destroyed the economics of the traditional S&L banks in the United States, opening them to takeover by the large commercial banks.

The sky was to be the interest rate limit under the new dogma of what the British called 'neoliberal monetarism.' Money was to be King, and the world, its dutiful servants. And Wall Street bankers were to be the Gods of Money.

The global impact of the Volcker high interest rates was devastating to the industrial and developing world. By the early 1980s, worldwide spending on long-term government-funded infrastructure and capital investments -- such as railroad, highway, bridge, sewer, and electricity plant construction -- had collapsed. According to the International Iron and Steel Institute's calculations, from the time of the first oil shock in 1975 until 1985, the total share of all government expenditure in major industrial nations devoted to construction of public infrastructure had fallen to one half its level of the mid-1970s. The world's production of steel, shipping ton-miles, and other indicators of real physical economic flows reflected the catastrophic Anglo-American monetary shock policy. The world's steel industry was forced deeper into its worst depression since the 1930s. [4]

Paul Volcker's monetary shock and the resulting US economic downturn were the major factors – along with Republican sabotage of Carter's Iran hostage negotiations -- causing Jimmy Carter's defeat in the November 1980 election.

Imposing the monetarist medicine

An arch-conservative Republican President, former Hollywood movie actor Ronald Reagan, had no hesitation in backing the Volcker shock treatment. Reagan had been tutored while Governor of California by the guru of monetarism, University of Chicago economist, Milton Friedman. Friedman was also an adviser to Britain's Margaret Thatcher.

One of Reagan's first acts as President in early 1981—after he had magically released the US Embassy hostages from captivity in Tehran within minutes of his inauguration—was to use his powers to dissolve PATCO, the trade union of the airline traffic controllers. This served to signal other unions not to attempt to seek Government relief from the soaring interest rates. Reagan was mesmerized by the same ideological zeal to "squeeze" out inflation as was his conservative British ally, Thatcher.

Reagan kept Milton Friedman as his unofficial adviser on economic policy. His administration was filled with disciples of Friedman's radical monetarism as well as followers of Austrian free market economist Ludwig von Mises.

The powerful US banking circles of New York were determined to use the same radical measures on the US economy that had earlier been imposed by Friedman to break the back of Chile's economy under the dictatorship of Augusto Pinochet. Friedman's policies had also been implemented by the Argentinean military juntas during the late 1970s and early 80s, to break Argentina's unions and destroy the country's middle classes.

This model of 'laissez faire' was now to be introduced on the home market in the United States with disastrous consequences for the long-term economic stability of the country, although it was not immediately clear just how severe that would be.

The power of American finance was given a new lease on life with the Volcker shock therapy, just as intended. The byproduct of Volcker's soaring interest rate policy -- a policy he held firmly to until October 1982 -- was a resurgence of the US dollar as capital flowed into US bonds and other assets to earn the very high interest rate returns.

Volcker explodes the debt bomb

The Latin American debt crisis, an ominous foretaste of the 2007 US sub-prime crisis, erupted as a direct result of Volcker's interest rate shock therapy. In August 1982 Mexico announced it could no longer pay the interest on its staggering dollar debt. Mexico, along with most of the Third World from Argentina to Brazil, from Nigeria to Congo, from Poland to Yugoslavia, had fallen for the New York banks' debt trap.

The trap was as follows: huge quantities of recycled OPEC petrodollars were invested in the major New York and London banks -- the 'Eurodollar banks' -- which then lent the dollars to desperate Third World borrowers. The loans were set initially at "floating rates" or adjustable rates tied to the London LIBOR interbank interest rates. [5]

However, when LIBOR rates unexpectedly rose some 300% within months as a result of Volcker's shock therapy, those debtor countries that had borrowed dollars at floating interest rates from the international banks in New York and London were unable to continue servicing their debt. It was exactly the same scenario the same New York banks repeated in the housing finance securitization bubble after 2000, with 'teaser rates' and 'ARM' or Adjustable Rate Mortgage and other tricks.

The IMF was then brought in to run things in the debtor or victim country, brought there by the major New York banks and the US Treasury. The greatest looting binge in world history to that date—misnamed the Third World Debt Crisis—was on. The scale of the big banks' looting binge during the 1980s was exceeded only by their gains from the 2000-2007 mortgage securitization swindles.

Volcker's shock policy had triggered the crisis, and the New York and London banks cleaned up on that debt crisis.

By 1986, after seven years of relentlessly high interest rates by the Volcker Fed, the internal state of the US economy was horrendous. Much of America had come to resemble a Third World country, with its sprawling slums, double-digit unemployment, rising crime rates, and endemic drug addiction. A Federal Reserve study showed that 55% of all American families were net debtors. Federal budget deficits were running at unprecedented levels of more than $200 billion annually.

In reality, Volcker, who had worked under David Rockefeller at Chase Manhattan Bank, had been sent by Rockefeller to Washington to do one thing—save the dollar from a free fall collapse that threatened the role of the US dollar as global reserve currency, and with it, to save the bond markets for the wealthy upper stratum of American elite society, the money interests. It was, in effect, the financial oligarchs' counter-revolution against the concessions they had been forced to give to the 'lower classes' during and after the Great Depression.

That role of the US dollar as world reserve currency was the hidden key to American financial power.

With US interest rates going through the roof, foreign investors flooded in to reap the gains by buying US bonds. Bonds, US Government debt, were the heart of Wall Street's control of the international financial system. Volcker's shock therapy for the economy reaped astronomical profits for the New York financial community.

Volcker succeeded all too well in his mission.

The dollar rose to all-time highs against the currencies of Germany, Japan, Canada and other countries from 1979 through the end of 1985. The over-valued

US dollar made US manufactured exports prohibitively expensive on world markets, however, and led to a dramatic decline in US industrial exports.

Already high interest rates from the Volcker Fed since October 1979 had led to a major decline in domestic construction, the ultimate ruin of the US automobile industry and with it, steel, as American manufacturers moved to outsource production offshore where the cost advantages were greater.

Referring to Paul Volcker and his free-market backers inside the Reagan White House, even staunch Republican Robert O. Andersen, chairman of Atlantic Richfield Oil Co. complained, "they've done more to dismantle American industry than any other group in history. And yet they go around saying everything is great. It's like the Wizard of Oz." [6]

The IMF helps plunder the Third World

There would not have been a Third World debt crisis during the 1980s, had there not been Margaret Thatcher's and Paul Volcker's radical monetary shock policies.

Beginning in June 1979 with the shock of the Thatcher government's interest rate hike, followed in October by that of Volcker's Federal Reserve, the interest rate burdens of Third World debtor countries compounded overnight, as London's LIBOR interest rates climbed from an average of 7 % in early 1978, to almost 20% by early 1980, the effects ricocheting across the globe.

As interest rate burdens on the Third World's foreign debt obligations soared to the stratosphere after 1980, the market for their commodity exports to the industrial countries, critical to repay those debt burdens, also collapsed, as the industrial economies were plunged into the deepest economic downturn since the world depression of the 1930s. The Thatcher-Volcker monetary shock 'cure' triggered global chain reactions.

Third World debtor countries were being squeezed in the blades of a vicious scissors of deteriorating terms of trade for their commodity exports, falling export earnings, and a soaring debt service ratio. This was what Washington and London referred to condescendingly as the "Third World debt crisis." The crisis had been made in London, New York and in Washington, not in Mexico City, Brasilia, Buenos Aires, Lagos or Warsaw.

The debtor countries paid many times over, literally with the proverbial 'pound of flesh,' to the modern-day Shylocks of New York and London, Tokyo and Frankfurt. The large Third World debtor nations had the pistol to their heads, under IMF pressure, to sign what the banks euphemistically termed 'debt work-outs' with American private banks, most often led by Citicorp or Chase Manhattan of New York.

The powerful private banking interests had banded together following a closed-door meeting in England's Ditchley Park during the fall of 1982. Their agenda was to create a creditors' cartel of leading banks, headed by the New York and London banks, called the Institute for International Finance or informally, the Ditchley Group. They imposed what one observer characterized as a "bankers' socialism," in which the private banks "socialized" (distributed) their lending risks and potential losses to the majority of the taxpaying public, while privatizing to themselves all the gains, similar to the Bush Administration's bank bailout policy in 2008.

Once the bankers and their allies inside the Reagan Administration, such as Treasury Secretary Donald Regan, sufficiently terrorized President Reagan over the situation, the White House called on Paul Volcker, the banks, and the IMF to impose a program of strict "conditionalities" on each debtor country.

The idea to place the IMF and its strict conditionalities into the middle of the debt negotiating process was an American idea. In substance, it was almost an exact copy of what the New York bankers had done after 1919 against Germany and the rest of Europe under the ill-fated Dawes Plan, and later attempted under the Young Plan. [7]

The IMF conditionalities and a country's agreement to sign with the IMF were part of a program developed by an American official then at the IMF, Irving Friedman, who was later to be rewarded for his work with a senior post at Citibank. The IMF, as noted earlier, had originally been created in 1944 at Bretton Woods to stabilize currency and trade relations among the industrial nations. It was now turned to an entirely new task -- that of debt policeman for New York banks.

The IMF prescription 'medicine,' the conditionalities, was invariably the same from one country to the next. The victim debtor country was told, if it ever wanted to see a penny of foreign bank lending again, it must slash domestic imports to the bone, cut the national budget savagely (most often targetting state subsidies for food and other necessities) and devalue the national currency in order to make its exports 'attractive' to industrial countries -- that is, to make them dirt cheap, while simultaneously making the costs of importing advanced industrial goods prohibitively expensive. All this, the officials of the IMF argued, was necessary in order to earn hard currency to service the debt. [8]

The IMF Structural Adjustment Program was only Step One to make the 'candidate' country eligible for consideration of Step Two—an agreement with its foreign creditor banks for 're-structuring' the repayment schedule of their foreign debt or a major portion of it. In this second stage, the banks won huge future rights over debtor countries, as they added defaulted interest arrears onto the face amount of total debt owed, interest capitalization as bankers termed it.

The end result of the countless debtor restructurings after 1982 was an enormous increase in the amount of debt owed to creditor banks. According to data from a leading Swiss insurance firm, Swiss Re, total foreign debt of all developing countries, long-term and short, rose steadily after 1982 from just over $839 billion to almost $1,300 billions by 1987. Virtually all of it consisted of the every-increasing burden of refinancing the unpayable old debt, added to the economic burden of the future, not new loans.

The IMF had become the global financial 'policeman,' enforcing payment of usurious debts through imposition of the most draconian austerity in history. With the crucial voting bloc of the IMF firmly controlled by an American-British axis, the IMF became the global enforcer of a *de facto* Anglo-American neo-colonial monetary and economic dictatorship, one imposed by a supranational institution immune from any democratic political controls.

The American banks, by far the largest group involved in lending to Latin America, strongarmed their bank counterparts in Western Europe and Japan that they must 'solidarize' and follow the same IMF script or face the prospect of collapse of the international banking system.

As debtor after debtor was coerced to come to terms with the IMF and the creditor banks, the result was a reversal in capital flows of titanic dimension. According to the World Bank, between 1980 and 1986, for a group of 109 debtor countries, payment of interest alone to the creditors on foreign debts totaled $326 billions. Repayment of principal on the same debts totaled another $332 billion, for a combined debt service total payment of $658 billions on what originally was a debt of $430 billions.

But despite this huge effort, those 109 countries still owed the creditors a sum of $882 billions in 1986. It was an impossible debt vortex. Thus worked the wonders of compound interest and floating LIBOR interest rates. [9]

The debtor countries had been caught in a debt trap from which the only way out, offered conveniently by the creditor banks of New York and London, was to surrender their national sovereign control over their economy, especially over valuable national resources such as oil and raw materials.

One study, by Hans K. Rasmussen of Danish UNICEF, pointed out that what had taken place since the early 1980s was a massive transfer of wealth from the capital-starved Third World, primarily into the financing of deficits in the United States. It was *de facto* imperialism or, as some called it, neo-colonialism under the disguise of IMF technocracy. [10]

Rasmussen estimated that during the 1980s, the combined nations of the developing sector transferred a total of $400 billion into the United States alone. This allowed the Reagan Administration to finance the largest peacetime deficits in world history, while falsely claiming credit for "the world's longest peacetime recovery." [11]

With high US interest rates, a rising dollar, and the security of American government backing, 43% of the record high US budget deficits during the 1980s were financed by this looting of capital from the debtor countries of the once-developing sector. As with the Anglo-American bankers in the post World War I Versailles reparations debt process, the debt was merely a vehicle for establishing *de facto* economic control over entire sovereign countries.

Even looting the debt-burdened developing world was not enough, however. The debt strategy of the Reagan Administration, Volcker and the New York banks was also taking its toll on the domestic US economy. In May 1986, the Joint Economic Committee of the US Congress prepared a Staff Study on the "Impact of the Latin American Debt Crisis on the US Economy." The report documented the devastating losses of US jobs and exports as IMF austerity measures forced Latin America to virtually halt industrial and other imports in order to service the debt. The report noted:

> *It is now becoming clear that Administration policies have gone above and beyond what was needed for protecting the money center banks from insolvency...the Reagan Administration's management of the debt crisis has in effect, rewarded the institutions that played a major role in precipitating the crisis and penalized those sectors of the US economy that had played no role in causing the debt crisis.[12]*

The institutions that precipitated the crisis were, of course, the Volcker Federal Reserve and the New York banks. The Congressional report was ignored in the major media and was promptly buried.

Africa fared even worse than other regions as a result of the American debt strategy. The oil shocks and the ensuing 20% interest rates and collapsing world industrial growth in the 1980s dealt the death blow to almost the entire Continent. Until the 1980s, Black Africa had been 90% self-sufficient in exporting its raw materials to finance its development. Beginning in the early 1980s, the world dollar price of such raw materials--everything from cotton to coffee to copper, iron ore and sugar -- began an almost uninterrupted freefall.

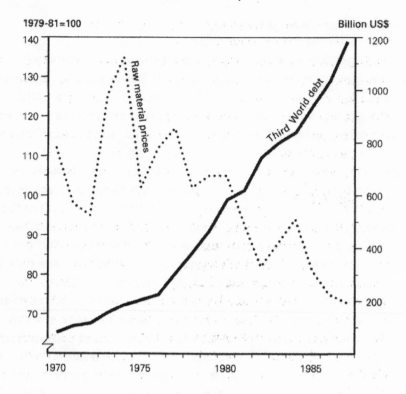

*Petrodollar loans to the Third World created a debt bubble that Volcker burst
in 1979 to lock the developing world into IMF conditions benefitting the industrial north
— a rerun of 1880's British financial imperialism in Egypt and Ottoman Turkey.*

By 1987 such raw materials prices had fallen to their lowest levels since the Second World War, as low as their level in 1932, a year of deep global economic depression. The 1980s collapse, which would last almost twenty years until China's economic boom began to reverse it in the early years of the next century, was a deliberate policy of the American financial interests to fuel an economic growth based on dirt-cheap raw materials in a 'globalized' economy.

If the prices for such raw material exports had remained at merely the levels of the early1980 period, Black Africa would have earned an additional 150 billion US dollars during the 1980s. In 1982, at the beginning of the 'debt crisis,' Africa owed creditor banks in he United States, Europe and Japan, some $73 billion. By the end of the decade, this sum, through debt 'rescheduling' and various IMF interventions into their economies, had more than doubled to $160 billion, almost exactly the amount that these countries would have earned at a stable export price level.

Chickens come home to roost

The aftermath of the oil shocks and the high interest rate monetary shocks of the 1970s was all too similar to the 1920s. In place of the Versailles reparations burden on world productive investment, the world now had the IMF's Third World debt "restructuring" process. The incredible rates of inflation during the early part of the 1980s -- typically 12-17% -- dictated the conditions of investment returns.

The IMF's 'structual adjustment' policies imposed after October 1982 to collect billions from Third World countries brought a huge windfall of financial liquidity to the American banking system. At the same time, Wall Street's and Treasury Secretary Donald Regan's zeal for lifting government 'shackles' off financial markets resulted in an extravaganza of financial excess. When the dust settled by the end of that decade, some began to realize that Reagan's free market had all but destroyed an entire national economy: the USA's.

President Ronald Reagan signed the largest tax reduction bill in postwar history in August 1981. The bill contained provisions that gave generous tax relief for certain speculative forms of real estate investment, especially commercial real estate. Government restrictions on corporate takeovers were also removed, and Washington gave the clear signal that 'anything goes, so long as it stimulated the Dow Jones Industrials stock index.

By summer 1982, as the White House secured agreement from Paul Volcker and the Federal Reserve that interest rate levels would finally begin a steady downward turn, the speculative bonanza was ready to go.

A bankruptcy of a small oil and real estate bank, Penn Square Bank, in Oklahoma that spring had combined with the Mexico debt crisis to convince Volcker that it was time to ease up on his strangulation of the money supply. A chain reaction collapse of the banking system was looming were he to continue with his high interest rates.

Between summer and December 1982, the US Federal Reserve Discount Rate was lowered seven times, to a level 4% lower than the previous August. The financial markets began to go wild with the low rates. Bonds and stocks boomed. Foreign capital flooded into New York financial markets to get in on the bonanza, pushing the dollar ever higher.

Reagan's 'economic recovery' did little to encourage investment in improving the technology and productivity of industry -- with the exception of a handful of military and aerospace firms that got record government defense contracts. Money went instead into speculation in real estate, into speculation in stocks, into oil wells in Texas or Colorado -- all of them 'tax shelters.'

As Volcker's interest rates moved lower, the fever grew hotter. Debt was the new fashion. People reasoned it was 'cheaper' to borrow today and repay tomorrow at lower interest levels. It didn't quite work. While American cities continued their 20-year long decline, bridges fell in, roads cracked for lack of maintenance, schools went unrepaired, and new shopping centers often enclosed empty stores.

Breaking organized Labor

As a central part of Reagan's policy, like Thatcher's, trade unions were identified as 'part of the problem.' A 1920's style class confrontation was set up between labor and management, and the result was the cracking of the organized labor movement.

Deregulation of government control over transportation was a key part of Reagan's anti-union policy. Trucking and airline transportation were 'set free.' Non-union, cut-rate airlines and trucking companies proliferated, often with few or no safety standards. Accident rates climbed; wage levels of union workers plunged.

While the Reagan 'recovery' was turning young stock traders into multi-millionaires with a seeming push of a computer key, it was forcing the skilled blue-collar workforce into lower standards of living. No one in Washington paid much attention. The conservative Reagan Republicans argued that trade unions were "almost like communists." A 19th century British-style cheap labor policy dominated official Washington.

The once-powerful International Brotherhood of Teamsters, the powerful transport and truckers' union, the United Auto Workers union, Oil, Chemical and Atomic Workers union, United Mine Workers, steel unions and others gave concession after concession, in a desperate attempt to secure benefits for older workers about to be pensioned, or to hold onto existing jobs. Real living standards for the majority of Americans steadily declined, while the wealth of a tiny minority skyrocketed as never before. Society was becoming extremely polarized around income differentials.

The new dogma of 'post-industrial society' was being preached from Washington to New York to California. No longer was America's economic prosperity linked to investment in the most modern industrial and manufacturing capacities. Steel had been declared a 'rust-belt' or 'sunset' industry, as steel plants were allowed to rust and blast furnaces were actually dynamited. Shopping centers, McMansions, glittery new Atlantic City or Las Vegas gambling casinos, and luxury resort hotels were where the money was to be made.

During the speculative boom of most of the Reagan years, the money flowed in from abroad to finance this wild spree. By the mid-1980s the United States had passed from being the world's largest creditor, to becoming a net debtor nation for the first time since 1914. Debt was cheap and it grew exponentially. American families went into record levels of debt to buy houses, cars, appliances, and even college tuition. The Government went into debt to finance the huge loss of tax revenue and the expanded Reagan defense buildup.

By 1983, annual Government deficits began to climb to an unheard of level of $200 billion. The National Debt expanded along with the record deficits, all paying Wall Street bond dealers and their clients record sums in interest income. Interest payments on the total debt of the US Government doubled in six years, from $52 billion in 1980 to more than $142 billion by 1986, almost a 300% rise, equal to one-fifth of all government revenue. Money flowed in from Germany, from Britain, from Holland, from Japan, to take advantage of the high dollar and the speculative gains in real estate and stocks.

Washington's 'reverse' Oil Shock

Storm clouds began to gather on the US economic horizon during 1985, threatening the future presidential ambitions of Vice President George H. W. Bush. Once again, oil would come to the rescue. This time, however, the tactic of manipulating global oil prices was run very differently from the Bilderberg oil shocks of the 1970s. Washington apparently reasoned, "if we can run the price up, why can't we run it down?"

The reasons included a growing concern over the weakness of the US economy, something that would receive a calculated boost were world oil prices to fall by 30-40%, as a top secret US Treasury Department study review in October 1985 concluded. The study noted, "lower oil prices would be good for the world economy...Our policy should be...to discourage OPEC and other producers from *artificially* propping up prices..." [13] In fact, as speeches and public statements from US Energy Secretary Donald Hodel and others made clear, to the loud protest of Saudi Oil Minister Sheikh Yamani, Washington was engaged in a covert operation to bring down oil prices while publicly talking as if the opposite was their policy.

In March 1985, US Secretary of State George Shultz sent a classified internal telegram to the US Embassy in London which read in part, "The Secretary is extremely interested in the Department producing quickly a study of the impact of a precipitous drop in the price of oil." [14] Saudi King Fahd had just come to

Washington on February 11 to meet with President Reagan to discuss "oil and economic relations." During the trip of the Saudi King, his oil minister Yamani also met with Vice President George H.W. Bush, Treasury Secretary James Baker and Energy Secretary John Herrington, who told Yamani that "the market" should be allowed to set prices.

By September 1985 Washington pressure on Saudi Arabia to raise its production levels at a time of high stock prices began to push world oil prices down. Assistant Secretary of State Morton Abramowitz wrote in a memo to Secretary Shultz, "By raising production and offering market related pricing...the Saudis seek to reform OPEC...If a price war were to occur oil prices could well plunge to the $20 a barrel range." They were at $35 when the action began. Abramowitz continued, "Most of the world, including the US, would benefit..." [15]

Then, Vice President George Bush traveled to Riyadh in April 1986. According to a declassified State Department account of the talks, Bush told the Saudi King that "market forces could best set oil price and production levels" -- code for having the Saudis collapse world prices by turning on the oil spigots full throttle. [16]

Significantly, in addition to a turbo boost to the US economy that would kick in conveniently in time for the anticipated Presidential campaign of George Bush in 1988, Abramowitz noted that as a result of a sharp drop in oil prices, "the Soviet Union would suffer a net unfavorable impact in the near term since it relies heavily on oil exports for hard currency earnings." [17]

At the same time he was involved in the Saudi reverse oil price shock that impacted Soviet hard currency earnings, Abramowitz was also involved in secret negotiations to provide highly effective Stinger missiles to Afghan Mujahadeen guerillas, whose numbers included a young Saudi named Osama bin Laden.[18] Appropriately, after Abramowitz left the State Department, he became president of the Carnegie Endowment for International Peace. The Stinger missiles were credited with dealing a significant blow to Soviet air force in Afghanistan.

Washington convinced Saudi Arabia's King Fahd, over the objections of his Oil Minister Yamani, to run the "reverse oil shock" and flood the depressed world oil market with its abundant oil.[19] The price of OPEC oil dropped like a stone, from an average of nearly $26 a barrel in the winter of 1985, to below $10 per barrel by the late spring of 1986. Magically, Wall Street economists proclaimed the final 'victory' over inflation, while conveniently ignoring the role of oil in creating the inflation of the 1970s or in reducing it in the 1980s.

Saudi Oil Minister Sheikh Zaki Yamani, who had openly opposed what he called a US oil price conspiracy, was made the scapegoat for a policy authored in Washington, and was fired by King Fahd. Oil prices stabilized at a conveniently low level of around $15 per barrel by 1987, in time to ensure a nice boost to the US economy as Presidential elections neared.

This 1986 oil price collapse unleashed a stock market surge that was comparable to the 1927-29 Wall Street stock bubble. Interest rates dropped even more dramatically, as money flowed in to make a 'killing' on the New York stock markets. A new financial mode became fashionable on Wall Street -- the Leveraged Buy-Out.

With money costs falling and stock prices rising, and the Reagan Administration promoting the religion of the unfettered 'free market,' anything and everything was allowed if it made money. A sound, 100-year old industrial company that had been conservatively managed – perhaps producing tires, or machines or textiles -- became a target for the new corporate 'raiders,' as the Wall Street scavengers were called.

Colorful personalities such as T. Boone Pickens, Mike Milken, or Ivan Boesky became billionaires on paper, as frontmen in the Leveraged Buy-Outs. A new corporate management philosophy of 'market efficiency' was proclaimed from such august institutions as the Harvard Business School and the University of Pennsylvania's Wharton School, to rationalize this madness.

Over the decade of the Reagan years, almost $1 trillion flowed into speculative real estate investment, a record sum, almost double the level of previous years. Banks, desiring to secure their balance sheets against troubles in Latin America and elsewhere, went directly into real estate lending for the first time, rather than traditional corporate lending.

The banks loot the S&Ls

Savings & Loan banks, established as separately regulated banks during the depression years to provide a secure source of long-term mortgage credit to family home buyers, were 'deregulated' in the early 1980s as part of Treasury Secretary Donald Regan's Wall Street 'free market' push. They were allowed to 'bid' for wholesale deposits, termed 'brokered deposits,' at a high cost. To facilitate this, the Reagan Administration removed all regulatory restraints in October 1982 with passage of the Garn-St. Germain Act which allowed S&L banks to invest in any scheme they desired, with US Government depositors insurance of $100,000 per account guaranteeing the risk in case of failure.

Using a Las Vegas image, President Reagan enthusiastically told an audience of invited S&L bankers, as he signed the new Garn-St. Germain Act into law, "I think we've hit the jackpot." His jackpot was the beginning of the collapse of the $ 1.3 trillion Savings & Loan banking system, at taxpayers' expense. Before the dust had settled, some 747 S&Ls had failed, costing US taxpayers more than $125 billion.

US Savings & Loan Bank (S&L) crisis in the 1980s that cost taxpayers hundreds of billions was a forerunner to the sub-prime bubble.

The new law had opened the doors of the S&Ls to wholesale financial abuses and wild speculative risks as never before. Moreover, it made S&L banks an ideal vehicle for organized crime to launder billions of dollars from the growing cocaine and narcotics business in 1980s America. Even so-called 'reputable' and high gloss firms joined the fray. It was Merrill Lynch, the former firm of Donald Regan, whose Lugano Switzerland office was implicated in laundering billions of dollars of heroin mafia profits in the so-called 'Pizza Connection.'

The wild and woolly climate of deregulation created an ambience in which normal, well-run, savings banks were surpassed by banks that catered to dubious money with no questions asked. Banks laundered funds for covert operations of the CIA, as well as covert operations of organized crime families. The son of the Vice President, Neil Bush, was a director of the Silverado Savings and Loan in Colorado, later indicted by the government for illegal practices. Son Neil had the good taste to resign the week his father received the Republican nomination for president in 1988. [20]

In order to compete with the newly deregulated banks and S&L's, the most conservative of all financial sectors, life insurance companies, also entered the speculative real estate market in a major way during the 1980s. But unlike banks and S&L's, insurance companies -- perhaps because they had been so conservative in the past -- never had been placed under national supervision or regulation. There was no national Government insurance fund to protect policyholders of insurance companies as there was for bank depositors. By 1989, insurance companies were holding an estimated $260 billion in real estate on their books, an increase from about $100 billion in 1980. But by then, real estate was collapsing in the worst depression since the 1930s, forcing failures of insurance companies for the first time in postwar history, as panicked policyholders demanded their money.

The ultimate cost of the 1980s S&L debacle came to more than $160 billion. Some calculated that real costs to the economy ran as high as $900 billion. Between 1986 and 1991, the number of new homes constructed dropped from 1.8 million to 1 million, the lowest rate since World War II.

The simple reality was that New York financial power had so overwhelmed all other national interests since the oil shocks of the 1970s, that almost no other voice was heard in Washington thereafter. Debt grew by astonishing amounts. When Reagan won the 1980 election, total private and public debt of the United States stood at $3,873 billion. By the end of the decade, it touched $10 trillion, or $10,000 billion. This meant a staggering increased in debt of more than $6,000 billion during this brief span.[21]

With the debt burden carried by the productive economy rising, and US industrial plant and labor force deteriorating, the cumulative effects of two decades of neglect began to manifest in wholesale collapse of vital public infrastructure of the United States. Highways cracked for lack of regular maintenance; bridges became structurally unsound and in many cases collapsed; urban water systems were allowed to become contaminated in depressed areas; hospitals and schools in major cities fell into disrepair; housing stock for the less wealthy decayed dramatically. By 1989 the association for the construction industry, Associated General Contractors of America, estimated that a net investment of $3.3 trillion was urgently needed merely to rebuild America's crumbling public infrastructure up to modern standards. No one in Washington listened.

The Bush Administration proposed 'free market' private initiative to solve the problem. Washington was in a budget crisis by 1990. The unequal distribution of the benefits from the Reagan recovery was indicated by US Government figures on the number of Americans living below the poverty level.

In 1979 when Paul Volcker began his monetary shock in the midst of the second oil crisis, the Government recorded 24 million Americans below the poverty level, defined as an income of less than $6,000 per year. By 1988, the figure had expanded by more than 30%, to 32 million Americans. Reagan-Bush tax policies had concentrated wealth into a tiny elite, as never before in US history. Since 1980, according to a study carried out by the US House Ways and Means Committee of Congress, real income for the top 20% increased a full 32%. That wealth gap was to explode when Bush's son, George W. Bush took office and pushed through the most radical tax cuts in American history. He was following the script written by the Money Trust back in 1973.

Costs of American health care, meanwhile, a reflection of the strange combination of privatization, free enterprise and government subsidy, rose to the highest levels ever; as a share of GNP, it was double that of the UK. Yet, 37 million Americans had no health insurance whatever – a number that surpassed 50 million in 2009. Health levels in large American cities, with impoverished ghettoes of black and Hispanic unemployed, resembled those of a Third World country, not what was supposed to be the world's most advanced industrial nation.

Japan comes to Bush's rescue

On October 19, 1987 the stock bubble burst. On that day the prices on the Dow Jones Index traded at the New York Stock Exchange collapsed more than in any single day in history, by 508 points. The bottom had fallen out of the Reagan 'recovery.'

But the bottom had most assuredly not fallen out of the strategy of the Bush and Rockefeller wing of the American establishment. They were determined to ensure that sufficient funds were invested to keep their hot air balloon aloft until the new President, George Herbert Walker Bush, could impose the Money Trust's grand strategy for the century's end.

The October 1987 stock crash signaled the beginning of the end of the deregulated financial speculation that had kept the American Century afloat since the early 1970s.

George Bush, anticipating election to the presidency the following November 1988, enlisted the efforts of his former campaign manager and close friend, Treasury Secretary James Baker, along with a powerful faction of the American establishment, to guarantee that despite the implications of the October 1987 crash, foreign capital would continue to flow into US bond and stock markets to sustain the illusion of a Reagan-Bush economic 'recovery' in the minds of voters.

Washington appealed to the Japanese government of Prime Minister Naka-sone, arguing that a Democratic Party president would damage Japanese trade with the US. Nakasone pressed the Bank of Japan and the Ministry of Finance to be accommodating. Japanese interest rates after October 1987 went lower and lower, making US stocks and bonds as well as real estate appear cheap by comparison.

Billions of dollars streamed out of Tokyo into the United States. During 1988 the dollar remained strong and Bush was able to secure election against his Democratic opponent. To secure this support, Bush gave private assurances to senior Japanese figures that a Bush presidency would 'improve' US-Japanese relations. The result of various Japanese financial concessions was the creation of the greatest world speculative bubble since the 1920s in Japanese stocks and real estate.

When it all came crashing down in 1990, as a worried Bank of Japan -- fear-ful of losing economic control -- began to raise interest rates, Japan was plunged into a decade-long depression and deflation from which it never fully recovered.

The actual plan of the new Bush Administration was to direct pressures on select US allies, especially Germany and Japan, for increased 'burden sharing' to manage the gigantic US debt burdens. Bush argued that Germany, Japan and other major economic and military allies of America should increase their financial support to maintain the American Superpower. It was a thinly veiled threat.

Despite the extraordinary measures taken by Wall Street and their friends in Washington during the 1980s, by the end of that decade the prospects for American superpower dominance looked worse than ever. Its domestic econo-my had essentially been relegated to Third World status after two decades of neglect, after Volcker's interest rate shock therapy, and as a result of America's corporate elite outsourcing jobs to lower wage countries from Mexico to Asia.

The large New York money center banks were in bad shape by 1989. That year, Senator Robert Dole called an emergency closed-door meeting in the White House to discuss a confidential Senate report showing that eleven of America's largest banks were technically insolvent. The largest, Citibank, was described as 'brain dead' by one Wall Street bank analyst. The Money Trust needed to take drastic measures. Alan Greenspan, who was named to replace Volcker as head of the Federal Reserve, would prove amenable to almost any wish of his old Wall Street friends.

Endnotes:

[1] Robert O. Anderson, cited in William Greider, *Secrets of the Temple: How the Federal Reserve runs the country* (New York: Simon & Schuster, 1987), p. 648.

[2] Sam Aaronovitch, *The Road From Thatcherism* (London: Lawrence & Wishart, 1981).

[3] William Greider, op. cit., p 156.

[4] International Iron and Steel Institute. *Infrastructure: Problems and Prospects for Steel.* Brussels. 1985.

[5] The LIBOR or London Interbank Offered Rate is the rate at which banks lend to one another in the major international wholesale money market in London. It is a standard financial index used in US and international capital markets. When this index goes up, interest rates on any loans tied to it also go up.

[6] Robert O. Anderson, op. cit.

[7] Following the defeat of Germany in World War I and several years of German hyperinflation lasting until 1923, the House of Morgan stepped in to take control of the German war reparations repayments. In effect J.P. Morgan took the German economy and its finances into its receivership. Morgan, acting through the US Government, named an Agent-general for Reparations, S. Parker Gilbert, a J.P. Morgan partner, installed in Berlin to collect the repayments for the Allies. Gilbert had power to impose new taxes, take control over the German central bank and insure that Britain, France and Italy got their reparations paid. That in turn allowed Morgan to be repaid for its war loans to the British, French and Italian governments which, conveniently, more or less exactly equaled the sum set by the Allied Powers for German War Reparations. The issue of Versailles reparations created a deep bitter resentment among the German elites and the population, a resentment that later the NSDAP party of Hitler exploited. See F. William Engdahl, *A Century of War: Anglo-American Oil Politics and the New World Order*, Chapter 6, pp.68-71. When reparations finally broke down in 1929, another Morgan scheme, the Young Plan, was proposed which called for establishing a supranational institution, the Bank for International Settlements situated just across the German boorder in Basle Switzerland to do the job.

[8] One of the most damaging consequences of IMF conditions imposed on debtor countries was the forced removal of state food subsidies and the forced opening of developing debtor countries to US Department of Agriculture subsidized agriculture products. Third World countries were flooded with mass produced food from US agribusiness – bananas, melons, chickens, rice, onions, whatever had previously been produced by local farmers. The US food industry always undercut the local prices and drove the farmers out of business.This made the local population import-dependant in food where they had been self-sustaining. The case of Jamaica was exemplified in the documentary video, *Life and Debt in Jamaica*, www.livevideo.com.

[9] Ibid. 1987.

[10] Hans Kornoe Rasmussen, *The Forgotten Generation: a debate book concerning children and the debt crisis*, (Copenhagen: Danish UNICEF Committee, 1987).

[11] Ibid. Also useful for background, see Marko Milivojevic, *The Debt Rescheduling Process* (New York: St. Martin's Press, 1985). See also, the annual United Nations reports, *Economic Survey of Latin America*, for useful data.

[12] US Congress, Joint Economic Committee, Staff Study, *Impact of the Latin American Debt Crisis on the US Economy*, May 1986, Washington DC.

[13] Richard T. McCormack, *Information Memorandum on Oil Prices to Secretary of State George Shultz*, October 25, 1984, Washington DC, document S001, declassified.

[14] George Shultz, Telegram, March 1985, # 081715, declassified.

[15] Morton I. Abramowitz, Assistant Secretary for Intelligence, *Implications of the Saudi Oil Price Cut,* September 19, 1985, US Department of State, Washington DC, declassified 6/4/1992.

[16] Edwin S. Rothschild, *The Reagan-Bush Administration's Role in the 1986 Oil Price Crash,* memorandum provided to the author in 1991.

[17] Ibid.

[18] Diana Johnstone, *Fool's Crusade* (London: Pluto Press, 2002), p. 9.

[19] Edwin S. Rothschild, *An Oil Card Up his Sleeve? How the Saudis could give Bush a $30 billion tax cut,* The Washington Post, November 24, 1991. Rothschild wrote, "in 1986 the Reagan-Bush Administration persuaded Fahd to open Saudi oil spigots to reduce world oil prices from $29 to $18 a barrel. Together with the devaluation of the US dollar engineered by then-Secretary of the Treasury James Baker, the oil price boosted US economic growth."

[20] Stephen Pizzo, *Inside Job: The looting of America's Savings & Loans* (New York: McGraw-Hill, 1989).

[21] US Congress Joint Economic Committee, *Economic Indicators,* Washington, 1990.

CHAPTER SIXTEEN

Greenspan's 'Revolution in Finance' Goes Awry

'As we move into the twenty-first century, the remnants of nineteenth-century bank examination philosophies will fall by the wayside...affiliation with banks need not--indeed, should not--create bank-like regulation of affiliates of banks.'

    –   Alan Greenspan, 1999, calling for deregulation of banks [1]

A long-term Greenspan agenda

Seven years of Volcker monetary shock therapy had ignited a payments crisis across the Third World. Billions of dollars in recycled petrodollar debts, loaned by major New York and London banks to finance oil imports after the oil price increases of the 1970s, suddenly became non-payable.

In August 1987, just a year away from the 1988 Presidential elections, in which George H.W. Bush was determined to succeed Reagan as President, Bush persuaded Reagan to name a new chairman of the Federal Reserve, a man more amenable to bowing before Wall Street. Bush did not trust Paul Volcker to be sufficiently partisan and feared he would choke off economic growth for fear of inflation just in time to deprive Bush of election victory; he preferred Alan Greenspan.

Greenspan would rarely disappoint his Wall Street patrons during the 18 years when he controlled the Fed with an almost iron grip. Those 18 years were marked by financial deregulation, successive speculation bubbles and instability.

With Greenspan at the helm, and after the large New York banks had looted all that was of value in the domestic US savings banks, the stage was set for the next phase in the Rockefeller financial deregulation agenda.. The next phase would entail nothing less than a revolution in the very nature of money—the Greenspan 'New Finance' Revolution.

A carefully cultivated public relations fest in the US media persuaded most Americans to believe that Alan Greenspan was essentially just a dedicated public servant who might make mistakes, but in the end always saved the day and the nation's economy and banks through extraordinary feats of financial crisis management, winning the appellation, "Maestro."[2] The truth was somewhat different.

Maestro serves the Money Trust

Alan Greenspan, like every Chairman of the Board of Governors of the Federal Reserve System, was a carefully picked, institutionally loyal servant of the actual owners of the Federal Reserve. The Federal Reserve owners, it will be recalled, consisted of the network of private banks, insurance companies, and investment banks which had created the Fed in December 1913 by rushing its statutory authorization through an almost empty Congress the day before Christmas recess. In Lewis v. United States, the United States Court of Appeals for the Ninth Circuit confirmed the true nature of the misnamed Federal Reserve when the court stated that "the Reserve Banks are not federal instrumentalities...but are independent, privately owned and locally controlled corporations." 3

Alan Greenspan, who served Wall Street Money Trust 18 years as Federal Reserve head, fostered the 'Revolution in Finance' that created the sub-prime mortgage crisis.

Greenspan's entire tenure as Fed chairman was dedicated to advancing the interests of American world financial domination in a nation whose domestic economic base had been essentially destroyed in the years following 1971.

Greenspan knew who buttered his bread and as Federal Reserve head he loyally served what the US Congress in 1913 had termed "the Money Trust," in reference then to the cabal of bankers behind the 1913 creation of the Federal Reserve.

Not surprisingly, many of the same banks which were pivotal in the securitization revolution of the 1990s and into 21st Century, including Citibank and J.P. Morgan had been at the center of the 1913 Money Trust as well. Both had share ownership of the key New York Federal Reserve Bank, the heart of the system. The real goal of the Money Trust whether in 1913 or in 1987 was to consolidate their control over major industries, economies and ultimately, over the economy of the entire world through what would be called the globalization of finance.

Alongside well-known institutions like J.P. Morgan and Citicorp and AIG, another shareholder of the New York Fed was a little-known company called Depository Trust Company (DTC), the largest securities depository in the world. Based in New York, the DTC held in custody more than 2.5 million US and non-US equity, corporate, and municipal debt securities issues from over 100 countries, valued at over $36 trillion. DTC and its affiliates handled over $1.5 quadrillion in securities transactions a year. That was to say, $1,500,000,000,000,000 -- a lot of responsibility in the hands of a company that most people never heard of.

The Depository Trust Company had a monopoly on the debt securities depository business in the USA. They had become in effect the back office of the world financial system. DTC advertised itself as a safe way for buyers and sellers of securities to make their exchange, and thus "clear and settle" transactions. It also provided custody of securities. They had simply bought up all other contenders, becoming in the process an essential part of New York's continued dominance of global financial markets, long after the American economy had become largely a hollowed-out, 'post-industrial' wasteland.

While free market purists and dogmatic followers of Greenspan's close friend 'self interest' ideologue Ayn Rand accused the Fed Chairman of hands-on interventionism, in reality there was a common thread running through each major financial crisis during Greenspan's near two decades reign as head of the world's most powerful financial institution. As Federal Reserve chairman, Greenspan managed to use each successive financial crisis to advance and consolidate the influence of US-centered finance over the global economy, almost always to the severe detriment of the US domestic economy and general welfare of the American public.

In each crisis, Greenspan used the situation to advance an agenda of globalization of risk and liberalization of market regulations to allow unhindered operation of the major financial institutions. Whether it was the October 1987 stock crash, the 1997 Asia Crisis, the 1998 Russian state default and ensuing collapse of Long Term Capital Management, or his refusal to make technical changes in Fed-controlled stock margin requirements to cool the dot.com stock bubble, or his encouragement of ARM variable rate mortgages (when he knew rates were at the bottom), Greenspan's manipulations of each crisis had the same goal. Moreover, most of the crises had been spawned or triggered by his widely read commentaries and publicly announced rate policies in the first place, as we will see.

When Alan Greenspan arrived in Washington in 1987, he had been hand picked by Wall Street and the big banks to implement their Grand Strategy. Greenspan was a Wall Street consultant whose clients included J.P. Morgan Bank, among others. Before taking the post as head of the Federal Reserve, Greenspan had also sat on the boards of some of the most powerful corporations in America, including Mobil Oil Corporation, Morgan Guaranty Trust Company and JP Morgan & Co. Inc. Greenspan had also served as a director of the Council on Foreign Relations since 1982. As Federal Reserve Chairman his first test in October 1987 would be the manipulation of stock markets using the then-new derivatives markets.

The 1987 Greenspan derivatives paradigm

In October 1987, Greenspan led a bailout of the stock market after the spectacular October 20 crash by pumping huge infusions of liquidity to prop up stocks. He simultaneously engaged in behind-the-scene manipulations of the market via purchases of Chicago stock index derivatives backed quietly by Fed liquidity guarantees. It was an unprecedented step by the central bank to intervene to manipulate stock markets covertly, something whose legality, should it be discovered, would have been highly questionable.

Since that October 1987 event, the Fed had made abundantly clear to major market players that they were, to use Fed jargon, TBTF—Too Big To Fail. No worry if a bank risked tens of billions speculating in Thai baht or dot.com stocks on margin. If push came to liquidity shove, Greenspan made clear he would be there to bail out his banking friends.

The October 1987 crash saw the sharpest one day fall in the Dow Industrials in history—508 points. The depth of the one day fall was exacerbated by new computer trading models based on the so-called Black-Scholes Options Pricing theory, whereby stock share derivatives were now being priced and traded just as hog belly futures had been before. As former Wall Street trader and author Michael Lewis described it,

> *A new strategy known as portfolio insurance, invented by a pair of finance professors at the University of California at Berkeley, had been taken up in a big way by supposedly savvy investors. Portfolio insurance evolved from the most influential idea on Wall Street, an options-pricing model called Black-Scholes. The model is based on the assumption that a trader can suck all the risk out of the market by taking a short position and increasing that position as the market falls, thus protecting against losses, no matter how steep.* [4]

The Black-Scholes model had recently come out of the university onto major Wall Street trading floors at the time of the 1987 crash. During the 1970s, academic economists Fischer Black and Myron Scholes designed a model that appeared to give a scientific basis to predict the price of an option on financial products in the future based on the price of the actual or underlying stock, currency, or other financial commodity such as oil. The new instruments, which were sold to Wall Street and then to corporate America as a form of cheap "financial insurance" against sharp price swings, were priced in a relation to -- i.e., derived from -- an underlying product such as crude oil, hence the term "derivatives."

The use of such financial derivatives has been compared to "trying to replicate a fire-insurance policy by dynamically increasing or decreasing your coverage as fire conditions wax and wane. One day, bam, your house is on fire, and you call for more coverage?" [5]

The 1987 crash and the role of financial derivatives for the first time in a major market crisis made clear was that there was no real liquidity in the markets when it was needed. All fund managers tried to do the same thing at the same time: to sell short the derivatives -- stock index futures in this case -- in a futile attempt to hedge their stock positions.

But the selling spree triggered an automated trading spiral – in effect, a computer-driven freefall. Financial derivatives, in effect sophisticated bets on the future direction of stock prices, had made their debut on Wall Street by helping trigger the largest one-day fall in the stock market's history. It was a shaky start and not by any means the last crisis to be fed by the exotic new financial derivatives.

Stephen Zarlenga, then a trader who was in the New York trading pits during the crisis days in 1987, gave a first hand trader's view of the impact of the new derivatives on stock prices:

> *They created a huge discount in the futures market...The arbitrageurs who bought futures from them at a big discount, turned around and sold the underlying stocks, pushing the cash markets down, feeding the process and eventually driving the market into the ground.*

> *Some of the biggest firms in Wall Street found they could not stop their pre-programmed computers from automatically engaging in this derivatives trading. According to private reports, they had to unplug or cut the wiring to computers, or find other ways to cut off the electricity to them (there were rumors about fireman's axes from hallways being used), for they couldn't be switched off and were issuing orders directly to the exchange floors.*

> *The New York Stock Exchange at one point on Monday and Tuesday seriously considered closing down entirely for a period of days or weeks and made this public...It was at this point...that Greenspan made an uncharacteristic announcement. He said in no uncertain terms that the Fed would make credit available to the brokerage community, as needed. This was a turning point, as Greenspan's recent appointment as Chairman of the Fed in mid 1987 had been one of the early reasons for the market's sell off.* [6]

What was significant about the October 1987 one-day crash was not the size of the fall, some 23%. It was the fact that the Fed, unannounced to the public, intervened through Greenspan's trusted New York bank cronies at J.P. Morgan and elsewhere on October 20 to manipulate a stock recovery through use of the new financial instruments, the derivatives.

The visible or presumed cause of the October 1987 market recovery seemed to occur when the Chicago-based MMI (Major Market Index) future price of select New York Stock Exchange blue chip stocks began suddenly to trade at a premium to the underlying actual stocks, midday Tuesday, at a time when one after another Dow stock had been closed down for trading. That was interpreted as a sign that "smart money" knew a rebound was about to happen. Brokers cautiously began buying the real stocks.

The meltdown began to reverse. Arbitrageurs, high-risk securities gamblers, bought the underlying stocks, re-opening them, and sold the MMI futures at a premium. The New York stock market had magically and for no clear reason begun a dramatic recovery. It was created in the trading pits of the Chicago MMI futures exchange, far from view of most of the public.

Greenspan and his New York financial cronies had successfully engineered a stock market recovery using the same derivatives trading models in reverse, to drive the price of stocks sharply higher just as they had driven the same stocks to the bottom only days earlier. It was the dawn of the era of financial derivatives, a world of potential manipulation beyond belief.

For most mundane Wall Street traders, financial derivatives gradually became accepted as a highly profitable new instrument to make money out of money. A few savvy financial insiders realized that those who could gain control of the market for the new financial derivatives, and control of their exchanges, had the potential to make or break entire financial markets. It was the start of one of the most colossal projects in the history of finance—the derivatives revolution.

Historically, so most people were led to believe, the role of the Federal Reserve as the Comptroller of the Currency, among others things, was to act as independent supervisor of the largest banks to insure stability of the banking system and prevent a repeat of the bank panics of the 1930s by serving as 'lender of last resort.'

Under the Greenspan regime, after October 1987, the Fed increasingly became the 'lender of first resort,' as the Fed widened the circle of financial institutions worthy of the Fed's rescue.

It was the birth of an insider game sold to the public during the late 1980s as the 'democratization' of capital, using the argument that because millions of Americans were investing their pension funds into mutual funds and money market funds, that meant that 'the people' actually controlled finance, not the financial oligarchs of old like J.P. Morgan or John D. Rockefeller. Nothing was farther from the truth.

The Greenspan Federal Reserve's *laissez faire* policy towards supervision and bank regulation after 1987 was crucial to implementing the broader deregulation and financial securitization agenda that Greenspan had hinted at in his first Congressional testimony in 1987.

On November 18, 1987, only three weeks after the October stock crash, Alan Greenspan told the US House of Representatives Committee on Banking that, "repeal of Glass-Steagall would provide significant public benefits consistent with a manageable increase in risk." [7]

Greenspan would repeat this mantra until Glass-Steagall, the law that had required separation of investment and commercial banking, was finally repealed in 1999. The support of the Greenspan Fed for unregulated treatment of financial derivatives after the 1987 crash was instrumental in the explosion of derivatives trading worldwide. The global derivatives market grew by 23,102% between 1987 and the end of 2006 when it was a staggering $370 trillion. The volumes were incomprehensible.

Destroying Glass-Steagall Restrictions

One of Greenspan's first acts as Chairman of the Fed had been to call for repeal of the Glass-Steagall Act, something that his old friends at J.P.Morgan and Citibank had ardently campaigned for. [8] Glass-Steagall, officially the Banking Act of 1933, had introduced the separation of commercial banking from Wall Street investment banking and insurance. Glass-Steagall originally was intended to curb the practices that had caused the severity of the 1930s wave of bank failures and depression.

One problem that Glass-Steagall was designed to address was that, prior to 1929, banks had been investing their own assets in securities, with consequent risk to commercial and savings depositors in the event of a stock crash. Unsound loans were made by the banks in order to artificially prop up the price of select securities or the financial position of companies in which a bank had invested its own assets. A bank's financial interest in the ownership, pricing, or distribution of securities inevitably tempted bank officials to press their banking customers into investing in securities which the bank itself was under pressure to sell. It was a colossal conflict of interest and invitation to fraud and abuse. That era was appropriately dubbed the 'Roaring Twenties' as the stock market roared to new inflated highs.

Banks that offered investment banking services and mutual funds were subject to conflicts of interest and other abuses, thereby harming their customers, including borrowers, depositors, and correspondent banks. The Glass-Steagall Act of 1933 was specifically intended to prevent this.

After the law was repealed in 1999, with no more Glass-Steagall restraints, banks offered securitized mortgage obligations and similar products via wholly owned Special Purpose Vehicles they created to get the risk 'off the bank books.' They were directly and knowingly complicit in what will go down in history as the greatest financial swindle of all times—the sub-prime securitization fraud.

Commenting on the origins of the 1930's Glass-Steagall act, Harvard economist John Kenneth Galbraith noted,

Congress was concerned that commercial banks in general and member banks of the Federal Reserve System in particular had both aggravated and been damaged by stock market decline partly because of their direct and indirect involvement in the trading and ownership of speculative securities.

The legislative history of the Glass-Steagall Act shows that Congress also had in mind and repeatedly focused on the more subtle hazards that arise when a commercial bank goes beyond the business of acting as fiduciary or managing agent and enters the investment banking business either directly or by establishing an affiliate to hold and sell particular investments.

....During 1929 one investment house, Goldman, Sachs & Company, organized and sold nearly a billion dollars' worth of securities in three interconnected investment trusts--Goldman Sachs Trading Corporation; Shenandoah Corporation; and Blue Ridge Corporation. All eventually depreciated virtually to nothing.[9]

Deregulation means 'Too Big To Fail'

From the 1980s Reagan era through the 1990s, major banks and Wall Street institutions consolidated unprecedented power over the United States and its economic life. The deregulation agenda proposed in 1973 by the Rockefellers was the driver of the power consolidation. For most of the period the consolidation took place under the watchful eye of the Greenspan Federal Reserve.

In the United States, between 1980 and 1994, more than 1,600 banks insured by the Federal Deposit Insurance Corporation (FDIC) had been closed or had received FDIC financial assistance. That was far more than in any other period since the advent of federal deposit insurance in the 1930s. It was part of a process of concentration into giant banking groups that would continue into the next century.

In 1984 the largest bank insolvency in US history seemed imminent. Chicago's Continental Illinois National Bank, the nation's seventh largest, and one of the world's largest banks, was on the brink of failure. To prevent such a large failure the Government, through the Federal Deposit Insurance Corporation, stepped in to bail out Continental Illinois by announcing 100% deposit guarantee instead of the limited guarantee provided by FDIC insurance.

This came to be called the doctrine of "Too Big to Fail" (TBTF). The argument was that certain very large banks, because they were so large, must not be allowed to fail for fear it would trigger a chain-reaction of failures across the economy. It didn't take long before the large banks realized that the bigger they became through mergers and takeovers, the more certain they were to qualify for TBTF treatment. So-called 'Moral Hazard' was becoming a prime feature of US big banks. [10]

The TBTF doctrine, during Greenspan's tenure as Chairman of the Federal Reserve, would be extended to cover very large hedge funds (LTCM), very large stock markets (NYSE), and virtually every large financial entity in which the US financial establishment had a strategic stake. Its consequences would be devastating. Few outside the elite circles of the largest institutions of the financial community even realized the TBTF doctrine had been established.

Once the TBTF principle was made clear, the biggest banks scrambled to get even bigger. The traditional separation of banking into local S&L mortgage lenders, on the one hand, and large international money center banks like Citibank or J.P. Morgan or Bank of America, on the other – as well as the prohibition on banking in more than one state -- were systematically dismantled. It was a new version of 'leveling the playing field,' whereby the biggest banks simply bulldozed and swallowed up the smaller ones, thereby creating financial cartels of unprecedented dimensions.

By 1996 the number of independent banks had shrunk by more than one-third from the late 1970s -- from more than 12,000 to fewer than 8,000. The percentage of banking assets controlled by banks with more than $100 billion doubled to one-fifth of all US banking assets. The trend was just beginning. The banks' consolidation was formalized in the 1994 Interstate Banking and Branch Efficiency Act which removed geographic restrictions on bank branching and holding company acquisitions by the individual states. Under the rubric of more efficient banking a Darwinian struggle for 'survival of the biggest' ensued. The biggest were by no means, however, the fittest. The consolidation was to have significant consequences a decade or so later as securitization exploded at a scale beyond even the banks' wildest imagination.

Operation Rollback: Enter Greenspan

The major New York money center banks had long had in mind the rollback of that 1933 Congressional restriction, Glass-Steagall. And Alan Greenspan as Fed Chairman was their man. The major US banks, led by Rockefeller's influential

Chase Manhattan Bank and Sanford Weill's Citicorp, spent over one hundred million dollars lobbying and making campaign contributions to influential Congressmen to get deregulation of the Depression-era restrictions on banking and stock underwriting.

Within two months of taking office, on October 6, 1987, just days before the greatest one-day crash on the New York Stock Exchange, Greenspan told Congress that US banks, victimized by new technology and "frozen" in a regulatory structure developed more than 50 years ago, were losing their competitive battle with other financial institutions and needed to obtain new powers to restore a balance: "The basic products provided by banks - credit evaluation and diversification of risk - are less competitive than they were 10 years ago."

As the *New York Times* noted, "Mr. Greenspan has long been far more favorably disposed toward deregulation of the banking system than was Paul A. Volcker, his predecessor at the Fed." [11]

Greenspan's first testimony to Congress as Chairman of the Fed was of signal importance to understand the continuity between the policies he implemented right from that moment up to the securitization revolution after 2001 -- the New Finance securitization revolution. Again quoting the *New York Times* account,

> *Mr. Greenspan, in decrying the loss of the banks' competitive edge, pointed to what he said was a 'too rigid' regulatory structure that limited the availability to consumers of efficient service and hampered competition. But then he pointed to another development of 'particular importance' - the way advances in data processing and telecommunications technology had allowed others to usurp the traditional role of the banks as financial intermediaries. In other words, a bank's main economic contribution - risking its money as loans based on its superior information about the creditworthiness of borrowers - is jeopardized.*

The *Times* quoted Greenspan on the challenge in 1987 to modern banking posed by technological change:

> *'Extensive on-line data bases, powerful computation capacity and telecommunication facilities provide credit and market information almost instantaneously, allowing the lender to make its own analysis of creditworthiness and to develop and execute complex trading strategies to hedge against risk,' Mr. Greenspan said. This, he added, resulted in permanent damage 'to the competitiveness of depository*

institutions and will expand the competitive advantage of the market for securitized assets,' such as commercial paper, mortgage pass-through securities and even automobile loans.

He concluded, 'Our experience so far suggests that the most effective insulation of a bank from affiliated financial or commercial activities is achieved through a holding-company structure.' [12]

However, in a bank holding company, the Federal Deposit Insurance fund, a pool of contributions to guarantee bank deposits at that time up to $100,000 per account, would only apply to the core bank, not to the various subsidiary companies created to engage in exotic hedge fund or other off-the-balance-sheet activities. The upshot was that in a crisis such as the unraveling post-2007 securitization meltdown, the ultimate Lender of Last Resort, the insurer of bank risk, becomes the taxpaying American public.

The issues provoked a hard fight in Congress that lasted until the final repeal of Glass-Steagall – the Gramm-Leach-Bliley Act -- was signed into law by Clinton in November 1999. Clinton presented the pen he used to sign the repeal as a gift to Sanford Weill, the powerful chairman of Citicorp, a curious gesture for a Democratic President, to say the least. It seemed Clinton, too, knew how to follow the money.

In 1999 Citigroup head Sandy Weill (center), with the support of Clinton Treasury Secretary Robert Rubin (R), won repeal of the 1933 Glass-Steagall Act.

Alan Greenspan had played the decisive role in moving Glass-Steagall repeal through Congress. Testifying before the House Committee on Banking and Financial Services on February 11, 1999, Greenspan declared,

> ...[W]e support, as we have for many years, major revisions, such as those included in H.R. 10, to the Glass-Steagall Act and the Bank Holding Company Act to remove the legislative barriers against the integration of banking, insurance, and securities activities. There is virtual unanimity among all concerned--private and public alike-- that these barriers should be removed. The technologically driven proliferation of new financial products that enable risk unbundling have been increasingly combining the characteristics of banking, insurance, and securities products into single financial instruments.[13]

In his same 1999 testimony Greenspan made clear that repeal meant less, not more, regulation of the newly allowed financial conglomerates, opening the floodgate to the fiasco that occurred less than a decade later:

> As we move into the twenty-first century, the remnants of nineteenth-century bank examination philosophies will fall by the wayside. Banks, of course, will still need to be supervised and regulated, in no small part because they are subject to the safety net. My point is, however, that the nature and extent of that effort need to become more consistent with market realities. Moreover, **affiliation with banks need not--indeed, should not--create bank-like regulation of affiliates of banks** [14] (emphasis added—f.w.e.)

Congress had passed Glass-Steagall in the first place precisely in order to break up the bank holding companies with their inherent conflicts of interest that had led tens of millions of Americans into joblessness and home foreclosures in the 1930s depression. In 1999, this protection vanished.

'Strategies unimaginable a decade ago...'

The *New York Times* described the new financial world created by repeal of Glass-Steagall in a June 2007 profile of Goldman Sachs, just weeks prior to the eruption of the sub-prime crisis: "While Wall Street still mints money advising companies on mergers and taking them public, real money - staggering money -

is made trading and investing capital through a global array of mind-bending products and strategies unimaginable a decade ago." They were referring to the securitization revolution.

The *Times* quoted Goldman Sachs chairman Lloyd Blankfein on the new financial securitization, hedge fund and derivatives world: "We've come full circle, because this is exactly what the Rothschilds or J. P. Morgan, the bankers were doing in their heyday. What caused an aberration was the Glass-Steagall Act."[15]

Lloyd Blankfein, like most of Wall Street's bankers and financial insiders, saw the New Deal as an aberration, openly calling for return to the early, unregulated heyday of J. P. Morgan and other tycoons, the 'Gilded Age' of abuses in the 1920s.

Glass-Steagall, Blankfein's 'aberration,' had been finally eliminated by Bill Clinton. Goldman Sachs had been a prime contributor to the Clinton campaign and even sent its chairman, Robert Rubin, to the Clinton Administration in 1993, first as "economic czar" then in 1995 as Treasury Secretary.

In October 2007 Robert Kuttner, co-founder of the Economic Policy Institute, testified before US Congressman Barney Frank's Committee on Banking and Financial Services, evoking the specter of the Great Depression:

> *Since repeal of Glass Steagall in 1999, after more than a decade of de facto inroads, super-banks have been able to re-enact the same kinds of structural conflicts of interest that were endemic in the 1920s - lending to speculators, packaging and securitizing credits and then selling them off, wholesale or retail, and extracting fees at every step along the way. And, much of this paper is even more opaque to bank examiners than its counterparts were in the 1920s. Much of it isn't paper at all, and the whole process is supercharged by computers and automated formulas.* [16]

Dow Jones *Market Watch* commentator Thomas Kostigen, writing in the early weeks of the unravelling sub-prime crisis, remarked about the role of Glass-Steagall repeal in opening the floodgates to fraud, manipulation and the excesses of credit leverage in the expanding world of securitization:

> *Time was when banks and brokerages were separate entities, banned from uniting for fear of conflicts of interest, a financial meltdown, a monopoly on the markets, all of these things.*

In 1999, the law banning brokerages and banks from marrying one another — the Glass-Steagall Act of 1933 — was lifted, and voila, the financial supermarket has grown to be the places we know as Citigroup, UBS, Deutsche Bank, et al. But now that banks seemingly have stumbled over their bad mortgages, it's worth asking whether the fallout would be wreaking so much havoc on the rest of the financial markets had Glass-Steagall been kept in place.

...No one really questioned the new fad of collateralizing bank mortgage debt into different types of financial instruments and selling them through a different arm of the same institution. They are now...(emphasis added, f.w.e).

....Glass-Steagall would have at least provided what the first of its names portends: transparency. And that is best accomplished when outsiders are peering in. When every one is on the inside looking out, they have the same view. That isn't good because then you can't see things coming (or falling) and everyone is subject to the roof caving in.

*Congress is now investigating the subprime mortgage debacle. Lawmakers are looking at tightening lending rules, holding secondary debt buyers responsible for abusive practices and, on a positive note, even bailing out some homeowners. These are Band-Aid measures, however, that **won't patch what's broken: the system of conflicts that arise when sellers, salesmen and evaluators are all on the same team.** [17] (emphasis added--f.w.e.)*

Greenspan's 'Dot.com' bubble

Before the ink was dry on Bill Clinton's signature repealing Glass-Steagall, the Greenspan Fed was fully engaged in hyping their next crisis—the deliberate creation of a stock bubble to rival that of 1929, a bubble which the Fed would then deliberately burst, just as it had in 1929.

The 1997 Asian financial crisis and the ensuing Russian state debt default of August 1998 created a sea change in global capital flows to the advantage of the dollar. With Korea, Thailand, Indonesia and most emerging markets in flames following a coordinated, politically-motivated attack by a trio of US hedge funds, led by George Soros' Quantum Fund, Julian Robertson's Jaguar and Tiger funds and Moore Capital Management, according to Swiss and City of London financial insider reports, the Connecticut-based LTCM hedge fund of John Merriweather.[18]

The impact of the Asia Crisis on the dollar was notable and suspiciously positive. Andrew Crockett, the General Manager of the Bank for International Settlements, the Basle-based organization of the world's leading central banks, noted that in 1996 the East Asian countries had been running a combined current account deficit of $33 billion. Then, as speculative hot money flowed in, "1998-1999, the current account swung to a surplus of $87 billion." By 2002 the surplus had reached the impressive sum of $200 billion. Most of that surplus returned to the US in the form of Asian central bank purchases of US Treasury debt, in effect financing Washington policies, pushing US interest rates way down and fuelling an emerging 'New Economy,' the NASDAQ Dot.com IT boom. [19]

During the extremes of Asia's 1997-1998 financial crises, Greenspan refused to act to ease the financial pressures until after Asia had collapsed and Russia had defaulted in August 1998 on its sovereign debt, and deflation had spread from region to region. Then, when he and the New York Fed stepped in it was to rescue the huge LTCM hedge fund that had become insolvent as a result of risky bets it had made that came unstuck as a result of the Russian crisis.

To save the big New York financial institutions that had given the credit lines to LTCM and other hedge funds, Greenspan made an unusually sharp cut in Fed Funds interest rates for the first time in his tenure as Fed chief, by 0.50%. That was followed a few weeks later by a 0.25% cut. That gave the nascent dot.com IT bubble in the stock market a nice little 'shot of whiskey' as cheap money poured into stocks, fueling a new bubble in prices unrelated to any long-term economic reality. The financial crises in Asia and Russia had, in effect, supplied the new cash for the Wall Street stock market casino to play the next round.

Towards the end of 1998, amid successive cuts in Fed interest rates and pumping in of ample liquidity, the US stock markets, led by the NASDAQ and NYSE, went ballistic. In 1999 alone, as the New Economy bubble got into full swing, a staggering $2.8 trillion increase in the value of stock shares was regis-tered. That was more than 25% of annual GDP, all in paper values.

Gone were the Glass-Steagall restrictions on savings & loan banks and in-vestment banks promoting the stocks they had brought to market. The exact conflict of interest that Glass-Steagall had been designed to prevent was now the centerpiece of the New Economy. Wall Street stock promoters were earning tens of millions in bonuses for fraudulently hyping Internet and other stocks such as WorldCom and Enron. It was the 'Roaring 1920s' all over again, but with an electronic, computerized turbo-charged kicker. Blankfein and his Wall Street cronies were no doubt satisfied that the 'aberration' of regulation had given way to the 'norm' of free-wheeling speculative frenzy.

The March 2000 speech

In March 2000, at the very peak of the Dot.com stock mania, Alan Greenspan delivered an address to a Boston College *Conference on the New Economy* in which he repeated his standard mantra in praise of the IT revolution and its impact on financial markets. In this speech he went even beyond previous praises of the IT stock bubble and its putative "wealth effect" on household spending which he claimed had kept the US economy growing robustly:

> *In the last few years it has become increasingly clear that this busi-*
> *ness cycle differs in a very profound way from the many other cycles*
> *that have characterized post-World War II America," Greenspan*
> *noted. "Not only has the expansion achieved record length, but it*
> *has done so with economic growth far stronger than expected.*

He went on, waxing almost poetic as he built momentum:

> *My remarks today will focus both on what is evidently the source*
> *of this spectacular performance--the revolution in information*
> *technology...When historians look back at the latter half of the*
> *1990s a decade or two hence, I suspect that they will conclude we*
> *are now living through a pivotal period in American economic*
> *history...Those innovations, exemplified most recently by the mul-*
> *tiplying uses of the Internet, have brought on a flood of startup*
> *firms, many of which claim to offer the chance to revolutionize*
> *and dominate large shares of the nation's production and distri-*
> *bution system.*

Then the Maestro revealed his real theme, the ability to spread risk by using technology and the Internet, a harbinger of his thinking about the unfolding securitization phenomenon, then in its infancy:

The impact of information technology has been keenly felt in the financial sector of the economy. Perhaps the most significant innovation has been the development of financial instruments that enable risk to be reallocated to the parties most willing and able to bear that risk. Many of the new financial products that have been created, with financial derivatives being the most notable, contribute economic value by unbundling risks and shifting them in a highly calibrated manner. Although these instruments cannot reduce the risk inherent in real assets, they can redistribute it in a way that induces more investment in real assets and, hence, engenders higher productivity and standards of living. Information technology has made possible the creation, valuation, and exchange of these complex financial products on a global basis.... [20]

Most notable about Greenspan's euphoric paean to the benefits of the IT stock mania was its timing. He knew very well that the impact of the Fed's six interest rate increases that he had instigated in late 1999 were sooner or later going to chill the buying of stocks on borrowed money.

Sure enough, the dot-com bubble burst one week after Greenspan's speech. On March 10, 2000, the NASDAQ Composite index peaked at 5,048, more than double its value just a year before. On Monday, March 13, the NASDAX fell by an eye-catching 4%.

Then, from March 13, 2000 through to the market bottom, the market lost paper values worth more than $5 trillion, as Greenspan's rate hikes brought a brutal end to a bubble he repeatedly claimed he could not confirm until after the fact. In dollar terms, the 1929 stock crash was peanuts compared with Greenspan's Dot.com crash. Greenspan had raised interest rates six times by March, a fact which had a brutal, chilling effect on the leveraged speculation in dot.com company stocks.

Stocks and 'Regulation T'

Greenspan had been present every step of the way to nurture the Dot.com stock "irrational exuberance." When it was clear even to most ordinary members of Congress that stock prices were soaring out of control, and that banks and investment funds were borrowing tens of billions of credit to buy more stocks "on margin," a call went out for the Fed to exercise its power over stock margin buying requirements.

By February 2000, margin debt had hit $265.2 billion, up 45% in just four months. Much of the increase came from increased borrowing through online brokers -- and the borrowing was being channeled into the NASDAQ New Economy stocks.

Under Regulation T, the Fed had the sole authority to set initial margin requirements for the purchase of stocks on credit, which had been at 50% since 1974. In other words, 50% of the funds needed to purchase a stock could be borrowed.

If the stock market were to take a serious fall, margin calls would turn a mild downturn into a crash as broker lenders were forced to demand more cash as collateral for their margin loans in a falling stock market, forcing most investors to sell their stocks to raise cash, a move that turned a market decline into a rout in 1929. Congress believed that this was what happened in 1929, when the total of margin debt held by investors equaled 30% of the stock market's entire capitalization or worth. That was why it gave the Fed power to control initial margin requirements in the Securities Act of 1934.

The margin requirement after the 1929 crash had been as high as 100%, meaning that none of the purchase price could be borrowed. Gradually it was relaxed and since 1974, it had been unchanged at 50%, allowing investors to borrow as much as half the purchase price of equities directly from their brokers. By 2000 this margin mechanism acted like gasoline poured on a raging bonfire.

Congressional hearings were held on the issue. Investment managers such Paul McCulley of PIMCO, the world's largest bond fund at that time, told Congress,

> *The Fed should raise that minimum, and raise it now. Mr. Green-span says "no," of course, because (1) he cannot find evidence of a relationship between changes in margin requirements and changes in the level of the stock market, and (2) because an increase in margin requirements would discriminate against small investors, whose only source of stock market credit is their margin account.* [21]

On the Margin

In the face of the obvious 1999-2000 US stock bubble, not only did Greenspan repeatedly refuse to tighten stock margin requirements or even forbid any buying of stocks with borrowed margin debt at all, which was in his power to do.

But in the late 1990s, the Fed chairman actually began to talk in glowing terms about the New Economy, arguing that IT and related technology had helped increase overall economic productivity. He was consciously fuelling the market's "irrational exuberance."

Between June 1996 and June 2000, the Dow rose 93% and the NASDAQ rose 125%. The overall ratio of stock prices to corporate earnings reached record highs not seen since the days before the 1929 crash.

Then in 1999, Greenspan initiated a series of interest rate hikes, when inflation was even slower than it was in 1996 and productivity was growing even faster. But by refusing to tie rate rises to a rise in margin requirements, which would clearly have signaled that the Fed was serious about cooling the speculative bubble in stocks, Greenspan impacted the economy with higher rates, evidently designed to increase unemployment and press labor costs lower to further raise corporate earnings, not to cool the stock buying frenzy of the New Economy. Accordingly, the stock market ignored it.

Influential observers, including financier George Soros and Stanley Fischer, deputy director at the International Monetary Fund, advocated that the Fed let the air out of the credit boom by raising margin requirements.

Greenspan refused this more sensible strategy.

At his re-confirmation hearing before the US Senate Banking Committee in 1996, he had claimed that he did not want to discriminate against individuals who were not wealthy and therefore needed to borrow in order to play the stock market (sic). As he well knew, the traders buying stocks on margin were not the 'poor and needy,' but professional traders out for a free lunch. Interestingly, however, this argument was precisely the one that Greenspan would use repeatedly to justify his advocacy of lending to lower income earners who were poor credit risks, ensnaring them into the sub-prime home ownership bonanza that his policies after 2001 had created. [22]

The stock market began to tumble in the first half of 2000, not because labor costs were rising, but because limits of investor credulity were finally reached. The financial press, including the *Wall Street Journal*, a year earlier had extolled Dot.com executives as pioneers of the New Economy; now, they were ridiculing the public for having believed that the stock of companies that would never make a profit could go up forever.

It was typical of the Wall Street mentality that regards 'the public' as suckers who deserve to be tricked and robbed blind by the smart big guys with all the money. One former derivatives trader at Morgan Stanley who got out in the mid-1990s described the prevailing attitude on Wall Street towards their derivatives clients: "When they weren't performing complex computer calculations they were screaming about how they were going to 'rip someone's face off'...The battlefields of the derivatives world are littered with our victims...at Orange County (California), at Barings Bank, and Daiwa Bank and Sumitomo Corporation...." [23]

The New Economy with all its derivatives manipulations, as one Wall Street Journal writer put it, "looks like an old-fashioned credit bubble." [24] In the second half of that year American consumers, whose debt-to-income ratios were at a record high, began to pull back. Christmas sales plunged, and by early January 2001 Greenspan reversed himself and lowered interest rates. In twelve successive rate cuts, the Greenspan Fed brought US Fed funds rates -- rates that determined short-term and other interest rates in the economy -- from 6% down to a postwar low of 1% by June 2003, where he held them until June 30, 2004.

Those historic lows had not been seen for that length of time since the Great Depression. In July 2004, Greenspan began the first of what were to be fourteen successive rate increases before he left office in 2006. He took Fed funds rates from the low of 1% up to 4.5% in nineteen months. In the process, he killed the bubble that was laying the real estate golden egg.

In speech after speech, the Fed chairman made clear that his ultra-easy money regime after January 2001 had, as its prime focus, the encouragement of investing in home mortgage debt. The sub-prime phenomenon—something only possible in the era of asset securitization and Glass-Steagall repeal, combined with unregulated OTC or Over-The-Counter derivatives trades between private financial institutions—was the predictable result of deliberate Greenspan policy. A close look at the historical record made that abundantly clear.

Endgame: Unregulated private money creation

What had emerged after the 1999 repeal of Glass-Steagall was an awesome transformation of American credit markets into what would soon become the world's greatest unregulated private money-creating machine.

The New Finance was built on an incestuous, interlocking, if informal, cartel of players, all reading from the script written by Alan Greenspan and his friends at J.P. Morgan, Citigroup, Goldman Sachs, and the other major financial houses of New York. Securitization was going to secure a 'new' American Century and US financial domination of the world, as its creators clearly believed on the eve of the millennium.

Key to the 'revolution in finance,' in addition to the unabashed backing of the Greenspan Fed, was the complicity of the Executive, Legislative and Judicial branches of the US Government, up to and including the Supreme Court. Also required in order to make the game work seamlessly, was the active complicity of the two leading credit agencies in the world—Moody's and Standard & Poors.

The revolution in finance required a Congress and Executive branch that would repeatedly reject rational appeals to regulate over-the-counter financial derivatives, bank-owned or financed hedge funds, and would systematically remove all of the mechanisms for supervision, control, and transparency that had been painstakingly built up over the previous century or more. It required that the major government-certified rating agencies give their AAA credit imprimatur to a tiny handful of poorly regulated insurance companies called 'monolines,' all based in New York. The monolines were another essential part of the New Finance.

The structural interlinks and ideological consensus behind the massive expansion of securitization among all these institutional players was so clear and pervasive it might as well have been incorporated as "America New Finance, Inc." and its shares sold over NASDAQ.

Alan Greenspan had anticipated and encouraged the process of asset securitization for years, even before his actual nurturing of the phenomenal real estate bubble in the beginning of the first decade of the new Century. In a clearly deceptive attempt to deny his central role after the collapse of the subprime real estate bubble, Greenspan claimed in late 2007 that the problem was not mortgage lending to sub-prime customers but the securitization of the sub-prime credits. In April 2005, however, he had sung a quite different hymn to sub-prime securitization. Addressing the Federal Reserve System's Fourth Annual Community Affairs Research Conference, the Fed chairman declared,

> *Innovation has brought about a multitude of new products, such as subprime loans and niche credit programs for immigrants. Such developments are representative of the market responses that have driven the financial services industry throughout the history of our country. With these advances in technology, lenders have taken advantage of credit-scoring models and other techniques for efficiently extending credit to a broader spectrum of consumers...The mortgage-backed security helped create a national and even an international market for mortgages, and market support for a wider variety of home mortgage loan products became commonplace. This led to securitization of a variety of other consumer loan products, such as auto and credit card loans.* [25]

This 2005 speech was delivered in the midst of what he later claimed was a sudden epiphany that securitization was getting out of hand. In September 2007, once the crisis was in full force, CBS' Leslie Stahl asked Greenspan why he had done nothing to stop "illegal or shady practices you knew were taking place in sub-prime lending." Greenspan replied, "Err, I had no notion of how significant these practices had become until very late. I didn't really get it until late 2005 and 2006..." [26]

What he omitted to say was that, even if "late 2005" was when he really 'got it,' he still did nothing, then or later, to stop the out of control fraudulent Ponzi bubble that his policies had done so much to create.

Already in 2002 when the subprime scheme was in its early days, the Mortgage Bankers' Association of America had made clear the huge risks in the booming subprime real estate securitization market. "Preliminary evidence indicates that the probability of default is at least six times higher for nonprime loans (loans with high interest rates) that prime loans," noted a report published in the magazine of the St. Louis Federal Reserve Bank in January 2006. The St. Louis Fed is one of the member banks of the Federal Reserve System. That Fed study pointed out that the risks of subprime lending were known long before Alan Greenspan's epiphany:

The Mortgage Bankers' Association of America reports that subprime loans in the third quarter of 2002 had a delinquency rate five and a half times higher than for prime loans and the rate at which foreclosures were begun for subprime loans was more than ten times that for prime loans. [27]

As far back as November 1998, only weeks after the near-meltdown of the global financial system through the collapse of the LTCM hedge fund, Greenspan had gleefully told an annual meeting of the US Securities Industry Association,

> *Dramatic advances in computer and telecommunications technologies in recent years have enabled a broad unbundling of risks through innovative financial engineering. The financial instruments of a bygone era, common stocks and debt obligations, have been augmented by a vast array of complex hybrid financial products, which allow risks to be isolated, but which, in many cases, seemingly challenge human understanding.* [28]

Greenspan's speech clearly signaled Wall Street to move into asset-backed securitization in a big way. After all, hadn't Greenspan just demonstrated -- through the harrowing Asian crises of 1997-98 and the systemic crisis triggered by the August 1998 sovereign debt default -- that the Federal Reserve and its liquidity spigot stood more than ready to bailout the banks in the event of any major mishap? The big banks were now, after all, clearly TBTF-- Too Big To Fail.

The Federal Reserve, the world's largest and most powerful central bank, headed now by arguably the world's most market-friendly Chairman, Greenspan, would back its major banks in the bold new securitization undertaking. When Greenspan mentioned risks "which seemingly challenge human understanding," he signaled that he understood at least in a crude way that this was a whole new domain of financial obfuscation and complication.

Traditionally, central bankers were known for their pursuit of transparency among banks and for conservative lending and risk management practices by member banks.

Not 'ole Alan Greenspan.

Most significantly, Greenspan's 1998 speech had reassured his Wall Street securities underwriting friends that he would do everything possible to ensure that in the New Finance, the securitization of assets would remain for the banks alone to self-regulate.

Under the Greenspan Fed, the foxes would be trusted to guard the henhouse. He stated:

> It is, thus, all the more important to recognize that twenty-first century financial regulation is going to increasingly have to rely on private counterparty surveillance to achieve safety and soundness. There is no credible way to envision most government financial regulation being other than oversight of process. As the complexity of financial intermediation on a worldwide scale continues to increase, the conventional regulatory examination process will become progressively obsolescent--at least for the more complex banking systems. [29]

Again in October 1999, amid the frenzy of the Dot.com IT stock market bubble mania, Greenspan had praised the role of financial derivatives and "new financial instruments...reallocating risk in a manner that makes risk more tolerable. Insurance, of course, is the purest form of this service. All the new financial products that have been created in recent years, financial derivatives being in the forefront, contribute economic value by unbundling risks and reallocating them in a highly calibrated manner." He was speaking of securitization on the eve of the repeal of the Glass-Steagall Act.[30]

The Fed's much-touted "private counterparty surveillance" had brought the entire international inter-bank trading system to a screeching halt in August 2007, as panic spread over the value of the trillions of dollars in securitized Asset Backed Commercial Paper and, in fact, most securitized bonds. As of this writing, the effects of the shock have only just begun, as banks and investors slash values across the US and international financial system. But that's getting ahead of our story.

J.P.Morgan's 'Weapons of Financial Mass Destruction'

In 1995, well into the Clinton-Rubin era, Alan Greenspan's former bank, J.P. Morgan, introduced an innovation that would revolutionize banking over the next decade. Blythe Masters, a 34-year old Cambridge University graduate hired by the bank, developed the first Credit Default Swaps, a financial derivative instrument that ostensibly enabled a bank to insure against loan default; and Collateralized Debt Obligations, bonds issued against a mixed pool of assets, a kind of credit derivative giving exposure to a large number of companies in a single instrument.

Their attraction was that it was entirely 'off' the bank's own books, hence away from the Basel Accord's 8% capital rules. In 1988, largely in a vain attempt to curb the growing speculative excesses of bank lending in Japan and the USA, world central bankers had agreed on a set of rules requiring international banks to hold capital equal to 8% of outstanding loans.

The goal of the new off-balance-sheet Credit Default Swaps was to increase bank returns while eliminating the risk, a kind of 'having your cake and eating it too,' something which in the real world can only be very messy.

J.P. Morgan thereby paved the way for the transformation of US banking -- from traditional commercial lenders, into traders of credit -- in effect, into securitizers. The new idea was to enable the banks to shift risks off their balance sheets by pooling their loans and remarketing them as securities, while buying 'default insurance' -- Credit Default Swaps -- after syndicating the loans for their clients with other international banks. It was to prove a staggering development, and would soon expand to volumes measured in the trillions for the banks.

By the end of 2007 there were an estimated $45,000 billion worth of Credit Default Swap contracts out there, giving bondholders the illusion of security. That illusion, however, was built on bank risk models that projected assumptions of default rates which were hidden from the public. Had they been open to scrutiny, it would likely have killed the entire securitization market.[31] Like other such risk models, they were wildly optimistic.

Yet the mere existence of the illusion was sufficient to lead the major banks of the world, lemming-like, into buying mortgage bonds collateralized or backed by streams of mortgage payments of unknown credit quality, and to accept at face value a Moody's or Standard & Poors AAA rating. Little wonder that conservative investors like Warren Buffett called financial derivatives "weapons of financial mass destruction."[32] He would be proven correct.

Just as new Fed chairman Greenspan had turned to his old cronies at J.P. Morgan when he wanted to find a loophole to the strict Glass-Steagall Act in 1987, and as he had turned to J.P. Morgan to covertly work with the Fed to buy derivatives on the Chicago MMI stock index to artificially manipulate a recovery from the October 1987 crash, so the Greenspan Fed worked with J.P. Morgan and a handful of other trusted friends on Wall Street to support the launch of securitization in the 1990s. It soon became clear what the staggering potential gains would be for the banks who were first in line and who could shape the rules of the new game, the New Finance.

J.P. Morgan & Co. had led the march of the big money center banks, beginning in 1995, away from traditional customer bank lending towards the pure trading of credit and of credit risk. The goal was to amass huge fortunes for the bank's balance sheet – and its executives -- without having to carry the risk on the bank's books. It was an open invitation to greed, fraud and ultimate financial disaster. Almost every major bank in the world -- from Deutsche Bank to UBS to Barclays to Royal Bank of Scotland to Société Générale -- soon followed Chase, J.P Morgan and Citibank like eager, blind lemmings.

When it came to eagerness, however, none came even close to the handful of US banks which created and dominated the new world of securitization and derivatives after 1995. The big New York banks were the first to begin to shift credit risk off the bank balance sheets by pooling credits and remarketing portfolios, buying default protection after syndicating loans for clients. The era of New Finance had begun. Like every major innovation in finance, it began slowly.

Very soon, the new securitizing banks such as J.P. Morgan began to create portfolios of debt securities, then to package and sell off tranches or risk-based chunks based on default probabilities. 'Slice and dice' was the name of the new game, to generate revenue for the issuing underwriting bank, and to give 'customized risk to return' results for investors. Soon Asset Backed Securities, Collateralized Debt Securities, even emerging market debt were being bundled and sold off in bite-sized chunks to pension funds, university endowments, foreign banks and other yield-hungry investors lured by the false sense of security of a Moody's or S&P AAA credit rating or monoline insurance, or more often, both.

The Mortgage Securitization scam begins

On November 2, 1999, only ten days before Bill Clinton signed the Act repealing Glass-Steagall – allowing banks unrestricted acquisition of brokerage firms, investment banks, insurance companies and a variety of other financial institutions -- Alan Greenspan turned his attention to encouraging the process of bank securitization of home mortgages.

In an address to America's Community Bankers, a regional banking organization, at a 1999 conference on mortgage markets, the Fed chairman stated:

> *The recent rise in the homeownership rate to over 67 percent in the third quarter of this year owes, in part, to the healthy economic expansion with its robust job growth. But part of the gains have also come about because innovative lenders, like you, have created a far broader spectrum of mortgage products and have increased the efficiency of loan originations and underwriting. Ongoing progress in streamlining the loan application and origination process and in tailoring mortgages to individual homebuyers is needed to continue these gains in homeownership...Community banking epitomizes the flexibility and resourcefulness required to adjust to, and exploit, demographic changes and technological breakthroughs, and to create new forms of mortgage finance that promote homeownership. As for the Federal Reserve, we are striving to assist you by providing a stable platform for business generally and for housing and mortgage activity.* [33]

Earlier that year, Greenspan had addressed the Mortgage Bankers' Association where he strongly pushed real estate mortgage backed securitization as the wave of the future. He told the bankers there,

> *Greater stability in the supply of mortgage credit has been accompanied by the unbundling of the various aspects of the mortgage process. Some institutions act as mortgage bankers, screening applicants and originating loans. Other parties service mortgage loans, a*

function for which efficiencies seem to be gained by large-scale op-
erations. Still others, mostly with stable funding bases, provide the
permanent financing of mortgages through participation in mort-
gage pools. Beyond this, some others slice cash flows from mortgage
pools into special tranches that appeal to a wider group of investors.
In the process, mortgage-backed securities outstanding have grown
to a staggering $2.4 trillion.... Automated underwriting software is
being increasingly employed to process a rapidly rising share of
mortgage applications.

..... One key benefit of the new technology has been an increased
ability to manage risk (sic). Looking forward, the increased use of
automated underwriting and credit scoring creates the potential for
low-cost, customized mortgages with risk-adjusted pricing. By tai-
loring mortgages to the needs of individual borrowers, the mortgage
banking industry of tomorrow will be better positioned to serve all
corners of the diverse mortgage market. [34]

Several more steps were needed, however, before asset securitization really
took off. Only after the Fed punctured the Dot.com stock bubble in 2000, and
after Greenspan dropped Fed funds interest rates to the lowest levels since the
Great Depression, did asset securitization literally explode into a multi-trillion
dollar enterprise.

Securitization—The 'Un-Real' Deal

Because the very subject of securitization was embedded with such complexity
no one, not even its creators, fully understood the diffusion of risk, let alone the
simultaneous concentration of systemic risk.

Securitization was a process in which assets were acquired by some entity,
sometimes called a Special Purpose Vehicle (SPV) or Special Investment Vehicle
(SIV). At the SIV, the diverse home mortgages, let's say, were assembled into
pools or 'bundles' as they were called. A specific pool, say, of home mortgage
receivables, now took life in the new form of a bond, an asset backed bond, in
this case a mortgage backed security. The securitized bond was backed by the
cash flow or value of the underlying assets.

To grasp those little steps involved a complex leap of faith. It was based on
illusory collateral backing whose real worth -- as is now dramatically clear to all

banks everywhere -- was unknown and unknowable. Already at this stage of the process the title to the home mortgage of a specific home in the pool was legally ambiguous. Who in the chain actually had in his or her physical possession the real, 'wet signature' mortgage deeds to the hundreds and thousands of homes in collateral? It would take hundreds of lawyers many years to sort out Wall Street's brilliant opacities.

Securitization usually applied to assets that were illiquid -- ones that were not easily sold -- hence it became common in real estate. And US real estate in 2008 was one of the world's most illiquid markets. Everyone wanted out and few wanted in, at least not at those prices.

Securitization was applied to pools of leased property, to residential mortgages, to home equity loans, student loans, credit cards or other debts. In theory all assets could be securitized as long as they were associated with a steady and predictable cash flow. That was the theory.

In practice, securitization allowed US banks to skirt tougher new Basel Capital Adequacy Rules. Basel II was designed explicitly, in part, to close the loophole in Basel I that let US and other banks shove loans wholesale into the SIVs, the 'off-the-books' Special Investment Vehicles.

Financial Alchemy: Where the fly hits the soup

Securitization, thus, converted illiquid assets into liquid assets. It did this, in theory, by pooling, underwriting and selling the ownership claims to the payment flows, as asset-backed securities (ABS). Mortgage-backed securities were one form of ABS, the largest by far since 2001.

Here is where the fly hit the soup and the meal got messy.

Beginning in 2006, the US housing market went into a sharp downturn, and rates on Adjustable Rate Mortgages (ARMs) started moving sharply higher across the country. This forced hundreds of thousands of homeowners to simply 'walk away' from their now un-payable mortgages, or be foreclosed on by one or another party in the complex securitization chain, very often illegally, as an Ohio judge recently ruled. Home foreclosures for 2007 were 75% higher than in 2006 and the trend was just beginning. The mortgage securitization fraud will produce a real estate disaster to rival or likely exceed that of the Great Depression. In California, foreclosures in 2007 were already up an alarming 421% over the year before.

The cascading process of mortgage defaults in turn left gaping holes in the underlying cash payment stream intended to back up the newly issued Mort-

gage Backed Securities. Because the entire system was totally opaque, no one --
least of all the banks holding this paper -- knew which asset-backed security was
good, and which was bad. Just as nature abhors a vacuum, bankers and investors, especially global investors, abhor uncertainty in financial assets they hold.
They treated all mortgage-backed securities, not just those on sub-prime
mortgages, like toxic waste.

The architects of this New Finance based on the securitization of home
mortgages, however, found that bundling hundreds of disparate mortgages of
varying credit quality from across the USA into a big MBS bond wasn't enough. If
the Wall Street MBS underwriters were to be able to sell their new MBS bonds to
the well-endowed pension funds of the world, they needed some extra juice. The
ratings game began.

Most pension funds are restricted to buying only bonds rated AAA, highest
quality. But how could a rating agency rate a bond which was composed of a
putative stream of mortgage payments from 1,000 different home mortgages
across the USA? They couldn't send an examiner into every city to look at the
home and interview its occupant. Who could stand behind the bond? Not the
mortgage issuing bank. They sold the mortgage immediately, at a discount, to
get it off their books. Not the Special Purpose Vehicle; they were just there to
keep the transactions separate from the mortgage underwriting bank. No,
something else was needed. In stepped the Big Three (actually Big Two) credit
rating agencies.

'Then the music just stopped'

Never ones to despair when confronted by new obstacles, clever minds at J.P.
Morgan, Morgan Stanley, Goldman Sachs, Citigroup, Merrill Lynch, Bear Stearns
and others in the game of securitizing exploding volumes of home mortgages after
2002, turned to the Big Three rating agencies to get their prized AAA.

This rating step was necessary because with Asset Backed Securities, no
corporation stood behind the debt. Unlike the issuance of a traditional corporate bond, say by GE or Ford, where a known, physical, blue chip, 'bricks 'n
mortar' company with a long-term credit history stood behind the bond in event
of default, an ABS was backed by nothing but a lot of promises and highly
convoluted chains of putative ownership.

The ABS or bond was a 'stand alone' artificial creation, whose legality under
US law has been called into question. That meant a rating by a credit rating
agency was essential to make the bond credible, or at least give it the 'appear-

ance of credibility,' as the world was soon to realize from the unraveling of the subsequent securitization debacle.

At the very heart of the new financial architecture, facilitated by the Greenspan Fed and more than two decades of US Administrations, was a semi-monopoly held by three *de facto* unregulated private companies that provided credit ratings for all securitized assets -- for fees, of course. For very nice fees.

Three rating agencies dominated the global business of credit ratings, the largest in the world being Moody's Investors Service. In the boom years of securitization, Moody's regularly reported well over a 50% profit on gross rating revenues. Doing ratings of Mortgage Backed Securities had become a main profit stream for Moody's.

The other two in the global rating cartel were Standard & Poor's and Fitch Ratings. All three were American companies intimately tied into the financial sinews of Wall Street and US finance. The fact that the world's rating business was a *de facto* US monopoly was no accident. It had been planned that way, as an integral part of the main pillar of the financial domination of New York. The control of the world's credit ratings was to US global financial power projection, almost the equivalent of what US domination in nuclear weapons was to US global political power.

The de facto monopoly role of the three US credit rating agencies in the financial crisis of 2007 has been carefully pushed to the side.

Former Secretary of Labor, economist Robert Reich, identified a core issue of the raters and their ratings system -- their built-in conflict of interest. As Reich noted,

Credit-rating agencies are paid by the same institutions that package and sell the securities the agencies are rating. If an investment bank doesn't like the rating, it doesn't have to pay for it. And even if

it likes the rating, it pays only after the security is sold. Get it? It's as if movie studios hired film critics to review their movies, and paid them only if the reviews were positive enough to get lots of people to see the movie.

Until the collapse, the result was great for credit-rating agencies. Profits at Moody's more than doubled between 2002 and 2006. And it was a great ride for the issuers of mortgage-backed securities. Demand soared because the high ratings had expanded the market. Traders didn't examine anything except the ratings...a multibillion-dollar game of musical chairs. And then the music stopped. [35]

That put three global rating agencies—Moody's, S&P, and Fitch—directly under the investigative spotlight when the crisis broke in late 2007. They were, in effect, the only ones in the business of rating the collateralized securities—Collateralized Mortgage Obligations, Collateralized Debt Obligations, Student Loan-backed Securities, Lottery Winning-backed Securities and a myriad of others—for Wall Street and other banks.

According to an industry publication, *Inside Mortgage Finance*, some 25% of the $900 billion in sub-prime mortgages issued over the two years beginning in 2005 had been given top AAA marks by the rating agencies. That came to more than $220 billion of sub-prime mortgage securities carrying the highest AAA rating by either Moody's, Fitch, or Standard & Poors. By the summer of 2007, the ratings system was coming unglued as home mortgage defaults snowballed across the land.

Here, the scene got ugly. Their model assumptions on which they gave their desired AAA seal of approval were a proprietary secret. "Trust us..."

According to an economist this author spoke with who was working within the US rating business, and who had access to the actual model assumptions used by Moody's, S&P and Fitch to determine whether a mortgage pool with sub-prime mortgages got a AAA or not, their methods were *pre-determined* to give the highest possible ratings to the dicey new securities. The raters used past default rates from a period in history when the lowest interest rates since the Great Depression were in force. In other words, they based their ratings on a period with abnormally low default rates, to declare by extrapolation that the sub-prime paper was -- and would be into the distant future -- of AAA quality. They also used data showing that a recession rarely took place across the entire fifty states, but rather in just one or several states at a time, so that if mortgages from many different regions were packaged into a security, the risk of default would also be insignificant.

The risk of default on even a more risky sub-prime mortgage, so went the argument, "was historically almost infinitesimal." That AAA rating from Moody's, in turn, allowed the Wall Street investment houses to sell the CMOs to pension funds, or to just about anybody seeking 'yield enhancement' but with no risk. That was the theory.

As Oliver von Schweinitz pointed out in a very timely book, *Rating Agencies: Their Business, Regulation and Liability*, "Securitizations without ratings are unthinkable." And because of the special nature of asset backed securitizations of mortgage loans, von Schweinitz points out, those ABS, "although being standardized, are one-time events, whereas other issuances (corporate bonds, government bonds) generally affect repeat players. Repeat players have less incentive to cheat than one time issuers." [36]

In other words, there was more incentive to cheat and to commit fraud with asset backed securities than with traditional bond issuance, a lot more.

Moody's, S&P enjoy unique status

The top three rating agencies under US law enjoyed an almost unique status. They were recognized by the Government's Securities and Exchange Commission (SEC) as Nationally Recognized Statistical Rating Organizations (NRSROs). There existed only four in the USA as of 2009. The fourth was Dominion Bond Rating Service Ltd., a far smaller, Canadian rater. Essentially, the top three held a quasi monopoly on the credit rating business worldwide.

The only US law regulating rating agencies, the Credit Agency Reform Act of 2006, was a toothless statute, passed in the wake of the Enron collapse. Four days before the collapse of Enron, the rating agencies gave Enron an "investment grade" rating, and a shocked public called for some scrutiny of the raters. The effect of the Credit Agency Reform Act of 2006 on the rating monopoly of S&P, Moody's and Fitch was null.

The European Union, also reacting to Enron and to the similar fraud of the Italian company Parmalat, called for an investigation into whether the US rating agencies rating Parmalat had conflicts of interest (they did), how transparent their methodologies were (not at all), and the lack of competition (evident).

After several years of 'study' and presumably a lot of behind-the-scenes maneuvering from big EU banks involved in the securitization game, the EU Commission in 2006 announced only that it would "continue scrutiny" (sic) of the rating agencies. Moody's and S&P and Fitch dominated EU ratings as well. There were no competitors in the rating game.

'It's a free country, ain't it?'

Under US law, the raters were not liable for their ratings, despite the fact that investors worldwide depend often exclusively on the AAA or other rating by Moody's or S&P as validation of creditworthiness, most especially in securitized assets. The Credit Agency Reform Act of 2006 did not address the issue of liability of the rating agencies. It was in this regard a worthless "reform." It was the only law dealing with the raters at all.

As von Schweinitz pointed out, "Rule 10b-5 of the Securities and Exchange Act of 1934 is probably the most important basis for suing on the grounds of capital market fraud." That Rule states that, "It shall be unlawful for any person...to make any untrue statement of a material fact." It sounded like something concrete. But then the US Supreme Court stated, in a 2005 ruling, *Dura Pharmaceuticals, Inc. v Broudo*, that ratings are not "statements of a material fact" as required under Rule 10b-5. The ratings given by Moody's or S&P or Fitch are rather, "merely an opinion." They were thereby protected as "privileged free speech," under the US Constitution's First Amendment.[37]

Moody's or S&P could say any damn thing it wanted to about Enron or Parmalat or sub-prime securities. 'It's a free country ain't it? Doesn't everyone have a right to their opinion?'....

Unless investors could prove that there had been a deliberate and material misrepresentation of fact that directly, or "proximately" caused the investors' economic loss – and not just the fact that the stock was overpriced and subsequently fell – then the investors were out of luck. The only way the rating itself could be the "proximate cause" of an investor's economic loss would be in the event of 1) proof that the investor had relied on the rating as accurate; 2) the rating had been exposed as fraudulent; and 3) the fraud caused the stock price to fall, thus causing the investor's economic loss. Proving such things in court turned out to be quite difficult.

US courts had repeatedly described financial markets as "efficient." As such, these 'efficient' markets would of their own nature detect any fraud in a company or security and price it accordingly...eventually. No need to worry about the raters then... [38]

That was the "self-regulation" that Alan Greenspan apparently had in mind when he repeatedly intervened to oppose any regulation of the emerging asset securitization revolution.

The entire securitization revolution was underwritten by a kind of 'hear no evil, see no evil' US government policy that said, 'what is good for the Money Trust is good for the nation.' It was a perverse twist on the already perverse saying from the 1950's of then General Motors chief, Charles E. Wilson, "what's good for General Motors is good for America."

The 'Rolling Crises' game

Greenspan's 18-year tenure could be described as rolling the financial markets from successive crises into ever larger ones, in the process to accomplish the over-riding objectives of the Money Trust guiding the Greenspan agenda—the extension of their power over the world monetary system.

By early 2009 it was becoming clear to much of the world that Greenspan's securitization revolution was a 'bridge too far,' spelling the end of the domination of the dollar and of dollar financial institutions' global dominance for decades or more to come. The deliberate intentions of the securitization revolution were evident in the following:

- Greenspan's adamant rejection of every attempt by Congress to impose some minimal regulation on OTC derivatives trading between banks;
- his refusal to change margin requirements on buying stock on borrowed money;
- his repeated support for securitization of sub-prime low quality high-risk mortgage lending;
- his relentless decade-long push to weaken and finally repeal Glass-Steagall restrictions on banks owning investment banks and insurance companies;
- his support for Bush's radical tax cuts which exploded federal deficits after 2001;
- his support for the privatization of the Social Security Trust Fund in order to funnel those trillions of dollars cash flow into his cronies in Wall Street finance.

All of these policies had been well planned and thoroughly considered; their consequences were knowable and foreseeable. The securitization revolution aimed at the creation of a world of New Finance where risk would be detached from banks and spread across the globe to the point where no one could identify where real risk lay.

Monoline Insurance: Viagra for Securitization

For those CMO sub-prime securities that fell short of AAA quality, there was also another crucial fix needed. The minds on Wall Street came up with an ingenious solution.

The issuer of the Mortgage Backed Security could take out what was known as Monoline insurance. Monoline insurance for guaranteeing against default in asset backed securities was another spin-off of the Greenspan securitization revolution.

Monoline insurance became a very essential element in the fraud-ridden Wall Street scam known as securitization. By paying a certain fee, a specialized (hence the term monoline) insurance company would insure or guarantee a pool of sub-prime mortgages in the event of an economic downturn or recession in which the poor sub-prime homeowner could not service his monthly mortgage payments.

Although monoline insurance had begun back in the early 1970s as a guarantee for municipal bonds, it was the Greenspan securitization revolution that gave it its leap into prominence. The monoline insurers were actually eleven poorly capitalized, loosely regulated insurance companies, who called themselves 'financial guarantors.' They were all based in New York and regulated by that state's insurance regulator.

As their industry association stated, "The monoline structure ensures that our full attention is given to adding value to our capital market customers." Add value they definitely did. As of December 2007, it was reliably estimated that the monoline insurers had given their insurance guarantee to enable the AAA rated securitization of over $2.4 trillion worth of Asset Backed Securities.

The official website of the monoline trade association stated, "The Association of Financial Guaranty Insurers, AFGI, is the trade association of the insurers and re-insurers of municipal bonds and asset-backed securities. A bond or other security insured by an AFGI member has the unconditional and irrevocable guarantee that interest and principal will be paid on time and in full in the event of a default." No doubt, they regret ever having made such a promise, as sub-prime mortgage resets, growing recession, and mortgage defaults are presenting hyperbolic insurance demands on the tiny, poorly capitalized monolines.

The main monoline insurers were hardly household names: ACA Financial Guaranty Corp., Ambac Assurance, Assured Guaranty Corp. BluePoint Re Limited, CIFG, Financial Guaranty Insurance Company, Financial Security Assurance, MBIA Insurance Corporation, PMI Guaranty Co., Radian Asset Assurance Inc., RAM Reinsurance Company and XL Capital Assurance.

A cautious reader might ask the question, "Who insures these eleven mono-line insurers who have guaranteed billions, indeed trillions, in payment flows over the past five or so years of the ABS financial revolution?"

"No one, yet," was the short answer. They state, "Eight AFGI member firms carry a Triple-A claims paying ability rating and two member firms carry a Double-A claims paying ability rating." Moody's, Standard & Poors and Fitch gave the monolines their AAA or AA ratings.

By having a guarantee from a bond insurer with an AAA credit rating, the cost of borrowing was less than it would normally be and the number of inves-tors willing to buy such bonds was greater.

For the monolines, guaranteeing such bonds seemed risk-free, with average default rates running at a fraction of 1 per cent in 2003-2006. As a result, mono-lines leveraged their assets to build their books, and it was not uncommon for a monoline to have insured risks 100 to 150 times the size of its capital base. Until recently, Ambac had capital of $5.7 billion against guarantees of $550 billion.

In 1998, the NY State Insurance Superintendent's office, the only regulator of monolines, had agreed to allow monolines to sell credit-default swaps (CDSs) on asset-backed securities such as mortgage-backed securities. Separate shell companies would be established, through which CDSs could be issued to banks for mortgage-backed securities.

The move into insuring securitized bonds was spectacularly lucrative for the monolines. MBIA's premiums rose from $235m in 1998 to $998m in 2007. Year on year premiums increased 140% in 2007. Then along came the US sub-prime mortgage crisis, and the music stopped dead for the monolines. Stone dead.

As the mortgages within bonds from the banks defaulted -- sub-prime mortgages written in 2006 were already defaulting at a rate of 20% by January 2008—the monolines were forced to step in and cover the payments.

On February 3, 2008, MBIA revealed $3.5 billion in write downs and other charges in three months alone, leading to a quarterly loss of $2.3 billion. That was likely just the tip of a very large and very cold iceberg. Insurance analyst Donald Light remarked, "The answer is no one knows," when asked what the potential downside loss was. "I don't think we will know to perhaps the third or fourth quarter of 2008." By then, losses were catastrophic.

Credit ratings agencies began downgrading the monolines, taking away their prized AAA ratings, which means a monoline could no longer write new business, and the bonds it guarantees no longer would hold a AAA rating.

By 2008, the only monoline to receive downgrades from two agencies - usually required for such a move to impact on a company - was FGIC, cut by both Fitch and S&P. Ambac, the second largest monoline, had been cut to AA by

Fitch, with the other monolines on a variety of different potential warnings. One of the largest insurers of Wall Street securitization bonds, AIG, was not even under regulatory control as it hid its activity in a London subsidiary and almost brought down the entire financial house of cards in September 2008 when its losses were finally made public. [39]

The rating agencies did "computer simulated stress tests" to decide if the monolines could "pay claims at a default level comparable to that of the Great Depression." How much could the monoline insurers handle in a real crisis? By their calculations, "Our claims-paying resources available to back members' guarantees...totals more than $34 billion." [40]

That $34 billion was a drop in the bottomless bucket of 2008 "bailouts." It was estimated that in the Asset Backed Securities market, roughly one-third of all transactions were "wrapped" or insured by AAA monolines. Investors demanded surety wraps for volatile collateral or products without a long performance history. [41]

According to the Securities Industry and Financial Markets Association, a US trade group, at the end of 2006 there was a total of some $3.6 trillion worth of Asset Backed Securities in the United States -- including home mortgages, prime and sub-prime, home equity loans, credit cards, student loans, car loans, equipment leasing and the like. Fortunately not all $3.6 trillion of securitizations are likely to default, and not all at once. But the AGFI monoline insurers had insured $2.4 trillion of that mountain of asset backed securities over the past several years. Private analysts estimated by early February 2008 that the potential insurer payout risks, under optimistic assumptions, could exceed $200 billion.

Off the books...

The entire securitization revolution allowed banks to move assets off their books into unregulated and opaque vehicles. They sold the mortgages at a discount to underwriters such as Merrill Lynch, Bear Stearns, Citigroup, and similar financial securitizers.

The underwriters then, in turn, sold the mortgage collateral to their own separate Special Investment Vehicle or SIV. The attraction of a stand-alone SIV was that they and their potential losses were --theoretically at least -- isolated from the main underwriting bank. Should things ever, God forbid, run amok with the various Asset Backed Securities held by the SIV, only the SIV would suffer, not Citigroup or Merrill Lynch.

The dubious revenue streams from subprime mortgages and similar low quality loans, once bundled into the new Collateralized Mortgage Obligations or similar securities, then often got an injection of monoline insurance, a kind of financial Viagra for junk quality mortgages such as the NINA (No Income, No Assets) or "Liars' Loans," or so-called 'stated-income' loans. Such loans were commonplace during the colossal Greenspan Real Estate economy up until July 2007.

According to the Mortgage Brokers' Association for Responsible Lending, a consumer protection group, by 2006 Liars' Loans were a staggering 62% of all US mortgage originations. In one independent sampling audit of stated-income mortgage loans in Virginia in 2006, the auditors found, based on IRS records, that almost 60% of the stated-income loans were exaggerated by more than 50%. Those stated-income chickens are now coming home to roost, or far worse. The defaults on these Liars' Loans swept across the entire US real estate market after 2001. [42]

None of that would have been possible without securitization, without the full backing of the Greenspan Fed, without the repeal of Glass-Steagall, without monoline insurance, without the collusion of the major rating agencies, and without the transfer of risk by the mortgage-originating banks to underwriters who bundled them, rated them and insured them all AAA.

In fact the Federal Reserve's New Finance revolution literally opened the floodgates to fraud on every level -- from home mortgage brokers to lending agencies to Wall Street and London securitization banks to the credit rating agencies. Entrusting oversight of the new securitized assets -- hundreds of billions of dollars worth of them -- to private 'self-regulation' between issuing banks like Bear Stearns, Merrill Lynch or Citigroup and their rating agencies, was tantamount to pouring water on a drowning man. It did not take long before that would be obvious to the entire world when the financial equivalent of a Tsunami was unleashed in 2007.

Endnotes:

[1] Alan Greenspan, *Testimony before the House Committee on Banking and Financial Services*, February 11, 1999.

[2] Bob Woodward, *Maestro: Alan Greenspan's Fed and the American Economic Boom* (New York: Simon & Schuster, 2000). Woodward's book is an example of the charmed treatment Greenspan was accorded by the major media. Woodward's boss at the Washington Post, Catharine Meyer Graham, daughter of the legendary Wall Street investment banker Eugene Meyer, was an intimate Greenspan friend. The book can be seen as a calculated part of the Greenspan myth-creation by the influential circles of the financial establishment.

[3] *Lewis v. United States*, 680 F.2d 1239 (9th Cir. 1982).

[4] Michael Lewis, *Inside Wall Street's Black Hole,* Portfolio.com, February 19, 2008, accessed in http://www.portfolio.com/news-markets/national-news/portfolio/2008/02/19/Black-Scholes-Pricing-Model/?print=true.

[5] Ibid.

[6] Stephen Zarlenga, *Observations from the Trading Floor During the 1987 Crash*, in http://www.monetary.org/1987%20crash.html.

[7] Alan Greenspan, *Testimony before the Subcommittee on Financial Institutions Supervision, US House of Representatives*, Nov. 18, 1987.
http://fraser.stlouisfed.org/historicaldocs/ag/download/27759/Greenspan_19871118.pdf.

[8] Robert D. Hershey jr., *Greenspan Backs New Bank Roles*, The New York Times, October 6, 1987.

[9] John Kenneth Galbraith, cited in Michael J. Laird, *The Glass-Steagall Banking Act, its Demise,*
Managerial Auditing Journal, 1998, Vol.13, no. 9, pp. 509-514.

[10] Federal Deposit Insurance Corporation, *History of the 80s, Volume I: An Examination of the Banking Crises of the 1980s and Early 1990s,* in
www.fdic.gov/bank/historical/history/vol1.html, p.1.

[11] Hershey, op.cit.

[12] Ibid.

[13] Alan Greenspan, *Testimony before the House Committee on Banking and Financial Services*, February 11, 1999.

[14] Alan Greenspan, *Statement by Alan Greenspan, Chairman, Board of Governors of the Federal Reserve System, before the Committee on Banking and Financial Services*, U.S. House of Representatives, February 11, 1999, in Federal Reserve Bulletin, April 1999.

[15] Jenny Anderson, *Goldman Runs Risks, Reaps Rewards*, The New York Times, June 10, 2007.

[16] Robert Kuttner, *Testimony of Robert Kuttner Before the Committee on Financial Services*, Rep. Barney Frank, Chairman, U.S. House of Representatives, Washington, D.C., October 2, 2007

[17] Thomas Kostigen, *Regulation game: Would Glass-Steagall save the day from credit woes?*, Dow Jones MarketWatch, Sept. 7, 2007, in
http://www.marketwatch.com/news/story/would-glass-steagall-save-day-credit.

[18] Various market traders in private telephone discussion with the author during the 1997-98 Asia crisis reported on the first hand knowledge of the three hedge funds in executing coordinated military-like attacks on the various Asian currencies. One source, a Swiss financial regulator, speaking off-record in 2002, told the author he had been

present in the office of the President of Thailand's largest bank when a call came from the head of one of the three mentioned hedge funds telling him of a planned coordinated assault on the Thai currency and of the futility of trying to resist.

[19] F. William Engdahl, *Hunting Asian Tigers: Washington and the 1997-98 Asia Shock*, reprinted in http://www.jahrbuch2000.studien-von-zeitfragen.net/Weltfinanz/Hedge_Funds/hedge_funds.html.

[20] Alan Greenspan, *The Revolution in Information Technology, before the Boston College Conference on the New Economy*, Boston, Massachusetts, March 6, 2000.

[21] Paul McCulley, *A Call For Fed Action: Hike Margin Requirements!*, testimony before The House Subcommittee on Domestic and International Monetary Policy on March 21, 2000.

[22] Alan Greenspan as Fed chairman repeatedly asserted it was impossible to judge if a speculative bubble existed during the rise of such a bubble. In August 2002, after his clear strategy of Fed rate increases was obvious to market players, he reiterated this: "*We at the Federal Reserve considered a number of issues related to asset bubbles--that is, surges in prices of assets to unsustainable levels. As events evolved, we recognized that, despite our suspicions, it was very difficult to definitively identify a bubble until after the fact--that is, when its bursting confirmed its existence.*"---Alan Greenspan Remarks by Chairman Alan Greenspan Economic volatility At a symposium sponsored by the Federal Reserve Bank of Kansas City, Jackson Hole, Wyoming August 30, 2002.

[23] Frank Partnoy, *F.I.A.S.C.O.:The Inside Story of a Wall Street Trader* (New York: Penguin Press, 1999), pp. 14-15.

[24] Jeff Faux, *The Politically Talented Mr. Greenspan*, Dissent Magazine, Spring 2001.

[25] Alan Greenspan, *Consumer Finance*, Remarks at the Federal Reserve System's Fourth Annual Community Affairs Research Conference, Washington, D.C., April 8, 2005, in www.federalreserve.gov/BoardDocs/speeches/2005/20050408/default.htm

[26] Alan Greenspan, *Greenspan Defends Low Interest Rates* Interview CBS 60 Minutes, September 16, 2007, in www.cbsnews.com/stories/2007/09/13/60minutes/main3257567.shtml

[27] Souphala Chomsisengphet and Anthony Penning, "The Evolution of the Subprine Mortgage Market," *Federal Reserve Bank of St. Louis Review*, January/February 2006, 88(1), pp 31-56.

[28] Alan Greenspan, *The Markets*, Excerpts From Greenspan Speech on Global Turmoil, reprinted in The New York Times, November 6, 1998.

[29] Alan Greenspan, *Remarks by Chairman Alan Greenspan: TheStructure of the International Financial System*, at the Annual Meeting of the Securities Industry Association, Boca Raton, Florida, November 5, 1998.

[30] Alan Greenspan, *Measuring Financial Risk in the Twenty-first Century*, Remarks Before a conference sponsored by the Office of the Comptroller of the Currency, Washington, D.C., October 14, 1999, in www.federalreserve.gov/boarddocs/speeches/1999/19991014.htm. Here Greenspan states, "...to date, economists have been unable to anticipate sharp reversals in confidence. Collapsing confidence is generally described as **a bursting bubble, an event incontrovertibly evident only in retrospect.** To anticipate a bubble about to burst requires the forecast of a plunge in the prices of assets previously set by the judgments of millions of investors, many of whom are highly knowledgeable about the prospects for the specific investments that make up our broad price indexes of stocks and other assets."

[31] A first-hand description of the risk assumptions in the major risk models employed by the major credit rating agencies was provided to the author. He confirmed that the assumptions had no relation to economic reality whatsoever. Evidently, nobody in a position to question had bothered to do so. It was too lucrative to close one's eyes.

[32] Warren Buffett, cited in Richard Dooling, *Machines of mass destruction*, International Herald Tribune, October 13, 2008.

[33] Alan Greenspan, *Mortgage markets and economic activity*, Remarks before a conference on Mortgage Markets and Economic Activity, sponsored by America's Community Bankers, Washington, D.C., November 2, 1999, in www.federalreserve.gov/boarddocs/speeches/1999/19991102.htm.

[34] Alan Greenspan, *Remarks to Mortgage Bankers' Association*, Washington, D.C., March 8, 1999.

[35] Robert Reich, *Why Credit-rating Agencies Blew It: Mystery Solved*, October 23, 2007, Robert Reich's Blog, in robertreich.blogspot.com/2007/10/they-mystery-of-why-credit-rating.html.

[36] Oliver Von Schweinitz, *Rating Agencies: Their Business, Regulation and Liability*, (Bloomington, IN: Unlimited Publishing LLC, 2007), pp. 35-36.

[37] *Dura Pharmaceuticals, Inc. v. Broudo* , 544 U.S. 336 (2005).

[38] Von Schweinitz, op. cit., pp. 67-97.

[39] Andrew Ross Sorkin, Too Big To Fail: Inside the Battle to Save Wall Street, (London, Allen Lane, 2009), pp. 236-237.

[40] Association of Financial Guaranty Insurers, *Our Claims-Paying Ability*, in www.afgi.org/who-fact.htm.

[41] James P. McNichols, *Monoline Insurance & Financial Guaranty Reserving*, in www.casact.org/pubs/forum/03fforum/03ff231.pdf.

[42] Dan Dorfman, *Liars' Loans Could Make Many Moan*, The New York Sun, Dec. 20, 2006.

CHAPTER SEVENTEEN

The End of the Dollar System?

'Behold, there come seven years of great plenty throughout all the land of Egypt: and there shall arise after them seven years of famine; and all the plenty shall be forgotten in the land of Egypt; and the famine shall consume the land'
  – Book of Genesis, 41:28-30

A little bank makes a big splash

The multi-trillion dollar US-centered securitization debacle began to unravel in June 2007 with the liquidity crisis in two hedge funds owned by the New York investment bank, Bear Stearns. One of the world's largest and most successful investment banks, it was also reportedly the bank used by the Bush family to handle a share of their vast wealth.

The world financial system crisis and depression first emerged around the small IKB bank in Germany in summer 2007 when their sizeable US sub-prime mortgage assets were revealed.

The two hedge funds were heavily invested in subprime mortgage securities. The damage soon spread across the Atlantic to a small German state-owned bank, IKB. In July 2007, IKB's wholly-owned funding conduit or subsidiary, Rhineland Funding, had approximately $24 billion in Asset Backed Commercial Paper (ABCP). In mid-July, investors refused to accept Rhineland Funding's ABCP. That triggered a global panic in the entire market for Asset Backed Securities as news spread like wildfire that IKB was insolvent. The panic forced the European Central Bank to inject record volumes of liquidity into the market to keep the banking system liquid.

Rhineland Funding asked IKB to provide a credit line. In turned out that IKB didn't have enough cash or liquid assets to meet the request, and was saved only by an emergency $10 billion credit from its state-owned major shareholder bank, the Kreditanstalt für Wiederaufbau (KfW). Ironically this was the same bank that had led the Marshall Plan reconstruction of war-torn Germany in the late 1940s. It was soon to become evident to the world that a new Marshall Plan, or some financial equivalent, was urgently needed, this time for the United States economy.

The intervention of KfW, rather than stopping the panic, led to widespread bank reserve hoarding and to a run on all commercial paper issued by international banks' off-books Structured Investment Vehicles (SIVs).

Asset Backed Commercial Paper was another one of the big products of the asset securitization revolution, described earlier, that had been fostered by Greenspan and Wall Street. They had been created to get risks off the balance sheets of the banks while at the same time allowing the banks to book handsome profits from the SIV gains. It was another example of having your cake and eating it too, only in the end it didn't function as Wall Street had planned.

A bank's SIV would typically issue Commercial Paper securities backed by a flow of payments from the cash collections received from the SIV's underlying asset portfolio. ABCP was short-term debt, generally no more than 270 days. Crucially, however, it was exempt from the registration requirements of the US Securities Act of 1933. They were unregistered securities, a huge loophole in terms of transparency.

ABCPs were typically issued from pools of trade receivables, credit card receivables, auto and equipment loans and leases, or collateralized debt obligations. An issuer would collect perhaps hundreds or several thousand small individual car loans from local banks, buy them at a discount, create a new bond whose value was based on the estimated future monthly cash inflow of those car loans, or credit card loans or similar sources.

In the case of IKB in Germany, the cash flow was supposed to come from its portfolio of sub-prime US home mortgages, mortgage-backed Collateralized Debt Obligations (CDOs). It was more than questionable what a European bank dedicated to lending to medium size German industry was doing buying such dicey securities as ultra-high-risk US subprime mortgage securities.

The main risk faced by ABCP investors was what bankers call asset deterioration—that the individual loans making up the security, whether home mortgage loans or car loans or whatever, would go into default—which is precisely what began to rumble through the US home mortgage markets during the summer of 2007.

The problem with CDOs was that once issued, they were rarely traded. They were new and no one had yet tested them in a distress sale. Their value, rather than being market-driven, was based on complicated theoretical models.

When CDO holders around the world in August 2007 suddenly and urgently needed liquidity to face the market sell-off, they found that the market value of their CDOs was far below their book value. So, instead of generating liquidity by selling CDOs, they instead were forced to sell high-quality liquid blue chip stocks, government bonds, and precious metals to raise urgently needed cash to cover losses.

That meant the CDO crisis led to a collapse of value in both CDOs and stocks. The drop in the price of stocks spread to hedge funds. The possibility of a dramatic price collapse had not ever been factored into the theoretical models used by all the quantitative hedge funds, and it resulted in large losses in that part of the market, led by Bear Stearns' two in-house hedge funds. Major losses by leading hedge funds further fed increasing uncertainty and amplified the crisis.

That was the beginning of colossal collateral damage, a destruction of wealth without historical precedent. The banks' risk models all had manifestly broken down.

Lack of transparency was at the root of the crisis that had finally and inevitably erupted in mid-2007. The lack of transparency, as outlined earlier, was due to the fact that instead of spreading risk in a transparent way, as foreseen by accepted economic theory, market operators chose ways to 'securitize' risky assets by promoting high-yielding, high-risk assets, without clearly marking their risk. Additionally, credit-rating agencies turned a blind eye to the inherent risks of the products. They used the same flawed risk models to rate the securities. The fact that the bonds were rarely traded meant that even the approximate value of these financial products was not known. [1]

Ignoring lessons from LTCM

Among banks, confidence in the international inter-bank market -- the heart of a global banking system that relied on Asset Backed Commercial Paper -- collapsed in August 2007. And with that collapse, the banking system stared a systemic crisis in the face. The crisis now threatened a domino collapse of banks akin to what had happened in Europe in 1931, when French banks, for political reasons, had pulled the plug on the Austrian Creditanstalt. The Federal Reserve's New Finance was revealing itself to be but a colossal source of new instability.[2]

The world financial system had faced the threat of a systemic crisis as recently as the September 1998 collapse of the Long-Term Capital Management (LTCM) hedge fund in Greenwich, Connecticut. Only extraordinary, coordinated central bank intervention then, led by Greenspan's Federal Reserve, had prevented a global meltdown.

The LTCM crisis contained the seed crystal of all that was going wrong with the multi-trillion dollar asset securitization markets, and that, a mere decade later. Curiously, Greenspan and others in positions of responsibility systematically refused to take those LTCM lessons seriously.

One source of the awe over LTCM before it's colossal collapse in 1998 was the 'dream team' who ran it. The fund's CEO and founder was John Meriwether, a legendary Wall Street trader who had left Salomon Brothers following a scandal over purchase of US Treasury bonds. The scandal hadn't dented his confidence. Asked whether he believed in efficient markets, he once modestly replied, "I *MAKE* them efficient."

The LTCM hedge fund's principal shareholders included the two eminent experts in the 'science' of risk, Myron Scholes and Robert Merton. The Swedish Academy of Sciences had awarded the 1997 Nobel Prize for economics to Scholes and Merton for their work on derivatives. Myron Scholes and his colleague Fisher Black had developed the original options pricing theories in 1973, the Black-Scholes model, mentioned in the previous chapter that laid the basis for the multi-trillion dollar derivatives explosion twenty years later. LTCM also had on board a dazzling array of professors of finance, doctors of mathematics and physics and other "rocket scientists" capable of inventing extremely complex, daring and profitable financial schemes.

Black-Scholes—Fundamental flaws in risk models

There was only one flaw. Scholes' and Merton's fundamental axioms of risk, the assumptions on which all their models were built, were simply wrong. They had been built not just on sand, but on quicksand. They were profoundly and catastrophically wrong.

Their mathematical options pricing model assumed that there were 'perfect markets,' markets so extremely large or deep that individual traders' actions could not affect prices. They assumed that markets and players were also rational. Reality suggested the opposite—markets were fundamentally irrational in the long-term. But the risk pricing models of Black-Scholes and others over the previous two or more decades had allowed banks and financial institutions to argue that traditional lending prudence was old fashioned. With suitable options as a kind of insurance, risk was no longer a worry. Or so Wall Street believed. Eat, drink and be merry, and collect your million dollar bonuses....

The assumptions of the risk models developed by Black, Scholes and Merton, however, ignored actual market conditions as prevailed in every major market panic since the Black-Scholes model had been introduced in 1973 on the Chicago Board Options Exchange. They ignored the fundamental role of options and 'portfolio insurance' in the Crash of 1987; they ignored the causes of the panic that in 1998 brought down Long Term Capital Management – the firm where Scholes and Merton were both partners. Wall Street, along with the economists and governors in the Federal Reserve, most especially Alan Greenspan, blissfully ignored the obvious.

Financial markets, contrary to the religious dogma that had been taught at every US and UK business school for decades, were not smooth, well-behaved entities following the Gaussian Bell-shaped Curve as if it were a fundamental law of the universe. The fact that the main architects of modern theories of financial engineering—now given the serious-sounding name 'financial economics'—had all been awarded Nobel prizes, surrounded the flawed models with the aura of Papal infallibility.

Only three years after the 1987 crash, a crash which had been driven by derivatives and the flawed risk models, the Nobel Committee in Sweden gave Harry Markowitz and Merton Miller the prize for advancing the same flawed risk notions. In 1997, amid the Asian financial crisis, where derivatives had played a central role, it gave the Nobel award to Robert Merton and Myron Scholes. [3]

The most remarkable aspect of the flawed risk models in use since the origins of financial derivatives in the 1980s and throughout the explosive growth of asset securitization twenty years later, was how rarely the risk models themselves were questioned.

The traders at LTCM, and all those who followed them to the edge of the financial abyss in August 1998, did not have a hedge against the one thing they now confronted—systemic risk. Systemic risk was precisely what they confronted when an 'impossible event,' the Russian state default, proved possible.

Despite the clear lessons from the harrowing LTCM debacle—that there was and is no derivative an investor or speculator can buy that insures against systemic risk—Greenspan, Robert Rubin and the New York banks continued to rely on their flawed risk models as if nothing had taken place. The Russian sovereign default was dismissed as a "once in a Century event."

The Wall Street bankers were moving forward to build the Dot.com bubble and, in its aftermath, the greatest financial bubble in human history—the asset securitization bubble of 2002-2007. The Wall Street strategy was to move risk off the banks' balance sheets through derivatives and other instruments such as securitization. Then by selling these novel securities to the rest of the world, they clearly saw a way to build their money power over the rest of the world almost without limit. Wall Street banks became literally intoxicated with their own hype and their own flawed risk models. They regarded themselves as literally the "Gods of money."

Life is no Bell Curve

Risk and its pricing however did not behave like a bell-shaped curve, not in financial markets any more than in oilfield exploitation. In 1900, an obscure French mathematician and financial speculator, Louis Bachelier, had argued that price changes in bonds or stocks followed the bell-shaped curve that the German mathematician, Carl Friedrich Gauss, had devised as an idealized working model to map statistical probabilities for various events. Bell curves assumed a 'mild' form of randomness in price fluctuations, just as the standard I.Q. test, by design, defines 100 as 'average,' the center of the bell. It was a kind of useful alchemy, but alchemy nonetheless.

The assumption that financial price variations behaved fundamentally like the bell curve allowed Wall Street's 'rocket scientists' to roll out an unending stream of new financial products, each more arcane and complex than its predecessor. 'Rocket scientist' was the name given by Wall Street to the math geeks and physicists they were hiring to figure out complex new financial angles to make a bundle on financial derivatives. With America's industrial base long in terminal decline, the nation's most talented scientific minds were being pulled into Wall Street.

The 'Law of Large Numbers' was added to the cocktail of risk models, to argue that when the number of events became sufficiently large, like flips of a coin or rolls of dice, the value converged on a stable value over the long term. The 'Law of Large Numbers,' which in reality was no scientific law at all, allowed banks like Citigroup or Chase to issue hundreds of millions of Visa cards without so much as a credit check, based on data showing that in 'normal' times, defaults on credit cards were so rare as not to be worth considering.[4]

The problem with models based on bell curve distributions or laws of large numbers arose when times were not normal -- such as a steep economic recession of the sort the United States economy went into after 2007, comparable perhaps only to that of 1931-1939. Even worse, the risk models in play actually led to the creation of the asset bubble that collapsed with a thud in August 2007.

The remarkable thing was that America's academic economists and Wall Street investment bankers, Federal Reserve governors, Treasury secretaries, Sweden's Nobel Economics Prize judges, England's Chancellors of the Exchequer, her High Street bankers, her Court of the Bank of England, to name just the leading icons -- all were willing to turn a blind eye to the fact that no economic theories, no theories of market behavior, no theories of derivative risk pricing, were capable of predicting, let alone preventing, non-linear surprises. [5]

The theory on which trillions of dollars of worldwide credit obligations ultimately rested was incapable of predicting the ultimate burst of speculative bubbles -- not in October 1987, not in February 1994, in March 2002, and most emphatically not since June 2007. It couldn't because the very model used had created the conditions that led to the ever larger and more destructive bubbles in the first place. Financial Economics was but another word for unbridled speculative excess, a process that inevitably would create bubbles, followed by collapsing of bubbles.

Nobel prizes notwithstanding, a theory incapable of explaining such major, defining, 'non-linear' surprise events was not worth the paper it was written on. Yet the US Federal Reserve Governors and Treasury Secretaries—from Alan Greenspan to Ben Bernanke, and US Treasury secretaries Robert Rubin, Larry Summers, Henry Paulsen and Tim Geithner—prevailed to make sure that Congress never lay a legislative or regulatory hand on the exotic financial instruments that were being created, instruments that had been created based on a theory that contradicted reality.

On September 29, 1998, Reuters reported,

> *Any attempts to regulate derivatives, even after the collapse—and rescue—of LTCM, have not met with success. The CFTC [the government agency with nominal oversight over derivatives trading-w.e.] was barred from expanding its regulation of derivatives under language approved late on Monday by the US House and Senate negotiators. Earlier this month the Republican chairmen of the House and Senate Agriculture Committees asked for the language to limit the CFTC's regulatory authority over over-the-counter derivatives echoing industry concerns.*

"Industry," of course, meant the big banks. Reuters added that,

> *When the initial subject of regulation was broached by the CFTC both Fed chairman, Alan Greenspan, and Treasury Secretary Rubin leapt to the defense of the industry claiming that the industry did not need regulation and that to do so would drive business overseas.[6]*

Relentless refusal to allow regulatory oversight of the explosive new financial instruments -- from Credit Default Swaps to Mortgage Backed Securities, and the myriad of similar exotic 'risk-diffusing' financial innovations – that had begun with the 1999 repeal of the Glass-Steagall Act strictly separating securities dealing banks from commercial lending banks, opened the gates in June 2007 to the second Great Depression in less than a century. It began what future historians will no doubt describe as the final demise of the United States as the world's dominant financial power.

Fraud à la Carte

The lessons of the 1998 LTCM systemic crisis were forgotten within weeks by the major players of the New York financial establishment. They reckoned clearly that they would be bailed out by the Government, more accurately, the taxpayer when the next crisis broke. Why change things...

When Glass-Steagall was finally repealed in late 1999, banks were free to snatch up rivals across the spectrum from insurance companies to consumer credit or finance houses. The landscape of American banking underwent a drastic change. The asset securitization revolution was ready to be launched.

With Glass-Steagall gone, the only banks directly monitored by the Federal Reserve were bank holding companies and subsidiary pure lending banks. If Citigroup opted to close its government regulated Citibank branch in a subprime neighborhood and instead have a new privately-owned non-regulated subsidiary like CitiFinancial, which specialized in subprime lending, work the area, CitiFinancial could operate under entirely different and lax regulation.

CitiFinancial could then issue mortgages separately from Citibank. And this is precisely what happened. Consumer groups accused CitiFinancial of specializing in 'predator loans' in which unscrupulous mortgage brokers or salesmen would push a loan on a family or person far beyond his comprehension or capacity to handle the risks, let alone the payments. And Citigroup was typical of most big US banks and mortgage lenders.

On January 8, 2008 Citigroup announced with great fanfare publication of its consolidated "US residential mortgage business," including mortgage origination, servicing and securitization. Curiously, the policy statement omitted CitiFinancial, precisely the subsidiary with the most risk on its books. [7]

Liars' loans, NINA and an orgy of bank fraud

It didn't take long before lending banks across the United States realized they were sitting on a bonanza bigger than the California gold rush. With no worry about whether a borrower of a home mortgage, say, would be able to service the debt for the next decades, banks realized they could make money on pure loan volume and loan resale to securitizers.

Soon it became commonplace for banks to outsource their mortgage lending to free-lance brokers. Instead of doing their own credit checks, the brokers relied, often exclusively, on various online credit questionnaires, similar to Visa card applications, where no follow-up was done. It became common practice for mortgage lenders to offer brokers bonus incentives to bring in more signed mortgage loan volume, another opportunity for massive fraud. The banks got more profit from making high volumes of loans, and then selling them on to Wall Street for securitization. The world of traditional banking was being turned on its head.

As a bank no longer had an incentive to assure the solidity of a borrower through minimum cash down payments and exhaustive background credit checks, many US banks, simply to churn loan volume and boost returns, gave out what they cynically called 'Liars' Loans.' They knew the person was lying about his credit and income to get that dream home. They simply didn't care. They sold the risk once the ink was dry on the mortgage.

A new terminology arose after 2002 for such loans, such as 'NINA' mortgages—No Income, No Assets. "No problem, Mr. Jones. Here's $400,000 for your new home. Enjoy."

With Glass-Steagall no longer an obstacle, banks could set up various separate entities to process the booming home mortgage business. The giant of the game was Citigroup, the largest US bank group, which had become a behemoth after repeal of Glass-Steagall, with assets totaling over $2.4 trillions (sic), an amount larger than the annual Gross Domestic Product of all but six nations of the world.

Citigroup included Travelers Insurance, a state-regulated but not nationally regulated insurer. It included the old Citibank, a huge retail lending bank. It included the Wall Street investment bank, Smith Barney. And it included the aggressive sub-prime lender, CitiFinancial, according to numerous consumer reports, one of the most aggressive predatory lenders pushing sub-prime mortgages on uninformed, ignorant or insolvent borrowers, often in poor black or Hispanic neighborhoods. [8] It included the Universal Financial Corp. one of the nation's largest credit card issuers, who used the so-called 'Law of Large Numbers' to grow its customer base among more and more dodgy credit risks.

Citigroup also included Banamex, Mexico's second largest bank and Banco Cuscatlan, El Salvador's largest bank. Banamex was one of the major banks in Mexico indicted for drug money laundering. That was nothing foreign to Citigroup. In 1999 the US Congress and GAO investigated Citigroup for illicitly laundering $100 million in drug money for Raul Salinas, brother of then-President of Mexico. The investigations also discovered that the bank had laundered money for corrupt officials from Pakistan to Gabon to Nigeria.

Citigroup, the financial behemoth, was typical of what happened to American banking after 1999. It was a different world entirely from anything that had existed before, with the possible exception of the excesses of the Roaring '20s. The degree of lending fraud and abuse that ensued in the new era of asset securitization was staggering to the imagination.

The Predators have a Ball

One US consumer organization opposing predatory lending by the banks documented some of the most common predatory lending practices during the real estate boom:

In the United States in the first decade of the 21st century there are
many storefronts offering such loans. Some are old -- Household Fi-
nance and its sister Beneficial, for example -- and some are newer-
fangled, like CitiFinancial. Both offer credit at rates over thirty per-
cent... Citibank pays under five percent interest on the deposits it
collects. Its affiliated loan sharks charge four times that rate, even
for loans secured by the borrower's home.

The business is global: the Hong Kong & Shanghai Banking Corpo-
ration, now HSBC, wants to export it to the eighty-plus countries in
which it has a retail presence....CitiFinancial and Household Fi-
nance both suggest to customers that insurance is needed. This they
serve in a number of flavors -- credit life and credit disability, credit
unemployment and property insurance -- but in almost all cases, it
is included in the loans and interest is charged on it... Midway you'll
be approached with a sweet-sounding offer: if you'll put up your
home as collateral, your rate can be lowered and the term be ex-
tended... The rate will be high and the rules not disclosed. For ex-
ample: if you satisfy the loan too quickly, you'll be charged a pre-
payment penalty. Or, you'll pay slowly and then be asked to pay
more, in what's called a balloon.

In prior centuries, this was called debt peonage. Today it is the fate
of the so-called sub-prime serf. Fully twenty percent of American
households are described as sub-prime. But half of the people who
get sub-prime loans could have paid normal rates, according to
Fannie Mae and Beltway authorities. Outside, it's the law of the
jungle; the only rule is Buyer Beware. [9]

In the 1980s, this author interviewed a senior Wall Street banker, at the time
recovering from career burnout. I asked about his bank's business in Cali,
Colombia where he worked during the heyday of the Cali cocaine cartel.
Speaking off the record, he related, "I was in Cali earlier. Men with sunglasses
literally walked into the bank with suitcases stuffed with 100 dollar bills. No
questions were asked. Banks would literally kill to get a slice of this business, it
was so lucrative." Those same banks moved on to sub-prime lending with
similar goals in mind, and with profits as huge as those of drug money laundering, according to government insiders.

And again, it was Alan Greenspan and the Federal Reserve who vigorously backed the extension of bank lending to the poorest ghetto residents, shamelessly pretending that this was some form of 'distributive justice.' Edward M. Gramlich, a Federal Reserve governor who died in September 2007, warned as early as 2001 when the real estate boom was in its early phase, that a fast-growing new breed of lenders was luring many people into risky mortgages they could not afford. When Gramlich privately urged Fed examiners to investigate mortgage lenders affiliated with national banks, he was rebuffed by Alan Greenspan. According to Fed insiders, Greenspan ruled the Fed with nearly the power of an absolute monarch. [10]

Revealing what was most certainly the tip of a gigantic iceberg of fraud, the FBI in January 2008 announced it was investigating 14 companies for possible accounting fraud, insider trading or other violations in connection with home loans made to risky borrowers. The FBI announced that the probe involved companies across the financial services industry, from mortgage lenders to investment banks that bundle home loans into securities sold to investors. Little more was heard of it.

At the same time, authorities in New York and Connecticut were investigating whether Wall Street banks had hidden crucial information about high-risk loans bundled into securities sold to investors. Connecticut Attorney General Richard Blumenthal said he and New York Attorney General Andrew Cuomo were investigating whether banks properly disclosed the high risk of default on so-called 'exception' loans — considered even riskier than subprime loans — when selling those securities to investors. In November 2007 Cuomo issued subpoenas to government-sponsored mortgage companies, Fannie Mae and Freddie Mac, in his investigation into what he claimed were conflicts of interest in the mortgage industry. He said he wanted to know about billions of dollars of home loans they had bought from banks, including the largest US savings and loan, Washington Mutual Inc., and how appraisals were handled.

The FBI said it was looking into the practices of subprime lenders, as well as potential accounting fraud committed by financial firms that hold these loans on their books or securitize them and sell them to other investors. Morgan Stanley, Goldman Sachs Group Inc. and Bear Stearns Cos. all disclosed in regulatory filings that they were cooperating with requests for information from various unspecified, regulatory and government agencies. [11]

One former real estate broker from the Pacific Northwest, who quit the business in disgust at the pressures on her to push mortgages on unqualified borrowers, described some of the more typical practices of predatory brokers in a memo to this author about the writing of Adjustable Rate Mortgages (ARMs):

The sub-prime fiasco is a nightmare alright. But the **prime** *ARMs hold potential for overwhelming disaster. The first 'hiccup' occurred in July/August 2007 - this was the 'Sub-prime Fiasco,' but in November 2007 the hiccup was more than that. It was in November 2007, that the prime ARMs adjusted upwards.*

What this means is that upon the 'anniversary date of the loan' the Adjustable Rate Mortgage adjusts up into a higher payment. This happens because the ARM was purchased at a 'teaser' rate, usually one or one and one half percent. Payments made at that rate, while very attractive, do nothing to reduce principal and even generate some unpaid interest which is tacked onto the loan. Borrowers are permitted to make the teaser rate payments for the entire first year, even though the rate is good only for the first month.

Concerns about 'negative amortization,' whereby the indebtedness on the loan becomes more than the market value of the property, were allayed by reference to the growth in property values due to the bank-created bubble, which it was said was normal and could be relied upon to continue. All that was promoted by the lenders who sent armies of account executives, i.e., salesmen, around to the mortgage brokers to explain how it would work.

Adjustable interest rates on home loans were the sum of the bank's profit - the margin - and some objective predictor of the cost of the borrowed funds to the bank, known as the index. Indexes generated by various economic activities - what the banks around the country were paying for 90 day Certificates of Deposit or what the banks in the London Interbank Exchange (LIBOR) were paying for dollars - were used. Adding the margin to the index produces the true interest rate on the loan - the rate at which, after 30 years of payments, the loan will be completely paid off ('amortized'). It is called the 'fully indexed rate.

I am going to pick an arbitrary 6% as the 'real' or inflation adjusted interest rate (3% margin + 3% inflation index). With a loan amount *of $250,000.00 the monthly payment at 1% would be $804.10; that is the 'teaser rate' payment, exclusive of taxes and insurance. This would adjust with changes in the index, but the margin remains static for the life of the loan.*

This loan is structured so that payment adjustments only occur once per year and are capped at 7.5 % of the previous year's <u>payment</u>. That can go on, stair stepping, for a period of 5 years (or 10 years in the case of one lender) without regard to what is happening in the real world. Then, at the end of the 5 years, the caps come off and everything adjusts to payments under the "fully indexed rate."

If the borrower has been making only the minimum required payments the whole time, this can result in a payment shock in the thousands. If the value of the home has decreased twenty-five percent, the borrower, this time someone with excellent credit, is encouraged to give it back to the bank, which devalues it at least another twenty-five percent and that spreads to the surrounding properties. [12]

According to a Chicago banking insider, during the first week of February 2008, bankers in the US were made aware of the following:

Chase Manhattan Bank ("CMB") has sent out an unlimited number of statements to its customers about Lines of Credit ("LOC's"). The terms of its LOC's, which, have been popular in the past, are now being manipulated and the values of the properties securing them are being unilaterally adjusted down, sometimes as much as 50 percent. This means homeowners are faced with making payments on a loan to buy an asset that is apparently worth half of the principal amount of the loan and paying interest on top of that. The only sensible thing to do in many cases is walk away, which results in a major loss in equity, reducing the value of all surrounding properties and adding to the avalanche of foreclosures.

This is especially aggravated in cases of "Creative Financing" LOCs - those that were drawn on equal to between ninety and one hundred percent of the value of the property before the bubble burst...

> *CMB has automatically closed credit lines that have "open" credit on them - meaning that the borrower left some money in the LOC for the future - over an80% ratio of the amount of the loan to the value ("LTV") of the property. This has been done on a mass basis without any reference to the"property owners."* [13]

"Loan to Value" limits mean that the amount of money that the lender is willing to loan cannot exceed the stated percentage of the property value. In common practice, an appraiser would be hired to assess the value of the property. The appraisal is informed by comparable sales of other properties which have sold in an area that, with a few exceptions, must be no more than one mile away from the subject property.

Those practices were merely the tip of the mortgage fraud bonanza that preceded the unfolding Tsunami.

The Tsunami was only beginning

The more home prices fell after the bubble burst in 2007, the more mortgages faced sharply higher interest rate resets, the more unemployment spread across America from Ohio to Michigan to California to Pennsylvania to Colorado and Florida. As more and more workers became unemployed or under-employed, the inevitable occurred: the dramatic increase in auto loan and credit card payment defaults. That process set off a vicious, self-feeding spiral of asset price deflation across America and in many parts of the world. By the early weeks of 2008 the process was just beginning to become ugly.

The subprime sector was merely the first manifestation of what was to unravel. The process would take years to wind down. The 'toxic waste' products, Asset Backed Securities, had been used as collateral for yet further bank loans, for leveraged buyouts by private equity firms, by corporations, even by municipalities. The vast pyramid of debt built on securitized assets began to go into reverse leverage as reality dawned in global markets that no one knew the worth of the securitized paper they held.

With shameless guile hiding their criminal negligence, trivializing its tragic impact on millions of Americans and others around the world, Standard & Poors, the second largest rating agency in the world, stated in October 2007 that they had "underestimated the extent of fraud in the US mortgage industry."

Alan Greenspan feebly tried to exonerate himself by claiming that lending to subprime borrowers was not wrong, that it was only the later securitization of the loans that had been the problem. The very system the bankers had labored to created over the preceding decades had been premised on fraud and non-transparency. They were clearly not naïve to that.

As hundreds of thousands of Americans over the coming months found their monthly mortgage payments dramatically reset according to their Adjustable Rate Mortgage terms, hundreds of billions of dollars in home mortgage debt went into default. That, in turn, led to a snowball effect in terms of job losses, credit card defaults and another wave of securitization crises in the huge market for securitized credit card debt.

The sinews of the entire American financial system were tied in to the colossal housing bubble and the related mortgage securitization debacle. There had never been a crisis of such magnitude in American history.

At the end of February 2008, the *Financial Times* of London revealed that US banks had 'quietly' borrowed $50 billion in funds from a special new Federal Reserve credit facility to ease their cash crisis. Losses at all the major banks -- from Citigroup to J.P. Morgan Chase to most other major US bank groups --- continued to mount as the economy sank deeper into a recession that clearly would turn into a genuine depression over the coming months.

During the 2008 Presidential campaign, neither candidate had dared utter a serious word about their proposals to deal with what was becoming the greatest financial and economic meltdown in American history.

The bizarre Lehman Bros. debacle

By early 2008 it had become clear that Financial Securitization was shaping up to become the Last Tango for the United States as the sole global financial superpower. Urgent measures were called for to save Wall Street's power, if it indeed could be saved.

In September 2008, amid growing panic within the Bush White House and, above all, in the office of Treasury Secretary Henry Paulson, the Administration made several decisions about which financial institutions to save and, most fatefully, which to let go bankrupt.

The large insurance company, AIG, whose founder, Hank Greenberg, had been accused several years before of gross fraud in manipulating the company's financial books, was given a US Government bailout of tens of billions of dollars. At the same time, the Government essentially nationalized the two huge privately owned national mortgage-underwriting companies, Fannie Mae and Freddie Mac. [14]

Then on September 15, 2008 a serious banking crisis in the US exploded into a global systemic financial crisis. Federal Reserve chairman Ben Bernanke met in closed-door session with New York Fed President Tim Geithner -- later to be Obama's Treasury Secretary -- and former Goldman Sachs CEO, Treasury Secretary Henry Paulson. They fatefully decided to let the fourth largest Wall Street investment bank, Lehman Bros., an institution with a history going back 153 years, go bankrupt.

Wall Street banker Henry Paulson, as Bush Treasury Secretary, funneled hundreds of billions of taxpayer dollars to his Wall Street cronies in 2008.

Financial markets from Tokyo to London and Frankfurt began to panic as they suddenly realized there was now no clear or at least consistent guideline indicating which US financial institutions were 'too big to fail.' No longer could any bank anywhere be confident that its counterparty in New York was solvent or, if not, that it would be supported by the US Government. A far smaller investment bank, Bear Stearns, had been rescued with Fed money a few months earlier. There was no clear logic. Yet that was precisely the intent of Paulson's decision.

Within hours, around the world, markets plunged as news about the decision on Lehman Bros. leaked out. What had been until then a major crisis in a smaller segment of the US subprime mortgage securitization market, at a scale of perhaps $800 billion, suddenly became a global systemic crisis in which banks questioned every asset they were asked to accept from other banks. A global crisis of confidence had erupted for the simple reason that, in the midst of a major crisis, the US Government and the private Federal Reserve had decided to deliberately let a major bank fail. Clearly, they did so with full knowledge of the consequences.

Within seconds of the announcement that Lehman Bros. would not be bailed out as Bear Stearns had been a few months earlier meant that suddenly US financial policy, the doctrine of Too Big To Fail, the insurance policy that world banks had relied on since the crises of the 1980s, no longer was a basis on which to calculate risk in dealing with other banks, especially American banks.

Had Henry Paulson at the Treasury and Geithner and Bernanke at the Fed decided instead to rescue Lehman Bros. and let Bear Stearns fail, perhaps the impact would have been significantly less. At least bankers around the world would have been assured that there was a consistent US Government bailout policy that financial institutions above a certain size were "too big to fail." Even former Goldman Sachs chairman, New Jersey Governor Jon Corzine came out and attacked his former Goldman partner, Paulson for being "inconsistent" and furthering the market panic by creating uncertainty. [15]

The only plausible explanation for the Lehman shock was that Wall Street and the US Treasury Secretary desperately needed an event to frighten Congress into giving Paulson a literal Carte Blanche or blank check to bail out his Wall Street cronies. September was two months from the 2008 elections, and Congress was in no mood to approve a politically explosive taxpayer bailout for the big banks that most people regarded as the cause of the crisis. The Lehman shock brought the financial world to the brink of global meltdown. It also concentrated the attention of Congress.

On September 23, Paulson announced an emergency bank bailout fund, the appropriately named TARP or Troubled Asset Relief Program. As the public later learned, with TARP the cover was also pulled over the banks; who got what was kept from the public by Paulson and by his Democratic successor Geithner.

In presenting the staggering bailout demand to Congress, Paulson and Bernanke said only that TARP would be $700 billion. They produced a hastily written 2-1/2 page draft of legislation with no mention of oversight or restrictions on the use of the money. At that point it was clear to the world that the US authorities had lost control. No bank dared trust any other international bank in such a climate. [16]

Then madness went into turbo-gear. TARP assumed the problem was that banks lacked 'liquidity.' TARP handed out hundreds of billions in taxpayer money to Citigroup, JP Morgan Chase, Goldman Sachs -- the very perpetrators of the gigantic Ponzi fraud of securitization in the first place.

By October 2008 the US Government moved to bailout troubled Citigroup, the world's largest bank and the most aggressive sub-prime lender.

The problem after September 2008, as former Under Secretary of Treasury John Taylor pointed out, was not interbank liquidity. It was lack of confidence among all major banks that their bank counterparty was solvent. No one knew, as Taylor put it, 'who is holding the Queen of Spades.'[17] Pumping hundreds of billions of taxpayer dollars into select banks was the wrong medicine for the wrong disease. But not for the Gods of Money.

The Citigroup Paradigm

Recipient banks like Citigroup loved TARP. Taxpayers were forced to pay the costs of the banks' unrestrained casino gambling. Vikram Pandit, Citigroup chief executive stated, "We completely remain in day-to-day charge of the company. We are going to run Citi for shareholders." The price of shareholders' stock at Citi was less than one dollar as he spoke. Citigroup had become a penny stock.

In effect Pandit said that the government's injection of capital would not change strategy, operations, or governance of Citigroup. 'Business as usual, boys.' However, prudence would have suggested his priority should have been to put the bank in a state in which it could operate without government support, and to reorganize its business so that such a disaster never again would happen. The interests of shareholders must be the last priority. That was the strict logic of risk in a real capitalist system. Wall Street preferred what some called 'bankers' socialism' instead: socialize the losses to the taxpayers and privatize the profits.

The Lehman Brothers bankruptcy spread panic around the world. Suddenly routine trade finance was frozen. In China, the world's primary exporter, companies were unable to obtain routine trade financing and factories began to close across the country. In the European Union, the European Central Bank turned on the liquidity spigot to try desperately to prevent wholesale bank failures.

In the UK, a bank panic had begun in early 2008 as Northern Rock, one of the country's largest mortgage banks, failed. It had a joint venture with Lehman Brothers in selling US sub-prime real estate securities in Britain. The bank had to be nationalized in a humiliating blow to the Labour Government of Gordon Brown. Brown had earlier been responsible for introducing bank-friendly legislation that deregulated banks like Northern Rock and opened the door to US-style casino banking.

What was to take place after the inauguration of a new US President, a President whose sole campaign slogan had been "for change," was soon clear to the world. It wasn't reassuring to those who expected real change.

Endnotes:

[1] UNCTAD Secretariat, *Recent developments on global financial markets: Note by the UNCTAD secretariat,*
TD/B/54/CRP.2, Geneva, 28 September 2007.
[2] For a treatment of the little-known political background to the 1931 Creditanstalt crisis that led to a domino collapse of German banks, see Engdahl, F. William, *A Century of War: Anglo-American Oil Politics and the New World Order* (London: Pluto Press, 2004), Chapter 6.

[3] John Oswin Schroy, *Fallacies of the Nobel Gods: Essay on Financial Economics and Nobel Laureates*, in http://www.capital-flow-analysis.com/investment-essays/nobel_gods.html.

[4] For a fascinating treatment of the fundamental theoretical flaws of economic and financial market models used today, and what he calls the high odds of catastrophic price changes, I recommend the book by Benoit Mandelbrot, the Yale mathematician and inventor of fractal geometry. Benoit Mandelbrot and Richard L. Hudson, *The (mis) Behavior of Markets: A Fractal View of Risk, Ruin and Reward*, (London: Profile Books Ltd, 2004).

[5] Donald MacKenzie, *An Engine, Not a Camera: How Financial Models Shape Markets* (Cambridge, MA: The MIT Press, 2008). MacKenzie documents the process by which the founder of the Chicago Mercantile Exchange hired University of Chicago economist, Milton Friedman to draft an argument for allowing trading of foreign exchange futures and options in the early 1970's and how the development of options pricing theory by Black and Scholes, after a time, gave Wall Street executives the certainty that their derivatives trading was based on 'real science.' It wasn't, of course, as the collapse of the securitization world in 2007 confirmed.

[6] Reuters, September 29, 1998.

[7] Cited by Inner City Press, *The Citigroup Watch*, January 28, 2008, accessed in www.innercitypress.org.citi.html.

[8] Rainforest Action Network, *Citigroup Becomes Mexico's Largest Bank after Banamex Merger*, August 10, 2001, in http://forests.org/archive/samerica/cibemexi.htm.

[9] Matthew Lee, *Predatory Lending: Toxic Credit in the Inner City*, 2003, InnerCityPress.org.

[10] Edmund L. Andrews, *Fed Shrugged as Sub-prime Crisis Spread*, The New York Times, Dec.18, 2007.

[11] Alan Zibel, *FBI Probes 14 Companies Over Home Loans*, AP, January 29, 2008.

[12] Private communication to the author from a former mortgage broker with a large US mortgage lender.

[13] Confidential email correspondence to the author.

[14] For a blow-by-blow description of the alleged discussions inside the US Government over the decision to bailout AIG and the role then New York Federal Reserve President, Tim Geithner, later Obama Treasury Secretary played, see Andrew Ross Sorkin, *Too Big To Fail*, (London, Allen Lane, 2009), pp. 234-237.

[15] Andrew Ross Sorkin, op. Cit., p. 470.

[16] Ibid., pp. 487-489.

[17] John B. Taylor, *The Financial Crisis and the Policy Responses: An Empirical Analysis of What Went Wrong*, November 2008, accessed in http://www.stanford.edu/~johntayl/FCPR.pdf.

CHAPTER EIGHTEEN

The Theft of a Nation

'Money is the root of all evil, money is the root of all evil, money is the root of all evil—take it away, take it away, take it away...'
  - The Andrews Sisters, 1945 Hit Parade song [1]

The 'Change' President

It didn't take long into the first year of Barack Obama's Presidency for people to grasp what candidate Obama had meant by his one-word campaign slogan, "change." The change was not in the direction of American economic or finance policy, nor was it change in the direction of American military policy or its overall foreign policy.

A closer look at Obama's choices for cabinet members and advisors made clear that the much heard mantra of change was not one of direction, as most of his supporters had naively hoped. Rather it was a change in intensity. If anything, Obama had revved up the policies of George W. Bush to a kind of 'Bush Mach II.'

In his choice of cabinet, President Obama made this fact clear. His national security team was the first tipoff. Robert Gates, a man who had been a close ally of the Bush family since he joined the CIA in 1966, was asked by President-elect Obama to remain as Defense Secretary. According to insiders, President George H.W. Bush had named Gates Director of the CIA in 1991 in order to help cover up Bush's involvement in the illegal Iran-Contra arms and drugs scandal. Gates became George W. Bush's Defense Secretary in 2006 when Don Rumsfeld left in a cloud of controversy. It was clear that as President, Obama intended to hold firmly to the Bush course in Pentagon policy.

Obama's National Security Adviser, General James Jones, had been Bush's NATO Commander in Europe during NATO's expansion towards Russia. The President's Director of National Intelligence, Admiral Dennis C. Blair, a career Navy man, had commanded US Forces in the Pacific under Bush. It was hardly a national security team that seemed likely to change the direction of the US as sole superpower, or to alter its focus on military might, even though no conceivable rival power was threatening America's security. Before the end of his first year as President, Obama had acted to increase the troop levels in Afghanistan by 30,000—even as he was accepting the Nobel Peace Prize.

Wall Street's greatest bank robbery... ever

The lack of real change was even clearer from Barack Obama's choices to head his financial and economic team. Here he named the very foxes that had opened the doors to the Wall Street banks a decade or so earlier, to guard the hen house.

Minutes after he was sworn in as President, Barack Obama made a dramatic about-face on his economic campaign promises and proceeded to name every key financial and economic post with either personal protégé's of either Citigroup vice chairman Robert Rubin or of Goldman Sachs to run his economic policy. Despite his clear victory with a mandate to make sweeping reforms of the bankrupt deregulated financial edifice, Obama proceeded with the most egregious Wall Street bailout in American history.

The President-elect on November 5, 2008 named his old Harvard Law School roommate and close friend, Michael Froman, then a high-ranking executive at Citigroup, to head Obama's Economic Transition Team—the group that would select all key cabinet posts dealing with banking and the economy. Froman had introduced candidate Obama to Citigroup Vice Chairman Rubin, former Clinton Treasury Secretary and former chairman of Goldman Sachs and mentor of every key Froman choice for the Obama Administration. [2]

The naming of Tim Geithner as Treasury Secretary and of Larry Summers as White House Director of the National Economic Council, a sort of Economy 'czar,' spoke volumes about whose piper Obama would be as President and who would name the tune. Wall Street was firmly in command, just as it had been for the previous century and more.

In 1999 and 2000 Summers, who had succeeded his former boss Robert Rubin as Secretary of the Treasury under President Clinton, and Tim Geithner, as his Assistant Secretary, drafted and pushed through Congress two fatal acts that would unleash the speculative frenzy of the Wall Street financial titans. They were the repeal of the Glass-Steagall Act of 1933 and the Commodity Futures Modernization Act of 2000, which allowed financial derivatives such as Credit Default Swaps to trade privately, "Over-The-Counter (OTC)" as it was termed, entirely free from government regulatory oversight.

Geithner came to Washington from his post as President of the powerful New York Federal Reserve, where he had played a decisive role in the decisions, along with Bernanke and Treasury Secretary Henry Paulson, to bail out AIG and to let Lehman Brothers go down. Geithner was Wall Street's man from his head to his toes.

The causes of the US-centered financial catastrophe that began in summer of 2007 had many deeply rooted components, as outlined in this book. The immediate causes stemmed from the deadly combination of deregulated financial structures, collusion in flawed risk models by the major credit rating agencies, and lax lending oversight by banks issuing mortgages.

Overseeing these policies were four successive US Presidents -- from Ronald Reagan to George H.W. Bush, to Bill Clinton, and to George W. Bush – all determined to enable the speculative debt binge destruction of the American economy by encouraging financial deregulation. The result was a drastic redistribution of wealth and power in the American population, enhanced by selective tax cuts for the wealthiest and tax hikes, direct and indirect, for the over-indebted American consumer – which in effect poured water on the drowning American public.

Wall Street investment banks -- such as Morgan Stanley, Goldman Sachs, Merrill Lynch, and Lehman Brothers – introduced securitization, a process supported by the authority that should have been restraining it, the Federal Reserve. This process led to the creation of the new instruments of fraud and deception—Asset Backed Securities. Banks issued 'liar's loans' and other easy credit to their customers, often misleading them as to ultimate risk. Banks behaved as if convinced that a new system existed which no longer placed a premium on conservative risk control.

Following the Asia Crisis of 1997-1998, a crisis that had been covertly and overtly ignited by the same Wall Street banks in order to draw Asian capital into the United States, the flood of money from Asia -- above all from China -- into US semi-public real estate giants Fannie Mae and Freddie Mac, gave securitization a turbo charge. The securitization of ordinary and even high-risk US home mortgages into new securities -- or Mortgage-Backed Securities that were then deceptively given the highest quality rating, AAA, by the major rating agencies, had seduced investors from Europe and Asia to plunge into the new American securities without examining the premises of that AAA credit rating.

The securitization structure had been created and designed to do just exactly what it did, with or without Asian liquidity. It was designed to fraudulently enrich those financial institutions that were at the heart of the American colossus -- Wall Street and their closest allies.

Ever since the first financial market 'rescue' by Alan Greenspan back in October 1987, the major market players had felt certain that should any crisis erupt as a consequence of their risky lending or financial dealings, the authorities would step in to save the day. The idea was put forward, and institutionalized, that some banks were 'Too Big to Fail.' It was the TBTF doctrine.

Too Big to Save?

A small handful of very big banks had grown so huge that they were deemed Too Big To Fail, thanks mainly to the deliberate Government policy of financial deregulation, most notably the 1999 repeal of the Glass-Steagall Act, engineered under Clinton by Summers and Geithner. That 1933 law, as was discussed, had restricted mergers among Wall Street investment firms -- commercial banks like Citibank or Bank of America -- and insurance companies. Indeed, by December 2008, despite their losses in the financial crisis to date, the assets of the four largest US banks exceeded the Gross Domestic Product of most countries in the world. They had indeed become the 'Gods of Money,' so large and so powerful that entire governments bowed down to their demands, worshipping at the alter of Wall Street.

The Bank of America, the largest, had a staggering $2.5 trillion in assets. It was followed by JP Morgan Chase at $2.2 trillion; Citigroup at $1.9 trillion and Wells Fargo at $1.3 trillion.[3] The four US mega-banks combined had a nominal asset value of almost $8 trillion. The four banks and perhaps another three to four major Wall Street investment banks -- as well as one giant insurance company turned gambling casino, AIG -- were at the eye of the storm of the global financial tsunami that exploded onto the scene at the beginning of the summer of 2007.

The power of money had concentrated into a very few hands. And those few hands were at the heart of subprime and other mortgage swindles and fraudulent Ponzi schemes that brought the world's greatest economy to its knees by 2009.

The key that allowed the unleashing of the tsunami was the extreme concentration of high risk in a small handful of US banks. As of June 2008, four US banks held the overwhelming majority of all contracts for complex financial derivatives. Among the fastest growing of the derivatives contracts were the Credit Default Swaps which were described by one banker as "similar to a man who goes and buys fire insurance, but on his neighbor's not his own house."[4] The temptations to abuse were awesome.

By far the largest derivatives bank was JP Morgan Chase with $91 trillion in notional or nominal derivatives exposure. Bank of America followed with $40 trillion; Citibank was close behind at $37 trillion, and the merged Wells Fargo-Wachovia after October 2008 held a combined $5.5 trillions. After those largest five banks, the derivatives holdings of the remaining US banks dropped dramatically lower. Derivatives risk was clearly a game of the biggest players and it had been dangerously concentrated in fewer than half a dozen institutions. [5] A failure of any one would unleash a global systemic crisis of unheard-of dimensions.

In the riskiest derivatives segment, the totally unregulated market for Credit Default Swaps (CDS) -- a market that, as noted, had been invented by JP Morgan Chase -- the four named US banks plus HSBC Bank USA, a subsidiary of Britain's largest bank, accounted for a staggering 95% of all trading by US banks in the complex CDS derivatives. Those five banks later refused to say how much of the AIG bailout money flowed to them to make good on those contracts. AIG's London office had served as a virtually unregulated insurance vehicle enabling the giant banks to make their huge bets. When the entire edifice came crumbling down after August 2007, the fraudulent schemes of AIG came down with it. [6]

Even more alarming, the concentration of risks in those five enormous banks was structured such that as the US and world economy fell deeper into recession, or even depression as in the case of the United States, future bank derivatives losses would explode exponentially. As of January 1, 2009, those five US banks reported a 'worst case' estimate of possible loss amounting to another $587 billion because of their derivatives exposures. Their estimated losses had ballooned by an alarming 49% since the September decision by the Government to let Lehman Brothers fail.[7]

One knowledgeable bank risk analyst called the situation a 'ticking time bomb' that was pre-programmed to get worse as the US economic crisis worsened.[8]

That was the hidden ugly secret that no one wanted to make public. Wall Street's giant banks, the new 21st Century version of the Money Trust -- based on exotic new derivative instruments -- went to extraordinary lengths to hide the real cause of the financial system losses – the bankers' own fraudulent schemes -- and to panic American taxpayers into covering the banks' losses. And the giant banks were aided and abetted every step of the way by their friends in the Federal Reserve and the US Treasury, and in the White House.

The losses had been entirely predictable. They resulted from a deregulated banking and financial system that had been carefully and deliberately put in place, step-by-step, by the banks' owners. It was a system of laissez faire finance, created through intensive lobbying by the Money Trust banks over the years. Wall Street banks and their satellite institutions in the related US financial sector had spent the impressive sum of at least $5 billion from 1998 through 2008, essentially buying the votes of the US Congress through campaign contributions and 'lobbying' expenses.

A former US bank regulator during the Savings & Loan crisis of the 1980s, William Black, described the transformation of the United States over a period of decades into a *de facto* financial oligarchy, where rights were increasingly equated with a person's wealth:

> *Forty years ago, our real economy grew better with a financial sector that received one-twentieth as large a percentage of total profits (2%) than does the current financial sector (40%). The minimum measure of how much damage the bloated, grossly overcompensated finance sector causes to the real economy is this massive increase in the share of total national income wasted through the finance sector's parasitism.*
>
> *Second, the finance sector is worse than parasitic.... The financial sector functions as the sharp canines that the predator state uses to rend the nation. In addition to siphoning off capital for its own benefit, the finance sector misallocates the remaining capital in ways that harm the real economy in order to reward already-rich financial elites harming the nation.... Corporate stock repurchases and grants of stock to officers have exceeded new capital raised by the US capital markets this decade. That means that the capital markets decapitalize the real economy. Too often, they do so in order to enrich corrupt corporate insiders through accounting fraud or backdated stock options.... The US real economy suffers from critical shortages of employees with strong mathematical, engineering, and scientific backgrounds. Graduates in these three fields all too frequently choose careers in finance rather than the real economy because the financial sector provides far greater executive compensation.... The financial sector's fixation on accounting earnings leads it to pressure US manufacturing and service firms to export jobs abroad, to deny capital to firms that are unionized, and to encourage firms to use foreign tax havens to evade paying US taxes.*

Black concluded the study of the effects of the concentration of power into the hands of finance noting that the system by its very nature must create ever newer and ever larger financial bubbles that inevitably burst:

> *Instead of flowing to the places where it will be most useful to the real economy, capital gets directed to the investments that create the greatest fraudulent accounting gains. The financial sector is particularly prone to providing exceptional amounts of funds to what I call accounting "control frauds". Control frauds are seemingly-legitimate entities used by the people that control them as a fraud "weapon"... Accounting control frauds are so attractive to lenders and investors because they produce record, guaranteed short-term accounting 'profits.' They optimize by growing rapidly like other Ponzi schemes, making loans to borrowers unlikely to be able to re-pay them (once the bubble bursts), and engaging in extreme leverage. Unless there is effective regulation and prosecution, this misallocation creates an epidemic of accounting control fraud that hyper-inflates financial bubbles.*[9]

Black's diagnosis of the destructive and self-feeding concentration of power into finance and into Wall Street -- most notably since the abandonment of the strictures of a dollar gold standard in August 1971 -- was tragically all too accurate.

Champagne for the Bankers; toxic waste for the Public

While Wall Street bankers from Goldman Sachs to Citigroup reveled in their government bailouts, continuing their business as usual and paying out lavish bonuses to their people, the rest of the nation -- including for the first time since the 1930s, large portions of the middle-income strata -- faced the grim reality of what was clearly becoming an economic depression, something that was 'not supposed to happen again.' But it was happening.

The ensuing economic depression in the United States was not difficult to understand. American families had been seduced by their bankers into a decade-long debt pile-up unlike any the world had ever witnessed.

It seemed to many that banks had so much money, they were practically giving it away. Tens of millions of Americans had been lured into buying one or even several homes as the bubble inflated after 2002, fully convinced that prices would rise forever. The Federal Reserve had encouraged them, after all, and the Congress of the United States was passing law after law to fuel the bonanza of speculation.

Once the bubble burst with the crisis at the small German IKB bank in August 2007, the entire domino chain of speculation and debt began to implode. Home prices, instead of rising as they had for several years, suddenly began to reverse in late 2007. Interest rates, so-called 'teaser rates' that lured homebuyers with deceptively low initial interest rates a few years earlier, began, as per contract, to 'reset' to market rates in late 2007 for the most risky mortgages, the so-called subprime mortgages.

As home prices declined, borrowers with adjustable-rate mortgages could not refinance to avoid the higher payments associated with rising interest rates. They began to default. During 2007, lenders began foreclosure proceedings on nearly 1.3 million properties, a 79% increase over 2006. That increased to 2.3 million in 2008, an 81% increase over 2007. By August 2008, 9.2% of all US mortgages outstanding were either delinquent or in foreclosure. By September 2009, the number of home mortgages either in foreclosure process or one payment behind had risen to 14.4%, an historical record not seen since the statistics were begun in 1972. [10]

Homeowners, facing huge increases in monthly mortgage payments, began to fall behind or to cease paying altogether. Banks repossessed homes in a process that had been made easier by Bush Administration actions to defend the banks rather than the victim home-owners.

One elected official, New York Governor Elliott Spitzer, an ambitious politician who had made his career in the Democratic Party as an ardent foe of Wall Street, and in particular of Hank Greenberg's AIG, sounded the alarm. When he warned about the devious moves of the Bush White House to feed the mortgage fraud and to rob states of Depression-era protections of homeowners from dispossession by banks, Spitzer became the victim of an FBI sting operation that forced him to resign.

Spitzer had testified before the US House of Representatives Financial Services subcommittee on the problems in New York-based specialized insurance companies, the "monoline" insurers. In his statements to Congress, he laid the blame for the financial crisis directly on the actions of the Bush Administration. A few days later, the *New York Times*, reportedly acting on a confidential Justice Department tip, revealed Governor Spitzer's tryst with an expensive prostitute in a Washington hotel.

In a national TV interview the same day, Spitzer had pointed out that several years earlier the US Office of the Comptroller of the Currency had gone to court and blocked New York State efforts to investigate the mortgage activities of national banks. Spitzer argued that the OCC had not put a stop to questionable loan marketing practices or upheld higher underwriting standards. "This could have been avoided if the OCC had done its job," Spitzer said in the interview. "The OCC did nothing. The Bush Administration let the housing bubble inflate and now that it's deflating we're dealing with the consequences." [11]

America's real economy deflates

Like all speculation bubbles or Ponzi schemes throughout history, once confidence in the process collapsed, the bubble burst in all directions. As Americans began losing their new homes in serious numbers, the housing construction boom also ground to a halt. Real estate had become the employer of last resort after the collapse of the IT bubble in the early decade. Millions of high-paid construction and white-collar real estate-related jobs vanished overnight. That led to a second wave of bankruptcies of small businesses that drove unemployment levels according to reliable private and unofficial estimates to above 22% of the available work force, a level reminiscent of the depths of the Great Depression. [12]

Officially, through ever-more drastic statistical revisions and manipulations of data, the Obama White House tried to downplay the reality, claiming an unemployment level of 10% by October 2009, alarming enough, but less than half as bad as the reality. Hourly wage earners who were lucky enough to still hold on to their jobs found their work hours drastically curtailed. The average hours per workweek declined to 33, the lowest level since the government began collecting the data in 1964, and hourly pay fell as well.[13] Many salaried employees found their work loads doubled as colleagues were laid off.

Because the bubble of American consumer spending had been built on a pyramid of debt, as the pyramid imploded and debts went unpaid, the entire credit system began to collapse. Banks refused to lend, even to other established banks, fearing the unknown. The American economy had entered into its own version of a Third World debt trap.

Every remedy, whether using taxpayer dollars to bailout the largest Wall Street banks, or pumping billions more of taxpayer dollars into trying to save the Detroit auto industry, only made the overall problem that much worse. As private consumers drastically cut back debt purchases—homes, cars and credit cards—the US Government exploded its public debt ledger.

The Brookings Institution reported in June 2009 that US consumption had comprised an astonishing one third of the growth in the entire global consumption between 2000 and 2007. That US consumption had been financed increasingly by debt. "The US economy has been spending too much and borrowing too much for years and the rest of the world depended on the US consumer as a source of global demand," they noted. As the US economy went into free-fall at the end of 2008, the rest of the world felt the seismic shocks. On an annual basis GDP fell by double-digits across the world from Mexico to Germany to Latvia to Great Britain to Japan and beyond. [14]

By March 2009, the Arab world had lost an estimated $3 trillion due to the crisis and the shrinking economy growth; unemployment in the Arab world was described as a 'time bomb,' as record high oil prices plunged in late 2008. Countries from Russia and Ukraine to China suffered sharp economic declines after September 2008 and the Lehman Brothers collapse crisis. [15]

Yet by all measures, the heart of the financial storm was located inside the United States economy and its banking system. The world's sole Superpower was sinking in a mire of debt and default, official and private corruption, unemployment and economic decline unlike anything it, or the world, had seen even in the 1930s.

In November 2009, White House Budget director Peter Orzag announced grim numbers. As the United States Government finished the Fiscal Year with a staggering deficit of $1.4 trillion, Orzag predicted that US Government deficits would likely add another $9 trillion to a national debt of $12 trillion over the following decade. He called the prospect, "serious and ultimately unsustainable."[16] Orszag was reporting vastly understated, cosmetic numbers. The reality was dramatically worse.

One critic of official Government economic data, John Williams, head of Shadow Government Statistics, noted in January 2009 that if one were to account for the annual change in the net present value of unfunded Social Security and Medicare liabilities, as a corporation would for its pension and healthcare liabilities for retirees, "the 2008 annual deficit was $5.1 trillion, versus $1.2 trillion in 2007."

By that measure, Williams continued, "total US Government obligations — gross federal debt outstanding plus the net present value of unfunded liabilities — at $66 trillion, was roughly 4.6 times the level of reported US GDP, and greater than total estimated global GDP. These numbers are unsustainable...and already are deteriorating severely for fiscal 2009." [17]

That exploding public debt burden in turn began to threaten international confidence in the value of the United States dollar and the entire dollar system edifice so painstakingly built up after the 1944 Bretton Woods talks, as China, Middle East oil producers, several Latin American states and Russia began to look seriously for alternatives to the US dollar.

An American Rome

A brief glance into the economic reasons for the fall of the Roman Empire some sixteen centuries earlier was instructive. The roots of the decline and ultimate collapse of the Roman Empire, in its day also the world's sole superpower, lay in the political decision by a ruling aristocracy, more accurately an oligarchy of wealth, to extend the bounds of empire through wars of conquest and plunder of foreign lands to feed their private wealth and personal power, not to the greater good of the state. The economic model of the Empire of Rome was based on the plunder of conquered territories. As the empire expanded, it installed remote military garrisons to maintain control and increasingly relied on foreign mercenaries to man those garrisons.

In the process of military expansionism the peasantry, the heart of the empire, became impoverished. They were forced to leave their farms, often for years to fight foreign wars of conquest. The south of Italy was devastated as one result. Those with money were able to buy land as the only stable investment, becoming huge latifundistas or landowners. [18]

That led to the concentration of land in a few hands, and the land in turn was worked by slaves captured in wars of conquest. Small farmers were bankrupted and forced to flee to Rome to attempt a living as proletarians, wage laborers. They had no voting rights or other citizen rights. In the eyes of the rich, they were simply the 'mob' that could be bought, manipulated, and directed to attack an opponent; they were the 'demos,' the masses, the public. Roman 'democracy' was all about mass manipulation in the service of empire.

The government of Imperial Rome didn't have a proper budget system, and squandered resources maintaining the empire while itself producing little of value. When the spoils from conquered territories were no longer enough to cover expenses, it turned to higher taxes, shifting the burden of the immense military structure onto the citizenry. Higher taxes forced many more small farmers to let their land go barren. To distract its citizens from the worsening conditions, the Roman ruling oligarch politicians handed out free wheat to the poor and entertained them with circuses, chariot races, throwing Christians to the lions and other entertainments, the notorious "bread and circuses" strategy of keeping unrest at bay.

Political offices increasingly were sold to those with wealth. The masses, in turn, 'sold' their votes to various politicians for favors, the charade of democracy.

The next fundamental change that vitally wounded the Roman Empire was the shift from a draft army made up of farmer soldiers to one of paid professional career soldiers as the ever-more distant wars became more unpopular. It was not unlike what took place in America in the years after the Vietnam War when President Nixon abolished the draft in favor of an "all volunteer" Army, after the popular protest became a threat to the future of the military.

As conditions for Roman soldiers in far away wars became more onerous, more incentives were needed to staff the legions. Limiting of military service to citizens was dropped and Roman citizenship could be won in exchange for military service, not unlike what is taking place now as immigrant teenagers are being promised US citizenship if they risk their lives for America's wars in Afghanistan, Iraq or elsewhere. At a certain point, Roman soldiers were forced to take an oath of service to their commander, not to the state.

Small farms were gradually replaced by huge latifundia, bought for booty, and the gap between the Roman rich and the poor increased. When the two brothers Gracchus tried in the second century AD to ease the growing gap between rich and the rest by introducing agriculture reforms that limited the powers of the wealthy Senators, they were assassinated by the men of wealth.

The Roman oligarchy grew increasingly degenerate. Towards the end of the reign of Roman emperors, gluttony was so commonplace among the rich that vomitoriums were constructed so that people who had eaten or drunk too much could throw up and go and eat and drink some more.

Emperor Nero at one point declared, "Let us tax and tax again. Let us see to it that no one owns anything!" The purchasing of exotic spices, silks, and other luxuries from the Orient bled Rome of its gold, gold that didn't return. Soon Rome didn't have enough gold to produce coins. And so it debased its coins with lesser metals until there was no gold left. Another emperor in order to reduce production and raise the price of wine, ordered the destruction of half of the vineyards in Rome's provinces.

Over time the costs of maintaining this huge global military structure became overwhelming. By the Third Century people were seeking every means to avoid the onerous taxes imposed to maintain the military. The army itself had doubled in size from the time of Augustus to the time of Diocletian, in the course of an inflationary spiral, inflation brought on by a systematic debasing of the gold and silver content of the Roman currency. In addition, costs of the state administration had grown enormously. By the time of Diocletian there was not one emperor but four emperors—which meant financing four imperial courts, four Praetorian Guards, four palaces, four staffs. The cost of policing the Roman state became increasingly enormous.[19] The cost of the Roman state bureaucracy ballooned as the size and cost of the US Executive Branch Federal Bureaucracy after 1971.

Ultimately, as Rome's territorial expansion stalled and began to contract, less and less loot was available to support the empire's global ambitions as well as its domestic economy. The outsourcing of the military led to lethargy, complacency, and decadence.

The Roman Empire gradually lost power. Barbarians in the north frequently went on raids against the disintegrating empire. The empire became steeped in debt as emperors tried desperately to buy the loyalty of the army, and the moral condition of its subjects continued to spiral downward.

Rome steadily lost control of its frontiers, and roads and bridges were not maintained, leading to a breakdown in trade and communication. Riots and revolts became commonplace in Rome itself. As the government fell deeper into debt, it raised taxes. The armies of different generals seized any supplies they needed from local people. Food became a precious commodity, and for the first time in centuries, large numbers of people went hungry.

Further wars of conquest plunged the Empire into internal chaos. Roman wars extended to Asia and Africa and corruption within the political ruling class increased dramatically. Money was king. Rome had become a plutocracy, an oligarchy where power was synonymous with wealth.

End of the Republic?

By 2009 the Government of the United States, authorized by the Congress of the United States, had spent more than one trillion dollars on two wars so far from American shores that most citizens could not comprehend their necessity. Iraq and Afghanistan were exposing the frayed edges of what the British called "imperial overstretch." Despite the most advanced military technology, including drone remote bombers piloted from special centers as far away from Afghan targets as Las Vegas, the United States war machine was losing rather than gaining. America had become transformed, much as ancient Rome, into a *de facto* military state, a national security garrison. By 2009 the Government was officially spending a total of more than $1 trillion annually on its military machinery, more than the total of the next forty five nations combined. [20]

Depending on where one dated the irreversible decline, it took the Roman Empire almost two centuries to collapse. By the first months of the end of the first decade of the 21st Century, it looked as though it might have taken the American Empire, the self-proclaimed American Century, little more than six decades to accomplish its destruction from within. In both cases the corruption of an oligarchy, a plutocracy in which power was equated to wealth, was at the heart of the collapse.

In March 2008, David M. Walker, the Comptroller General of the United States and head of the Government Accountability Office, resigned 5 years before the end of his 15-year term expired. His reason for resigning as he stated publicly in speeches across the country, was that as Comptroller he was limited in what he could do and that the United States was in danger of collapsing in much the same manner as the Roman Empire. Drawing parallels with the end of the Roman Empire, Walker warned there were "striking similarities" between America's current situation and the factors that brought down Rome.[21]

The American Century that had been proclaimed by Time chairman Henry Luce, the Rockefeller brothers, Averell Harriman and others of the wealthiest circles of the establishment in 1941, had been based as had Rome on a system of looting and plunder of foreign lands. It took a different form from that of Rome over time, using the supranational technocrats IMF to plunder the wealth of countries from Argentina to Brazil to the nations of resource-rich Africa. It used the unique financial advantage after 1971 of being the world's reserve currency and at the same time its unchallenged military superpower to extend its power and influence far beyond what its internal economy could have sustained. As Roman emperors diluted the gold and silver content of the coins of the realm to continue an unsustainable system, the Gods of Money on Wall Street used a free-floating dollar and virtual money in the form of financial derivatives to maintain a facade of solvency. That facade cracked in August 2007 with the collapse of Germany's IKB bank.

It was an open question whether the rest of the world or even future generations of Americans would appreciate the lessons of Rome, let alone of the American Century. William Jennings Bryan had warned against letting the nation be hanged "on a cross of gold," before the Democratic National Convention of 1896, as he was nominated the party's Presidential candidate. A life-long opponent of the Money Trust, of the oligarch's creed of "social Darwinism," as Secretary of State under Woodrow Wilson, Bryan had resigned in 1915 in protest against Wilson's manipulation of the circumstances surrounding sinking of the *Lusitania* in order to build a case for entering the European war. Bryan noted prophetically in a 1906 speech, little more than a century before the collapse of the US economy and its financial system,

Plutocracy is abhorrent to a republic; it is more despotic than monarchy, more heartless than aristocracy, more selfish than bureaucracy. It preys upon the nation in time of peace and conspires against it in the hour of its calamity...The time is ripe for the overthrow of this giant wrong.[22]

Endnotes:

[1] The Andrews Sisters, *"Money is the Root of All Evil,"* in The Golden Age Of The Andrews Sisters CD 2/4, first recorded in 1945, CD remastered from original, 2002, Jasmine Music.
[2] Matt Taibbi, *Obama's Big Sellout,* Rolling Stone, December, 2009, accessed in http://www.rollingstone.com/politics/story/31234647/obamas_big_sellout/2.
[3] SNL Financial, cited in Barron's, *The Numbers,* March 23, 2009, p. 16.
[4] Kim Asger Olsen, Luxembourg investment banker in a private conversation with the author, February, 2009.
[5] George Washington Blog, *Data of Top 25 Investment Banks with Largest Derivatives Exposures,* Scribd, accessed in http://www.scribd.com/doc/6486125/Data-of-Top-25-Investment-Banks-with-Largest-Derivatives-Exposures-from-GeorgeWashingtonBlog.
[6] Greg Gordon and Kevin G. Hall, *Regulatory reports show 5 big banks face huge loss risk,* McClatchy Newspapers, March 9, 2009, accessed in http://www.mcclatchydc.com/227/story/63606.html.
[7] Ibid.
[8] Ibid.
[9] William K. Black, Senior Regulator during S&L crisis, *How the Servant Became a Predator: Finance's Five Fatal Flaws,* accessed in http://www.huffingtonpost.com/william-k-black/how-the-servant-became-a_b_318010.html.
[10] Mortgage Bankers' Association, *Delinquencies Continue to Climb in Latest MBA National Delinquency Survey,* Press Release, November 19, 2009, accessed in http://www.mbaa.org/NewsandMedia/PressCenter/71112.htm.
[11] Paul Campos, *Was Spitzer targeted?,* Rocky Mountain News, March 12, 2008, accessed in http://www.rockymountainnews.com/news/2008/mar/12/campos-was-spitzer-targeted/. See also the author's article, *Why Bush Watergated Eliot Spitzer,* by F. William Engdahl, 17 March 2008, in www.engdahl.oilgeopolitics.net.
[12] John Williams, *Shadow Government Statistics,* accessed in http://www.shadowstats.com/.
[13] Moria Herbst, *Even the Employed Lose with Hour and Wage Cuts,* Business Week, July 10, 2009.
[14] Martin N. Baily and Douglas J. Eliott, *The U.S. Financial and Economic Crisis: Where Does It Stand and Where Do We Go From Here?* The Brookings Institution, Washington D. C., June 15, 2009.
[15] Doron Peskin, *Following crisis: Arab world loses $3 trillion,* IPR, March 31, 2009, accessed in http://infoprod.co.il/main/siteNew/index.php?langId=1&mod=article&action=article&Admin=qwas&stId=247.

[16] Walter Alarkon, *OMB director warns growing deficit a threat to American economy*, The Hill, November 3, 2009, accessed in
http://thehill.com/homenews/administration/66085-omb-director-warns-growing-deficit-a-threat-to-us-economy.

[17] John Williams, op. cit., accessed in http://www.shadowstats.com/article/gaap-based-federal-deficit.

[18] Mateusz Romanowski, *Ancient Rome: Downfall of the Empire*, accessed in http://www.ancient-rome.biz/downfall.html.

[19] Josef Peden, *Inflation and the Fall of the Roman Empire*, Mises Institute, October 27, 1984, accessed in http://www.marketoracle.co.uk/Article12831.html.

[20] General Accountability Office, Report 2008, p. 35.

[21] Charles Wisniowski, *Interview with Comptroller general of the United States David M. Walker*. Mortgage Banking, June 1 2007.

[22] William Jennings Bryan, *Speech at Madison Square Garden*, New York, August 30, 1906, in *Speeches of William Jennings Bryan* (New York: Funk & Wagnalls, 1909), pp. 90-91.

Index